The ways in which literary works begin have proved fascinating to readers and critics at least since Aristophanes. This collection of essays gives new life to a topic of perennial interest by presenting a variety of original readings in nearly all the major genres of Greek and Latin literature. The subjects of these essays range from narrative voices in the opening of the *Odyssey* to ideological reasons for Tacitus' choice of a beginning in the *Histories*, and from a survey of opening devices in Greek poetry to the playwright's negotiations with the audience in Roman comedy. Other papers discuss "false starts" in Gorgias and Herodotus, the prologues of Greek tragedy, Plato's "frame" dialogues, delayed proems in Virgil, the role of the patron in Horace, aristocratic beginnings in Seneca, and "inappropriate" prefaces in Plutarch. By embracing a variety of authors and a broad range of approaches, from formal analysis of opening devices to post-structural interpretation, these twelve contributions by both younger and established scholars offer an exciting new perspective on beginnings in classical literature.

The range of this volume will make it of interest both to classicists and to students of literature in general.

YALE CLASSICAL STUDIES

YALE CLASSICAL STUDIES
EDITED FOR THE DEPARTMENT OF CLASSICS

by

FRANCIS M. DUNN

Assistant Professor of Classics, Northwestern University

and

THOMAS COLE

Professor of Greek and Latin, Yale University

VOLUME XXIX
BEGINNINGS IN CLASSICAL
LITERATURE

CAMBRIDGE UNIVERSITY PRESS

CAMBRIDGE

LONDON   NEW YORK   PORT CHESTER

MELBOURNE   SYDNEY

Published by the Press Syndicate of the University of Cambridge
The Pitt Building, Trumpington Street, Cambridge CB2 1RP
40 West 20th Street, New York NY 10011-4211, USA
10 Stamford Road, Oakleigh, Victoria 3166, Australia

© Cambridge University Press 1992

First published 1992

Printed in Great Britain at the University Press, Cambridge

*A catalogue record is available for this title
from the British Library*

Library of Congress cataloguing in publication data
Beginnings in classical literature / edited for the Department of
Classics by Francis M. Dunn and Thomas Cole.
p. cm. – (Yale classical studies: v. 29)
ISBN 0 521 41319 2 HARDBACK
1. Classical literature – History and criticism. 2. Openings
(Rhetoric) I. Dunn, Francis M. II. Cole, Thomas, 1933–
III. Series.
PA25.Y3 vol. 29
[PA3014.064]
870'.9 s – dc20
[880'.09] 91–12089
CIP

ISBN 0 521 41319 2 hardback

UP

Contents

Introduction: beginning at Colonus   page
   FRANCIS M. DUNN   *Northwestern University*   1

How Greek poems begin
   WILLIAM H. RACE   *Vanderbilt University*   13

The Muse corrects: the opening of the *Odyssey*
   VICTORIA PEDRICK   *Georgetown University*   39

Sappho 16, Gorgias' *Helen*, and the preface to Herodotus' *Histories*
   HAYDEN PELLICCIA   *Cornell University*   63

Tragic beginnings: narration, voice, and authority in the prologues of Greek drama
   CHARLES SEGAL   *Harvard University*   85

Plato's first words
   DISKIN CLAY   *Duke University*   113

Plautine negotiations: the *Poenulus* prologue unpacked
   NIALL W. SLATER   *Emory University*   131

Proems in the middle
   GIAN BIAGIO CONTE   *Università degli Studi di Pisa*   147

Openings in Horace's *Satires* and *Odes*: poet, patron, and audience
   BARBARA K. GOLD   *Hamilton College*   161

An aristocracy of virtue: Seneca on the beginnings of wisdom
   THOMAS N. HABINEK   *University of California at Berkeley*   187

Contents

Beginnings in Plutarch's *Lives*
THOMAS G. ROSENMEYER   *University of California at Berkeley*   205

"Initium mihi operis Servius Galba iterum T. Vinius consules..."
THOMAS COLE   *Yale University*   231

Introduction: beginning at Colonus

FRANCIS M. DUNN

"Well, now I'll turn to his prologues," Euripides exclaims, "and the first part of the tragedy will be the very first thing of this clever man's that I put to the rack." The earliest surviving example of literary criticism in antiquity is the riotous parody in Aristophanes' *Frogs*, where Euripides subjects the beginning of Aeschylus' *Choephori* to hair-splitting sophistic torture, and Aeschylus responds with verbal slap-stick, pummeling his opponent's prologues with a barrage of "little oil flasks."[1] Clearly enough, an author's opening words – μῆνιν ἄειδε, θεά, *arma virumque cano* – are charged with special meaning; and consequently, as Aristophanes reminds us, these opening words are an obvious target of criticism.[2] The following collection of essays seeks to place in perspective literary openings and our readings of them by bringing together a broad sample of authors and critics. Before reviewing this range of approaches, I start with an example that renders problematic the very act of making a beginning.

The stage is empty. Slowly, two figures approach from the left. They hesitate, unsure which way to turn. Finally, they reach the center of the stage and pause. One is a frail old man and the other a younger woman, both in rags. The man turns to speak:[3]

> Child of a blind old man, Antigone, what
> place have we come to, or what city of men?
> Who will take in the wandering Oedipus
> today, with meager gifts?
> I ask for little, get even less,
> and that's enough for me.

---

1. Aristophanes, *Frogs* 1119ff. and 1198ff.
2. On criticism of openings by Protagoras and Prodicus, see C. Segal, "Protagoras' *Orthoepeia* in Aristophanes' Battle of the Prologues (*Frogs* 1119–97)," *RhM* 113 (1970) 158–62.
3. Quotations are my own translation of Pearson's text (Oxford 1928).

> Patience I have learned from suffering, from the
> long years attending me, and from noble birth.
> But child, if you see any seat
> by public ground or holy grove,
> stop me and sit me down, so we can find out
> where we are; we come as strangers, to learn
> from the people and do as we are told.   (1–13)

What does Oedipus tell us? Many years after discovering his crimes, he is an outcast with his daughter Antigone, and his long exile from Thebes seems to have taught him humility. But this opening information is slight compared to the questions that remain. Why are they in exile? Did Creon indeed banish Oedipus after his terrible discovery? And where are they now? It is this last question which Oedipus insistently repeats, and which Antigone can only partially answer:

> Suffering father, Oedipus, the towers
> crowning the city seem far away;
> but surely this place here is holy, teeming
> with laurel, olive, and vine; and densely
> winged nightingales sing inside.
> So bend your limbs here on this uncut rock
> since you've traveled a long way for an old man.   (14–20)

Already our interest is focused upon a central issue of the play. This holy spot will turn out to be the grove of the Eumenides, and Oedipus will insist on staying here despite the objections of the inhabitants, and despite the threats of Creon and the pleas of Polyneices. The opening lines anticipate this theme indirectly, arousing curiosity with the old man's persistent questions:

> O. Well, sit me down and guard the blind.
> A. After all this time, no need to teach me that.
> O. But can you tell me where we are?
> A. I recognize Athens, but not this place.
> O. Everyone we met told us that!
> A. Shall I go and find out what place it is?
> O. Yes, child, at least if it's inhabited.   (21–27)

Of course, the opening anticipates much more than a single theme. This impatient exchange, for example, may suggest the strain of years on the road together and anticipate Oedipus' short temper with Creon and his son. But more significant is the unusual way in which the setting is introduced. Unlike other

Introduction: beginning at Colonus

tragedies, this one begins not by describing the scene, but by asking what it is. *Oedipus the King* likewise begins with questions, as Oedipus asks why the people are dressed as suppliants, but in that play the setting is deftly sketched in and is never in doubt.[4] *Philoctetes* places much more emphasis upon its setting – the desolate island and the cripple's squalid cave – but here the scene is clearly identified from the start: "This is the shore of the land of Lemnos, surrounded by waves," Odysseus begins, and he proceeds to describe the island and the cave where he abandoned Philoctetes many years before. Although there is a short delay before Neoptolemus finds the cave itself, we are never uncertain where we are. The second *Oedipus*, on the other hand, begins by making the setting a problem – a question to be asked and a mystery to be unraveled. This is all the more remarkable because at least some members of the audience would have heard an outline of the plot a few days earlier at the Proagon.[5] Yet even though these spectators know that the play will portray Oedipus' arrival at Colonus, the opening scenes make the identity of the setting a central issue, and the remainder of the play revolves around discovering its full significance.

It is hard to exaggerate the importance of the setting.[6] It is the source of conflict with the Stranger and with the Chorus, both of whom try to expel Oedipus from the holy spot; it gives rise to more spectacular conflicts with Creon and Polyneices, the former trying to remove the blind man physically from the stage; and it culminates in the religious awe surrounding the secret spot where Oedipus dies, a spot that will guarantee the security of Athens. But the insistent questions of the prologue (1–4, 9f., 11f., 23, 26f., 38, 41, 52) do more than anticipate a theme: they generate an uncertainty and curiosity which will not be exhausted until the report of the hero's death at the end of the play.[7] By launching us,

---

4. For a detailed comparison of the two opening scenes, see B. Seidensticker, "Beziehungen zwischen den beiden Oidipusdramen des Sophokles," *Hermes* 100 (1972) 255–74.

5. On the day before the festival began, the poets announced in the Odeion the subjects of their plays; see A. Pickard-Cambridge, *The Dramatic Festivals of Athens*, 2nd edn (Oxford 1968) 63 and 67–68.

6. See for example John Jones, *On Aristotle and Greek Tragedy* (Oxford 1962) 222–28, R. P. Winnington-Ingram, *Sophocles: An Interpretation* (Cambridge 1980) 339–40 and D. Birge, "The Grove of the Eumenides," *CJ* 80 (1984–85) 11–17.

7. On the opening scenes as a miniature version of the entire drama, see K. Reinhardt, *Sophocles*, tr. H. and D. Harvey (Oxford 1979) 197ff.

as viewers, upon a search for the full meaning of the setting, the prologue defines a central concern of the drama.

Of course, Oedipus and Antigone *do* eventually learn where they are. The Stranger identifies the place as Colonus ("the fields nearby claim this horseman, Colonus, as their founder," 58ff.) and Oedipus in turn describes its importance to him: "Apollo said... that here I would close my wretched life, founding blessings for those who received me, and ruin for those who exiled and banished me," 87ff. But until then, for the first sixty lines of the play, we remain unsure of the setting, provoked by questions and teased by hints. Our own prolonged uncertainty becomes an objective correlative to the blindness of Oedipus and the homelessness of Antigone: in a sense we, too, must grope around an empty stage. Because we share their uncertainty, we identify more closely with the protagonists – although with an important irony. From the opening lines, the blind man seems to know there is a seat (9) and a holy grove (10) nearby.[8] Oedipus, who cannot see, senses the setting and repeatedly asks where he is, while Antigone can see a city in the distance and a grove at hand, but cannot say where she is, and the audience can see the stage and its properties, but is unsure what they represent. The dramatic irony of the earlier *Oedipus* is thus reversed. Now the old man knows and understands the oracles before we do; and while we grope slowly toward understanding, Oedipus at once recognizes the fateful sign:

> O. What place is it? What god does it belong to?
> S. Untouched and uninhabited. Here the terrible goddesses live, daughters of Earth and Darkness.
> O. Tell me what holy name I should pray to.
> S. The all-seeing Eumenides, someone here would say; elsewhere other names are right.
> O. May they graciously receive this suppliant, since I shall never leave this seat.
> S. What do you mean?
> O.   It is the sign of my fate.
> (38–46)

Oedipus then sends for Theseus, and when the chorus asks him to explain his cryptic message, Oedipus says only: "The words I say

---

8. Perhaps he also knows that he will be instructed to make sacrifice, χἂν ἀκούσωμεν τελεῖν, 13; cf. 469ff.

Introduction: beginning at Colonus

will see everything" (74). The irony culminates at the end of the play when Oedipus makes his final exit, a blind man leading the sighted toward the place of his appointed death.

Ironic treatment of the setting thus anticipates the ironic play of blindness and knowledge later in the drama.[9] But the setting – and our incomplete understanding of it – plays a more important role. The opening lines do not simply ask "Where are we? What land or city of men is this?" They also ask, in a remarkably detailed and literal manner, what each part of the stage represents. It is likely that the stage settings were fairly simple:[10] a rock seat was placed somewhere near center stage; the central door may have been flanked by paintings of trees and vines; and a low wall, probably the one separating stage from orchestra, ran across-stage.[11] In the opening section of the play, each part of the physical stage is carefully and deliberately identified as part of the dramatic setting. In her first answer to Oedipus, Antigone identifies the skene as a grove or thicket (16–18), and she appropriates the rock at center stage as a seat for her father (19–20). In the following exchange we learn that the exit stage-right leads to Athens (24), and when the Stranger enters he at once announces that the stage area represents holy ground (36ff.). We later learn that the grove represented by the skene is sacred to the Eumenides, and that the action takes place in Colonus, just outside Athens. Finally, as the Chorus enters from the right, Oedipus uses the central door to hide within the grove (113ff.), and the townsmen are shocked, explaining that behind the door is the holiest part of the grove (155ff.) and directing Oedipus to come forward and sit outside the sanctuary. The choreography is fastidious. When Antigone tells her father to follow their advice, he takes her hand and begins this lyrical exchange:

   O. Further?
   Ch.   Yes, go further.

9. See more generally D. Seale, *Vision and Stagecraft in Sophocles* (London 1982) 113ff.

10. Jebb's elaborate reconstruction of stage properties leaves no room for the imagination, R. C. Jebb, *Sophocles: The Plays and Fragments*, vol. 2 (Cambridge 1928) xxxvii–viii; Arnott's spare setting is much closer to the mark, P. Arnott, *Greek Scenic Conventions* (Oxford 1962) 35f., 99f., but may err in the other direction.

11. Line 59 suggests there may also have been a statue of a horseman onstage: τόνδ' ἱππότην Κολωνόν. If so, the investment of the stage with meaning includes identifying this figure for the audience (unlike a statue of Athena, for example, its identity would not have been self-evident).

O. More?
Ch.   Lead him forward,
    girl, since you can see.
A.   Follow this way, father, follow
    with your blind foot where I lead you.
    ...
O.   Lead me child, where we
    may speak and listen
    walking in holiness;
    let's not fight necessity.
Ch. There! don't turn your foot
    past the ledge of rock.
O.   Like this?
Ch.   Enough, I say.
O.   Shall I sit?
ch.   Crouch down
    low on the edge of the stone.
A.   Father, let me help. Gently
    join step with step —
O.   Ah, me!
A.   — leaning your old body
    on my loving arm.

(179–201)

This touching portrait of the old man's helplessness will be answered by his staggering self-confidence in the finale. And the obsessive concern with where he may and may not sit, defining the low ledge as a boundary, completes the remarkably detailed process of investing each feature of the stage with meaning.

But this is only the first step. At the beginning we lacked bearings and the stage seemed a blank. Now, at the end of the parodos, each part of the physical setting has been clearly defined. By mid-play the scene is invested with deeper meaning, as Oedipus proclaims and defends his resolve to die at Colonus. And at the end of the play, the grove offstage is charged with his awesome and ineffable death. This process of gradually learning the meaning of the scene entails a novel kind of drama. Tragedy usually begins by describing a setting against which the action takes place, and definition of the scene is no more than a necessary antecedent to the play and a routine step in establishing dramatic illusion. In this play, however, definition of the setting is postponed and becomes a central concern of the action itself; when the full meaning of the setting is clear, the *Oedipus at Colonus* is over. In a sense the drama is stripped down to a single aspect of stage convention: from beginning to end we are occupied in discovering what the scene represents. This narrow focus gives the action a relentless linear movement and an intense, concentrated power. Yet the problem of defining the scene leaves us stuck at the beginning, rendering problematic the very process of beginning. If we cannot complete the dramatic illusion, how do we begin to make sense of the action onstage?

We do so with great effort. Just as the prologue challenged us to make sense of a setting which Oedipus already understood, so the action as a whole demands us to make sense of his resolve to remain here. And in meeting this demand, the audience becomes engaged in constructing a new form of drama. Instead of witnessing the conflicts that arise from known characters in a known situation, we are involved in the more personal and subjective process of finding our bearings and learning what this place means. As we struggle to see what Oedipus already sees, we gradually realize the importance of the grove and begin to understand the old man's decision to die here. Yet we never learn the scene's full meaning. Its deepest significance remains veiled by the ineffable mystery of the hero's death and by its secret location offstage. We hear the rumble of thunder behind the skene, and we hear reports from those who accompanied Oedipus: first a messenger, then his daughters, and finally Theseus who shares – and guards – his secret. Just as we seem blind to the setting at the beginning of the play, we are walled off from its fullest meaning at the end. Rather than watching a reenactment, we take an active role in this play of presence seen and unseen, access offered and denied. In this respect, Sophocles' posthumous play has a remarkable parallel in that of Euripides. The action of the *Bacchae* likewise revolves around a single stage convention, the role of the mask in bestowing identity and authority.[12] The protagonist begins by proclaiming that he appears in disguise, and in the ensuing action we see Dionysus progressively reveal his identity and power until the final, terrifying epiphany which destroys Pentheus offstage. The epilogue spoken by the unmasked god then confirms his identity without fully exposing his power. Both

---

12. See H. Foley, "The Masque of Dionysus," *TAPA* 110 (1980) 107–33 and C. Segal, *Dionysiac Poetics and Euripides' Bacchae* (Princeton 1982) 223ff.

late plays involve the spectator in a gradual access to transcendent meaning, and both are in some ways closer to mystery play than to tragedy.

When we begin at Colonus, the playwright not only introduces us to important themes but also engages us in a new way of responding to drama. He does so by inverting the way in which we expect him to begin, making our initial understanding of the scene a problem which exercises us throughout the play. In the Greek literary tradition, to begin is to acknowledge both derivation and separation from the voice of authority. The Homeric bard calls upon the memory of the Muses, the lyric poet invokes the greater power of Apollo and his lyre, and even Herodotus takes the mythical paradigms as his point of departure. The new beginning seeks to recover the power of a higher authority, and in so doing launches the author upon sublunar seas, cast off from that privileged origin. In the Latin tradition, authority tends to be vested in literary models and precedents, but the beginning just as clearly marks the end of an earlier privileged condition. The beginning at Colonus is remarkable because of the radical manner in which it presents these concerns. The slate is literally wiped clean. Not only is the stage empty, it is stripped of the conventions that normally establish its meaning. We are forced to construct anew the stage and its properties step by laborious step, and in so doing we find ourselves constructing a new form of drama as well. One is tempted to compare this radical break with the flood of Deucalion: the known world is destroyed and from the barren waste new forms gradually arise. But the new world restored by Deucalion is similar to and continuous with the old, suggesting a continuity in change that is more characteristic of beginnings in general than of the beginning at Colonus in particular.[13] The opening of Sophocles' last play should make us think instead of the flood in Ovid: *partimque figuras | rettulit antiquas, partim nova monstra creavit*, "in part [the earth] restored old shapes, in part it created strange prodigies."[14] The prodigy Sophocles creates from his empty stage marks a radical end to traditional tragedy – and it marks an equally radical return to the beginning. In a city and a theater torn by conflict and doubt, the playwright

---

13. Thus Edward W. Said, *Beginnings: Intention and Method* (New York 1975) 34.
14. Ovid, *Metamorphoses*, 1 436f.

Introduction: beginning at Colonus

reconstructs the direct and primitive power of mystery rites for the dead; he seeks to recover not an earlier beginning but *the* beginning itself, a presence and authority too overpowering to behold. Perhaps it is no coincidence that Sophocles' radical new beginning marks the end of Greek tragedy as we know it, and the beginning of the more personal and subjective concerns of fourth-century literature.

Different beginnings can and will suggest different interpretations. But the questions we ask about beginnings are often similar: why does the author choose to begin here? How does the beginning define allegiance to a genre or independence from predecessors? What devices of suspense or flattery does the author use to gain the interest of an audience? What purpose or project does the beginning announce or betray? These questions tend to focus attention upon the tradition or authority from which the author begins, and upon his or her strategies in addressing the audience. The papers which follow reflect the wide variety of useful answers to these questions, and together they testify to the importance of beginnings in classical literature.

The first piece in the collection sets the stage by describing the formal opening patterns available to the poet. William Race offers a broad review of beginnings in Greek poetry, proposing a general division into narrative, dramatic, discursive, and hymnal openings. Narrative openings begin reporting events without introduction; dramatic openings enter into a scene or dialogue; discursive openings present a thesis by arguing from similarity, difference, or universal truth (e.g. similes, priamels, and gnomes); and hymnal openings include the rhapsodic invocation of epic poetry and the lyric poet's cultic address to a god. Race discusses variations of these patterns, and innovative combinations in Hesiod, Pindar, and Callimachus.

The second essay shows how a dramatic or dialectical version of the rhapsodic invocation introduces the theme of the *Odyssey*. Victoria Pedrick argues that the epic begins with a proem in which the narrator asks the Muse to help in an ambivalent project: a traditional tale of return with an unconventional focus upon the character of its hero. In a second proem, his Muse corrects this request by offering a new beginning for the narrative

(Calypso's island) and a new emphasis upon the demands (wife, home, gods) that will begin to define this initially nameless hero.

A variation upon the priamel opening may illustrate how an author's purpose departs from that of his predecessors. Hayden Pelliccia shows that the explicit priamel in Sappho becomes an unexpected break-off in Gorgias and Herodotus; Gorgias varies his Sapphic model to heighten the effect of his sophistic defense of Helen, while Herodotus uses a similar "false start" to reject the approaches of earlier historians. Formal similarities between the two prose works may also situate them within a rhetorical rivalry in defense of Helen.

These formal devices are not available in dramatic genres. Charles Segal surveys opening strategies in Greek tragedy, noting that tragic prologues lack epic authority and clarity since there is no narrative voice outside the drama. The action itself must suggest seriousness and arouse curiosity and sympathy, and Segal considers in detail three solutions to the problem. Suppliant prologues arouse sympathy and create a crisis; "conspiratorial" prologues arouse interest in an absent or silent protagonist; and detached prologues not only supply information but also draw attention to the poet's role as a creator of fictions.

In Plato, a dramatic scene introduces, and then narrates, an earlier conversation of Socrates. As Diskin Clay points out, despite the care lavished on these scenes, and despite Plato's insistence on the strict necessity of part to whole, the way in which Plato begins is seldom strictly necessary to the dialogue that follows. On the other hand, the beginning is not irrelevant "scenery," and Clay shows at greater length how the opening scenes of the *Phaedo* and the *Republic* introduce the central philosophical concerns of those dialogues.

Unlike Greek tragedy, Roman comedy begins with an extra-dramatic speaker, but this authorial voice does not invoke a higher authority. Niall Slater shows how the *Poenulus* prologue negotiates reception of the drama by playing upon the roles and authority of actors and audience. The beginning of the *Poenulus* thus bears a double burden: it draws the spectators into the world of the play, and it anticipates the themes and the double structure of the following action.

The next two essays discuss programmatic beginnings in Latin

Introduction: beginning at Colonus

poetry from different perspectives. In a revision of a paper first published in Italian, Gian Biagio Conte traces a historical development in which Hellenistic and Latin poets came to use the proem to present not only a theme but also a literary program. Conte argues that in Virgil the proem is relatively traditional, with a programmatic statement reserved for a second "proem in the middle," and he traces this division of emphasis back to Ennius and Lucretius.

In Horace the programmatic opening defines the poet's relationship to his patron and his audience. Barbara Gold shows that the opening poem of the *Satires* moves from address to Maecenas to the inclusion of other types of audience, arguing that this anticipates his patron's diminished role in the rest of the Book and helps to define his satiric technique. The opening poem of the *Odes*, on the other hand, portrays the poet as both dependent upon Maecenas and detached from his audience; this parallels his ambivalent use of the priamel and reflects the problematic status of Roman lyric.

The last three essays, on prose writers of the Empire, reflect the very different concerns of didactic philosophy, moral biography, and historical narrative. Thomas Habinek is less concerned with the opening itself than with the source of authority to which the opening and the work as a whole appeal. Seneca's *Dialogues* and *Letters* seek to supplant their beginnings, even as they depend upon the authority of these beginnings, whether literary (the paternal, hortatory mode), cultural (a traditional, aristocratic conception of virtue), or mythological (the privileged model of the Golden Age).

Beginnings thus look backward and outward, situating the author among literary and cultural precedents; they also look forward and inward to the particular project that follows. Thomas Rosenmeyer examines how Plutarch introduces his *Lives*, drawing attention to the indirect and freakish manner in which proem leads up to biography. He suggests that the failings of these prefaces reflect a weakness in the larger project: Plutarch's historical material resists his moral and didactic intention, and so the *Lives* in a larger sense are unsure where to begin.

Finally, the beginning is an apparently arbitrary point: that place in the seamless web of events where the author chooses to begin his narrative. Thomas Cole asks why Tacitus began his *Histories* not at an obvious turning point in events but in the middle of the unrests of 68–70 A.D. Aside from useful literary effects, Cole argues for an ideological purpose in excluding (prior) unsavory deeds of Galba and Verginius, and including (later) events which foreshadow the promise of Nerva and Trajan; an arbitrary point is thus invested with the Roman reader's own hope for a new beginning.

This collection makes no attempt to be exhaustive. Many other genres and authors are equally worthy of attention, and I am sure that other approaches will prove equally rewarding. But if these essays succeed in raising new questions and promoting further dialogue in the study of classical literature, that will be enough of a beginning.[15]

15. My thanks to Sheila Murnaghan and Thomas Cole for helpful comments on this essay. The preparation of this volume owes much to the encouragement of John Herington, the diligence of Thomas Cole, and the patience of all the contributors.

How Greek poems begin

WILLIAM H. RACE

Greek and Roman rhetorical treatises provide many observations on the topics and aims of prose introductions (προοίμια, *exordia*, *principia*), but have little to say about poetic introductions and practically nothing about their formal elements.[1] The purpose of this article is to explore the forms that underlie the beginnings of Greek poems. No system of classification can provide an exhaustive account of the various ways in which Greek poems open, but a few formal patterns do predominate, and in order to discuss them I have divided the openings of Greek poems (whether epic, dramatic, or lyric) into four main types: narrative, dramatic, discursive, and hymnal.[2] The narrative opening begins by telling about an event without any prefatory statements. The dramatic opening presumes a situation in which the speaker of the poem finds himself; although it naturally occurs in drama, it is also found in non-dramatic poetry, increasingly in the Hellenistic period. The discursive opening sets forth a proposition, either explicitly or implicitly, for which it argues; common forms include comparisons and contrasts, priamels, gnomes, and justifications of the poet's role. The hymnal opening, the earliest and most pervasive of these types, really comprises two kinds of hymns, rhapsodic and cultic. After a brief review of each type, we shall conclude with examples that illustrate innovative combinations of them.

---

1. H. Lausberg, *Handbuch der literarischen Rhetorik* (Munich 1960) 150–63 provides a convenient survey, although he omits the important instructions of Menander Rhetor for composing a prose hymn to Apollo; see D. A. Russell and N. G. Wilson, *Menander Rhetor* (Oxford 1981) 206–25.
2. Occasionally poems open with a *descriptio*. One example is Iby. 286 *PMG*, if indeed we have the beginning of the poem; another is Alk. 338 L–P, which reflects a practice, common among *carpe diem* poems, of describing a natural scene before issuing a *carpe diem* injunction (cf. Athen. 430AB and Horace, *Carm.* 1.4, 1.9, and 4.7). Because of their great number and variety, I have not included epigrams in this study, although they exemplify the types surveyed.

I. The narrative opening

As far as our evidence shows, the narrative opening is a relatively late development. The earliest examples of poems that begin by narrating events without any preliminary invocation or explanation are Parmenides' philosophical poem, which begins with horses conveying him (πέμπον, 2) on his journey, and two of Bakchylides' dithyrambs. Bakch. 17 opens as Minos' ship carrying Theseus and the Athenian youths is en route to Krete (Κυανόπρωρα μὲν ναῦς...Κρητικὸν τάμνε{ν} πέλαγος, 1–4); the imperfect verb establishes the setting for the action to come. The fragmentary Bakch. 20 begins with a narrative, signalled by the temporal adverb ποτέ (Σπάρτᾳ ποτ' ἐν ε[ὐρυχόρῳ). Although precedents exist,[3] it was Euripides who used the narrative opening to greatest advantage in so many of his prologues by introducing a character who provides the background of the situation: *Alk.*, *Med.* (note ποτέ in line 3), *Hipp.*, *And.* (note ποτέ in line 2), *Hek.*, *El.* (note ποτέ in line 2), *Her.* (note ποτέ in line 2), *Tr.* (note ἐξ οὗ in line 4), *I.T.*, *Ion*, *Hel.*, *Bakch.* (note ποτέ in line 2), and *I.A.*[4] The pattern continues with Menander's *Dysk.* Eleven of Theokritos' *Idylls* begin with narratives.[5] A notable example is the opening of *Idyll* 7: Ἧς χρόνος ἁνίκ' ἐγών τε καὶ Εὔκριτος εἰς τὸν Ἄλεντα | εἵρπομες ἐκ πόλιος, where ἇς χρόνος ἁνίκ' is the equivalent of ποτέ.[6] Apart from these examples, some epigrams, and poems in the *Anakreontea* (e.g., 6; note ποτ'), the narrative opening rarely occurs; for example, not a single epinician of Pindar or of Bakchylides opens with a narrative.

II. The dramatic opening

Often the poet opens with a supposed scene, in which the speaker is involved either as an onlooker or as a participant. This is the typical opening of plays without a prologue, where speakers

---

3. For example, after identifying itself, the chorus in Aischylos' *Persai* proceeds with a narrative of recent events.
4. Cf. also the prologue of Sophokles' *Phil.* (note the ποτέ in line 5).
5. The list includes *Idd.* 6, 7, 8, 18, 19, 20, 23, 24, 25, 26, and 30 (note the narrative ποκά/ποτέ in 6, 18, 19, and 24). The opening of *Id.* 18 (Ἔν ποκ' ἄρα Σπάρτᾳ) closely resembles that of Bakch. 20 (quoted above).
6. Cf. the narrative opening of Plato's *Republic*: Κατέβην χθὲς εἰς Πειραιᾶ μετὰ Γλαύκωνος.

address or question one another. It is a favorite of love poets because of the vividness it imparts. Sappho opens *fr.* 31 by placing herself in a dramatic scene (φαίνεταί μοι κῆνος ἴσος θέοισιν) and Anakreon portrays himself as once again the sport of Eros in *fr.* 358 *PMG* (σφαίρη δηῦτέ με πορφυρῇ | βάλλων χρυσοκόμης "Ἔρως). In *fr.* 360 *PMG* he addresses a boy (ὦ παῖ παρθένιον βλέπων) and in *fr.* 417 *PMG* an elusive girl (πῶλε Θρηκίη, τί δή με λοξὸν ὄμμασι βλέπουσα | νηλέως φεύγεις, δοκεῖς δέ μ' οὐδὲν εἰδέναι σοφόν;).[7] A remarkable example is the dithyramb of Bakchylides (18), which opens with dramatic dialogue as the chorus questions Aigeus about the alarm that has just been sounded.

Pindar occasionally creates a dramatic setting for the opening of his epinicians by depicting the conditions of the ode's performance. We shall treat three examples (*Isth.* 1, *Nem.* 3, and *Ol.* 10) in the final section. Another example, *Isth.* 8, opens with a series of commands to the youths who are present to go begin the celebration:

> Κλεάνδρῳ τις ἁλικίᾳ
> τε λύτρον εὔδοξον, ὦ νέοι, καμάτων
> πατρὸς ἀγλαὸν Τελεσάρχου παρὰ πρόθυρον
> ἰὼν ἀνεγειρέτω
> κῶμον...

This dramatic opening is especially effective because it becomes apparent in the succeeding lines that this celebration is taking place soon after the expulsion of the Persians from Greece and therefore takes place within a context of even greater rejoicing.[8]

The dramatic opening becomes especially popular with Hellenistic writers, who employ it as part of their effort to achieve realistic effects. Lykophron gives his *Alexandra* a dramatic setting by putting the poem (in iambic trimeter) in the mouth of a slave reporting to Priam the words of Kassandra. Herodas' mimes all open with dramatic dialogue in realistic settings. *Mime* 4 is especially innovative; it combines an opening cultic hymn to Asklepios (1–18), full of typically Hellenistic ἠθοποιία (in the woman's description of her poverty), with naturalistic dramatic

---

7. Two fragments of Alkaios may also be dramatic openings of poems, 208 L–P (ἀσυν⟨ν⟩έτημμι τῶν ἀνέμων στάσιν) and 332 L–P (νῦν χρὴ μεθύσθην).
8. Cf. *Pyth.* 6, which opens with a command to the audience for silence: Ἀκούσατε.

dialogue and even an *ekphrasis*. The first five *Idylls* of Theokritos open with dramatic dialogues, beginning with the conversation that opens *Id.* 1 ('Ἁδύ τι τὸ ψιθύρισμα καὶ ἁ πίτυς, αἰπόλε, τήνα).[9] As we shall see, Kallimachos also employs dramatic openings in his hymns.

III. The discursive opening

A. Sappho and Alkaios

Many poems open with an argument, often advanced through comparisons and contrasts, which sometimes are extended into priamels. One of the most famous is Sappho, *fr.* 16: ο]ἰ μὲν ἰππήων στρότον οἰ δὲ πέσδων. The logical basis of this poem has long been recognized: Sappho sets forth a proposition and attempts to prove it, first by an appeal *per exemplum* to the authority of tradition, and then by adducing her own experience, that ἔρως determines what is κάλλιστον.[10] By contrasting the figures of Helen and Thetis, Alkaios, *fr.* 42 appears to advance an opposing proposition, that ethical correctness determines what is best:

ὡς λόγος, κάκων ἄ[χος ἔννεκ' ἔργων
Περράμῳ καὶ παῖσ[ί ποτ', Ὤλεν', ἦλθεν
ἐκ σέθεν πίκρον, π[ύρι δ' ὤλεσε Ζεῦς
Ἴλιον ἴραν.

οὐ τεαύταν...

If we had more of Alkaios' poems we might find a number of discursive openings, for we are told that he constructed his poems on the model of political rhetoric,[11] but the remains of early lyric provide few certain examples.[12]

---

9. Cf. *Idd.* 2, 3, 4, 5, 9, 10, 12, 14, 15, 27, and Bion 1. For a good treatment of realistic techniques in Hellenistic poetry, see G. Zanker, *Realism in Alexandrian Poetry: A Literature and its Audience* (London 1987), and in particular his analysis of *Id.* 15 on pages 9–18.

10. See G. W. Most, "Sappho Fr. 16.6–7 L–P," *CQ* 31 (1981) 11–17. W. H. Race, "Sappho, *fr.* 16 L–P and Alkaios, *fr.* 42 L–P: Romantic and Classical Strains in Lesbian Lyric," *CJ* 85 (1989) 16–20 discusses the sophistic nature of her logic. This poem is also an early example of a poetic *recusatio*, a type of argument which became frequent in introductory poems from the "Prologue" of Kallimachos' *Aitia* to Oppian's *Kynegetika* 1.20–40.

11. Cf. Dion. Hal. *Imit.* 6.205 U–R: τὸ μέτρον τις εἰ περιέλοι, ῥητορείαν ἂν εὕροι πολιτικήν and Quint. 10.1.63, who says that he is *plerumque oratori similis*.

12. The famous assertion of Mimnermos may have begun a poem: τίς δὲ βίος, τί δὲ τερπνὸν ἄτερ χρυσῆς Ἀφροδίτης;

B. Pindar

The case is different with Pindar, who opens many epinicians with discursive arguments before introducing the particular topic of the ode. Two odes open with priamels (*Ol.* 1.1–7 and *Ol.* 11.1–5) and two open with gnomic statements of general truths that are exemplified by the victor (*Pyth.* 5.1–4 and *Isth.* 3.1–3).[13] Four odes begin with elaborate similes (*Ol.* 6, 7; *Nem.* 2; *Isth.* 6), one of which discusses the nature of the opening itself. At the beginning of *Ol.* 6, one of his most impressive discursive openings, Pindar invokes the rule (cf. χρή, 4) for the proper way to begin a poem when the subject is particularly conspicuous:

> Χρυσέας ὑποστάσαντες εὐ-
> τειχεῖ προθύρῳ θαλάμου
> κίονας ὡς ὅτε θαητὸν μέγαρον
> πάξομεν· ἀρχομένου δ' ἔργου πρόσωπον
> χρὴ θέμεν τηλαυγές.

The final word τηλαυγές is especially important: it indicates that the beginning of the poem, like the façade of a heroic palace, must be boldly conspicuous from afar. The point is that Hagesias' achievements are so resplendent that there is no need for elaborate indirection.[14]

Another kind of discursive opening sets forth similarities and contrasts, a type for which Pindar shows a particular fondness. *Nem.* 6 opens with a meditation on the similarities and differences between gods and men (Ἐν ἀνδρῶν, ἓν θεῶν γένος· ἐκ μιᾶς δὲ πνέομεν | ματρὸς ἀμφότεροι) to provide a context for the victory, announced in the following lines (8ff.). More dramatic is the abrupt opening

---

13. Bakch. 14.1–20 is a particularly complex example. Some dramatic prologues open similarly with a general proposition that is fulfilled in the present instance. Cf. Soph. *Trach.* 1–5; Eur. *Herakl.* 1–6, *Or.* 1–3 (introducing a genealogical priamel); Aristoph. *Acharn.* 1–3 (introducing a priamel) and *Plout.* 1–14.

14. Cicero probably alludes to this passage at *Orat.* 50: *Vestibula nimirum honesta aditusque ad causam faciet illustris.* Cf. also *de Or.* 2.320: *oportet, ut aedibus ac templis vestibula et aditus, sic causis principia pro proportione rerum praeponere.* The metaphor of the porch (πρόθυρον = προοίμιον) with its columns of gold and the heroic associations of the word μέγαρον indicate that the poem promises a grand treatment of an obviously preeminent person. The outline of Hagesias' distinctions in the following lines (4–9) fully bears this out. At *Pyth.* 7.1–4 (quoted below, note 70) Pindar uses the metaphor of the foundation (κρηπῖδ' ἀοιδᾶν, 3) to describe the straightforward *prooimion*, which is called for because his subject is so conspicuous (cf. ἐπιφανέστερον, 7).

of *Pyth.* 10 ('Ολβία Λακεδαίμων, | μάκαιρα Θεσσαλία. πατρὸς δ' ἀμφοτέραις ἐξ ἑνός | ἀριστομάχου γένος Ἡρακλέος βασιλεύει. | τί κομπέω παρὰ καιρόν;). In *Nem.* 4.1ff. Pindar develops a contrast between physical relaxation after victory and the permanence of fame that song bestows ("Αριστος εὐφροσύνα πόνων κεκριμένων | ἰατρός· αἱ δὲ σοφαί | Μοισᾶν θύγατρες ἀοιδαὶ θέλξαν νιν ἁπτόμεναι). Other examples include *Ol.* 9.1–10, where the present celebration is contrasted with the spontaneous cheers at the site of the games; *Nem.* 5.1–2, which contrasts poetry with statues that stand still on their bases; *Isth.* 2.1–11, which contrasts the spontaneity of older love poets with the venality of the modern encomiastic poet; and *Isth.* 6, which compares the victories of Lampon's sons to libations at a symposium.

C. Theokritos

Hellenistic poets also employ discursive openings. The "Prologue" to Kallimachos' *Aitia* is a well-known example.[15] Theokritos opens *Id.* 11 with an abbreviated priamel:

> Οὐδὲν ποττὸν ἔρωτα πεφύκει φάρμακον ἄλλο,
> Νικία, οὔτ' ἔγχριστον, ἐμὶν δοκεῖ, οὔτ' ἐπίπαστον,
> ἢ ταὶ Πιερίδες...

This argument, dramatically presented in an address to Nikias the doctor, sets the scene for the love-sick Polyphemos' poetic appeal to Galateia (19–79), which is rounded off by a recapitulation at the end of the poem (οὕτω τοι Πολύφαμος ἐποίμαινεν τὸν ἔρωτα | μουσίσδων, ῥᾷον δὲ διᾶγ' ἢ εἰ χρυσὸν ἔδωκεν, 80–81). *Id.* 16 begins with the longest and most complex argument in the *corpus*:

> Αἰεὶ τοῦτο Διὸς κούραις μέλει, αἰὲν ἀοιδοῖς,
> ὑμνεῖν ἀθανάτους, ὑμνεῖν ἀγαθῶν κλέα ἀνδρῶν.
> Μοῖσαι μὲν θεαὶ ἐντί, θεοὺς θεαὶ ἀείδοντι·
> ἄμμες δὲ βροτοὶ οἵδε, βροτοὺς βροτοὶ ἀείδωμεν.
> τίς γὰρ...

These proemial lines justify the poet's selection of a human subject for his song. The rhapsodic question beginning with τίς initiates a long *zetesis* (5–80) that eventually selects Hieron II as the subject of the song.[16]

---

15. If we have the beginning of Choirilos' epic, it is an early example of discursive opening.   16. *Idd.* 13, 21, and 29 also have discursive openings.

IV. Hymnal openings

The most pervasive and important type of opening is the hymnal, whose influence extends throughout Greek poetry, from Homer to Nonnos. One reason for this longevity is the adaptability of hymnal openings, for, in spite of their stereotypical formulas, they allow a great deal of room for variation, not only in free-standing hymns, but also in introductions to longer works. There are two basic hymnal types, rhapsodic and cultic; we shall treat them separately, although they share some elements.

A. The rhapsodic tradition

Hymns and prayers of many kinds can be found in other cultures, but rhapsodic (or "epic") hymns are a specific creation of Greek poets. They are self-consciously poetic and formally consistent with one another. In the first verse they present the poet as a *composer*, whose intention is to sing of a god (ἀείδειν) or recall his deeds (μεμνῆσθαι), and they designate the poem itself as an ἀοιδή or ὕμνος. The god himself is named at the beginning, described in the middle, and saluted with χαῖρε (or ἴληθι) at the end of the hymn.[17] Their impersonal character and their connection with public performance in the Homeric vein (cf. *h. Hom.* 3.146–76) made them readily adaptable to introducing major works,[18] and

---

17. Accordingly, there arises the rhapsodic assurance to sing of the god "first, middle, and last," whether or not the hymnist actually carries through with the promise. See West *ad* Hes. *Th.* 34 and Gow *ad* Theok. *Id.* 17.1 for lists of instances. For studies of Greek hymnology, see E. Norden, *Agnostos Theos* (Leipzig 1913) 143–76, R. Wünsch, "Hymnos," *RE* 9 (1916) 140–83, K. Keyssner, *Gottesvorstellung und Lebensauffassung im griechischen Hymnus* (Stuttgart 1932), H. Meyer, "Hymnische Stilelemente in der frühgriechischen Dichtung" (Diss. Cologne 1933), H. Koller, "Das kitharodische Prooimion," *Philologus* 100 (1956) 159–206, E. von Severus, "Gebet," *RAC* 8 (1972) 1134–52, and W. H. Race, "Aspects of Rhetoric and Form in Greek Hymns," *GRBS* 23 (1982) 5–14. For a lucid and succinct description of the characteristics of rhapsodic and cultic hymns, see A. M. Miller, *From Delos to Delphi: A Literary Study of the Homeric Hymn to Apollo* (Leiden 1986) 1–5. Especially valuable for its analysis of hymnal form in Pindar and Kallimachos is E. L. Bundy, "The 'Quarrel Between Kallimachos and Apollonios' Part 1: The Epilogue of Kallimachos's *Hymn to Apollo*," *CSCA* 5 (1972) 39–94.

18. Indeed, the later tradition called such hymns προοίμια, a designation corroborated by many of their endings, which announce another song to come: ἄλλης μνήσομ' ἀοιδῆς or μεταβήσομαι ἄλλον ἐς ὕμνον. For the designation of the Homeric Hymns as προοίμια (whether or not they actually introduced a separate poem), cf. Pindar, *Nem.* 2.1–3, Thouk. 3.104, and Plato, *Phaido* 60D. G. Nagy, "Hesiod," in *Ancient Writers I*, ed. J. T. Luce (New York 1982) 53 argues, following Koller (above note 17), that ἄλλης ἀοιδῆς means "the rest of my

epic poets regularly adapted the openings of rhapsodic hymns to introduce their narrative subject.

1. Homeric Hymns and epic

All rhapsodic openings exhibit variations on two formulas, exemplified by the beginnings of *h. Hom.* 2 (Δήμητρ' ἠΰκομον σεμνὴν θεὰν ἄρχομ' ἀείδειν) and *h. Hom.* 5 (Μοῦσά μοι ἔννεπε ἔργα πολυχρύσου Ἀφροδίτης). In the first example the hymnist declares his intention (in the first person) to sing about a particular god; in the second he requests (in the second person) the Muse to sing. Of the thirty-two preserved openings of the Homeric Hymns eighteen follow the first model, ten the second.[19] The *Iliad* and *Odyssey* conform to the second, as does the *Thebaid* ("Ἄργος ἄειδε θεὰ πολυδίψιον ἔνθεν ἄνακτες). The *Little Iliad*, however, follows the first ("Ἴλιον ἀείδω καὶ Δαρδανίην εὔπωλον).[20]

As in typical rhapsodic openings, where the subject is immediately named in an oblique case in the first line,[21] the initial invocation to the Muse in both the *Iliad* and *Odyssey* briefly identifies the subject and proceeds to expand its significance by means of a relative clause: Μῆνιν...Ἀχιλῆος, ἣ μυρί'... (*Iliad*) and Ἄνδρα...πολύτροπον, ὃς μάλα πολλά... (*Odyssey*).[22] But once the subject is presented and magnified, and a δεῖγμα given of the forthcoming work, the problem remains of where to begin the narrative. This narrative ἀρχή is indicated in the *Iliad* by line 6: ἐξ οὗ δὴ τὰ πρῶτα διαστήτην, where the temporal οὗ marks the

song," which is a possible implication, but in light of *h. Hom.* 31.18–19, 32.18–20, and the later tradition (see Bundy [above note 17] 49–57), the emphasis falls on the *change of theme*, not on the rest of the performance.

19. See A. Lenz, *Das Proöm des frühen griechischen Epos: Ein Beitrag zum poetischen Selbstverständnis* (Bonn 1980) 21–26. The remaining four hymns consist mainly of cultic elements: 8 (to Ares), 21 (to Apollo), 24 and 29 (to Hestia).

20. The opening of the *Epigonoi* combines the two formulas ("I begin to sing" and "sing Muse") by making ἄρχομαι a first-person plural imperative: νῦν αὖθ' ὁπλοτέρων ἀνδρῶν ἀρχώμεθα Μοῦσαι. An interesting anomaly is presented by the ungrammatical inscription on the Douris cup (c. 485 B.C.) in Berlin: Μοῖσά μοι ἀ(μ)φὶ Σκάμανδρον ἐΰ(ρ)ο(ο)ν ἄρχομ' ἀ(ε)ίδειν, which combines both types of beginning, with the formulaic expressions Μοῖσά μοι and ἄρχομ' ἀείδειν occupying their normal positions in the hexameter line. For a brief discussion of the inscription in the context of epic *prooimia*, see B. A. van Groningen, *La composition littéraire archaïque grecque* (Amsterdam 1958) 63 note 2.

21. See R. Janko, "The Structure of the Homeric Hymns: A Study in Genre," *Hermes* 109 (1981) 9–10.

22. See S. E. Bassett, "The Proems of the *Iliad* and the *Odyssey*," *AJP* 44 (1923) 340–41 for a formal comparison of the two proems and A. Heubeck et al., *A Commentary on Homer's Odyssey* I (Oxford 1988) 67–68 for bibliography.

precise moment (cf. δή) which initiates (cf. τὰ πρῶτα) the rest of the narrative.

Forms of πρῶτος, which often mark an event as the starting-point for the ensuing account, whether at the beginning of a work or at important junctures within a longer one,[23] tend to suggest the importance of an event rather than its absolute priority in time. Here, the point of τὰ πρῶτα is not that this is the very first quarrel of Achilleus and Agamemnon,[24] but rather that this particular quarrel is of primary importance in initiating the narrative.[25] Once he has established his ἀρχή, however, the poet moves even further back in time in order to provide the αἰτία for the event itself, and to accomplish this he uses another technique, common in the epic (or rhapsodic) tradition, the "rhapsodic question": τίς τ' ἄρ σφωε θεῶν ἔριδι ξυνέηκε μάχεσθαι; (8). Such questions can sometimes initiate priamels which ultimately culminate in the correct choice,[26] but often they are "rhetorical" questions, as here, where the poet immediately provides the answer: Λητοῦς καὶ Διὸς υἱός (9). The ensuing γάρ-clause (9ff.) finally begins the narrative proper with the events leading up to that "primary" quarrel.[27]

In contrast, the *Odyssey* does not posit an explicit ἀρχή; rather, the poet requests the Muse to begin the narration at any point she chooses: τῶν ἁμόθεν γε (10). There is no πρῶτον to mark the

23. Among many examples, cf. *Il.* 16.113 (πρῶτον) and *Od.* 8.268 (τὰ πρῶτα), the latter marking the beginning of Demodokos' narrative of Ares and Aphrodite.
24. The later tradition, at least, attests to an earlier quarrel between them; cf. Proclus, *Chr.* 104.23–24 (Allen). The quarrel between Achilleus and Odysseus sung by Demodokos at *Od.* 8.75ff. suggests that a νεῖκος was a favorite theme for epic narration.
25. See W. Leaf and M. A. Bayfield, *The Iliad of Homer* (London 1959) 274: "The quarrel of Agamemnon and Achilles is the foundation of all that follows." G. S. Kirk, *The Iliad: A Commentary* I (Cambridge 1985) 53 appears to take τὰ πρῶτα as strictly temporal: "from the point at which he and Agamemnon first quarrelled." A translation such as "from that time when they first began to quarrel" captures its full force.
26. Cf. *h. Hom.* 3.19–25, where the question πῶς γάρ σ' ὑμνήσω; is answered by a single choice, Apollo's birth: ἢ ὥς σε **πρῶτον** Λητὼ τέκε χάρμα βροτοῖσι. The expanded version at 207–14 culminates in the establishment of Apollo's oracle as the theme: ἢ ὡς τὸ **πρῶτον** χρηστήριον... (214). In each instance, the word πρῶτον marks the primary event that serves as the ἀρχή of the narrative. For a close examination of these passages in the developing program of the hymn, see A. M. Miller (above note 17) 20–26 and 70–72, who notes that the "first" in such passages "is, strictly speaking, *aetiological* in its force," but also takes on a programmatic function by signalling "the starting-point for a longer discourse" (26).
27. This maneuver of announcing the primary event and subsequently providing background is evident at *h. Hom.* 3.29–115 (the travels and travails of Leto leading to Apollo's birth), at Hdt. 1.7–25 (the establishment of the Mermnad dynasty), and Thouk. 1.24ff. (the events leading to the breaking of the truce).

"primary" event, since there is no such event, given the multitude of Odysseus' experiences (cf. πολύτροπον... πολλά... πολλῶν... πολλά in lines 1–4) and the complexity of the situation on Ithaka. Hence, the poet begins with a brief sketch of Odysseus' situation (11–21) before turning to councils of the gods in Books 1 and 5 which set in motion the journeys of son and father that will eventually converge in the complicated resolution of the plot.[28]

2. *Hesiod's* Theogony

The two preserved Hesiodic poems open with variations on each type of rhapsodic prelude: Μουσάων Ἑλικωνιάδων **ἀρχώμεθ᾽ ἀείδειν** (*Th.* 1) and Μοῦσαι Πιερίηθεν ἀοιδῇσι κλείουσαι, | δεῦτε Δί᾽ **ἐννέπετε**, σφέτερον πατέρ᾽ ὑμνείουσαι (*Op.* 1–2). Both poems, however, exhibit sophisticated adaptations of hymnal form.[29] Since the pioneering work of Friedländer, it has been generally recognized that the opening of the *Theogony* (1–115) consists of a rhapsodic hymn in two parts, clearly marked by similar beginnings: Μουσάων Ἑλικωνιάδων **ἀρχώμεθ᾽** ἀείδειν, | αἵ (1–2) and Μουσάων **ἀρχώμεθα**, ταί (36).[30] In the first part (1–35) the word πρώτιστα (24) marks the beginning of Hesiod's career when the Muses "at the very first" commissioned him as their poet.[31] The second part, which

---

28. See S. E. Bassett (above note 22) 344–48. Eust. *ad Od.* 1.10 points out that in contrast to the *Iliad*, which the poet begins directly with Achilleus' wrath, the starting-point of the *Odyssey* is left to the Muse διὰ τὸ πάνυ πολλὰ πάθη τῆς πλάνης. The background is finally provided in Books 9–12. The "openness" of the *Odyssey* in contrast to the closed circularity of the *Iliad* (on which see W. G. Thalmann, *Conventions of Form and Thought in Early Greek Epic* [Baltimore 1984] 76) is foreshadowed by the contrast between the precise ἐξ οὗ δή and the more frankly arbitrary ἁμόθεν γε.

29. The opening of the *Works and Days* is treated below, pages 31–32.

30. P. Friedländer, "Das Proömium der Theogonie," *Hermes* 49 (1914) 1–16. See also H. Koller (above note 17) 181–82, 201–3, W. G. Thalmann (above note 28) 134–43, and most recently J. S. Clay, "What the Muses Sang: *Theogony* 1–115," *GRBS* 29 (1988) 323–33 and R. Hamilton, *The Architecture of Hesiodic Poetry* (Baltimore 1989) 10–14. The *Theogony* is the first instance of a work introduced by more than one *prooimion*, a procedure often employed by Isokrates and recommended by later rhetorical handbooks; see below note 41. In emphasizing the *formal* elements of the proem I do not mean to discount the extraordinary innovations in its content, for this rhapsodic hymn to the Muses contains some of the most sophisticated poetry of the archaic period, as a comparison with the compressed *h. Hom.* 25 readily shows; see Nagy (above note 18) 54. For a profound analysis of the Muses' integrative discourse and its implications for literary theory, see W. Trimpi, *Muses of One Mind* (Princeton 1983).

31. Cf. Kall. *Aitia, fr.* 1.21–22: καὶ γὰρ ὅτε **πρώτιστον** ἐμοῖς ἐπὶ δέλτον ἔθηκα | γούνασιν, Ἀπόλλων εἶπεν ὅ μοι Λύκιος. Here again the word πρώτιστον marks the point at which a decisive event in the poet's life occurred, whether or not it means that Apollo appeared to him "the very first time" he took up writing.

How Greek poems begin

follows the dramatic break-off in line 34,³² contains a more elaborate depiction of the Muses, and reserves a δεῖγμα of the coming narrative for the rhapsodic envoi beginning at 104: χαίρετε τέκνα Διός, in which the poet requests the Muses to "celebrate" (κλείετε, 105) the race of the gods and, more specifically, to "relate how first" (εἴπατε ὡς τὰ πρῶτα, 108) the gods came into being and "how first" (ὡς τὰ πρῶτα, 113) they occupied Olympos. In lines 114–16 all these themes are summed up (cf. ταῦτα, 114) with another rhapsodic introductory formula (ταῦτά μοι ἔσπετε Μοῦσαι),³³ which indicates, in a final flourish of terms, the actual beginning of the narrative:

ταῦτά μοι ἔσπετε Μοῦσαι Ὀλύμπια δώματ' ἔχουσαι
ἐξ ἀρχῆς, καὶ εἴπαθ', ὅτι **πρῶτον** γένετ' αὐτῶν.
ἤτοι μὲν **πρώτιστα** Χάος γένετ'·

Forms of πρῶτον occur four times in the proem to indicate starting-points (34, 44, 108, 113), but the superlative πρώτιστα, which occurs only in lines 24 and 116 in the entire *Theogony*, designates the two beginnings of fundamental importance: 1) when Hesiod began his career as a poet, and 2) when the kosmos began from primal Chaos.³⁴ The word πρῶτος (*primus*) rings throughout classical literature to mark primary events for narration, from the *Iliad* (ἐξ οὗ δὴ **τὰ πρῶτα** διαστήτην, 1.6), to Herodotos (τὸν δὲ οἶδα αὐτὸς **πρῶτον** ὑπάρξαντα ἀδίκων ἔργων ἐς τοὺς Ἕλληνας, 1.5),³⁵ to Virgil (*Troiae qui **primus** ab oris*, Aen. 1.1), to Propertius (*Cynthia **prima** suis miserum me cepit ocellis*, 1.1.1), and to Milton ("Of man's **first** disobedience," P.L. 1.1).³⁶

32. For a defense of verse 35, called an "unconvincing device" by Janko (above note 21) 20, see W. H. Race, "Some Digressions and Returns in Greek Authors," *CJ* 76 (1980) 6–7.

33. Cf. *h. Hom.* 5.1: Μοῦσά μοι ἔννεπε and *Od.* 1.1: Ἄνδρα μοι ἔννεπε Μοῦσα. Hesiod has converted the envoi (104–15), which terminates his rhapsodic hymn to the Muses (1–103), into a new rhapsodic introduction to his hymn of the Olympian gods.

34. Although πρώτιστα is often merely a synonym for πρῶτον, it appears to have significance in the *Theogony* and in Kallimachos' *Hymn to Delos* (see below, page 36).

35. Herodotos dismisses a false beginning, marked by πρῶτον... ἄρξαι (1.2), put forward by the Persians. On the opening of Herodotos' *Histories* as an adaptation of hymnal and lyric priamels, see W. H. Race, *The Classical Priamel from Homer to Boethius* (Leiden 1982) 111.

36. In all these instances, the author is seeking a starting-point for his narrative by stressing the *fundamental importance* of the event, not necessarily its temporal priority; hence the problems of interpretation occasioned by Virgil's and Propertius' use of the tradition. Commentators from the time of Servius have objected to *primus* at *Aen.* 1.1 on the grounds that Aeneas was not the first Trojan to settle in Italy, for as Virgil himself later relates, Antenor preceded him (cf. 1.242ff.). Likewise, scholars complain that Cynthia was not actually Propertius' first love (cf. 3.15.3–10). There is no need for quibbling; in both cases,

3. Pindar and Bakchylides

Pindar and Bakchylides frequently open poems with elements drawn from the rhapsodic tradition. Two straightforward examples are *Nem.* 10.1–2 and Bakch. 3.1–3:

> Δαναοῦ πόλιν ἀγλαοθρό-
> νων τε πεντήκοντα κορᾶν, **Χάριτες**,
> "Αργος "Ηρας δῶμα θεοπρεπὲς **ὑμνεῖτε**.

> 'Αριστο[κ]άρπου Σικελίας κρέουσαν
> Δ[ά]ματρα ἰοστέφανόν τε Κούραν
> **ὕμνει**, γλυκύδωρε **Κλεοῖ**, θοάς τ' 'Ο-
> λυμ]πιοδρόμους 'Ιέρωνος ἵππ[ο]υς.

In both examples the lyric poets have expanded the hymn's subject through numerous modifiers. Whereas Pindar provides an extensive list of Argive achievements before arriving at the present victory of Theaios (2–24),[37] Bakchylides immediately adds Hieron's victory as the final item in the invocation. In *Pyth.* 4.1–3 Pindar elaborates on both the subject and the rhapsodic imperative:

> Σάμερον μὲν **χρή** σε παρ' ἀνδρὶ φίλῳ
> **στᾶμεν**, εὐίππου βασιλῆι Κυράνας,
> **ὄφρα** κωμάζοντι σὺν 'Αρκεσίλᾳ,
> **Μοῖσα**, Λατοίδαισιν ὀφειλόμενον Πυ-
> θῶνί τ' **αὔξῃς οὖρον ὕμνων**...

The ὕμνει is expanded to χρή σε... στᾶμεν... ὄφρα... αὔξῃς οὖρον ὕμνων, while the human subject is successively given as ἀνδρὶ φίλῳ... βασιλῆι Κυράνας... 'Αρκεσίλᾳ.[38]

Although rhapsodic poets generally announce their theme as already chosen, they can also dramatize the process of choice by posing questions.[39] This technique initiates the narrative at *Iliad* 1.8–9: "Which, then, of the gods brought the two together to

as with τὰ πρῶτα at *Il.* 1.6, the force of the word *primus* is to designate a truly significant starting-point. Cf. also *primus* at Prop. 3.1.3 and *princeps* at Hor. *Carm.* 3.30.13.

37. Lines 2–22, an adaptation of a rhapsodic selection priamel, culminate in the games dedicated to Hera in which Theaios was victorious. The underlying rhapsodic question is: "Charites, which of the many achievements (cf. ἀρεταῖς | μυρίαις, 2–3) of Hera's Argos will you celebrate?" See E. L. Bundy, *Studia Pindarica* (Berkeley 1962) 7 and 13.

38. Other rhapsodic openings in Pindar include *Ol.* 3.1–4, *Pyth.* 9.1–4, and *Nem.* 9.1–3. Cf. also Bakch. 1.1–5, 9.1–6, and 12.1–4, all of which have additional cultic elements in the address to the Muses or Graces. For a more detailed discussion of rhapsodic and cultic elements in Pindar's opening hymns upon which the present discussion draws, see W. H. Race, *Style and Rhetoric in Pindar's Odes* (Atlanta 1990) 85–117.

39. The aporetic mode of rhapsodic hymns is discussed at length by Bundy (above note 17) 58–77.

contend in strife?" Pindar begins his first hymn (fr. 29) with a long series of "rhapsodic questions":

> Ἰσμηνὸν ἢ χρυσαλάκατον Μελίαν
> ἢ Κάδμον ἢ Σπαρτῶν ἱερὸν γένος ἀνδρῶν
> ἢ τὰν κυανάμπυκα Θήβαν
> ἢ τὸ πάντολμον σθένος Ἡρακλέος
> ἢ τὰν Διωνύσου πολυγαθέα τιμὰν
> ἢ γάμον λευκωλένου Ἁρμονίας
> ὑμνήσομεν;

In terms of form, these questions invert the direct opening, "I shall sing of" (ἀείσομαι), by posing the question, "What shall I hymn?" (ὑμνήσομεν;).[40] In this passage Pindar passes in review the various glories of Theban history before selecting one for narrative elaboration. He uses a similar strategy in the famous opening of *Ol.* 2: Ἀναξιφόρμιγγες ὕμνοι, | τίνα θεόν, τίν' ἥρωα, τίνα δ' ἄνδρα κελαδήσομεν; In this example the question (ὕμνοι... **κελαδήσομεν**;) is an elaboration of the question (ὑμνήσομεν;) in *fr.* 29: by addressing his songs, Pindar actualizes the dramatic potential of the question "What hymn shall I sing?" As in the opening of the *Iliad*, Pindar answers his question immediately in the following lines (3–7): Zeus, Herakles, Theron.[41]

4. *Theokritos*

Hellenistic authors continued the rhapsodic tradition, consciously adapting the inherited forms to new uses. *Idyll* 17 in praise of

40. In citing these lines at *encom. Demosth.* 19, Loukian shows a correct understanding of their rhetorical point: "If you were to turn your mind to dealing with the whole of Demosthenes once and for all, you would be in the greatest difficulty (ἂν ἀποροῖς) as you darted to and fro round your discourse without knowing what your mind should seize upon as its primary topic (ὅτου πρῶτον)... Just as Pindar [in *fr.* 29] turning his mind to many topics expressed his difficulties (ἠπόρηκεν)" (M. D. Macleod, tr.). Loukian recognizes the trope of ἀπορία and the force of the word πρῶτος in such contexts.

41. Menander Rhetor's instructions for constructing three *prooimia* to a prose hymn to Apollo sum up this rhetorical tradition. The first contains the topic of the speaker's obligation to praise the god, while the second contains the "modesty topos." The third is devoted to selecting an ἀρχή for his speech, where the rhetor is advised to say that if he were praising a hero he would not be at a loss (οὐκ ἂν **διηπόρησα** περὶ τῆς ἀρχῆς οὐδ' ὅθεν δεῖ **πρῶτον** τὴν **ἀρχὴν** τοῦ λόγου ποιήσασθαι, 437.27–30), but since he has undertaken to praise such a great god, he must follow Pindar's example and ask his hymns where to begin ("ἀναξιφόρμιγγες ὕμνοι" πόθεν με χρὴ τὴν **ἀρχὴν** ποιήσασθαι;), after which he immediately selects his starting-point, praise of the god himself (δοκεῖ δ' οὖν μοι **πρῶτον** ἀφεμένῳ τέως τοῦ γένους ὕμνον εἰς αὐτὸν ἀναφθέγξασθαι, 438.6–9). Of particular interest here is the consistent use of the terms ἀπορέω, ἀρχή, and πρῶτον, from Homer onwards, not only in poetry and oratory (e.g., Thouk. 2.36.1; Hyper. *Epitaph.* 9; Andok. *de Myst.* 8), but in the historians Herodotos (see above note 35) and Thoukydides (cf. ἀρξάμενος, 1.1.1; ἤρξαντο, 1.23.4; πρῶτον, 1.23.5). For further examples in late prose hymns, see Race (above note 17) 7–8.

Ptolemy II is in fact the first full-scale rhapsodic hymn composed in praise of a mortal.⁴² It opens by positing Zeus as its beginning (and ending): ʼΕκ Διὸς ἀρχώμεσθα καὶ ἐς Δία λήγετε Μοῖσαι (1), but it immediately shifts to its human subject: ἀνδρῶν δ' αὖ Πτολεμαῖος ἑνὶ **πρώτοισι** λεγέσθω | καὶ πύματος καὶ μέσσος (3–4).⁴³ Having established Ptolemy as his principal theme, Theokritos pauses to decide at what point to begin his praise by drawing an analogy with a woodcutter on Mt. Ida faced with a forest and not knowing where to start (πόθεν **ἄρξεται** ἔργου, 10); he asks: τί **πρῶτον** καταλέξω; ἐπεὶ πάρα μυρία εἰπεῖν, | οἷσι θεοὶ τὸν ἄριστον ἐτίμησαν βασιλήων.⁴⁴ The asyndetic ἐκ πατέρων (13) indicates his starting-point.⁴⁵

Idyll 22 is in the form of a rhapsodic hymn to the Dioskouroi. It opens with the straightforward declaration of its theme: Ὑμνέομεν... | Κάστορα καὶ... Πολυδεύκεα (1–2) and goes on to sketch the ἀρεταί of the brothers (3–22). Then, before embarking upon the actual narrative, the poet pauses to decide with which of the twins to begin: Κάστορος ἢ **πρώτου** Πολυδεύκεος **ἄρξομ' ἀείδειν**; (25). He solves the dilemma by declaring that he will hymn both, but will begin with Polydeukes: ἀμφοτέρους ὑμνέων Πολυδεύκεα **πρῶτον** ἀείσω (26).⁴⁶

5. *Apollonios Rhodios*

Apollonios begins three of the four books of the *Argonautika* with increasingly complex adaptations of rhapsodic techniques. The opening of the first book is brief and to the point: ʼΑρχόμενος σέο, Φοῖβε, παλαιγενέων κλέα φωτῶν | μνήσομαι. Here Apollonios has closely adapted the envoi of *h. Hom.* 32: σέο δ' ἀρχόμενος κλέα

---

42. The poem served as a model for praise of Roman emperors, as F. Cairns, *Generic Composition in Greek and Latin Poetry* (Edinburgh 1972) 100–12 has shown.

43. The πρώτοισι initially marks the "primacy" of his subject, which in the following line assumes a temporal aspect in light of the adjectives "last" and "middle" (the change of case neatly signals the surprising switch).

44. Theokritos is adapting the beginning of Odysseus' *apologia* at *Od.* 9.14–15: τί **πρῶτόν** τοι ἔπειτα, τί δ' ὑστάτιον **καταλέξω**; | κήδε' ἐπεί μοι πολλὰ δόσαν θεοὶ Οὐρανίωνες. At 16 he begins his narrative with νῦν δ' ὄνομα **πρῶτον** μυθήσομαι. See Gow *ad* Theok. 17.11.

45. This asyndeton is frequent (especially with proper nouns) after the writer has announced his ἀρχή and begins his narrative proper; cf. Bakch. 15.47–48: Μοῦσα, τίς πρῶτος λόγων ἄρχεν δικαίων; | Πλεισθενίδας Μενέλαος...; Hdt. 1.6.1: Κροῖσος ἦν...; and Thouk. 1.24.1: ʼΕπίδαμνός ἐστι πόλις. Cf. Λατοῦς καὶ Διὸς υἱός at *Il.* 1.9, Μῦς ποτε διψαλέος at *Batrach.* 9 (after ἀρχήν, 8), and Σηστὸς ἔην at Mousaios, *Hero and Leander* 16. The particles ἤτοι μέν also serve to mark the actual beginning; cf. Hes. *Th.* 116, Pindar, *Ol.* 2.3, and A. R. 4.6.

46. For further discussion of this topic, see Race (above note 17) 7–8. For a similar maneuver at Pindar, *Isth.* 1.1ff., see below note 65.

φωτῶν | ἄσομαι (18–19), in which the poet ends his hymn to Selene by announcing his intention to proceed with epic deeds.⁴⁷

More elaborate is the *prooimion* to Book 3, as the poet begins his narrative of the ill-fated love of Jason and Medea:

> Εἰ δ' ἄγε νῦν, Ἐρατώ, παρά θ' ἵστασο, καί μοι ἔνισπε,
> ἔνθεν ὅπως ἐς Ἰωλκὸν ἀνήγαγε κῶας Ἰήσων
> Μηδείης ὑπ' ἔρωτι. σὺ γὰρ καὶ Κύπριδος αἶσαν
> ἔμμορες, ἀδμῆτας δὲ τεοῖς μελεδήμασι θέλγεις
> παρθενικάς· τῷ καί τοι ἐπήρατον οὔνομ' ἀνῆπται.

The model for this opening is the appeal to the Muses before the catalogue of ships (*Il.* 2.484–87), where Homer draws upon the Muses' ability to remember exact details. Here he invokes Erato because (cf. γάρ at 3 and at *Il.* 2.485) of her knowledge of love (cf. ἔρωτι, emphatically reserved until the end of the announcement of the book's theme), an appeal justified by a *figura etymologica*.

The *prooimion* to Book 4 adds the motif of ἀπορία, which we have seen to be common in rhapsodic hymns for adding dramatic tension:

> Αὐτὴ νῦν κάματόν γε, θεά, καὶ δήνεα κούρης
> Κολχίδος ἔννεπε, Μοῦσα, Διὸς τέκος. ἦ γὰρ ἔμοιγε
> ἀμφασίη νόος ἔνδον ἑλίσσεται ὁρμαίνοντι,
> ἠέ μιν ἄτης πῆμα δυσίμερον, ἦ τόγ' ἐνίσπω
> φύζαν ἀεικελίην, ᾗ κάλλιπεν ἔθνεα Κόλχων.
> Ἤτοι ὁ μέν...

The γάρ-clause explains why the poet needs the Muse's help at this juncture of the work: he pretends not to know whether it was love-sickness or panic that impelled her to leave her family. Although both motivations are important, the order of the questions, coupled with the following account of her fear of being discovered, leaves little doubt about which is more important for the forthcoming narrative.⁴⁸

---

47. Cf. also *h. Hom.* 31.18. For an analysis of the opening addresses to the Muses, see C. R. Beye, *Epic and Romance in the Argonautica of Apollonius* (Carbondale 1982) 13–17, although I consider the ἀπορία expressed in the *prooimion* to Book 4 to be more traditional than he argues.

48. Perhaps the most famous Hellenistic rhapsodic *prooimion* is the hymn to Zeus which opens Aratos' *Phainomena*: Ἐκ Διὸς ἀρχώμεσθα, τόν. The praise of Zeus in lines 2–14 narrows the focus of his *aretai* to the σήματα he has established for the benefit of mankind. It is not fortuitous that these signs constitute the subject of the treatise. Rhapsodic hymns continue to be composed in various metrical forms in the Hellenistic period. Cf. Anon., *Paian Erythr.* (934 *PMG*), [Telesilla] 935 *PMG*, Anon., *Paian in Apol.* (Powell 141), Anon., *Hymn. in Vest.*

William H. Race

B. The cultic tradition

Cultic hymns are distinguished from rhapsodic by their consistent second-person address to the god or goddess ("Du-Stil") and by their more personal tone, for they portray the speaker as praying or supplicating (e.g., εὔχομαι, λίσσομαι) and attempting to establish a close "I-Thou" relationship with the god by requesting his attention (e.g. κλῦθι μευ/μοι) or presence (e.g., δεῦρο, ἐλθέ) and by reminding him of past interactions (e.g., εἴ ποτέ τοι). Unlike rhapsodic hymns, which consistently maintain an impersonal tone and envision generalized performances, they are often concerned with a specific occasion and contain a specific request. In a rhapsodic hymn the primary intention is to tell *about* the god, and when the poet includes a request it is either a simple petition to the Muse at the beginning (e.g., ὕμνει Μοῦσα) or a perfunctory one to the god in the envoi of the hymn; in a cultic hymn, in contrast, the request is so important that every element is designed to dispose the god favorably to it. When the request predominates, the cultic hymn becomes indistinguishable from a prayer.[49]

The following table shows the principal distinguishing features of rhapsodic and cultic hymns:

	rhapsodic hymns	cultic hymns
poet's role	composer (ἄρχομ᾽ ἀείδειν, Μοῦσά μοι ἔννεπε)[50]	suppliant (λίσσομαι, εὔχομαι)
divine subject	named in oblique case	directly addressed

(Powell 164–65), Isyllos, *Paian* (Powell 134–35), Limenios, *Paian* (Powell 149–50), and Heliodoros, *A.P.* 9.485. Late epics also begin with rhapsodic invocations (e.g., Nonnos, *Dion.* 1.1–45 and Mousaios, *Hero and Leander* 1–15), as do late didactic treatises (e.g., Oppian, *Kyn.* 1.1–46).

49. The model cultic prayer of Chryses at *Il.* 1.37–42 is called a κλητικὸς ὕμνος by Menander Rhetor (335.13). In this article I do not attempt to distinguish kletic hymns from prayers.

50. Since the request to the Muse is formally a prayer, it can be expanded with cultic features, as at *Il.* 2.484–85: Ἔσπετε νῦν μοι Μοῦσαι Ὀλύμπια δώματ᾽ ἔχουσαι· | ὑμεῖς γὰρ θεαί ἐστε πάρεστέ τε ἴστέ τε πάντα. The lyric poets also expanded introductory addresses to the Muses. A good example is Alkman 27 *PMG*: Μῶσ᾽ ἄγε Καλλιόπα θύγατερ Διός | ἄρχ᾽ ἐρατῶν ϝεπέων, ἐπὶ δ᾽ ἵμερον | ὕμνῳ καὶ χαρίεντα τίθη χορόν. The request for a pleasing song, in rhapsodic hymns reserved for the envoi (cf. *h. Hom.* 10.5: δὸς δ᾽ ἱμερόεσσαν ἀοιδήν), is here part of the invocation. Cf. also Alkm. 3 *PMG*: [Μώσαι Ὀλ]υμπιάδες, περί με φρένας | [ἱμέρῳ νέα]ς ἀοιδᾶς | πίμπλατε and 14 *PMG*: Μῶσ᾽ ἄγε Μῶσα λίγηα πολυμμελές | αἰὲν ἀοιδὲ μέλος | νεοχμὸν ἄρχε παρσένοις ἀείδην. According to a scholion (193 *PMG*) Stesichoros' two palinodes began with invocations to the Muse: δεῦρ᾽ αὖτε θεὰ φιλόμολπε and χρυσόπτερε παρθένε.

How Greek poems begin

	rhapsodic hymns	cultic hymns
treatment of subject	narrative (ὅς/ἥ...)	hypomnesis (εἴ ποτε)
selection of subject	rhapsodic questions (τίς; πῶς; ἤ...ἤ;)	aporia (concerning an attribute[51])
leave-taking	salutation (χαῖρε, ἴληθι); request for a pleasing song; announcement of another song to follow	request (κλῦθι, ἐλθέ)

Cultic hymns are much more flexible than rhapsodic hymns, because they consist of many more elements, any of which can be expanded *ad libitum* by the poet;[52] they play a much greater role in Greek poetry in general, whether as complete poems or as beginnings of longer ones. Since it is impossible to cover the full array of cultic hymns, we shall briefly treat three lyric examples, beginning with Sappho, *fr.* 1, which consists entirely of a hymn to Aphrodite (Ποικιλόθρον' ἀθανάτ'Ἀφρόδιτα). This poem masterfully employs a cultic hymn to make a programmatic statement. If, as D. A. Campbell has suggested, this poem stood at the head of Sappho's collection,[53] then it formed a striking hymnal introduction to her love poetry. The personal relationship which she depicts between herself and the goddess, whom she portrays in the lengthy *hypomnesis* as addressing her by name (ὦ | Ψάπφ', 19–20), well illustrates the intimacy possible in a cultic hymn – and, if this poem did introduce her works, her name neatly constitutes a σφραγίς. As is typical of cultic hymns, the request predominates.[54]

Anakreon similarly uses cultic hymns to set forth his program of erotic poetry. In 357 *PMG* he requests Dionysos, whose amorous

---

51. Rhapsodic hymns pose questions about which god to sing, which particular exploit to treat, or where to begin the narrative ("rhapsodic questions"); *aporia* in cultic hymns generally involves selecting the proper name, attribute, epithet, or sacrificial offering. For examples of *aporia* in cultic hymns, see Norden (above note 17) 144–47.

52. For a list and discussion of the parts of cultic hymns, see Race (above note 38).

53. See D. A. Campbell, *Greek Lyric Poetry* (New York 1967) 264 and Race (above note 10) 31–32.

54. There are actually six requests, arranged in the sequence a b b a c c. The imperatives ἀλλὰ τυίδ' ἔλθ' (5) and ἔλθε μοι καὶ νῦν (25), placed at the beginning of the second and final stanzas, demarcate the lengthy *hypomnesis* (αἴ ποτα...κωὐκ ἐθέλοισα, 5–24) from the preliminary and subsequent requests for release from unhappiness: μή μ' ἄσαισι μηδ' ὀνίαισι δάμνα (3) and χαλέπαν δὲ λῦσον ἐκ μερίμναν (26), which are topped off with the final two positive requests: τέλεσον...σύμμαχος ἔσσο (27–28). There are numerous fragments of cultic hymns by Sappho (*frr.* 2, 5, 17) and Alkaios (*frr.* 34, 45, 69, 129, 296b, and 308b, which opened the second book of his poems), but none is complete enough for sure analysis.

nature is emphasized through his companion deities, to come (ἔλθ' ἡμίν), to heed (ἐπακούειν) his prayer (εὐχωλῆς), and to persuade the reluctant boy, Kleoboulos:[55]

> ὦναξ, ᾧ δαμάλης Ἔρως
> καὶ Νύμφαι κυανώπιδες
> πορφυρῆ τ' Ἀφροδίτη
> συμπαίζουσιν, ἐπιστρέφεαι
> δ' ὑψηλὰς ὀρέων κορυφάς·
> γουνοῦμαί σε, σὺ δ' εὐμενὴς
> ἔλθ' ἡμίν, κεχαρισμένης
> δ' εὐχωλῆς ἐπακούειν·
> Κλεοβούλῳ δ' ἀγαθὸς γένεο
> σύμβουλος, τὸν ἐμόν γ' ἔρω-
> τ', ὦ Δεόνυσε, δέχεσθαι.

Pindar, whose hymnal *prooimia* are deservedly famous for their striking effects, opens sixteen epinicians with cultic hymns.[56] Who could forget the celebrated hymn to the Lyre that opens *Pyth.* 1 or the hymn to Theia in *Isth.* 5?[57] All of his opening hymns display similar creative energy. I select one example, *Nem.* 7.1-8:

> Ἐλείθυια, πάρεδρε Μοιρᾶν βαθυφρόνων,
> παῖ μεγαλοσθενέος, ἄκου-
> σον, Ἥρας, γενέτειρα τέκνων· ἄνευ σέθεν
> οὐ φάος, οὐ μέλαιναν δρακέντες εὐφρόναν
> τεὰν ἀδελφεὰν ἐλάχομεν ἀγλαόγυιον Ἥβαν.
> ἀναπνέομεν δ' οὐχ ἅπαντες ἐπὶ ἴσα·
> εἴργει δὲ πότμῳ ζυγένθ' ἕτερον ἕτερα. σὺν δὲ τίν
> καὶ παῖς ὁ Θεαρίωνος ἀρετᾷ κριθείς
> εὔδοξος ἀείδεται Σωγένης μετὰ πενταέθλοις.

55. Cf. also Anakr. 348 *PMG*: γουνοῦμαί σ' ἐλαφηβόλε. There are also proemial prayers in elegy. The prayer to the Muses which opens Solon's longest extant poem (13 W) shows an even further development towards an independent cultic invocation of the Muses (cf. κλῦτέ μοι εὐχομένῳ, 2), for he does not request them to begin or to guide his song, but to provide ὄλβος and δόξα. Theognis begins his collection of gnomic poetry with a series of hymns containing elements from both traditions, a mixture which perhaps reflects the diverse nature of the collection that follows. For a detailed treatment of the problems in these hymns and of their relationship to the collection, see B. A. van Groningen, *Theognis* (Amsterdam 1966) 9–18.

56. Opening cultic hymns include *Ol.* 4.1-10, 5.1-8, 8.1-7, 12.1-6a, 14.1-17; *Pyth.* 1.1-12, 2.1-7, 8.1-12, 11.1-12, 12.1-6; *Nem.* 1.1-6, 7.1-8, 8.1-3, 11.1-10; *Isth.* 1.1-6, and 5.1-10. Bakchylides opens five epinicians with cultic hymns: 2.1-10, 7.1-10, 10.1-8, 11.1-12, 14B.1-6.

57. For a good appreciation of the hymn to Theia, see H. Fränkel, *Early Greek Poetry and Philosophy*, tr. M. Hadas and J. Willis (Oxford 1975) 485–88. Contrast the effects of the προοιμίων ἀμβολάς of the *phorminx* in *Pyth.* 1 with the whirring of the timbrels that lead off (κατάρχει, 8) the celebration in *Dith.* 2 (*fr.* 70b).

Unlike rhapsodic hymns, which either name their subject in the opening lines or delay it through disjunctive lists, cultic hymns are often much more indirect, sometimes withholding the topic of concern for a long time. Here the hymn to Eleithyia, after providing her *sedes* (πάρεδρε Μοιρᾶν βαθυφρόνων) and genealogy (παῖ μεγαλοσθενέος Ἥρας), sketches her effects on humans, who all depend upon her for birth. And yet, from that birth we all have different aspirations and are constrained in different ways by destiny (here again is the motif of comparison and contrast). The point of Eleithyia's close association with the deep-counseling Fates becomes clear: we are born with certain limitations on our aspirations. Out of this diversity of human experience (cf. οὐχ ἅπαντες ἐπὶ ἴσα, 5; ἕτερον ἕτερα, 6), Sogenes, with Eleithyia's help, has emerged victorious as a pentathlete. The hymn has provided a context within which the victory takes on significance.[58] In the final section, we shall briefly examine two Pindaric examples of innovative use of hymnal forms.[59]

V. Combinations and innovations

To conclude, I wish to analyze briefly several hymnal openings of Hesiod, Pindar, and Kallimachos that combine features of two or more types we have surveyed.

A. Hesiod's Works and Days

Unlike the grand rhapsodic proem to the *Theogony*, whose overall function is to announce its main theme (θεῶν γένος, 44) and to establish a "beginning" for the narrative, the proem to the *Works and Days* introduces a more restricted subject, the poet's counsel to

---

58. The practical efficacy of opening cultic hymns or prayers is that they can highlight a subject by means of progressive specification. Often they function as priamels, as Bundy (above note 37) 36 has demonstrated. Very frequently the request asks the god to look favorably upon (e.g., δέξαι) the particular celebration (e.g., τόνδε κῶμον); cf. *Ol.* 4.9, 5.3, 8.10, 14.16; *Pyth.* 8.5, 12.5; *Nem.* 11.3; and *Isth.* 7.20–21.

59. Cultic hymns continue to play an important role in hexameter poetry (e.g., Kleanthes' *Hymn to Zeus* and Orphic Hymns) and in lyric poetry (e.g., Aristotle's *Hymn to Arete*). A number of plays open with prayers followed by narratives which explain the dramatic situation: Aisch. *Supp.* 1–4, *Ag.* 1–7, *Choe.* 1–3, *Eum.* 1–2; Eur. *Supp.* 1–4, *Phoi.* 1–3, *Kykl.* 1–2; and the mock hymn at Aristoph. *Ekkl.* 1–5. Theokritos opens *Id.* 28 with a mock hymn to a distaff.

his brother. Although it is formally similar to the shorter Homeric Hymns, it includes language and features from the cultic tradition. In the invocation, instead of the simple ὕμνει Μοῦσα, the poet adds an appeal, common in cultic hymns, to be present (δεῦτε, 2) and relegates the subject of the hymn (Zeus) to the second line, a procedure unique among rhapsodic hymns of the archaic period. In the body, the anaphoric listing of Zeus' powers is typical of cultic hymns (cf. the Orphic Hymns). Then, in the salutation, instead of the usual rhapsodic dismissal (χαῖρε), he uses a cultic request: κλῦθι ἰδὼν ἀίων τε, δίκη δ' ἴθυνε θέμιστας | τύνη· ἐγὼ δέ κε Πέρσῃ ἐτήτυμα μυθησαίμην (9–10). Here the rhapsodic closing formula αὐτὰρ ἐγὼ καὶ σεῖο καὶ ἄλλης μνήσομ' ἀοιδῆς, by which the rhapsode promises to keep the god in mind as he turns to another theme, is neatly adapted to announce his intention to counsel Perses.[60] These formal adjustments suggest that the forthcoming lines will not be in the epic narrative style (as the *Theogony*) but rather in a more personal vein. The prominence of βροτοὶ ἄνδρες (3) in the body of the hymn shows that Hesiod is primarily thinking of Zeus's general control over human affairs, while the request narrows the concern to justice. The portrayal of Zeus's power to effect sudden reversals in men's lives serves as the basis for the warning which Hesiod gives his brother.[61] By invoking the justice of Zeus as authority for his counsel, Hesiod uses the hymnal *prooimion* to lay the foundation for the entire work.

B. Pindar

By far the most innovative lyric poet is Pindar, whose creative adaptations and combinations of his inherited traditions paved the way for later experimentation.[62] The opening of every Pindaric ode is extraordinary in one way or another and repays repeated examination; I have selected just three examples. The

---

60. See West, *Hesiod Works and Days* (Oxford 1978) 141 and Janko (above note 21) 15–16 and 22. The optative μυθησαίμην is a polite form of the intentional future (μεταβήσομαι).
61. Cf. Odysseus' warning to Amphinomos (*Od.* 18.125–50), Solon's didactic elegy (13 W), and Thouk. 5.90, where the Melians remind the Athenians that they too might eventually need to invoke τὸ κοινὸν ἀγαθόν.
62. See A. W. Bulloch, *Callimachus, The Fifth Hymn* (Cambridge 1985) 7, who points out that "in tone and mode of writing [Pindar] is often the precursor of Hellenistic hymnal style."

How Greek poems begin

first is *Nem.* 2.1–5, which Pindar opens discursively, comparing the athlete's first major victory to a rhapsode's introduction:

> Ὅθεν περ καὶ Ὁμηρίδαι
> ῥαπτῶν ἐπέων τὰ πόλλ' ἀοιδοί
> ἄρχονται, Διὸς ἐκ προοιμίου, καὶ ὅδ' ἀνήρ
> καταβολὰν ἱερῶν ἀγώ-
>   νων νικαφορίας δέδεκται πρῶτον, Νεμεαίου
> ἐν πολυυμνήτῳ Διὸς ἄλσει.

Not only the comparison, but also the vocabulary, is drawn from rhapsodic hymns, including the reference to the epic tradition (Ὁμηρίδαι, ἐπέων), the designation of rhapsodes (ῥαπτῶν, ἀοιδοί), the technical term *prooimion* (προοιμίου), and the echo of ἄρχομ' ἀείδειν in ἀοιδοί | ἄρχονται. Even the starting-point of the narrative is designated by πρῶτον (4), as the poet predicts that the youthful athlete will go on to win more prestigious crowns.

The second is *Isth.* 1.1–6:

> Μᾶτερ ἐμά, τὸ τεόν, χρύσασπι Θήβα,
> πρᾶγμα καὶ ἀσχολίας ὑπέρτερον
> θήσομαι. μή μοι κραναὰ νεμεσάσαι
> Δᾶλος, ἐν ᾇ κέχυμαι.
> τί φίλτερον κεδνῶν τοκέων ἀγαθοῖς;
> εἶξον, ὦ 'Απολλωνιάς· ἀμφοτερᾶν
>   τοι χαρίτων σὺν θεοῖς ζεύξω τέλος...

In this famous passage treated in detail by Bundy,[63] Pindar combines three types of openings: a cultic address to the honoured divinity (Theba), a dramatic dilemma (he must interrupt composing a *paian* to Delos in order to celebrate Theba, since in the meantime Thebans have won six victories in one Isthmian festival),[64] and a discursive argument, in which he justifies beginning with Theba because of filial devotion, but reassures Delos that he will eventually hymn them both.[65]

---

63. Bundy (above note 37) 36–42. He also demonstrates the close formal relationship of this argument to those that open *Nem.* 6 and *Pyth.* 10.

64. For an analysis of the opening lines, which argues that Thebans won six crowns at the most recent Isthmian festival, see W. H. Race, "The Six Crowns at Pindar, *Isthmian* 1.10–12," *GRBS* 30 (1989) 27–39.

65. The poet's ἀπορία (which goddess should he hymn first?) is also typical of rhapsodic openings. Just as Theokritos chooses Polydeukes first but will eventually sing of both (ἀμφοτέρους; see above page 26), so Pindar begins with Theba but promises eventually to sing of both goddesses (ἀμφοτερᾶν, 6). The motif was adapted to prose *prooimia*, as at Andok., *de Myst.* 8 ("Shall I begin with x, y, or z?" cf. πάντα).

The opening of *Nem.* 3 is a complex interweaving of four types: rhapsodic, cultic, dramatic, and discursive.

> Ὦ πότνια Μοῖσα, μᾶτερ ἀμετέρα, λίσσομαι,
> τὰν πολυξέναν ἐν ἱερομηνίᾳ Νεμεάδι
> ἵκεο Δωρίδα νᾶσον Αἴγιναν· ὕδατι γάρ
> μένοντ' ἐπ' Ἀσωπίῳ μελιγαρύων τέκτονες
> κώμων νεανίαι, σέθεν ὄπα μαιόμενοι.
> διψῇ δὲ πρᾶγος ἄλλο μὲν ἄλλου,
> ἀεθλονικία δὲ μάλιστ' ἀοιδὰν φιλεῖ,
> στεφάνων ἀρετᾶν τε δεξιωτάταν ὀπαδόν·
> τᾶς ἀφθονίαν ὄπαζε μήτιος ἁμᾶς ἄπο·
> ἄρχε δ' οὐρανοῦ πολυνεφέλα κρέοντι, θύγατερ,
> δόκιμον ὕμνον· ἐγὼ δὲ κείνων τέ νιν ὀάροις
> λύρᾳ τε κοινάσομαι.

The passage consists of a rhapsodic core embellished by cultic elements. To isolate the rhapsodic elements we may compare the opening of *h. Hom.* 31: Ἥλιον ὑμνεῖν αὖτε Διὸς τέκος ἄρχεο Μοῦσα, where ὑμνεῖν = ὕμνον (11); Διός = οὐρανοῦ κρέοντι (10); τέκος = θύγατερ (10); ἄρχεο = ἄρχε (10); and Μοῦσα = Μοῖσα (1). The cultic elements consist of the verb of supplication λίσσομαι (1), the request to come (ἵκεο, 3), and the consistent "Du–Stil" (πότνια, 1; σέθεν, 5; ὄπαζε, 9), which establishes a close I–Thou relationship (cf. μᾶτερ ἀμετέρα, 1). The one element in the Homeric Hymn not directly accounted for is αὖτε "on this occasion." Pindar has, as it were, elaborated αὖτε into a dramatic situation. The ode is overdue (cf. ὀψέ, 80) and the coming of the Muse is urgent – the celebrants are eagerly awaiting her voice; their need for song, expressed as craving (cf. διψῇ, 6) and desire (cf. φιλεῖ, 7), is amplified by a discursive priamel (6–8). All of these elements combine to invest the opening with intensity and life.[66]

C. Kallimachos

Kallimachos' six hymns display sophisticated adaptations of rhapsodic techniques.[67] His most obvious innovation, in line with Hellenistic practice in general, consists of creating dramatic

---

66. *Ol.* 10, also a late ode, has a similarly complex opening based on rhapsodic formulas; see Race (above note 38) 113–15.

67. For a detailed analysis of Pindaric and Kallimachean innovations of the hymnal tradition, see Bundy (above note 17). See also Bulloch (above note 62) 7–8 for a brief but excellent description of Kallimachos' use of and departure from the hymnic tradition.

How Greek poems begin

settings, for with the exception of *Hymn* 3 to Artemis, he presents each hymn as actually occurring during a ceremony. Thus the *Hymn to Zeus* opens as libations are being offered (Ζηνὸς... παρὰ σπονδῆσιν, 1).[68] The *Hymn to Apollo* portrays an elaborate opening scene of rapt anticipation of Apollo's arrival (cf. the exclamatory openings of the first two lines, οἷον... οἷα), as the poet details the signs of his presence, the shaking of the laurel branch and of the temple, the nodding of the palm, and the singing of the swan. His addresses to the audience in lines 2, 4, and 7 present a lively scene of preparations for the epiphany of the god. The *Hymn to Demeter* also opens dramatically by calling attention to the moving basket in the ceremony: Τῶ καλάθω κατιόντος (1).[69]

The openings of Kallimachos' hymns contain variations of many rhapsodic features. For example, in the *Hymn to Zeus*, rather than stating outright the subject of the hymn, the poet poses a rhetorical question typical of rhapsodic hymns: Ζηνὸς ἔοι τί κεν ἄλλο παρὰ σπονδῆσιν ἀείδειν | λώιον ἢ θεὸν αὐτόν; This maneuver is already found in Pindar; in fact, the wording suggests that Kallimachos had Pindar in mind.[70] Having established Zeus as his subject, the poet pauses in ἀπορία before beginning his narrative,[71] because the god's birthplace is disputed: πῶς καί μιν, Δικταῖον ἀείσομεν ἠὲ Λυκαῖον (4). In a brief discursive argument (5–9), he masterfully adapts the strategy of *h. Hom.* 1.1ff. (cf. ψευδόμενοι, 6) by quoting the proverb "all Kretans are liars" (8), thereby selecting Arkadia as the correct place of his birth: ἐν δέ σε Παρρασίη Ῥείη τέκεν (10).

The *Hymn to Delos* begins with a variation of a rhapsodic

---

68. See the discussion of G. R. McLennan, *Callimachus, Hymn to Zeus: Introduction and Commentary* (Rome 1977) 26.
69. See N. Hopkinson, *Callimachus, Hymn to Demeter* (Cambridge 1984) 77, who rightly stresses the deictic use of the definite article and the mimetic effect of the opening.
70. Cf. *fr.* 89: Τί κάλλιον ἀρχομένοις ἢ καταπαυομένοισιν | ἢ βαθύζωνόν τε Λατώ | καὶ θοᾶν ἵππων ἐλάτειραν ἀεῖσαι; Aristophanes parodies this opening at *Eq.* 1264–67; see H. Kleinknecht, *Die Gebetsparodie in der Antike* (Stuttgart 1937) 109 note 2. Cf. also the much more extended version at *Pyth.* 7.1–8:

    Κάλλιστον αἱ μεγαλοπόλιες Ἀθᾶναι
    προοίμιον Ἀλκμανιδᾶν εὐρυσθενεῖ
    γενεᾷ κρηπῖδ᾽ ἀοιδᾶν ἵπποισι βαλέσθαι.
    ἐπεὶ τίνα πάτραν, τίνα οἶκον ναίων ὀνυμάξεαι
    ἐπιφανέστερον
    Ἑλλάδι πυθέσθαι;

71. We have seen that such ἀπορία is very common in rhapsodic openings; see above pages 24–26 with notes 26, 37, 39, 40, 41, and 65.

question, addressed to his θυμός, asking not what subject he should sing of, but when he shall sing. With the very question comes the answer, prominently displayed at the beginning of the second line, for he has already begun to sing of Delos. The rest of the *prooimion* is an elaborate explanation of the appropriateness of his choice of Delos first from among all the Kyklades: because Delos is held first in esteem (τὰ πρῶτα, 4) by the Muses and because she first (πρώτη, 6) accepted Apollo as a god. Here πρῶτος has both its rhapsodic senses: qualitative and temporal priority. After singling her out from among all the Kyklades in the following lines (16–27), the poet pauses to begin his narrative with the question (answered immediately):

εἰ δὲ λίην πολέες σε περιτροχόωσιν ἀοιδαί,
ποίῃ ἐνιπλέξω σε; τί τοι θυμῆρες ἀκοῦσαι;
ἦ ὡς τὰ πρώτιστα...

Here the superlative πρώτιστα (30) finally marks the very beginning of the narrative (in contrast to the previous uses of πρῶτος in 4, 6, 16, and 22).[72]

VI. Conclusion

By distinguishing these four types of openings, we have been able to highlight the creative adaptations and combinations that mark Greek poetry from its very beginnings to its late representatives in the empire. These forms proved to be remarkably durable, yet flexible enough to permit poets to adapt them to various sorts of poetic occasions and invest them with freshness and individuality. Outstanding in this regard are the innovations of Hesiod, the author of the Homeric *Hymn to Apollo*, Sappho, Pindar, Theokritos, and Kallimachos.

72. Cf. the importance of πρώτιστα at Hes. *Th.* 24 and 116 (discussed above page 23).

How Greek poems begin

Index locorum

Aischylos: (*Ag.* 1–7) 31 n. 59; (*Choe.* 1–3) 31 n. 59; (*Eum.* 1–2) 31 n. 59; (*Pers.* init.) 14 n. 3; (*Suppl.* 1–4) 31 n. 59
Alkaios: (*fr.* 34) 29 n. 54; (*fr.* 42.1ff.) 16; (*fr.* 45) 29 n. 54; (*fr.* 69) 29 n. 54; (*fr.* 129) 29 n. 54; (*fr.* 208) 15 n. 7; (*fr.* 296b) 29 n. 54; (*fr.* 308b) 29 n. 54; (*fr.* 332) 15 n. 7; (*fr.* 338) 13 n. 2
Alkman: (*fr.* 3) 28 n. 50; (*fr.* 14) 28 n. 50; (*fr.* 27) 28 n. 50
Anakreon (*fr.* 348) 30 n. 55; (*fr.* 357) 29–30; (*fr.* 358.1–2) 15; (*fr.* 360.1) 15; (*fr.* 417.1–2) 15
Anakreontea: (6) 14
Andokides: (*de Myst.* 8) 25 n. 4, 33 n. 65
Anonymous: (*Hymn. in Vest.* = Powell 164–65) 27 n. 48; (inscr. Douris cup) 20 n. 20; (*Paian Erythr.* = 934 *PMG*) 27 n. 48; (*Paian in Apol.* = Powell 141) 27 n. 48; (schol. 193 *PMG*) 28 n. 50
Apollonios Rhodios, *Argonautika*: (1.1–2) 26; (3.1–5) 27; (4.1–6) 27; (4.6) 26 n. 45
Aratos: (*Phainomena* 1–14) 27 n. 48
Aristophanes: (*Acharn.* 1–3) 17 n. 13; (*Ekkl.* 1–5) 31 n. 59; (*Eq.* 1264–67) 35 n. 70; (*Plout.* 1–14) 17 n. 13
Aristotle: (*Hymn to Arete* = 842 *PMG*) 31 n. 59
Athenaios: (430AB) 13 n. 2

Bakchylides: (1.1–5) 24 n. 38; (2.1–10) 30 n. 56; (3.1–3) 24; (7.1–10) 30 n. 56; (9.1–6) 24 n. 38; (10.1–8) 30 n. 56; (11.1–12) 30 n. 56; (12.1–4) 24 n. 38; (14.1–20) 17 n. 13; (14B.1–6) 30 n. 56; (15.47–48) 26 n. 45; (17.1–4) 14; (18 init.) 15; (20.1) 14, 14 n. 5
Bion: (1) 16 n. 9

Choirilos: (*fr.* 1) 18 n. 15
Cicero: (*de Or.* 2.320) 17 n. 14; (*Orat.* 50) 17 n. 14

Dionysios of Halikarnassos: (*Imit.* 6.205) 16 n. 11

Euripides: (*Alk.* init.) 14; (*And.* 2) 14; (*Bakch.* 2) 14; (*El.* 2) 14; (*Hek.* init.) 14; (*Hel.* init.) 14; (*Her.* 2) 14; (*Herakl.* 1–6) 17 n. 13; (*Hipp.* init.) 14; (*I.A.* init.) 14; (*I.T.* init.) 14; (*Ion* init.) 14; (*Kykl.* 1–2) 31 n. 59; (*Med.* 4) 14; (*Or.* 1–3) 17 n. 13; (*Phoi.* 1–3) 31 n. 59; (*Supp.* 1–4) 31 n. 59; (*Tr.* 4) 14
Eustathios: (*ad Od.* 1.10) 22 n. 28

Heliodoros: (*A.P.* 9.485) 27 n. 48
Herodas: (*Mime* 4.1–18) 15–16
Herodotos: (1.2) 23 n. 35; (1.5) 23; (1.6.1) 26 n. 45; (1.7–25) 21 n. 27
Hesiod, *Theogony*: (1–115) 23 n. 33; (1–116) 22–23; (24) 36 n. 72; (44) 31; (116) 26 n. 45, 36 n. 72
Works and Days: (1–2) 22; (1–10) 31–32
Homer, *Iliad*: (1.1–2) 20; (1.6) 20–21, 23, 23 n. 36; (1.8–9) 21, 24–25; (1.9) 26 n. 45; (1.37–42) 28 n. 49; (2.484–85) 28 n. 50; (2.484–87) 27; (16.113) 21 n. 23
Odyssey: (1.1) 23 n. 33; (1.1–2) 20; (1.1–4) 22; (1.10) 21; (1.11–21) 22; (8.268) 21 n. 23; (8.75ff.) 21 n. 24; (9.14–16) 26 n. 44; (18.125–50) 32 n. 61
Homeric Hymns: (1.1ff.) 35; (2.1) 20; (3.19–25) 21 n. 26; (3.29–115) 21 n. 27; (3.146–76) 19; (3.207–14) 21 n. 26; (5.1) 20, 23 n. 33; (8) 20 n. 19; (10.5) 28 n. 50; (21) 20 n. 19; (24) 20 n. 19; (25) 22 n. 30; (29) 20 n. 19; (31.1) 34; (31.18) 27 n. 47; (31.18–19) 19 n. 18; (32.18–19) 26–27; (32.18–20) 19 n. 18
[Homer]: (*Batrach.* 8–9) 26 n. 45; (*Epigonoi* init.) 20 n. 20; (*Little Iliad* init.) 20; (*Thebaid* init.) 20
Horace, *Carmina*: (1.4) 13 n. 2; (1.9) 13 n. 2; (3.30.13) 23 n. 36; (4.7) 13 n. 2
Hyperides: (*Epitaph.* 9) 25 n. 41

Ibykos: (*fr.* 286) 13 n. 2
Isyllos: (*Paian* = Powell 134–35) 27 n. 48

Kallimachos, *Aitia*: (prologue) 16 n. 10, 18; (*fr.* 1.21–22) 22 n. 31
Hymns: (1.1–10) 35; (2.1–7) 35; (3) 35; (4) 23 n. 34; (4.1–30) 35–36; (6.1) 35
Kleanthes: (*Hymn to Zeus*) 31 n. 59

37

Limenios: (*Paian* = Powell 149–50) 27 n.
  48
Loukian: (*encom. Demosth.* 19) 25 n. 40
Lykophron: (*Alexandra* init.) 15

Menander: (*Dysk.* init.) 14
Menander Rhetor: (335.13) 28 n. 49;
  (437.27–30) 25 n. 41; (438.6–9) 25
  n. 41
Milton: (*P.L.* 1.1) 23
Mimnermos: (*fr.* 1.1W) 16 n. 12
Mousaios, *Hero and Leander*: (1–15) 27 n.
  48; (16) 26 n. 45

Nonnos: (*Dion.* 1.1–45) 27 n. 48

Oppian, *Kynegetika*: (1.1–46) 27 n. 48;
  (1.20–40) 16 n. 10
Orphic Hymns: 31 n. 59, 32

Pindar, *Olympians*: (1.1–7) 17; (2.1–7) 25;
  (2.3) 26 n. 45; (3.1–4) 24 n. 38;
  (4.1–10) 30 n. 56; (4.9) 31 n. 58;
  (5.1–8) 30 n. 56; (5.3) 31 n. 58; (6
  init.) 17; (7 init.) 17; (8.1–7) 30 n.
  56; (8.10) 31 n. 58; (9.1–10) 18; (10
  init.) 15, 34 n. 66; (11.1–5) 17;
  (12.1–6a) 30 n. 56; (14.1–17) 30 n.
  56; (14.16) 31 n. 58
Pythians: (1 init.) 30, 30 n. 57; (1.1–12)
  30 n. 56; (2.1–7) 30 n. 56; (4.1–3)
  24; (5.1–4) 17; (6.1) 15 n. 8; (7.1–7)
  17 n. 14; (7.1–8) 35 n. 70; (8.1–12)
  30 n. 56; (8.5) 31 n. 58; (9.1–4) 24
  n. 38; (10 init.) 33 n. 63; (10.1–4)
  18; (11.1–12) 30 n. 56; (12.1–6) 30
  n. 56; (12.5) 31 n. 58
Nemeans: (1.1–6) 30 n. 56; (2 init.)
  17; (2.1–3) 19 n. 18; (2.1–5) 33; (3
  init.) 15; (3.1–12) 34; (3.80) 34;
  (4.1ff.) 18; (5.1–2) 18; (6 init.) 33 n.
  63; (6.1–8ff.) 17; (7.1–8) 30–31, 30
  n. 56; (8.1–3) 30 n. 56; (9.1–3) 24 n.
  38; (10.1–2) 24; (10.2–22) 23 n. 37;
  (10.2–24) 24; (11.1–10) 30 n. 56;
  (11.3) 31 n. 58

Isthmians: (1 init.) 15; (1.1ff.) 26 n. 46;
  (1.1–6) 30 n. 56, 33; (2.1–11) 18;
  (3.1–3) 17; (5 init.) 30; (5.1–10) 30
  n. 56; (6.1ff.) 18; (6.1–4) 17;
  (7.20–21) 31 n. 58; (8.1–4) 15
Fragments: (29) 25, 25 n. 40; (70b.8) 30
  n. 57; (89) 35 n. 70
Plato: (*Phaido* 60D) 19 n. 18; (*Rep.* init.)
  14 n. 6
Proclus: (*Chr.* 104.23–24) 21 n. 24
Propertius: (1.1.1) 23; (3.1.3) 23 n. 36;
  (3.15.3–10) 23 n. 36

Quintilian: (10.1.63) 16 n. 11

Sappho: (*fr.* 1) 29; (*fr.* 2) 29 n. 54; (*fr.*
  5) 29 n. 54; (*fr.* 16.1ff.) 16; (*fr.* 17)
  29 n. 54; (*fr.* 31.1) 15
Solon: (*fr.* 13W) 30 n. 55, 32 n. 61
Sophokles: (*Phil.* 1–5) 14 n. 4; (*Trach.*
  1–5) 17 n. 13

[Telesilla]: (935 *PMG*) 27 n. 48
Theognis: (1ff.) 30 n.55
Theokritos, *Idylls*: (1.1) 16; (2) 16 n. 9;
  (3) 16 n. 9; (4) 16 n. 9; (5) 16 n. 9;
  (6) 14 n. 5; (7) 14 n. 5; (7.1–2) 14;
  (8) 14 n. 5; (9) 16 n. 9; (10) 16 n.
  9; (11.1–3) 18; (11.19–81) 18; (12)
  16 n. 9; (13) 18 n. 16; (14) 16 n. 9;
  (15) 16 n. 9; (16.1–5) 18; (16.5–80)
  18; (17.1–13) 25–26; (18) 14 n. 5;
  (19) 14 n. 5; (20) 14 n. 5; (21) 18 n.
  16; (22.1–26) 26; (23) 14 n. 5; (24)
  14 n. 5; (25) 14 n. 5; (26) 14 n. 5;
  (27) 16 n. 9; (28) 31 n. 59; (29) 18
  n. 16; (30) 14 n. 5
Thoukydides: (1.1.1) 25 n. 41; (1.23.4)
  25 n. 41; (1.23.5) 25 n. 41; (1.24ff.)
  21 n. 27; (1.24.1) 26 n. 45; (2.36.1)
  25 n. 41; (3.104) 19 n. 18; (5.90) 32
  n. 61

Virgil, *Aeneid*: (1.1) 23, 23 n. 36;
  (1.242ff.) 23 n. 36

The Muse corrects: the opening of the *Odyssey*

VICTORIA PEDRICK

The first ten verses of the *Odyssey* are a peculiar proem;[1] as Stephanie West in a recent commentary summarizes:

> Despite the care which has obviously been bestowed on its composition, this is...an odd opening for our *Odyssey*. It covers only a third of the poem (V–XII), not very accurately, and gives disproportionate emphasis to a single incident...[And] the suitors' sins are of far more importance for the poem as a whole than those of Odysseus' comrades. Moreover...Odysseus' wanderings do not take him much among the cities of men (3), but far from human society. None of the *speciosa miracula* which we associate with Odysseus...is mentioned. We do not expect a comprehensive summary of what is to come; but if the poet's purpose was, as it would be natural to suppose, simply to indicate enough of his theme to catch his audience's attention, his choice of detail is strange.[2]

The proem is thus incomplete as an introduction and skewed in its focus: the loss of Odysseus' crew due to its recklessness in eating the cattle of the Sun hardly seems the cardinal thematic episode in the epic. The proem also suffers from vagueness; while it is apparently similar in its structure to the openings of other early Greek narratives, it does not explicitly name its hero or its theme. Explanations for the vagueness and imprecision have included the

---

1. I wish to thank Francis Dunn, James Morrison, Sheila Murnaghan, and the reviewers for their helpful suggestions on earlier drafts of his paper.

2. Alfred Heubeck, Stephanie West, and J. B. Hainsworth, eds., *A Commentary on Homer's Odyssey*, vol. 1 (Oxford 1988) at 1.1–10; see also C. M. Bowra, *Homer* (London 1972) 117f. Studies of the proem include: Samuel Bassett, "The Proems of the Iliad and Odyssey," *AJP* 44 (1923) 339–48; Jenny Strauss Clay, *The Wrath of Athena. Gods and Men in the Odyssey* (Princeton 1983) 9–53; George Dimock, *The Unity of the Odyssey* (Amherst, MA, 1989) 5–12; A. van Groningen, "The Proems of the *Iliad* and the *Odyssey*," *Meded. Ned. Akad. van Wetensch. Afd. Letterkunde*, n.s. 9:8 (1946) 279–94; Ansgar Lenz, *Das Proöm des frühen griechischen Epos. Ein Beitrag zum poetischen Selbstverständnis* (Bonn 1980); Pietro Pucci, "The Proem of the *Odyssey*," *Arethusa* 15 (1982) 39–62; and Klaus Rüter, *Odysseeinterpretationen. Untersuchungen zum ersten Buch und zur Phaiakis*, ed. K. Matthiessen, *Hypomnemata* 19 (1969) 28–52, valuable for its meticulous identification of both the traditional and untraditional elements in the opening of the *Odyssey*.

analytic: *these* verses are not the original opening to *this Odyssey*.[3] More recently, critics have argued for the autonomy of the proem as the poet's statement of his agenda before he merges his human efforts with divine inspiration; these opening verses thus reflect his own biases, especially for his hero.[4] These defenders note that the proem indicates, for all its indirection, both Odysseus' identity and the epic's theme (*nostos*). The purpose of this essay is to discuss the peculiarities of the *Odyssey's* proem in the context of the next eleven verses, the remainder of its introduction. In these lines the narrator's request to the Muse (v. 10) is ostensibly being answered with the choice of a place to begin, but the goddess' expansive description of the opening situation (vv. 11–21) actually corrects the proem, supplying much that West finds missing and introducing the poem with a more appropriate tone. Thus I am suggesting that we hear the opening of the *Odyssey* as an exchange between the narrator and his Muse in which she participates more actively than normally supposed.[5]

We can imagine such an exchange if we conceive of both the narrator, who sings the proem, and the goddess he addresses as participants of the text as discourse, and as such capable of expressing views on how the narrative is to proceed. The Homeric narrator is increasingly the focus of study as fundamental for our understanding of how the epics work as narrative.[6] Scott Richardson describes this figure:

He is not a fictional character living in the heroic world of the epic, nor is he the historical author known as Homer. He is, rather, a quasi-fictional projection whose relationship to the other creations in the epics is not one between equals but one resembling that between 'an omnipotent god' and the mortals subject to him... He is nevertheless a

---

3. Denys Page, *The Homeric Odyssey* (Oxford 1955) 168, note 2, for instance, takes the analytic line; see also Heubeck, West, and Hainsworth (above, note 2) at 1–10.

4. See Clay (above, note 2) 34–38; and Dimock (above, note 2) 8f. for example.

5. Dimock (above, note 2) 12f. also discusses vv. 11–21 as specifically the Muse's, calling them her "deceptively gentle opening."

6. See Scott Richardson, *The Homeric Narrator* (Nashville, TN, 1990); another recent study of the epic narrator that depends upon narrative theory (or narratology) is Irene de Jong, *Narrators and Focalizers. The Presentation of the Story in the Iliad* (Amsterdam 1987). See also Elizabeth Block, "The Narrator Speaks: Apostrophe in Homer and Virgil," *TAPA* 112 (1982) 7–22, whose first note contains a description of the distinction between the poet and his narrator. The value of distinguishing between the real, flesh-and-blood poet or author and the internal narrator has long been recognized, as these scholars acknowledge; see, for instance, Wayne Booth, *The Rhetoric of Fiction* (Chicago 1961) 149–65.

fictional character of sorts, a metacharacter, who plays his role not on the level of the story, but on the level of the discourse, the telling of the story.

(p.2)

Although the narrator is usually an unobtrusive voice, narrating in the third person without much apparent editorial comment, the proem is exceptional.[7] Here the narrator directly addresses the Muse in his own voice to request help for the song he has in mind.[8] He relies on a traditional form for the proem, but this form allows his energy and ideas to emerge vividly, as we shall see.[9] Moreover, the proem of the *Odyssey*, and in particular the request for a starting point in verse 10, are unusual and powerful enough to create the illusion that this narrator has a problem on his hands which needs the Muse's help.

Just as the narrator is a character within the epic at the level of discourse, so too is the Muse, when he asks her to recite the story.[10] Others have described how the narrator conceives of the Muses he invokes: these goddesses do more than merely inspire his poetic production; they supply the facts of the heroic tradition and the

---

7. But see De Jong (above, note 6) *passim* for the interpretive role of the entity she calls the "focalizer," that is, that aspect of the narrator which slants the apparently objective narrative with judgments and evaluation and is thus responsible in essence for the narrative's point of view; on pp. 18–20 she outlines earlier scholars' categories for considering the "subjective" aspects of the Homeric narrative. See also Booth (above, note 6) 4–6; and Richardson (above, note 6) *passim*.

8. He even refers to himself with first-person pronouns, but μοι ἔννεπε (v. 1) is a typical phrase. For the usage μοι ἔννεπε (ἔσπετε) in invocations to the Muse(s), see *Hymn to Aphrodite*; *Hymn* 19; Hes., *Theog.* v. 114; *Il.* 2.484, 761, 11.218, 14.508, 16.112 and compare *Hymn* 14. Hes., *Erg.*, uses ἔννεπετε without the μοι; compare *Hymn* 33. Pucci (above, note 2) 40 argues that it is precisely the μοι in v. 1 that allows us to see the poet's personality so vividly in the poem's opening.

9. Among critics who argue that the proem is a statement of the poet's independent purposes, the most cogent is Jenny Strauss Clay (above, note 2) 9–53, who perceives an interdependent relationship between the poet and the Muse and thus concludes: "The poet pronounces the first ten lines of the *Odyssey*; the rest of the poem belongs properly to the Muse – or, at least, the poet transformed by the inspiration of the Muse. These introductory lines are the only ones that can be ascribed to the poet *in propria persona*" (p. 34). Clay relies on the second invocation in v. 10 as a signal of the poet's relinquishing control of his art to the Muse. Verse 10 is unusual, but it has, I believe, a somewhat different effect; see below. Pucci (above, note 2) 40 accepts her notion, as it is put forth in an earlier article, "The Beginning of the *Odyssey*," *AJP* 97 (1976) 313–16, 317, but without examining how far such autonomy can be expected to extend.

10. Characters within the story also pay homage to the Muse; see especially *Od.* 8.487–91 and 22.344–49. Thus this goddess also functions as a figure of inspiration at the level of the story.

detailed information that only divine eyewitnesses can have.[11] More recently Richardson and Irene De Jong have argued that the Muses should also be understood in invocations as figures of the narrator's prowess: he depends on their aid but the fact that they give it heralds his own outstanding skill.[12] I wish to argue further that sometimes the narrator employs these goddesses even more self-consciously. At the opening of the *Odyssey*, for instance, he addresses the Muse as a character at his own level of discourse so that he can enact the process of inspiration that transpires between them.[13] Together his proem and the Muse's response are an artifice: there is no genuine change of speaker for verses 11–21, so we must perceive them as representing the Muse's answer *as it is rendered by the narrator*.[14] But the fact that she not only fulfills the request of verse 10 but also corrects the whole proem makes the artifice more conspicuous – a reflection, in effect, on the difficulty of beginning an innovative epic.

In this exchange the narrator puts himself into the posture of needing correction so that the power of the Muse becomes

---

11. See *Il.* 2.484–87. For the powers of the Muses as they are suggested in the epics, see Clay, (above, note 2) 9–25; Lenz (above, note 2) 27–37, esp. 34ff.; Dimock (above, note 2) 5–8; also Mark W. Edwards, *Homer. Poet of the Iliad* (Baltimore 1987) 18f.

12. See De Jong, p. 52, and Richardson, p. 181 (both above, note 6).

13. On the narrator's self-consciousness, see now Richardson (above, note 6) chap. 7. Douglas J. Stewart, *The Disguised Guest. Rank, Role and Identity in the Odyssey* (Lewisburg, PA 1976) 161–63, discusses the poet's sense of autonomy as an artist. William G. Thalmann, *Conventions of Form and Thought in Early Greek Epic Poetry* (Baltimore 1984) 157–60, discusses the text's self-consciousness, especially about poetry. Another instance of this sort of enactment occurs in the *Iliad*, at the invocation before the catalogue of ships (2.484ff.). There is every reason to suppose that the real poet responsible for the *Odyssey* believed that he sang as well as he did because of divine inspiration, but I do not think that we witness the process in the poem's opening, at least not for the poet. As De Jong notes (above, note 6) 36, 44, the real poet's beliefs are properly the object of those engaged in reception theory; see, for instance, Thalmann, 126–29.

14. The artifice lies in the fact that under the guise of reporting the Muse's answer, the narrator is actually creating it – because he creates all of the text, even that which he attributes to his characters through direct quotations as their words. On the narrator's other mechanisms for reporting characters' speeches, see Richardson (above, note 6) 70–88; at 86f. he describes the process by which Demodokos' second song is reported: "But beginning at line 272 [of Book 8] or so we sense a sort of narratorial anacoluthon – the intention to render the song by quoting the singer's words indirectly has given way to what must be taken as direct discourse. The detail, the elaboration, and, above all, the directly quoted speeches of the characters point to the conclusion that these are the very words used by Demodokos himself. Yet there is no transition from indirect to direct discourse. What has occurred is a usurpation of Demodokos's song by the narrator." This seems an intriguing inversion of what happens in the epic's opening: we do not have usurpation of the Muse's words, but an attempt by the narrator to pass off his own as hers.

manifest.[15] Thus throughout this essay I shall argue for a double vision of the proem: on the one hand, it shows great skill, especially in its language and ideas; on the other, it needs help in overcoming traditional constraints. This paradox is a deliberate ploy, and one of its effects is to make it apparent that the Muse does more than provide the narrator with facts; she also helps him shape his song. Furthermore, in enacting this exchange in which a human voice encounters corrections from his most concerned listener (the goddess he has invoked), the narrator sets up a paradigm for what happens elsewhere in the epic between other singers or story-tellers and their audiences.

I

The peculiarities of the proem are the product of a clash between two conflicting impulses. While much within the opening ten verses is boldly innovative, to judge from other early hexameter poetry, these same verses are quite traditional in their structure and, more importantly, in their conception of how the epic should proceed. A daring idea approached in a conventional way: this is the problem the narrator develops in the proem and which his Muse must correct.

Let us begin our examination of what is traditional about the *Odyssey's* opening, and what is not, by comparing other proems. As has often been noted, early Greek epics and hymns open with a set structure that allows the narrator, as he invokes his Muse for inspiration, to mention the subject of his song and to state its theme.[16] In the Homeric Hymns the name of the god being praised usually appears in the accusative case as the first word of the song; an epithet, which can be thematically significant, follows. Pendent to the main clause is a relative one which further characterizes the god or begins the narrative if the hymn contains one. The opening of the *Hymn to Demeter* is illustrative:

15. Richardson (above, note 6) 181 remarks on this phenomenon: "It is striking that the Homeric narrator refers to himself in the first person only in these passages whose purpose is, paradoxically, to deny his autonomy. He draws attention to himself most explicitly just when he is making the point that he is incapable of narrating except through divine aid."

16. See Bassett (above, note 2); Rüter (above, note 2) 28–34; Lenz (above, note 2) 21–26; and Richard Janko, "The Structure of the Homeric Hymns: A Study in Genre," *Hermes* 109 (1981) 9–24 for detailed studies.

Victoria Pedrick

Δήμητρ' ἠΰκομον σεμνὴν θεὸν ἄρχομ' ἀείδειν,
αὐτὴν ἠδὲ θύγατρα τανύσφυρον ἣν Ἀϊδωνεὺς
ἥρπαξεν...

(1–3)

The absence of an invocation is not surprising; one occurs in only about a third of the hymns.[17] The second verse is unusual in its reiteration of the goddess Demeter, but the narrator chooses thus to introduce her daughter, on whom the relative clause beginning the mythic story depends.[18]

In more substantial hexameter narratives this opening structure can be altered to indicate thematic concerns as well. The *Iliad* gives a straightforward illustration of the changes: the narrator now states his theme in the accusative (μῆνιν) with the epithet οὐλομένην, while his subject, the main hero, shifts into the genitive case (Ἀχιλῆος).[19] The following relative clause, instead of beginning the narrative proper as often in the hymns, indicates the focus of the coming narrative by sketching in general but graphic terms the great cost of Achilleus' anger; it also introduces the will of Zeus as a second motivating force in the narrative (v. 5). The proem of the *Theogony* proper, after the introductory hymn to the Muses, has a similar structure.[20] The *Hymn to*

17. *Hymns* 4, 5, 9, 14, 17, 19, 20, 31, 32, 33; see Janko (above, note 16) 11. Nine hymns do not name their subjects in the accusative: 3, 5, 8, 19, 21, 24, 25, 29, 33. Of these, two use the genitive case because of the verb: 3 and 25; see the opening of the *Theogony*, v. 1; and the *Epigoni* v. 1. Two other hymns use a periphrasis – 19 and 33. Janko, p. 11, notes that the relative clause introduces either as enumeration of the god's attributes in the timeless present tense, or a mythological narrative in the past tense. See, however, Jenny Strauss Clay, *The Politics of Olympus. Form and Meaning in the Major Homeric Hymns* (Princeton 1989) 25–29.
As for the epithets, ἠΰκομον may ironically foreshadow how Demeter spends much of the poem in the dishevelment of mourning, and σεμνὴν θεόν can signal Demeter's quest for proper respect from both gods and mortals. Since the same line also introduces *Hymn* 13, also to Demeter, care is needed in such interpretation. I follow N. J. Richardson, *The Homeric Hymn to Demeter* (Oxford 1974), in reading θεόν; see his remarks at 1–3. θεάν is read by Thomas Allen, *Homeri Opera*, vol. v (Oxford 1912, reprinted with corrections 1946), on whose edition of Homer I otherwise rely throughout this paper.
18. See Richardson (above, note 17) at 1–3.
19. The use of Achilleus' patronymic in the first verse of the epic may be thematically significant. Arguments can certainly be made that the hero's relationship to his father is significant in a way that Odysseus' is not; see Clay (above, note 2) 26. But Πηληϊάδεω is a standard epithet for the genitive of his name in this final position, occurring five other times in the *Iliad* and twice in the *Odyssey*. See James Redfield, "The Proem of the *Iliad*: Homer's Art," *CP* 74 (1979) 99f.
20. Χαίρετε, τέκνα Διός, δότε δ' ἱμερόεσσαν ἀοιδήν·
κλείετε δ' ἀθανάτων ἱερὸν γένος αἰὲν ἐόντων,
οἳ Γῆς ἐξεγένοντο καὶ Οὐρανοῦ ἀστερόεντος,...

(104ff.)

The opening of the "Odyssey"

Aphrodite, an anomaly among the hymns in many respects, shows the kind of clever manipulation that is possible with such openings:[21]

Μοῦσά μοι ἔννεπε ἔργα πολυχρύσου Ἀφροδίτης
Κύπριδος, ἥ τε θεοῖσιν ἐπὶ γλυκὺν ἵμερον ὦρσε...

As in the *Iliad* and *Theogony* (although nowhere else in the *Hymns*), the narrator uses the accusative to mention his theme and the genitive to introduce his subject. Ἔργα... Ἀφροδίτης turns out to be ambiguous: as an opening it sounds like a promise to describe the goddess' powerful deeds, and the relative clause about the desire she evokes in all beings strengthens this interpretation. In the course of the poem, however, we realize that the ἔργα could also be her actions under the influence of the desire inflicted upon her by Zeus.[22] These three examples indicate that in the typical proem the narrator can state explicitly both the hero of his song and its theme, and suggest how it is to proceed.

The *Odyssey*'s opening verses represent a striking departure from the tradition:

Ἄνδρα μοι ἔννεπε, Μοῦσα, πολύτροπον, ὃς μάλα πολλὰ
πλάγχθη, ἐπεὶ Τροίης ἱερὸν πτολίεθρον ἔπερσε·

Neither the presumed theme of *nostos* nor the hero's name is specified: the only direct object is "the man." This is not an omission but a daring innovation: the absence of a proper name in either the accusative or in the genitive reveals that the narrator's purpose is not simply to identify his subject but to engage in the process of defining this man. The innovation implies that the traditional use of his name is no longer adequate to embrace the complex identity of this hero. A further implication is that, for this narrator, the heroic subject of his narrative and its theme are inextricably linked, such that the traditional practice of carefully

---

Verse 104 is the final line of the hymn to the Muses – the singer's farewell, as it is called; see Janko (above, note 16) 15f. It accounts, however, for the absence of an invocation in v.105, the opening of the *Theogony* proper. These verses otherwise conform to the traditional structure of a proem. The poet names his subjects – the immortals – in the genitive case, to allow his theme – their birth – to appear as well. The relative clause indicates two further desiderata of the narrative: that it begin very early, with Earth and Sky; and that it proceed down to the Olympians (vv. 107–13). See M. L. West, ed., *Hesiod. Theogony* (Oxford 1966) at 112–13, for problems of balance in this summary.

21. On the hymn's maverick structure, see Janko (above, note 16) 19.
22. I owe this observation to Thomas Van Nortwick.

distinguishing theme and hero cannot suffice.[23] The ambiguous epithet that follows (πολύτροπον) suggests how the characterization of the hero is to proceed. This is a rare adjective and much has been written on its meaning.[24] It is worth noting here that the word is well suited to continue the complexity surrounding the hero: at once referring to his physical exertions ("much traveled") and pointing to his exceptional mental capacity ("turning in many ways [his thoughts]"), *polutropos* is an adjective whose verbal core is both transitive and intransitive at once, a quality of the hero himself, who both gives pain and endures suffering.[25] The narrator thus deploys a feature of the traditional proem with great technical virtuosity and innovation, selecting an epithet that can conjure up the many facets of his hero without explicitly fixing their meaning.

The first verse of the *Odyssey* is a bold beginning, but the narrator does not sustain his innovation.[26] The pendent relative clause, which evokes enforced wanderings as crucial to the man's identity does contain some clever ambiguity: is πλάγχθη intransitive or genuinely passive? Does the hero wander because he is compelled or not? But the clause very nearly ruins the subtlety of *polutropos* by acting as a gloss on it.[27] And the further subordinate clause,

23. Rüter (above, note 2) 34–38 has a good discussion of this innovation; Clay (above, note 2) 25–29 discusses the absence of the hero's name in terms of its frequent suppression in the rest of the epic. See also Pucci (above, note 2) 54ff. for an intriguing argument about why the name *must* be omitted if the polyvalence of πολύτροπον is to succeed.

24. It occurs only once more in the epic (10.330); see also *Hymn to Hermes* 13, 439. Its ambiguity in meaning is regularly accepted as deliberate; see P. Chantraine, *Dictionnaire étymologique de la langue grecque*, vol. 3 (Paris 1974) 927; and Heubeck, West, and Hainsworth (above, note 2) at 1. For discussions, see Clay (above, note 2) 29–32 and Pietro Pucci (above, note 2) 50–54; his book takes these ideas further: *Odysseus Polutropos, Intertextual Readings in the* Odyssey *and the* Iliad (Ithaca, NY 1987) *passim*, but especially 16–17 and 24.

25. On this quality of Odysseus, see now Pucci (above, note 24) 44–49 and 56–62. Of course, his very name carries this linguistic ambivalence of having both active and passive connotations; see Clay (above, note 2) 62ff.

26. Erwin Cook, "Worlds in Apposition: Towards a Synoptic Interpretation of the Homeric Odyssey," Diss. (Berkeley 1990) 79, quotes D. M. Jones: "We need have no esteem for the composer of this prologue, whose inspiration, after a good first line, has so lamentably failed." Cook, who kindly allowed me to see a draft of his dissertation, does not agree with Jones and goes on to consider that most thorny of issues arising from the epic's opening, the fact that the theology it suggests apparently contradicts that of the narrative.

27. On the clause as a gloss, see Pucci (above, note 2) 53; and Heubeck, West, and Hainsworth (above, note 2) at 1. Clay (above, note 2) 31 notes the passive force of πλάγχθη; see also Dimock (above, note 2) 9. Pucci translates it "wandered," i.e., intransitively; so also A. T. Murray, trans., *Homer, The Odyssey* (Cambridge, MA 1919) 3; and Walter Shewring, trans., *Homer, The Odyssey* (Oxford 1980) 1.

The opening of the "Odyssey"

ἐπεὶ Τροίης ἱερὸν πτολίεθρον ἔπερσε, while it ostensibly sets a *terminus post quem* for the beginning of the story, proves too emphatic. It introduces unmistakably the traditional theme of *nostos*, because wanderings after the fall of Troy are precisely that, and it identifies Odysseus as the song's hero by punning on an epithet (πτολίπορθος) that is his alone following the war.[28] Thus this clause upsets the balance between the narrator's innovative project and the traditional structure of the proem. The delicate identification between this hero's quality of mind and his wanderings that the first verse and a half effected is undone by the greater explicitness of the rest of verse 2, which so emphatically evokes the traditional cycle of *nostoi* arising from Troy's destruction.

Once the tradition of the *nostoi* intrudes, it begins to shape the narrator's proposal:

πολλῶν δ' ἀνθρώπων ἴδεν ἄστεα καὶ νόον ἔγνω,
πολλὰ δ' ὅ γ' ἐν πόντῳ πάθεν ἄλγεα ὃν κατὰ θυμόν,
ἀρνύμενος ἥν τε ψυχὴν καὶ νόστον ἑταίρων.

(3–5)

Critics have seen significant references to Odysseus' cognitive skills in these verses and they underscore the verb πάθεν as an allusion to his ability to endure. The anaphora of *pollon, polla* seems an echo of the first element in the epithet *polutropos* and points to the constellation of *polu*-compounds that cluster around this hero.[29] Thus the narrator's use of language remains intriguing. But verses 3–5 can also be read simply as a brief summary of the

---

28. In the *Iliad* he shares it only with Achilleus among the Greek heroes, who of course does not survive the war; otherwise the epithet modifies once each Otrynteus and Oileus, fathers of a Trojan and a Greek hero respectively, and the divinities Ares and Enyo. It is Odysseus' alone in the *Odyssey*. The pun comes from πτόλις and πορθέω, a collateral form of πέρθω.

29. See Norman Austin, *Archery at the Dark of the Moon. Poetic Problems in Homer's Odyssey* (Berkeley 1975) 179: "In the first three lines the [*Odyssey*] comes as close as Homer's Greek permits to announcing the poem's intent to explore man's discovery of mind." The allusion to the *polu*-compounded epithets is often discussed: see Heubeck, West, and Hainsworth (above, note 2) at 1; and Clay (above, note 2) 26–28. Pucci (above, note 2) 40–43 discusses in detail the effect of the anaphora in vv. 3–4 and the intertextual reverberations between the *Iliad* and the *Odyssey* that these verses set up. Dimock (above, note 2) 9–11 has an intricate analysis of the sounds in these verses, which he believes throw emphasis on the noun *psukhen* and hence on Odysseus' will to live. Note a general interpretive problem: our knowledge of the *Odyssey* as a text colors our reading of the proem; since we know how little it reflects the true shape of the epic, we impute special significance to what *is* there, for its thematic or paradigmatic value.

traditional adventures of any hero making his way home: he sees strange cities, becomes acquainted with the customs of their inhabitants, suffers dangers at sea, and tries to get both himself home alive and as many of his crew as he can.[30] Any listener whose appetite for innovation was whetted by the manipulation of the traditional opening in the first verse must settle back in disappointment by verse 5: another traditional *nostos* after all.

The proem is not over, however, contrary to the typical form, which does not encourage expansive elaboration: elsewhere, after the opening statement of their theme, epic narrators turn to a more specific indication of the time of the story's beginning.[31] The Odyssean narrator postpones this detail by a consideration of one incident in the hero's wanderings, the loss of his crew:

ἀλλ' οὐδ' ὧς ἑτάρους ἐρρύσατο, ἱέμενός περ·
αὐτῶν γὰρ σφετέρῃσιν ἀτασθαλίῃσιν ὄλοντο,
νήπιοι, οἳ κατὰ βοῦς Ὑπερίονος Ἠελίοιο
ἤσθιον· αὐτὰρ ὁ τοῖσιν ἀφείλετο νόστιμον ἦμαρ.

(6–9)

The inclusion of a specific event in the proem, in some detail, is itself unusual. Furthermore, although it introduces the motif of divine anger – a typical aspect of the traditional *nostos* – here the anger is not directed at the hero himself.[32] Nor is this incident appropriate as a paradigm for all of Odysseus' adventures, as others have noted.[33] Recently, critics have argued persuasively that the destruction of the crew is not raised to be such a paradigm. It is used instead to introduce the theme of reckless

---

30. Elements of this summary appear in the *nostoi* of Agamemnon (a storm with the loss of some of his crew; the loss of his life) and Menelaus (wanderings to Egypt). Another feature of the traditional *nostos*, which soon appears in the narrator's proem, is a divine anger; thus Aias Oileus loses his homecoming. The accumulation of vast wealth, also traditional, plays no role in the opening of the *Odyssey* but proves a large concern in the epic itself. See Bernard Fenik, *Studies in the Odyssey*, Hermes Einzelschriften 30 (1974) 167–70, for his analysis of the typical elements in Menelaus' account of his homecoming as well as those in Odysseus' lies about his wanderings.

31. Compare *Iliad* 1.6; Rüter (above, note 2) 38 notes that the proems to the *Iliad* and the *Hymn to Aphrodite* both reiterate their themes in closing.

32. Thus Aias Oileus' homecoming is marred by Poseidon's anger (4.499–505); Menelaus discovers from Proteus that he has incurred the wrath of Zeus and the other gods for want of an offering (4.472–74). See Fenik (above, note 30) 208.

33. See the quotation above, p. 39, for the opinion of Heubeck, West, and Hainsworth (above, note 2); also Page (above, note 3) 168, note 2; and Rüter (above, note 2) 39, 43. Clay (above, note 2) 35 notes that it is unsuitable as a "programmatic" event, but argues forcefully for its thematic usefulness.

disregard (ἀτασθαλίῃσιν, 7), which is to be of great importance in the slaughter of the suitors: *their* recklessness justifies Odysseus' ruthlessness in punishing them.[34]

The narrator's use of the cattle of the Sun incident is still curious, however, since it is an ambiguous analogy. In the actual episode, the sailors hardly seem guilty of *atasthaliai*; if anything, Odysseus pitches his narrative to exculpate them on grounds of necessity due to the gods' arbitrariness. Thus, what is of special note here is the narrator's different presentation of the event precisely to insinuate the problem of recklessness into his proem. This is an obliqueness reminiscent of the opening verses, and a clever manipulation of a traditional feature in the *nostos*, the theme of divine anger.[35] Yet valuable as the reference to *atasthaliai* is, we should recognize another, more direct motive underlying the mention of this incident. The narrator's defense of his hero against any blame is entirely in keeping with the traditional *nostos* set forth in verses 2–5, since the loss of a crew presumably must be explained if the glory of the hero's homecoming is not to suffer.[36]

The reference to the cattle of the Sun incident provides a *terminus ante quem* for the beginning of the story, if the narrative is to include it, which parallels the temporal clause in verse 2. In the final verse of the proem, the narrator exploits these boundaries: τῶν ἁμόθεν γε, θεά, θύγατερ Διός, εἰπὲ καὶ ἡμῖν (10). Behind the seemingly modest gesture of asking for a starting point, lies a confidence in his own powers: anywhere the Muse decides, the narrator expresses himself ready to begin. So much is evident; but a further self-confidence is at work, since by stipulating the *termini* the narrator is *not* leaving the choice strictly up to the Muse. She is constrained by a plan suggested by the information in the proem: the narrator wants to start after the fall of Troy but before the slaughter of Helios' cattle. These temporal boundaries reveal an inclination for the traditional shape of a *nostos*: in particular,

---

34. See Clay (above, note 2) 35–38, who translates ἀτασθαλίαι as "heedless recklessness." See also Sheila Murnaghan, *Disguise and Recognition in the Odyssey* (Princeton 1987) 67, note 13.

35. The narrator's omission of any reference to Poseidon's anger at Odysseus in his proemium is discussed as part of his partisanship by Clay (above, note 2) 37f. Odysseus' project of presenting his crew as blameless is an intriguing parallel to that of the main narrator's, whose concern is with Odysseus' own *kleos*.

36. See 3.188–92, where Nestor, reporting the heroes' returns, singles out Idomeneus for bringing home all of his companions safely, without one being lost at sea.

the narrator underscores an event that typically threatens the hero's *kleos* by insisting on its inclusion in his song.

The narrator has set up a problematic proem: bold in its innovative conception of a song that is to define a hero, and in its linguistic virtuosity; but curiously tied to the traditional boundaries of a *nostos* for its vision of the shape and themes of that song. He demonstrates that his skill in deploying ideas is sure but by verse 9 he has allowed it to become unclear what the relationship is to be between his innovation and his reliance on the tradition.

II

In the next eleven verses of the *Odyssey* the narrator presents the Muse's response to this proem. Under the guise of selecting the requested starting point, she in fact corrects his efforts by modifying the details and adjusting the imbalance. Her changes reveal the limitations of the traditional *nostos* and allow the innovative project of the first verse to re-emerge.

It is verse 10 that allows us to imagine the next few lines as an answer from the goddess. A second invocation of the Muse is unusual at the end of a proem; the Iliadic narrator, for instance, chooses his own starting point (vv. 6–7).[37] The closing verses of the proem to the *Theogony* proper offer an instructive parallel:

> ταῦτά μοι ἔσπετε Μοῦσαι Ὀλύμπια δώματ' ἔχουσαι
> ἐξ ἀρχῆς, καὶ εἴπαθ' ὅτι πρῶτον γένετ' αὐτῶν.
>
> (114–15)

These verses also pose a request for information, but their specificity (ταῦτα, ἐξ ἀρξῆς, πρῶτον) is markedly different from the apparent openness of the request in the *Odyssey*. It is possible to imagine that Hesiod's Muses are answering the request in verse 116, but not that they have much choice about it,[38] and it is this sense of leeway that enables us to envision the *Odyssey*'s Muse

---

37. See Rüter (above, note 2) 38. The following question about which god began the quarrel is rhetorical, addressed to no one and answered with emphatic brevity (vv. 8–9). Clay (above, note 2) 23 sees this question as the poet's to his Muse, paralleling verse 11 of the *Odyssey*; see also Richardson (above, note 6) 179. But the narrator of the *Iliad* sometimes uses rhetorical questions as a way of beginning new sections in his narrative; see 5.703f., 8.273, 11.299f. See Block (above, note 6) 11f.

38. Note that Hesiod has already outlined his program for his theogony three times: once explicitly at vv. 106–12; and twice in describing the song of the Muses, at vv. 44–52 and, in reverse order, at vv. 11–21.

actually deciding about where she will begin and what she will do to direct the narrator. That is, because verse 10 poses a real question, we can imagine someone answering it; the verses that follow immediately express the answer that was given.[39]

The Muse's corrections begin at once: she approves the theme but ignores the proposed *termini* for the beginning of the story, skipping far ahead to a point near its end (11–12, quotations below). In describing her choice she sets up a different contrast for highlighting this hero, not between him and those he could not save, but between him and all other survivors now safe at home. The next verses (13–15) underscore the new contrast by focusing upon the hero's longing to get home, not just to survive, and they give specific details about this urge and about what prevents his return – another crucial opposition, as we shall see. After the Muse strictly answers the narrator's request, she also elaborates her introduction, in verses 16–21, paralleling the expansion in verses 6–9. She mentions the role that the gods' kindly intent plays in the hero's return and alludes to the troubles he will encounter once on his own island (16–19).[40] She closes by stating Poseidon's anger with the hero himself (vv. 19–20), in direct contrast to the earlier stress on the anger of Helios with his crew. Finally, she gives the hero's name (v. 21).

The significance of the Muse's corrections becomes clear in their accumulation: if the narrator is to realize his project of defining this man, he must treat more subtly the traditional elements of the *nostos*. Her response implies that a different structure and thematic focus are needed, and her subtleties alter the vision of the coming epic to reflect more nearly the *Odyssey* we know.[41] Take, for instance, the choice of a starting point: when all other heroes are at home and only this one still languishes abroad, longing for his wife but kept back by a nymph.[42] If the narrator's

39. As noted above, it is actually the narrator who renders the Muse's answer.

40. For the possible interpretations of vv. 18–19, depending upon the punctuation, see W. B. Stanford, *The Odyssey of Homer* (New York 1959²) at vv. 18–20; and Heubeck, West, and Hainsworth (above, note 2) at vv. 18–19.

41. Aristotle's summary of the *Odyssey*'s *logos* in the *Poetics* (1455b 16–23), for instance, defines as essential (*idion*) only details or elaborations of details which appear in the Muse's introduction.

42. Reasons for this choice are considerably debated; for a recent summary of some explanations, see Clay (above, note 2) 39–53. I believe her own explanation, that the *Odyssey* begins where it does because the goddess Athena has finally ceased her anger at Odysseus, puts too much emphasis on that anger as a motivating force in the epic. See also

boundaries for a beginning and his summary in verses 4–5 imply a serial account of the hero's adventures, the Muse forestalls such a straightforward procedure.[43] Her choice has brilliant consequences both for the resulting structure of the poem and for its tone. Structurally, such a late starting point allows for an all but grown-up Telemachos, ready for his own adventures, although he does not know this himself, and chafing at his mother's tangled affairs in his father's absence. The Muse's choice makes room in the proposed narrative for the *Telemachy*, and, given the narrator's innovative theme, the value of this detailed, leisurely consideration of the hero's son is great.[44] Furthermore, a late start allows for Odysseus' account of his own adventures to the Phaiakians.[45]

As for the tone set by these verses, the Muse's starting point generates a crisis about the hero himself that is thematic for the whole of the *Odyssey*. Telemachos' problem at the start, his need of his father, reappears throughout the narrative: characters need the man himself or they want a version of him, and he must resist those versions which deny his true heroic identity.[46] Symbolic of this need is the epic's persistent interest in the problem of guests', but especially Odysseus', identity – how they will be recognized and accordingly treated.[47] The hero is also "needed" by the narrative itself when the narrator claims an unidentified man as his theme. But even though the proem's first verse sets up this theme, the remainder does little to generate any sense of crisis. The narrator does not indicate that much is at stake in distinguishing this heroic identity, since he stresses only Odysseus' longing to get himself and his crew home safely – a traditional

Dimock (above, note 2) 12f.; and Uvo Hölscher, "The Transformation from Folk-tale to Epic," *Homer: Tradition and Invention*, ed. B. Fenik (Leiden 1978) 55–58.

43. See Hölscher (above, note 42) 56.

44. See Murnaghan's remarks (above, note 34) 156–66 on the relationship of the *Telemachy* to the main project of the poem – Odysseus' homecoming; see also Bowra (above, note 2) 122f.; and Austin (above, note 29) 182–91.

45. A point often noted to explain why the epic begins where it does; see Clay (above, note 2) 39, who remarks that although Odysseus' *apologia* is a consequence of the epic's starting point, it is hardly a sufficient justification for the Muse's choice.

46. Penelope will settle for no one else and Nausikaa wants a husband just *like* him (6.244). The suitors want the beggar they can control, not the emerging hero they fear. Murnaghan (above, note 34) 56–90, especially 67ff., has a good discussion on the effect of Odysseus' disguises.

47. On this concern with identity, see Stewart (above, note 13) 17f., who connects it with a concern about "personal worth."

The opening of the "Odyssey"

longing that could be any hero's. The Muse, however, has a subtler notion of what is unique about Odysseus' heroic identity. She begins by revealing the startling fact that he is stuck. He is not wandering after all, as the narrator said, but he is trapped, unable to move and on the verge of a destiny desired for him by someone else, a nymph whose name specifies that destiny – concealment.[48] The Muse's starting point thus sets at risk the narrator's cardinal claim that his hero is πολύτροπος: if Odysseus cannot escape either Kalypso's cave or her definition, perhaps he is not so resourceful or polyvalent after all. The narrator's proposal that this hero's special identity could be defined by his homecoming adventures is now transformed into a study of this crisis about his very being.[49]

The Muse's choice of a starting point also improves the structure and thematic focus of the narrator's project by setting up a more sophisticated series of contrasts. The proem stresses just one, between Odysseus and his crew: his survival, their ruin; his lack of blame for the loss, their recklessness. In answer, the Muse presents three: between Odysseus and other survivors; between the competing lures of Penelope at home and Kalypso in her cave; and between the Olympians who wish Odysseus well and Poseidon who persists in his anger. As noted above, the narrator's contrast seems to spring from a traditional concern for the hero's *kleos* and the damage it might suffer from the loss of his crew. The Muse's first contrast, among the survivors, also arises from a concern about heroic fame, but it implies that the feat is not merely to survive, but to return home in some particular way:

> Ἔνθ' ἄλλοι μὲν πάντες, ὅσοι φύγον αἰπὺν ὄλεθρον,
> οἴκοι ἔσαν, πόλεμόν τε πεφευγότες ἠδὲ θάλασσαν
> τὸν δ' οἶον...
>
> (11–13)

The juxtaposition of πάντες and οἶον, while explicitly indicating

---

48. On the significance of Kalypso's name for the opening of the epic, see Heubeck, West, and Hainsworth (above, note 2) at 1.14; and Dimock (above, note 2) 12–15.

49. Note once again how the Muse reaffirms the vigor and innovation of the proem's first verse in its claims about the hero, as opposed to the traditional program of its remainder. See Hölscher (above, note 42) 57f., who also sees the epic as opening in a crisis but believes this originates in the "story of Penelope" and the coming of age of Telemachos; Clay (above, note 2) 234, also speaks of the "pressure of events on Ithaca" as the motivation behind Athena's abandoning her anger, which governed this starting point. See also Rüter (above, note 2) 41 on Odysseus' complete isolation.

that his homecoming took longer than anyone else's, also raises the possibility that it is to surpass all others in its quality. The narrative bears this implication out. Nestor and Menelaus each return home and take up the routines of heroic domesticity, but in both Pylos and Sparta we sense an air of lack.[50] Even the alternative *nostoi* posed by Odysseus in his lies in the second half of the epic all offer less than glorious visions of what he might have encountered. By the end of the *Odyssey* we see that every other homecoming is in some sense inadequate when measured against his.[51] The emphasis upon fleeing or escaping in this initial contrast underscores the narrator's reference to his hero's struggle to survive (v. 5), but the image cuts in two directions. It contrasts Odysseus' strength of will with that of other heroes but it also implies an element of chance beyond human effort. The Muse intimates here what she will shortly emphasize (in vv. 16–20): that more is at work in the hero's marvelous homecoming than his own efforts.

The juxtaposition in the next three verses, between Odysseus' longing for his wife and Kalypso's desire to keep him as her husband, strengthens the idea that an appropriate focus for his *nostos* extends beyond mere survival.

> τὸν δ' οἶον, νόστου κεχρημένον ἠδὲ γυναικός,
> νύμφη πότνι' ἔρυκε Καλυψώ, δῖα θεάων,
> ἐν σπέσσι γλαφυροῖσι, λιλαιομένη πόσιν εἶναι.
>
> (13–15)

The reference to Penelope implies that the key to Odysseus' especially glorious homecoming will be the restoration of his marriage. The state of any wandering hero's marriage ultimately determines the nature of his return, as both sons of Atreus discovered to their regret, but Odysseus' bond to Penelope is peculiarly close – he himself uses the word ὁμοφροσύνη to describe

---

50. Nestor has lost his favorite son Antilochos (3.111–12) and even Peisistratos, who never knew his brother, still grieves for him (4.186–88, 199–202). Nestor also seems curiously isolated in his recounting of news (3.184–85). Menelaus grieves for his lost heroic friends amidst his splendid wealth (4.93–112) and seems sometimes at a loss with guests and ill at ease with his own wife Helen; see Victoria Pedrick, "The Hospitality of Noble Women in the *Odyssey*," *Helios* 15 (1988) 88 and note 17. Agamemnon's return, which was ruined by what he found waiting for him, is continually contrasted with Odysseus'.

51. See Thalmann (above, note 13) 164–70; and Murnaghan (above, note 34) 148–75, who includes in her discussion the wanderings and adventures of Telemachos. Truncated in their scope and glory, presumably to prevent him upstaging his father, they are thus true to the pattern suggested by the Muse.

the best marriage at 6.181 – and undergoes sustained and varied attacks by different female figures. Her fidelity is also tested severely, both by the twenty-year absence and by the vigorous wooing of the suitors. Thus the hero's marriage is subjected to close scrutiny from both perspectives in the coming narrative. The oblique contrast between Penelope and Kalypso also modifies another feature in the narrator's proem. His emphasis is upon high adventures on land and sea among men – in other words, the traditional, masculine feats. The Muse offers this correction: to get an understanding of this hero, to define Odysseus, it is necessary also to focus on the women in his adventures.[52] It is not enough to know that his wife draws him home; we must also see that some of the greatest obstacles to his return are female – mortal, divine, and monstrous. Kalypso is representative of all females who try to stop him in his quest for home,[53] and from this perspective two details in verses 14–15 become powerful. The goddess exercises physical force (ἔρυκε) to keep the hero in her cave, symbolizing those physical dangers and hindrances posed by such figures as Scylla, Charybdis, the Sirens – even Kirke with her magic. Kalypso's desire for him (λιλαιομένη) represents the complex interplay of allurement between Odysseus and women that sometimes threatens his homecoming. His longing to re-establish his household on Ithaka is in constant tension with the possibility of forming other ones elsewhere, or being trapped in them.[54]

The third contrast, between the gods' general benevolence and Poseidon's wrath, is made in an excursus after the Muse has answered the specific request of verse 10:

ἀλλ' ὅτε δὴ ἔτος ἦλθε περιπλομένων ἐνιαυτῶν,
τῷ οἱ ἐπεκλώσαντο θεοὶ οἶκόνδε νέεσθαι
εἰς Ἰθάκην, οὐδ' ἔνθα πεφυγμένος ἦεν ἀέθλων,
καὶ μετὰ οἷσι φίλοισι. Θεοὶ δ' ἐλέαιρον ἅπαντες
νόσφι Ποσειδάωνος· ὁ δ' ἀσπερχὲς μενέαινεν
ἀντιθέῳ Ὀδυσῆϊ πάρος ἣν γαῖαν ἱκέσθαι.

(16–21)

52. Menelaus, when becalmed in Egypt, encounters Eidothea, daughter of Proteus (4.364ff.). On the relationship of this encounter to Odysseus', see Fenik (above, note 30) 26–28 and note 25, also p. 33.   53. Thus also Rüter (above, note 2) 41.
54. See Pedrick (above, note 50) 91–93; and Helene Foley, "'Reverse Similes' and Sex Roles in the *Odyssey*," now in *Homer's The Odyssey*, ed. Harold Bloom (New York 1988) 87–101.

These verses balance the structure of the poem, which also contained an expansion, and the parallel keeps alive the artifice that the narrator is still giving the Muse's answer. Her statement that the gods pity the hero and have now decided to bring him home corrects the earlier emphasis upon the hero's own efforts to save his life (ἀρνύμενος, v. 5; ἱέμενός περ, v. 6). Also, the reference to Poseidon's anger gives the proper traditional focus: this is the anger incurred by the hero himself.[55] The further implication is that the proem's narrow interest in Helios' anger against the crew misses the mark: the events on Thrinakia do not explain for us Odysseus' complicated relations with the gods. Our understanding of these must come instead through his own experience, especially of Athena's guardianship and of Poseidon's enmity. The god's anger proves crucial at two different levels of the narrative. First, within the story this wrath is more important for defining Odysseus because he is responsible for it. His own recounting of the Polyphemos episode makes clear that he understands the nature of his responsibility, despite the Cyclops' savage provocation, for in it he demonstrates both the cardinal feature of his mind – his *mētis* – and the danger that boasting about it can raise.[56] Poseidon's anger also proves useful structurally in the sequence that finally introduces Odysseus in person (Book 5), as a counterbalance to the planning of Zeus and Athena at its opening and to the wistful kindness of Kalypso. The contrast between the other gods' benevolence and Poseidon's vengeful storm creates a powerful vignette of the preoccupation Odysseus arouses in divinities. Here then is one instance in which the Muse,

55. On the traditional role of divine anger in a *nostos*, see above, note 32. Rüter (above, note 2) 45 notes the reference to the gods' positive attitude (*das einmütige Erbarmen*) as unusual.

56. He remains in the Cyclops' cave in the face of evident danger, his companions' warnings, and his own misgivings (9.213–15; 224–30); after he and his surviving companions have escaped to their ship, he errs in giving Polyphemos his name, again despite the warning of his crew (9.488–501). For an account of the significance of the Polyphemos episode, especially focused on the interplay of Odysseus' *mētis* and his failure to exercise restraint, see Ann Bergren, "Odyssean Temporality: Many (Re)Turns," *Approaches to Homer*, ed. Carl Rubino and Cynthia Shelmerdine (Austin 1983) 45–50. But to say that Odysseus is responsible for Poseidon's wrath is not to blame him in accordance with the ethically based theology outlined by Zeus in Book 1 (32–37). On the problem of the dual theology in the *Odyssey*, see Fenik, (above, note 30) 209–27; and Clay (above, note 2) 213–39, both of whom carefully distinguish the idiosyncratic anger of Helios and Poseidon from the notion of the gods as upholders of justice. See also now Cook (above, note 26).

for good reasons, affirms a traditional theme – divine anger directed at the hero himself – against the narrator's efforts to subvert it by alluding to a god's anger at another party.[57]

The reference in verses 18–19 to the troubles Odysseus will face "among his friends" is an allusion to Odysseus' confrontation with the suitors, a veiled reference that subtly balances the narrator's earlier obliqueness. He applied the theme of reckless disregard (*atasthaliai*) to Odysseus' crew, but the suitors are the men who display real disdain for all decency, all warnings, and all prophecy. Furthermore, in making this allusion the Muse suggests a shape of the narrative that is very different from that proposed by the narrator. His careful *termini* for the story's beginning indicate a desire to include an account of the crew's recklessness, and the structure of the Muse's version will fulfill this desire but without making the episode the center-piece of Odysseus' adventures. Her reference to the troubles on Ithaca corrects the preoccupation of the proem with adventures at sea and forecasts a narrative which emphasizes instead the suitors' moral obtuseness and hence Odysseus' lack of blame in punishing them.[58]

The Muse's corrections are radical but in a real sense complementary. The shifts in theme, the expanded sets of contrasts, even the choice of a starting point do not contradict the narrator's bold project of defining this hero. In fact, they give more acute perspectives on the man, those needed to get at his distinctive character and the peculiar glory of his homecoming. Nor do her corrections eliminate several valuable points made by the narrator's proem. Her starting point exposes a crisis with appropriate reverberations both for examining the essence of her hero and for testing the appropriateness of his cardinal epithet πολύτροπος. She does not discount the significance of the hero's will to live, but her series of contrasts indicates that the narrator must employ greater complexity to show how this survival surpasses all others. Finally, she strengthens the key theme of

---

57. Although, as argued above, the narrator had good reasons, both on the grounds of his theme and because of the tradition, for attempting this manipulation.

58. The Muse's corrections end at v. 21, which contains the first use of Odysseus' name. West comments on its appearance: "We have long realized that Odysseus was meant, but the name adds a certain emphasis to the conclusion of this section," Heubeck, West, and Hainsworth (above, note 2) at 20–21.

reckless disregard by alluding to the real villains of the piece.[59] Nevertheless, the Muse's version of this song more closely introduces the epic material the narrator himself actually sings, whereas little in his proem – seeing cities, learning the customs of men, even the loss of the crew – is told in his own, third-person voice. Most appears instead in Odysseus' first-person recounting of his adventures to the Phaiakians. This point is long noted and usually taken as a master stroke by Homer, since the proem thereby reflects the fact that a major portion of the epic is told in the hero's voice.[60] Instead, I think, it arises from an undue reliance on the shape and material of a traditional *nostos*, which the Muse has now corrected.

III

Between them, the narrator and his Muse have introduced the *Odyssey*, but oddly: the narrator presents a brilliant idea for a song but employs an imperceptive notion of how to proceed with it, although his technical virtuosity is evident. Furthermore, he then expresses the necessary corrections as though they were the Muse's. Why such a long, convoluted process? Compared with the spare elegance of the *Iliad*'s proem or the terseness of the Homeric Hymns, the opening of the *Odyssey*, including all twenty-one verses, seems remarkably expansive and comprehensive.[61] Such an impulse to make entirely clear what the narrator is to do suggests an anxiety about beginning this epic – fitting enough, given the innovative project and the evident inadequacy of relying on the traditional form and stories of the *nostos*. Yet the nervousness is in tension with the clever obliqueness and word-play that also characterize the opening of the *Odyssey* – we can

---

59. Note, however, that neither the narrator nor the Muse fully suggests the crucial connections among *atasthaliai*, the suitors' villainy, and the ethical theology about to be expounded by Zeus (1.32–37); see Fenik (above, note 30) 210f. and Clay (above, note 2) 218.

60. See Rüter (above, note 2) 45, who quotes A. Kirchhoff, *Die homerische Odyssee* (Berlin 1879²) 165.

61. Although it is not; to name just two omissions, note the absence of any allusion to the role Odysseus' son is to play and of explicit reference to Athena. A truism about early Greek epic narratives is that their proems do not need to be comprehensive. So West, quoted above: "We do not expect a comprehensive summary of what is to come," in Heubeck, West, and Hainsworth (above, note 2) at 1.1–10; see Rüter (above, note 2) 32. Clay (above, note 2) 35 notes concerning the presence of cattle of the Sun incident, "What one expects, instead, is, in some sense, a programmatic statement for the entire *Odyssey*."

infer that the narrator is feigning this anxiety. He is aware all along of the real nature of his project and the approach he should use; the exchange between himself and his Muse is an artful, staged enactment of the process of inspiration, and his willingness to participate as the lesser voice is testimony to his confidence that, although he is corrected, he suffers no loss of glory, since the help is divine.[62]

Beyond being a self-reflexive tribute, the *Odyssey*'s opening also serves as a paradigm for the difficulties singers and story-tellers alike face when they attempt a new song or tale.[63] Innovation is a risky business, as the first instance within the story shows. Phemios, the bard in Odysseus' household, is singing for the entertainment of the suitors (1.325ff.), but his theme, the painful homecoming of the Achaians, does not please Penelope, who asks him to choose another song – this one reminds her of her husband (337–44). Telemachos rebukes her for the complaint, remarking:

τὴν γὰρ ἀοιδὴν μᾶλλον ἐπικλείουσ' ἄνθρωποι,
ἥ τις ἀκουόντεσσι νεωτάτη ἀμφιπέληται.

(1.351–52)

Telemachos thinks listeners like new songs: the narrator thus reminds his audience about the effects of time upon the heroic tradition: the *nostos* may be for him a theme that needs renovation, but for the characters in this story, just ten years after the Trojan War's close, songs about the Achaians' return are the latest thing. More importantly, we see Phemios' risk in attempting this new song: he pleases some of his listeners, but of what sort? The uncouth suitors. Penelope, however, does not approve, and does not hesitate to tell him so, because Phemios' theme reminds her of the man whose homecoming is incomplete.[64] So it is with singers and story-tellers throughout the epic; their efforts can be met with disbelief, criticism, or – worst of all – indifference.[65]

62. Besides, as the mortal voice in the alliance, he has little choice but to play this role, as the example of Thamyris, the singer who contested with the Muses, teaches (*Il.* 2.594–600); see de Jong (above, note 6) 52. See Stewart (above, note 13) 159–61 on the poet's self-confidence.

63. On the notion of innovation when an audience is familiar with the oral tradition, see Thalmann (above, note 13) 123–25.

64. See Murnaghan (above, note 34) 154–56 for the further significance of this exchange; Thalmann (above, note 13) 158f. discusses Telemachos' evident immaturity in criticizing his mother's reaction.

65. Thalmann (above, note 13) 160–61 has some good observations on the conditions surrounding songs or stories that fail. Take, for instance, the freely invented tales of

When the story or song succeeds, its glory is truly remarkable, but in two closely positioned examples the narrator underlines the difference between the man who tells his own story and the singer who relies on his training and his Muse. As Odysseus begins the story of his wanderings, his rhetoric indicates that he knows how crucial the crafting of a story is:

> τί πρῶτόν τοι ἔπειτα, τί δ' ὑστάτιον καταλέξω;
> κήδε' ἐπεί μοι πολλὰ δόσαν θεοὶ οὐρανίωνες.
> νῦν δ' ὄνομα πρῶτον μυθήσομαι...

(9.14–16)

Yet Odysseus makes very different choices from the main narrator in the epic's opening. He begins directly with his name, and the verb he uses – καταλέγειν – reflects his intent to proceed straightforwardly in his account.[66] In fact he has no need of divine inspiration to aid his memory, or the oblique and artful structuring employed by the narrator. He can dispense with these because the story is his own: his troubles and his name – the theme and the subject of his tale – are so closely linked in his own understanding. His story is sheer revelation for his audience and utterly beguiles them.[67] Odysseus' choices in Book 9, however, are not the only way – or even the best way – to have one's story told. The origin of Demodokos' final song at the end of Book 8, just before the hero's own effort, depicts another possibility and provides a crucial analogy to what happens at the opening of the *Odyssey* between the narrator and his Muse.

The situation in Book 8 is not strictly parallel to the epic's beginning, because it is Odysseus – that is, the audience – who

---

Odysseus: those he tells to the suitors and their retainers are met with scorn and abuse; when he gives his story to his friends and family, they are charmed, but firmly disbelieve his central point (and the single truth in his tales) that Odysseus himself is alive and nearly home. Amphinomos is inclined to accept the warning in the version he receives but, befuddled by Athena, he finally turns away (18.153–56). See Fenik (above, note 30) 179f. and Clay (above, note 2) 227f. on how variations in Odysseus' lies depend upon the listener. This is not to argue that Odysseus' purpose in telling his lies is, or should be, to please and convince his audience, but rather to observe that the reception of his tales conforms to the lesson we learn early on in the epic: story-telling, especially when it is innovative, is risky.

66. On the use of this verb to stress as well the validity of an account, see Margalit Finkelberg, "Homer's View of the Epic Narrative: Some Formulaic Evidence," *CP* 82 (1987) 135f.; and Tilman Krischer, *Formale Konventionen der homerischen Epik*, *Zetemata* 56 (1971) 146–58, who concludes: "Das Wort bezeichnet somit die sachliche und genaue Darstellung dadurch, daβ es angibt, wie man sie herstellt."

67. See Stewart (above, note 13) 154–57; 161f. See Bergren (above, note 56) 57–60 for what is at stake for both Odysseus and the Phaiakians in the telling of these adventures.

The opening of the "*Odyssey*"

proposes a theme to Demodokos and suggests how it should proceed. Yet we see how the singer can modify such a request to move his audience beyond its expectations. Odysseus asks for a song that glorifies his trick of the Trojan Horse:

ἀλλ' ἄγε δὴ μετάβηθι καὶ ἵππου κόσμον ἄεισον
δουρατέου, τὸν Ἐπειὸς ἐποίησεν σὺν Ἀθήνῃ,
ὅν ποτ' ἐς ἀκρόπολιν δόλον ἤγαγε δῖος Ὀδυσσεύς,
ἀνδρῶν ἐμπλήσας οἵ Ἴλιον ἐξαλάπαξαν.

(8.492–95)

His subject is the Trojan Horse and his thematic word is *kosmos*.[68] the rest of his summary indicates that he envisions a song that proceeds step by step from the inception of the idea forward. That is, Epeios made it, Odysseus filled it with men and got it inside the city, etc. Again, Odysseus' final instructions and in particular the verb he uses, are revealing: … ταῦτα κατὰ μοῖραν καταλέξῃς (v. 496). Yet Demodokos does not sing about the plan of the Wooden Horse, or about its building, or about any of the preliminaries.

Ὣς φάθ', ὁ δ' ὁρμηθεὶς θεοῦ ἄρχετο, φαῖνε δ' ἀοιδήν,
ἔνθεν ἑλὼν ὡς οἱ μὲν ἐϋσσέλμων ἐπὶ νηῶν
βάντες ἀπέπλειον, πῦρ ἐν κλισίῃσι βαλόντες,
Ἀργεῖοι, τοὶ δ' ἤδη ἀγακλυτὸν ἀμφ' Ὀδυσῆα
ἥατ' ἐνὶ Τρώων ἀγορῇ κεκαλυμμένοι ἵππῳ·
αὐτοὶ γάρ μιν Τρῶες ἐς ἀκρόπολιν ἐρύσαντο.

(8.499–504)

As Rüter notes, Demodokos' choice of where to start and what to sing about parallels the Muse's because he also chooses a moment of grave crisis, both for the success of the trick and in the survival of the Trojan city. But Rüter believes that this simply shows how a singer, or a Muse inspiring that singer, can begin anywhere.[69] We are now in a position to see that Demodokos, exercising his god-given powers as a singer (ὁρμηθεὶς θεοῦ), has *corrected* his audience's proposal.[70] He accepts the theme but will not be bound

---

68. Note again the use of the genitive ἵππου for the subject and the accusative κόσμον for the theme. Here *kosmos* seems to mean something like "trick;" Heubeck, West, and Hainsworth (above, note 2) at 8.492–93, following the scholiasts, note that the word here means κατασκευήν, οἰκονομίαν ἤ ὑπόθεσιν.

69. Rüter (above, note 2) 39: "Der wirkliche Gesang des Demodokos … setzt mit der aufs äußerste gespannten Situation ein … Die Möglichkeit, den Angang beliebig zu wählen, wird eigens betont."

70. See Heubeck, West, and Hainsworth (above, note 2) at 8.499 for the force of the genitive.

by the rest of Odysseus' suggestion to a recounting of the whole from the pines on Mount Ida on.[71] Instead, he creates a song that sounds as if it captures the pathos of the ruse's success and the poignancy of Troy's fall, for at its end Odysseus is in tears, and he is compared to a woman grieving at the death of her husband as her city is sacked and she is led into slavery (8.521–31).[72] Later, the hero has only words of praise for Demodokos (9.3–4); he does not criticize him for the dramatic changes from his request. How could he, when the singer, relying on inspiration, shaped the song to do what he wanted? That is, Odysseus wanted glory and he thought he knew what kind of a song would do: a straightforward rehearsal of his trick. But Demodokos knew better: Odysseus chose a theme that was more complicated than he supposed; the trick of the Trojan horse won a grim kind of glory for the victors.

The narrator of the *Odyssey* constructs an opening to the epic with a similar lesson. The eager listener becomes his own voice, expressing what he would like to sing. The skilled singer becomes the Muse, who is wise not just in facts, it seems, but also in how to shape the song he wants, since she knows that his proposed theme of exploring Odysseus' heroic identity cannot be fully satisfied by the traditional forms. Human desire and talent must be coupled with the divine wisdom to create this epic, and once this lesson is presented as an opening paradigm, the narrator turns to his story, fully instructed in how best to proceed.

71. As Rüter (above, note 2) 39, following Apollodoros, *Epit.* 5.14, notes he could have.
72. For the significance of this simile, see Foley (above, note 54) 100.

Sappho 16, Gorgias' *Helen*, and the preface to Herodotus' *Histories*

HAYDEN PELLICCIA

In a recent article on Sappho and Alcaeus, William H. Race pointed out that the discussion of ἔρως in Gorgias' *Helen* is indebted to Sappho 16, and suggested that the sophist was directly indebted to the poet; in his book on the priamel, Race had already remarked upon the structural similarity of Herodotus' preface to the same poem, without suggesting any direct link.[1] My purpose here is to complete the triangle by demonstrating a connection, independent of Sappho 16, between the two prose authors: the similarities are of such a sort as to suggest either that both were written in a context that generated the similar matter independently in each, or that one work was written in awareness of the other – possibly in rivalry with it.

I

The similarities between the preface of the *Histories* (i.e., proem plus chapters 1–5) and Gorgias' *Helen* (epecially its own prefatory section) are thematic, rhetorical, and verbal. The thematic similarities are obvious: Herodotus reports what he claims to be the account of Persian λόγιοι of a series of rapes culminating in Paris, Helen, and the Trojan War; Gorgias devotes his work in its entirety to these last. Both accounts are legalistic in presentation: Herodotus' Persians carefully keep score, and when the incursions escalate to military engagements they offer a defense of themselves and criticism of the Greeks based upon an assignment of relative culpability. Herodotus scrupulously calls forth Phoenician witnesses to defend their people from the charge levelled by the

---

1. W. H. Race, "Sappho, *fr.* 16 L–P and Alkaios, *fr.* 42 L–P: Romantic and Classical Strains in Lesbian Lyric," *CJ* 85 (1989) 16–33, hereafter Race (1989) 19, and *The Classical Priamel from Homer to Boethius*, Mnemosyne Supplement 74 (Leiden 1982), hereafter Race (1982) 111. My debt throughout will be apparent to anyone familiar with these works.

Persians, and permits them to offer an explanation of the removal of Io which exculpates themselves without forcing a radical revision of the Persian account. Gorgias' encomium of Helen, on the other hand, is almost wholly devoted to a legalistic defense of her innocence. These legal themes will be discussed further below.

Since the rhetorical and verbal similarities merge I will treat them together. The passages share in common a technique I have elsewhere called the "false-start recusatio."[2] This device is not used in Sappho 16,[3] and Herodotus and Gorgias each use it to different effect; but they do use it, and its nature and function must be appreciated if we are properly to understand either the passages by themselves or their relationships to their predecessors.

I designate with the term false-start recusatio such passages as Pindar, *Olympians* 1.25–53 and 9.29–41, where the poet starts with one story, or version of a story, and begins to develop it, but before finishing decides, for some reason or other, to abandon it in favor of some other topic, version, or approach. The rhetorical purpose of this device is similar to that of the priamel: something is introduced, only to be rejected in favor of something else, which is thereby highlighted by the preceding foil. It might be conceived of as a dramatic form of the priamel: in the latter, the author

---

2. "Pindarus Homericus: *Pythian* 3.1–80," *HSCP* 91 (1987) 39–63, 47f. It is usual to confine the term *recusatio* to Latin poems such as Horace 1.6 and to trace the origin of the procedure to Callimachus; see, e.g., R. G. M. Nisbet and M. Hubbard, *A Commentary on Horace Odes Book 1* (Oxford 1970) p. 81. J. P. Barron, "Ibycus: To Polycrates," *BICS* 16 (1969) 119–149, p. 135, states that "the theme of *recusatio* is thoroughly Hellenistic in sentiment, and cannot in fact be paralleled before that period." This is overstatement: both Barron and Nisbet and Hubbard refer to Callimachus, *Aitia fr.* 1 Pf., lines 17–28 of which are generally acknowledged to be the ultimate model for Horace loc. cit. and Virgil, *Ecl.* 6.3–5, among other passages; but since Callimachus modelled his own passage on Pindar, *Pae.* 7b.10–12 (κελαδῆσαθ' ὕμνους, | 'Ομήρου [δὲ μὴ τρι]πτὸν κατ' ἀμαξιτόν | ἰόντες, ἀ[λλ' ἀλ]λοτρίαις ἀν' ἵπποις), what is the point of claiming that the procedure originated with him? I justify calling the procedure I examine a "recusatio" because it resembles that exhibited in the Latin poems usually so designated, and because the word Pindar uses in one of the paradigmatic passages (*Ol.* 1.52; see below) is ἀφίσταμαι, a Greek synonym of *recuso* (cf. Aesch. *Eum.* 413f., where Athena breaks off her potentially offensive musings with the thought that ἀποστατεῖ θέμις [i.e., from impolite personal comments]). Race (1989) p. 25 n. 23 briefly defends the application of the term to Sappho 16, and refers to L. Rissman, *Love as War: Homeric Allusion in the Poetry of Sappho, Beiträge zur klassischen Philologie* 157 (Königstein 1983) 30–54. D. C. Young had already in 1968 (*Three Odes of Pindar, Mnemosyne Supplement* 3 (Leiden) pp. 33–34) described Pindar, *Pyth.* 3 as a recusatio. See also Race (1982) p. 21, and the same author's *Classical Genres and English Poetry* (London 1988) pp. 1–34.

3. But see J. G. Howie, "Sappho Fr. 16 (LP): Self-Consolation and Encomium," *Papers of the Liverpool Latin Seminar* (1976) 207–35.

overtly offers alternatives, and for reasons that are more or less explicit, settles on one, usually the last mentioned. Many priamels are in the nature of intellectual exercises: we are invited to consider a range of alternatives, but the ultimate decision is, as a rule, presented as already determined. A number of other priamels, however, are aporetic: the alternatives are presented as rhetorical questions: "How shall I sing you, Apollo? As A or B or C?" or "In which of your former glories, Thebes, do you most pride yourself? In A or B or C?" In such cases the poet presents himself as undecided, or rather as making his decision on the spot before us. This type is obviously to some extent dramatic: the poet imitates a person pondering the decision, and so invites us to observe and thus to participate in the process of decision making.

With the false-start recusatio the author begins without giving any overt indication that there is a choice to be made;[4] sometimes, as in Pindar, he presents himself as being unsuspecting of or unprepared for the change in direction. Thus, in *Ol.* 9 Pindar becomes aware of the moral unsuitability of his Heracles *exemplum* only after he has gotten most of the way through it; when this awareness penetrates, he reacts (or depicts himself as reacting) vehemently: cast out this story, mouth! In *Ol.* 1 he refuses to continue: I simply cannot call any of the gods a glutton; I refuse.[5]

In neither Herodotus nor Gorgias have we anything so vivid as these. In both the device is toned down: there is no explicit statement that the opening move was a false or immoral one; it is simply begun, and then dismissed, without explanation, and the author moves on to the new approach. I will summarize the

---

4. On the question of whether Herodotus' preface should be classified as a priamel or a false-start recusatio, and the relevance of "overtness" to the decision, see below.

5. The Pindar passages have often been compared, by themselves and with other apparent instances of (self-)correction. The term, "false-start recusatio" is designed in part to stress the deliberateness of the technique, as against, e.g., R. Lattimore, "The First Elegy of Solon," *AJP* 68 (1947) 161–79 and "The Composition of the *History* of Herodotus," *CP* 53 (1958) 9–21, who speaks of "correction in stride" as more or less the result of a lack of foresight. In somewhat summarily assembling passages under the one rubric I do not mean to suggest that there are no significant differences among them; the shared element – deliberate, rhetorically motivated misdirection – seems clear enough. For an excellent recent discussion, see M. Griffith, "Contest and Contradiction in Early Greek Poetry," in *Cabinet of the Muses*, ed. M. Griffith and D. J. Mastronarde (Atlanta 1990) 185–207, who studies the passages as instances of innovation and the out-doing of predecessors, motivations I regard as relevant to Herodotus and Gorgias (section III below).

passages, describing their procedures, and then quote the verbal parallels.

Gorgias begins aphoristically, propounding general rules for praise and blame, which will, in the event, serve to guide his subsequent treatment of the particular subject, Helen: χρὴ τὸ μὲν ἄξιον ἐπαίνου ἐπαίνῳ τιμᾶν, τῷ δὲ ἀναξίῳ μῶμον ἐπιτιθέναι. This unexceptionable assertion reflects such traditional encomiastic formulations as Pindar, *Nem.* 8.39 αἰνέων αἰνητά, μομφὰν δ' ἐπισπείρων ἀλιτροῖς. The challenge Gorgias has set himself in the present work is to demonstrate that Helen belongs to the first category rather than to the second. For this reason he offers, in the next sentence, an argument in support of the encomiastic rule just propounded, based upon the self-evident impropriety of its contradiction: ἴση γὰρ ἁμαρτία καὶ ἀμαθία μέμφεσθαί τε τὰ ἐπαινετὰ καὶ ἐπαινεῖν τὰ μωμητά. This negative formulation enables Gorgias to embrace in his subsequent praise of Helen the negative (but complementary) activity of refutation, namely, of those who improperly attach blame to something worthy of praise;[6] thus; τοῦ δ' αὐτοῦ ἀνδρὸς λέξαι τε τὸ δέον ὀρθῶς καὶ ἐλέγξαι τοὺς μεμφομένους Ἑλένην. In this sentence λέξαι τὸ δέον refers to the earlier encomiastic rule introduced by χρή, while ἐλέγξαι κτλ. reiterates and particularizes the negative reformulation.[7] I will refer to these two distinct if complementary aspects of praise as the encomiastic and the elenctic. In the next sentence – that which concludes the proem – Gorgias states that his purpose in his speech is elenctic: ἐγὼ δὲ βούλομαι λογισμόν τινα τῷ λόγῳ δοὺς τὴν μὲν κακῶς ἀκούουσαν παῦσαι τῆς αἰτίας, τοὺς δὲ μεμφομένους ψευδομένους ἐπιδείξας καὶ δείξας τἀληθὲς παῦσαι τῆς ἀμαθίας.

In spite of this announcement of an elenctic approach, Gorgias now (§3) begins what appears to be the body of his speech with

---

6. He thereby anticipates the charge levelled by Isocrates in his *Helen* 14f.

7. It has been usual since Dobree to posit a lacuna after ἐλέγξαι, supplying for the sense of the lost text something like Diels' τὸ λεγόμενον οὐκ ὀρθῶς· προσήκει τοίνυν ἐλέγξαι. The objection to the text as transmitted cannot be any difficulty of sense, since it contains none; it is rather an objection to the boldness with which that sense is expressed. But the transmitted version forms a very effective introduction of Helen, and is not in thought radically dissimilar to such hyperbolically encomiastic passages as Pindar, *Pyth.* 9.87 κωφὸς ἀνήρ τις, ὃς Ἡρακλεῖ στόμα μὴ περιβάλλει and *Isth.* 5.19f. τὸ δ' ἐμόν, οὐκ ἄτερ Αἰακιδᾶν, κέαρ ὕμνων γεύεται. It is true that the abruptness with which Helen is brought in here is not reproduced in the Pindar passages, but the effect resembles that achieved by Aristotle in prefacing his lectures on rhetoric with the modified Euripidean line αἰσχρὸν σιωπᾶν, Ἰσοκράτην δ' ἐᾶν λέγειν (see Cicero, *de Orat.* 3.35).

a conventional topic of the encomiastic style: praise of the subject's γένος and φύσις:[8] ὅτι μὲν οὖν φύσει καὶ γένει τὰ πρῶτα τῶν πρώτων ἀνδρῶν καὶ γυναικῶν ἡ γυνὴ περὶ ἧς ὅδε ὁ λόγος, οὐκ ἄδηλον οὐδὲ ὀλίγοις. The reasons for Gorgias' introduction of this theme – the relevance of which to an elenctic defense of Helen is not readily apparent (had anyone charged her with poor breeding?) – will be given later; for the moment we need only note that he appeals to the authority of universal consensus to support his claim of Helen's genealogical supremacy. The remainder of the section is concerned with her parents, human and divine: Leda, Tyndareus, and Zeus.

The next section turns to a standard sub-category of the φύσις topic: the subject's inherited beauty;[9] the special relevance to Helen is obvious. Immediately, however, Gorgias turns to the effects of Helen's beauty on those who saw it, which is again a standard encomiastic device: the truthfulness of the encomiast's claims is proved by the evidence of actual witnesses, who are themselves praised in order to lend their testimony as much weight as possible.[10] This passage (§4), which is the last before the break-off, is lavished with all of Gorgias' most extravagant (and characteristic) stylistic devices:

πλείστας δὲ πλείστοις ἐπιθυμίας ἔρωτος ἐνειργάσατο, ἑνὶ δὲ
σώματι πολλὰ σώματα συνήγαγεν ἀνδρῶν ἐπὶ μεγάλοις μέγα
φρονούντων, ὧν οἱ μὲν πλούτου μεγέθη, οἱ δὲ εὐγενείας παλαιᾶς
εὐδοξίαν, οἱ δὲ ἀλκῆς ἰδίας εὐεξίαν, οἱ δὲ σοφίας ἐπικτήτου

8. On γένος (or ἡ γενεαλογία) as a topic of encomium, as well as its placement first after the proem, see *Rhet. ad Alex.* 1440b23–1441a14. On the appearance of this "program" in earlier poetry, see A. M. Miller, *From Delos to Delphi*, Mnemosyne Supplement 93 (Leiden 1986) pp. 6–9 and *passim*. For φύσις, see Menander Rhetor, περὶ ἐπιδεικτικῶν 371.14–15 (Russell and Wilson): μετὰ τὴν γένεσιν ἐρεῖς τι καὶ περὶ φύσεως, οἷον ὅτι ἐξέλαμψεν ἐξ ὠδίνων εὐειδὴς τῷ κάλλει καταλάμπων.
9. See the passage of Menander Rhetor quoted in n. 8 above, and cf. *Rhet. ad Alex.* 1440b17–18, where κάλλος is grouped together with εὐγένεια (as well as ῥώμη and πλοῦτος) to illustrate τὰ ἔξω τῆς ἀρετῆς.
10. This technique can be observed as early as Homer, where Nestor establishes his credentials (i.e., engages in self-praise) by stating that, e.g., "I consorted with men who were the mightiest of their times, such as Perithous and Theseus, for they summoned me, and no one of the men of today could compete with them; and they heeded my advice and obeyed my words..." (*Il.* 1.260–73). Cf. Pindar, *Nem.* 8.8–10 (Aeacus was born from Oenone and Zeus) πολλά νιν πολλοὶ λιτάνευον ἰδεῖν· ἀβοατὶ γὰρ ἡρώων ἄωτοι περιναιεταόντων ἤθελον κείνου γε πείθεσθ' ἀναξίαις ἑκόντες κτλ. Isocrates justifies the entire Theseus digression in his praise of Helen by the same principle (38): οὐ γὰρ δὴ μάρτυρά γε πιστότερον οὐδὲ κριτὴν ἱκανώτερον ἕξομεν ἐπαγαγέσθαι περὶ τῶν Ἑλένῃ προσόντων ἀγαθῶν τῆς Θησέως διανοίας.

δύναμιν ἔσχον· καὶ ἧκον ἅπαντες ὑπ' ἔρωτός τε φιλονίκου
φιλοτιμίας τε ἀνικήτου.

The virtuosity and ornateness of the style here mark the passage as one of special importance;[11] again, we may wonder what the motive is, especially since the subject of Helen's suitors inevitably leads to the subject of her marriage, a topic an encomiast might be forgiven for trying to steer clear of. In fact, that is precisely what Gorgias immediately does (§5):

> ὅστις μὲν οὖν καὶ δι' ὅτι καὶ ὅπως ἀπέπλησε τὸν ἔρωτα τὴν ῾Ελένην λαβών, οὐ λέξω· τὸ γὰρ τοῖς εἰδόσιν ἃ ἴσασι λέγειν πίστιν μὲν ἔχει, τέρψιν δὲ οὐ φέρει. τὸν χρόνον δὲ τῷ λόγῳ τὸν τότε νῦν[12] ὑπερβὰς ἐπὶ τὴν ἀρχὴν τοῦ μέλλοντος λόγου προβήσομαι, καὶ προθήσομαι τὰς αἰτίας, δι' ἃς εἰκὸς ἦν γενέσθαι τὸν τῆς ῾Ελένης εἰς τὴν Τροίαν στόλον.

It is in this transition that the recusatio resides, revealing the material of sections 3–4 to have been a "false start". Gorgias began, as we saw, with an announcement of his intention to praise Helen elenctically, that is, by refuting her detractors; he then devoted two sections to the praise of her genealogy and her beauty. I remarked that these conventional topics of encomium were surprising to find in what was announced to be an elenchos, but we can be certain that their very conventionality saved their presence from appearing unacceptably paradoxical. The opening

---

11. Polyptoton: πλείστας/πλείστοις; σώματι/σώματα; μεγάλοις/μέγα; paradox: ἑνὶ σώματι/πολλὰ σώματα; word-play: the interlaced εὐ- and φιλο- compounds (cf. D. Fehling, *Die Wiederholungsfiguren und ihr Gebrauch bei den Griechen vor Gorgias* [Berlin 1969] 247f.). The last four words are especially extravagant: not only the reiterations (φιλο- and νικ-), but also a phonetic figure discovered by Calvert Watkins (pervasively) in Pindar: close conjunction of the thematically appropriate (to epinician) and phonetically complementary pair τιμ-/νικ-: "the vowels are identical, and the sequence nasal sonorant-oral unvoiced stop of the one is reversed in the other" ("New Parameters in Historical Linguistics, Philology, and Culture History," *Language* 65 [1989] 783–99, 789). Apart from the Pindaric examples found by Watkins, cf. in prose [Lysias], *Epitaphios* 16: ἐπίπονον καὶ φιλόνικον καὶ φιλότιμον αὑτῷ καταστήσας τὸν βίον, and Thucydides 3.82.8: πάντων δ' αὐτῶν αἴτιον ἀρχὴ ἡ διὰ πλεονεξίαν καὶ φιλοτιμίαν· ἐκ δ' αὐτῶν καὶ ἐς τὸ φιλονικεῖν καθισταμένων τὸ πρόθυμον. The play on τιμ-/νικ- as it occurs throughout Greek literature is to be studied by A. B. Westervelt in a forthcoming article, to which I owe the reference to Thuc. 3.82.8.

12. Like Diels-Kranz, I do not follow Blass in supplying τῷ before νῦν, since if it is supplied "the present λόγος" can only be that encomiastic one begun in §3, and must be distinguished (as pointed out by Immisch ad loc.) from "the impending λόγος" now announced; this is unacceptable, since the skipping over of τὸν χρόνον τὸν τότε is not *part* of the encomium of §§3–4, but that which brings it to a close, a close which was announced earlier with the words οὐ λέξω. Accordingly, I prefer to leave νῦν as referring to the transitional moment between the two sections, rather than to use it (with Blass' definite article) to specify the former.

from φύσις and γένος will certainly have been understood by the audience as signalling that the course has been set and the speech under way. The real surprise, then, will come in section 5, when Gorgias suddenly changes direction. His reason for doing so at this point has already been suggested: Helen's marriage is the critical issue over which her encomiasts and her detractors will divide, and we can see in retrospect how naturally – almost innocently – this critical issue has been raised, simply by following the standard topics of encomium. Now that it has been reached, however, Gorgias reasonably moves to dismiss the discussion of the events that occurred, and turns to their interpretation, an approach that permits him both to refute τοὺς μεμφομένους Ἑλένην and to vindicate the woman herself. This approach is the one taken for the rest of the speech – it is its true program – and it is, paradoxically, also the one that the programmatic statements of the proem (§§ 1–2) had prepared us for: the recusatio returns us to the course originally chosen.

Why did Gorgias not simply proceed, after the proem, with the elenctic program he announces both there and here, two sections later? Certainly the intervening encomiastic material leads up to the issue of Helen's infidelity with a titillating inevitability, so that a certain dramatic effect is achieved by his letting us see him, as it were, paint himself into a corner; but he can hardly expect us to take this self-entrapment very seriously when he has stated at the start that his intention is to defend Helen from the charges that have been brought against her – for what are these charges all along supposed to have been, other than those stemming from her elopement with Paris? It is reasonable to infer that there is something in this encomiastic material – which is anomalous in the program he has announced – that he thinks will be useful to him later. The question is, what?

This kind of problem is recurrently posed by false-start recusatios, priamels, praeteritios, and other devices that reject foil in favor of some climax: what purpose does the rejected foil serve? The principle at work is often that of having your cake and eating it too.[13] The particular cake that Gorgias gets to eat and keep by the present maneuver is revealed later on in the speech, where

13. T. C. W. Stinton, "'Si credere dignum est': Some Expressions of Disbelief in Euripides and Others," *PCPS* n.s. 22 (1976) 60–89, 67f.

Gorgias appeals in Helen's defense to a claim that had already been made (and presumably accepted) in this earlier section (§§ 3–4) preceding the break-off. Note that the rejected section (§§ 3–4) presents claims that are beyond dispute – perfectly traditional and uncontroversial material, the keynote being the words which conclude its first sentence: οὐκ ἄδηλον οὐδὲ ὀλίγοις. The specific item here that will be exploited later is the sentence which follows the statement (at the beginning of §4) that Helen possessed from her parents an ἰσόθεον κάλλος, and which describes the effect of that beauty: πλείστας δὲ πλείστοις ἐπιθυμίας ἔρωτος ἐνειργάσατο, ἑνὶ δὲ σώματι πολλὰ σώματα συνήγαγεν ἀνδρῶν ἐπὶ μεγάλοις μέγα φρονούντων. Everybody knows that this was the effect that Helen's beauty had on her contemporaries – the statement is uncontroversial. By gaining the audience's tacit assent to this account, however, Gorgias implicitly extracts from them their assent to a more general proposition: that this is the effect that all beauty of a certain standard can be reasonably expected to have upon its beholders. At the end of the speech, this general principle will be stated explicitly.

In section 15 Gorgias turns to his final and most important argument in exculpation of Helen: that she was a victim of ἔρως. His argument about ἔρως is somewhat surprising in that it confines itself exclusively to the effect of sight, specifically comparing the effect of the sight of the beloved to that of hostilely deployed weapons: διὰ δὲ τῆς ὄψεως ἡ ψυχὴ κἀν τοῖς τρόποις τυποῦται. αὐτίκα γὰρ ὅταν πολέμια σώματα [καὶ] πολέμιον ἐπὶ πολεμίοις ὁπλίσῃ κόσμον χαλκοῦ καὶ σιδήρου, τοῦ μὲν ἀλεξητήριον τοῦ δὲ †προβλήματα, εἰ θεάσεται ἡ ὄψις, ἐταράχθη καὶ ἐτάραξε τὴν ψυχήν (§§ 15–16).[14] Race has correctly seen that this emphasis upon sight, and the combination of erotic and military objects of sight, derive from Sappho 16, which combines armies, Helen of Troy, and the vision of one's beloved:[15]

> οἱ μὲν ἰππήων στρότον οἱ δὲ πέσδων
> οἱ δὲ νάων φαῖσ' ἐπὶ γᾶν μέλαιναν
> ἔμμεναι κάλλιστον, ἔγω δὲ κῆν' ὄτ-
> τω τις ἔραται·

14. In this corrupt passage I have followed the text of D–K.
15. Race (1989) 19. All the elements are present in the Teichoskopeia, also discussed by Race, ibid.

πάγχυ δ' εὔμαρες σύνετον πόησαι
πάντι τοῦτ', ἀ γὰρ πόλυ περσκέθοισα
κάλλος ἀνθρώπων ' Ελένα τὸν ἄνδρα
τὸν [πανάρ]ιστον

καλλ[ίποι]σ' ἔβα 'ς Τροίαν πλέοισα
κωὐδ[ὲ πα]ῖδος οὐδὲ φίλων τοκήων
πά[μπαν] ἐμνάσθη, ἀλλὰ παράγαγ' αὔταν
           ]σαν

...
...
...]με νῦν 'Ανακτορί[ας ὀ]νέμναι-
σ' οὐ] παρεοίσας·

τᾶ]ς κε βολλοίμαν ἔρατόν τε βᾶμα
κἀμάρυχμα λάμπρον ἴδην προσώπω
ἢ τὰ Λύδων ἄρματα καὶ πανόπλοις
           ]άχεντας.

As Race notes, Gorgias generalizes the argument: sight *in general* possesses "psychologically compelling power." After this generalization, he proceeds to illustrate his claim with military and artistic examples, and then, again as noted by Race, applies the argument to Helen.[16] What needs to be added, however, is that Gorgias' new argument turns the usual account of Helen – the one espoused by himself in section 4 – on its head: she herself is now the victim of passion aroused by the beauty of her beloved; and, furthermore, that the means of accomplishing this inversion is that same generalization of the arguments explicitly presented in sections 15–18 and implied in section 4. This crucial passage comes in the transition at the end of section 18:

> οὕτω τὰ μὲν λυπεῖν τὰ δὲ ποθεῖν πέφυκε τὴν ὄψιν. <u>πολλὰ δὲ πολλοῖς πολλῶν ἔρωτα</u> καὶ πόθον ἐνεργάζεται πραγμάτων καὶ <u>σωμάτων</u>. εἰ οὖν τῷ τοῦ 'Αλεξάνδρου <u>σώματι</u> τὸ τῆς 'Ελένης ὄμμα ἡσθὲν προθυμίαν καὶ ἅμιλλαν ἔρωτος τῇ ψυχῇ παρέδωκε, τί θαυμαστόν;

The language has been chosen to recall that of section 4: <u>πλείστας δὲ πλείστοις ἐπιθυμίας ἔρωτος ἐνειργάσατο, ἑνὶ δὲ σώματι πολλὰ σώματα</u> συνήγαγεν ἀνδρῶν. The earlier account of Helen (§4) had

---

16. Race (1989) 19: "[B]efore discussing *eros* itself, Gorgias first illustrates the power of sight in effecting emotion in the soul. The very example he chooses strongly suggests that he had Sappho's poem in mind: he points out that the sight of military formations can cause panic in the viewer. Having thus demonstrated the psychologically compelling power of sight, Gorgias applies his argument (cf. οὖν) to the case of Helen's *eros* for Paris (§19)."

been, as I said, traditional and uncontroversial: everybody knows that this was the effect of Helen's beauty on those who saw it. It is an account that possesses unquestioned authority; by reminding the audience of it – and this will have been the purpose of its inclusion as the "false start" – Gorgias strengthens his position when, in sections 15–18, he comes to generalize and invert its usual application to Helen.[17] Thus, if anyone should now resist the new paradoxical claim that Helen was herself the victim of ἔρως, Gorgias is in a position to retort: "You placidly accepted that Helen's beauty had this effect upon her suitors back in section 4; how can you deny the principle here?"

Gorgias' unremarkable insight has been that the traditional account of Helen contains within it the material of her defense: if, with the traditional account, you accept that it is in the nature of beauty to exert a compulsion upon those who perceive it, then Helen's own notoriety serves as a powerful piece of evidence to defend her. The story of Helen has two parts: first she is the active victimizer, and then the victimized; the universal authority of the first can be used to demonstrate the reasonableness of the second (εἰκὸς ἦν γενέσθαι τὸν τῆς Ἑλένης εἰς τὴν Τροίαν στόλον, §4).[18]

All this sounds familiar; it is a sophistic reworking of the paradoxical argument of Sappho 16. Page, in his commentary on line 7, describes that argument well, if critically:

The sequence of thought might have been clearer. The preceding stanza had asked the question, 'What is τὸ κάλλιστον, the most beautiful thing on earth?' The answer was given, 'It is that which you love.' Helen is to prove the truth of this: τὸ κάλλιστον, for her, was 'the one whom she loved' – her paramour, for whose sake she deserted home and family. It seems then inelegant to begin this parable, the point of which is that Helen found τὸ κάλλιστον in her lover, by stating that she herself surpassed all mortals in this very quality.[19]

17. Race (1989): 19: "Here the eye (ὄμμα), delighted by physical appearance, initiates a passion (ἔρωτος) that is impossible to resist. Whereas Sappho makes ἔρως the basis for judgment of beauty without raising the problem of a moral issue, Gorgias deliberately confronts the moral questions only to argue that the compulsive nature of passion absolves Helen (and by extension anyone else) of moral responsibility."

18. As Race points out to me, this observation is corroborated by the portrayal of Helen in *Iliad* 3, "where the patronage of Aphrodite is both a blessing and a curse, and where Helen is both a victimizer of the Trojans (πῆμα) and the victim of Aphrodite's manipulation." He also points to the Homeric *Hymn to Aphrodite*, in which the goddess who makes everyone else fall in love is herself made to love Anchises.

19. D. L. Page, *Sappho and Alcaeus* (Oxford 1955) 53. For summary of various discussions of the problem described by Page, see G. W. Most, "Sappho Fr. 16.6–7 L–P," *CQ* 31

Gorgias would seem to have found an explanation – or at least a use – for this "inelegance": the point of reminding the audience of Helen's supreme beauty (referring to the earlier part of her career when that beauty actively exerted its well-known effects) is to give authority to the account of the later part of her career, when she herself operated under the compulsion of erotic beauty.[20] Compare Gorgias' general conclusion in section 18 (πολλὰ δὲ πολλοῖς πολλῶν ἔρωτα καὶ πόθον ἐνεργάζεται πραγμάτων καὶ σωμάτων) to Sappho's formulation (τὸ κάλλιστον is κῆν' ὄττω τις ἔραται);[21] both are statements of a radical relativism; Sappho's ostensible purpose is to propound this as general law, and she brings Helen in subsidiarily as corroborative evidence;[22] Gorgias' purpose is to defend Helen, and he formulates the general law in order to apply it to her particular case; otherwise the arguments are identical.

The purpose of this examination of Gorgias' *Helen* has been to discover the rationale for his inclusion of sections 3–4, that is, the

(1981) 11–17. Most himself correctly identifies Sappho's use of Helen as an argument from authority, as described by Aristotle (*Rhet.* 1398b19–1399a6).

20. The question is inevitably posed: does this Gorgianic "interpretation" of Sappho work for the poem itself? Most (see n. 19 above, p. 15) resolves the problem (stated by Page) thus: "as the καλλίστη of all mortals, Helen is uniquely competent to judge what is the κάλλιστον of all objects. Rhadamanthys' actions have the greatest authority for determining what is τὸ δικαιότατον; Achilles', for τὸ ἀνδρειότατον; and Helen's, for τὸ κάλλιστον." But this is simply to make a virtue out of the defect (Most, p. 13, concedes, or rather, stresses the "non-rational" element in such arguments from authority) and does not address the basic paradox that Sappho's two propositions contradict one another: there exists a universally acknowledged and objective standard of beauty (Helen), and beauty is purely subjective (κῆν' ὄττω τις ἔραται). Gorgias' "explanation" has the merit of side-stepping this pitfall by confining the whole argument to the subjective: it is not that Helen constitutes an objective standard of beauty, but rather that a lot of people (subjectively) found in her "that which they desired," and that therefore she illustrates the power of that effect. He would therefore (I suppose) understand ἃ πόλυ περσκέθοισα κάλλος ἀνθρώπων not as an objective statement (as it appears to be) of the existence of an objective κάλλος, but exclusively in terms of the proposition just formulated by Sappho: "she who among humans was the object of the greatest number of people's desire." The argument thus becomes something along the lines of "as all know, she inspired passion in everyone, and so could have had any, but she pursued the one who caused this effect in her." If this is what Sappho had in mind, then it must be agreed that her presentation is so abbreviated and inappropriately formulated as to justify Page's charge of inelegance.

21. Sappho's formulation is reminiscent of Hesiod's (*Th.* 120) Ἔρος, ὃς κάλλιστος κτλ., and the prominence of eros/Eros in theogonical aetiology, in mythological explanation in general, will not have been insignificant to Herodotus, on whom see below. Cf. Agathon's characterization of Eros as κάλλιστος (Plato, *Symposium* 195A) and Socrates' denial (201B: οὐκ ἔχει Ἔρως κάλλος).

22. Her ultimately revealed purpose – the praise of Anactoria – is encomiastic, like that of the *Helen*.

rationale for the false-start recusatio. We can regard this rationale as being a means of unpacking – and thereby avoiding the "inelegance" of – Sappho's ambidextrous use of Helen in poem 16: Helen's authority as an example of beauty's *active* power (Sappho's ἀ γὰρ πόλυ περσκέθοισα κάλλος ἀνθρώπων) is put by Gorgias into the preliminary sections (3–4: ἔσχε τὸ ἰσόθεον κάλλος κτλ.) that will be dismissed in the transitional recusatio of section 5; Helen's complementary function as exemplar of the effect of ἔρως on its victim (Sappho's παράγαγ' αὔταν; cf. *Helen* §4 πολλὰ σώματα συνήγαγεν) is kept by Gorgias to the end and climax of his argument (§§ 18–19), a passage which, as we have seen, designedly recalls and exploits the earlier.

II

Turning now to the preface of Herodotus' *Histories*, it will be a fairly simple task – thanks especially to the observations of Race – to discern the use of a comparable structure. Again, I will summarize and describe the procedures followed by the author.

Herodotus begins with the famous long and complicated sentence describing the purpose of his work:

> Ἡροδότου Ἁλικαρνησσέος ἱστορίης ἀπόδεξις ἥδε, ὡς μήτε τὰ γενόμενα ἐξ ἀνθρώπων τῷ χρόνῳ ἐξίτηλα γένηται, μήτε ἔργα μεγάλα τε καὶ θωμαστά, τὰ μὲν Ἕλλησι, τὰ δὲ βαρβάροισι ἀποδεχθέντα, ἀκλεᾶ γένηται, τά τε ἄλλα καὶ δι' ἣν αἰτίην ἐπολέμησαν ἀλλήλοισι.

Recent discussions have concentrated upon those features which appear to recall the epic tradition.[23] I draw attention to a negative or polemical element. It is clear from external and internal evidence that Herodotus regarded Hecataeus as both a model and foil for his own work.[24] The rather sarcastic account of Hecataeus' genealogical interests in Book 2.143, together with Herodotus'

---

23. See T. Krischer, "Herodots Prooimion," *Hermes* 93 (1965) 159–67 and G. Nagy, "Herodotus the *Logios*," *Arethusa* 20 (1987) 175–84. An epic passage that may have influenced the negative formulations in the double purpose clause and which, so far as I know, has not been mentioned by commentators, is *Il.* 22.304f. (Hector solemnly prays): μὴ μὰν ἀσπουδί γε καὶ ἀκλειῶς ἀπολοίμην, | ἀλλὰ μέγα ῥέξας τι καὶ ἐσσομένοισι πυθέσθαι.

24. See, e.g., F. Jacoby, "Die Entwicklung der griechischen Historiographie," *Abhandlungen zur griechischen Geschichtsschreibung* (Leiden 1956) 16–64, pp. 37–39 = *Klio* 9 (1909) 80–123, pp. 99–100 and, for qualification of Jacoby's view, C. W. Fornara, *The Nature of History in Ancient Greece and Rome* (Berkeley 1983) 29–31.

The preface to Herodotus' "Histories"

apparently programmatic disavowal of such interests himself, suggest that Hecataeus' *Genealogies* was a special target of Herodotus' disdain.[25] It seems to me at least possible that a rejection of genealogically organized *historia* in general motivates some of the language of the proem. The only other instance of ἐξίτηλος in Herodotus is in 5.38: the Spartan ephors tell the childless king Anaxandrides to get a new and fertile wife, since they cannot allow the race of Eurysthenes to die out; compare the language with that of the proem:

ὡς μήτε τὰ γενόμενα ἐξ ἀνθρώπων τῷ χρόνῳ ἐξίτηλα γένηται

ἡμῖν τοῦτό ἐστι οὐ περιοπτέον, γένος τὸ Εὐρυσθένεος γενέσθαι ἐξίτηλον[26]

The similarity raises the possibility that Herodotus chose γενόμενα in the first μήτε clause – balanced by ἔργα in the second – as something to replace what the subsequent ἐξίτηλα will bring to mind, namely, γένος/γένεα,[27] as found (together with ἔργα) in, for example, *A.P.* 9.64.7f. (= [Asclepiades] xlv Gow–Page), where Hesiod is addressed: μακάρων γένος ἔργα τε μολπαῖς καὶ γένος ἀρχαίων ἔγραφες ἡμιθέων. Compare *h. Hom.* 31.18*f.*, κλήσω μερόπων γένος ἀνδρῶν ἡμιθέων ὧν ἔργα θεοὶ θνητοῖσιν ἔδειξαν.[28] My inference assumes that ἐξίτηλα recognizably belonged to the vocabulary of genealogy, and that genealogy was, for the audience, a traditional and even expected topic or genre, as exemplified by the quoted epic phrase γένος ἀνδρῶν, which presumably announced a composition wherein events were related incidentally as they attached themselves to the individuals of the γένος, providing the overall organizing structure (like the *Catalogue of Women*, which begins νῦν δὲ γυναικῶν φῦλον ἀείσατε).[29] It seems to me fair to say that Herodotus, as part of his attempt to move beyond

---

25. πρότερον δὲ Ἑκαταίῳ τῷ λογοποιῷ ἐν Θήβῃσι γενεηλογήσαντι ἑωυτὸν καὶ ἀναδήσαντι τὴν πατριὴν ἐς ἑκκαιδέκατον θεὸν ἐποίησαν οἱ ἱρέες τοῦ Διὸς οἷόν τι καὶ ἐμοὶ οὐ γενεηλογήσαντι ἐμεωυτόν.

26. For another application of the word to extinction, see Aeschylus, *fr.* 162.4: οὔπω σφιν ἐξίτηλον αἷμα δαιμόνων.

27. Regardless of the fact that γενόμενα linearly precedes ἐξίτηλα, it still remains that γενόμενα ἐξ ἀνθρώπων is syntactically united with ἐξίτηλα γένηται, and they will thus have been taken together in the audience's mind.

28. Γένος and ἔργα (or πράξεις) form two major categories of encomium in later rhetorical theory; see Miller (n. 8 above) on this and on the poetic antecedents.

29. On Greek genealogical works in both poetry and prose, see M. L. West, *The Hesiodic Catalogue of Women* (Oxford 1985) 2–11.

genealogical history, inverted this organizational principle by subordinating men and their genealogies to events, and, furthermore, that the designation of his subject matter as γενόμενα ἐξ ἀνθρώπων,[30] as opposed to γένος ἀνδρῶν, satisfactorily announces this inversion. At any rate, Hecataeus seems in some way to have seen himself as the successor and continuer of the Hesiodic tradition, and it is notable that the same work of his is referred to under three names: Ἱστορίαι, Γενεαλογίαι, and Ἡρωολογία. The first is the word Herodotus uses to characterize his own approach, while the other two reflect just those aspects of Hecataeus' work that Herodotus rejects as organizing principles for his own.[31]

That Herodotus intended his proem to be understood to include a rejection of genealogically organized history remains speculative, though such a rejection is made explicitly in Book 2; but no one, I think, would deny that the remainder of his preface has the purpose of rejecting ἡρωολογία.[32] It is here that the false-start recusatio is found. Herodotus begins by reporting – without editorial comment, which is withheld until the recusatio proper in chapter 5 – the account of the Persians: Περσέων μέν νυν οἱ λόγιοι

---

30. The use of γενόμενα in the sense "things done," though characteristic of Herodotus, may also reflect the similar use of the participle in Hesiod *Th.* 31–33, again in conjunction with what Herodotus excludes, γένος: ἐνέπνευσαν δέ μοι αὐδὴν | θέσπιν, ἵνα κλείοιμι τά τ' ἐσσόμενα πρό τ' ἐόντα, | καί μ' ἐκέλονθ' ὑμνεῖν μακάρων γένος αἰὲν ἐόντων.

31. For Hecataeus as follower of Hesiod, see, e.g., Jacoby (n. 24 above) p. 20 (= 83): "Sie [i.e., Hecataeus' Γενεαλογίαι and Περίοδος Γῆς] ersetzen und lösen ab das 'hesiodeische,' das lehrhafte Epos und machen eben deshalb Epoche, weil sie den wissenschaftlichen Stoff auch in die Sprache der Wissenschaft kleiden." Note that criticism of Hecataeus on this point does not entail a rejection of genealogy *tout court*: as G. Nagy points out to me, "Herodotus simply has a more varied repertoire than Hecataeus."

32. Jacoby (n. 24 above) 37–39(= 99–100), saw this development less as a matter of polemic and more as a natural consequence of Herodotus' view of himself as continuer of the genealogical tradition for the *spatium historicum*: "Das sieht, wer sich sein Prooimion überlegt (1 1–5), in dem die ersten Stadien des weltgeschichtlichen Gegensatzes zwischen Orient und Occident ganz kurz abgemacht, eigentlich nur erwähnt und dem Leser einleitungsweise ins Gedächtnis gerufen werden. Eine ausführliche Darstellung dieses Teiles der griechischen Geschichte wird ausdrücklich abgelehnt, nicht etwa aus klar erfassten kritischen Bedenken gegen die Wahrheit und Geschichtlichkeit der Tradition über diese Zeit, sondern aus einem ganz äusserlich-praktischen Gesichtspunkt: diese Stadien – Jo Europa Helena – haben bereits eine ausgedehnte kritische d. h. rationalisierende und historisierende Behandlung durch Herodots Vorgänger erfahren." Where Jacoby sees a polite nod of the head to predecessors, I see (especially in the emphatic οἶδα αὐτός of 1.5.3, as it contrasts with the immediately preceding and dismissive "I shall not say about these things that they happened this way or that") criticism of their attempt to give an account of personages antedating ἡ ἀνθρωπηίη λεγομένη γενεή (3.122.2 – another swipe at the genealogists). Jacoby's opinion that Herodotus makes it a general principle not to repeat information available elsewhere is, however, corroborated by 6.55.

The preface to Herodotus' "Histories"

Φοίνικας αἰτίους φασὶ γενέσθαι τῆς διαφορῆς.[33] There follows for the next four chapters the stories of the successive rapes of Greek and Asian girls (Io, Europa, Medea) culminating (chs. 3–4) in the story of Paris' rape of Helen and the war that resulted. Chapter 5.1 summarizes this account, and 5.2 is given over to the Phoenician variant of the Io story. Looking back now to the first sentence we can see that the μέν (Περσέων μέν νυν κτλ.) is twice repeated, and twice answered with a δέ: the first repetition comes in the summary of 5.1 οὕτω μὲν Πέρσαι λέγουσι γενέσθαι κτλ., which is directly answered by the Phoenician variant: περὶ δὲ τῆς ᾿Ιοῦς οὐκ ὁμολογοῦσι Πέρσῃσι οὕτω Φοίνικες. The second repetition of the μέν, and the second δέ, come in 5.3, where the μέν-clause summarizes the whole preface (excluding the proem) so far, and the δέ-clause constitutes the recusatio: ταῦτα μέν νυν Πέρσαι τε καὶ Φοίνικες λέγουσι. ἐγὼ δὲ περὶ μὲν τούτων οὐκ ἔρχομαι ἐρέων ὡς οὕτως ἢ ἄλλως κως ταῦτα ἐγένετο, τὸν δὲ οἶδα αὐτὸς πρῶτον ὑπάρξαντα ἀδίκων ἔργων ἐς τοὺς ῞Ελληνας, τοῦτον σημήνας προβήσομαι ἐς τὸ πρόσω τοῦ λόγου κτλ.

Race, once again, has observed the similarity of technique to Sappho 16: "Although it is more diffuse than its poetic prototypes, the opening of Herodotus' *Histories* (1–5) is in the form of a priamel along the lines of *h. Hom.* 1.1–16 and Sappho *fr.* 16: οἱ μέν...οἱ δέ...ἐγὼ δέ, where the opinions of others are presented, only to be rejected *en masse* by the new approach offered by the writer... The form Sappho had used to exalt her love for Anactoria Herodotus uses to begin his histories with that which *he himself* knows."[34] I would dissent only on the point of describing the structure of Herodotus' opening as a priamel. An essential characteristic of priamels would seem to be that they are immediately recognizable as such, as in Sappho 16 and *h. Hom.* 1.1–16.[35] Psychological or rhetorical effect plays a part here, and it would be a preternaturally acute reader who could deduce from Περσέων μέν νυν κτλ. that the succeeding four chapters were merely the first element of a priamel; they are revealed as such only in retrospect, at 5.3. Until the break-off there, Herodotus would

33. Jacoby (n. 24 above) p. 38 (= 100) n. 65 entertains the hypothesis that Herodotus cites the Persian λόγιοι here because they had been used by Hecataeus as sources for the rationalistic accounts he opposed to the λόγοι πολλοί τε καὶ γελοῖοι of the Greeks (*FGrH* 1 F 1).
34. Race (1982) 111.
35. There is a concealed, "surprise" priamel at *h. Ap.* 30–49; see Race (1982) p. 49.

seem to expect his audience to take the account at face value; he perhaps even hopes that they will be taken in and assume that his own history is going to follow the same general lines. After all, the systematic and rationalized tracing of present day persons and things to origins in the mythic past is precisely what the *Histories* of Hecataeus will have taught them to expect from such projects – all dressed up with the apparatus of fastidious pedantry, a need which Herodotus himself (or his "Persian sources") here complaisantly supplies: "Io and the other women came to the Phoenician ships on the fifth *or sixth* day."[36] More telling still is his intervention in his own voice (1.2.1): μετὰ δὲ ταῦτα Ἑλλήνων τινάς (οὐ γὰρ ἔχουσι τοὔνομα ἀπηγήσασθαι) φασὶ τῆς Φοινίκης ἐς Τύρον προσσχόντας ἁρπάσαι τοῦ βασιλέος τὴν θυγατέρα Εὐρώπην. εἴησαν δ' ἂν οὗτοι Κρῆτες. Here he actually helps his informants out, supplementing their account with what he knows from Greek myths (that Europa ended up in Crete), and using that information to supply by inference the kidnappers' identity. Such co-operation is a form of endorsement, in that it takes the informant seriously. Since, as it seems, Herodotus to some extent conceals from his reader the procedure he is employing, I prefer to regard his preface not, with Race, as a priamel, but as a false-start recusatio.

The purpose of Herodotus' use of the device here is not as hard to detect as it was in the case of Gorgias' *Helen*. One type of purpose has already been mentioned: the historian wishes to declare that his own work will reject the mythological orientation of Hecataeus', and the recusatio is an effective means of accomplishing this end. It would not, however, seem to be solely the unscientific methodology of mythological history that Herodotus wants to distance himself from. Note that Sappho 16 contains an element that associates it with the recusatios of Roman elegy: the rejection of martial themes in favor of the personal and erotic. Note also that Herodotus – using, as Race pointed out, a structure reminiscent of Sappho 16 – exactly reverses this preference: the rejection of the traditional stories of rape and adultery that had been used, and supposedly were still being used, in the mythic aetiology of the east–west conflict, and

36. Cf. the quotation from Jacoby in n. 32 above.

the preferring of military and political history based upon what can be known. Helen of Troy is a pivotal figure in the arguments of both.[37]

At any rate, it is appropriate to acknowledge that Herodotus' preface, and his histories as a whole, reverse the preference expressed by Sappho for the erotic over the military, just as they reject Hecataeus' inclusion of genealogical and mythological material. The rejection of the Sapphic outlook was surely just as significant as that of the Hecataean, given the prominence awarded eros in both the quasi-scientific cosmologies from Hesiod (see especially *Th.* 120) to Empedocles, and in the epic "histories" of the heroic age, where the emblematic (and catalytic) figure is Aphrodite's sometimes unwilling protégée, Helen of Troy. Herodotus follows Homer in identifying the ἀρχὴ κακῶν as ships, but his νέες ἀρχέκακοι are deployed in the service of political conviction rather than sexual indulgence (5.97.3 versus *Il.* 5.62). His originality in locating political causality in the axes of power rather than in the whims of lust is not the least of his achievements. None the less, it must be emphasized that what Herodotus does – and this is standard procedure in the exploitation of "rejected" foil – is demote, not expel, eros as a force in world events: the Persian histories are framed by tales of erotic misadventure, beginning with Gyges and Candaules' wife and concluding with the horrific stories of Artaÿnte and of Artaÿktes. This is prominence of a kind, and yet, while the symmetrical positioning of these lubricious tales may reflect the historical theorist's sincere conviction that public events are often shaped by the most personal quirks of the great personages who enact them, it may contrarily do no more than reveal the hand of the wise raconteur who knows what his audience likes. Again, there is always an element of having your cake and eating it too in these techniques that deploy ostentatiously rejected foil.[38] In the case of the false-

---

37. It is a pleasing coincidence that the chariots rejected by Sappho (identified after the priamel and the climactic introduction of Anactoria) are of the same nationality (τὰ Λύδων ἄρματα) as the man with whom Herodotus begins his history proper after the conclusion of his preface (the recusatio): Κροῖσος ἦν Λυδὸς μὲν γένος.

38. Cf. E. L. Bundy, "The 'Quarrel between Kallimachos and Apollonius'," *CSCA* 5 (1972) 39–94, p. 71, n. 79 on Pindar *Ol.* 1: "Although Pindar's purposes here require that he rejects [the traditional account of the feast of Tantalus], yet the detail of the ivory shoulder is *too good to spare*..." (my emphasis).

start recusatio the author simply misleads the audience, creating the expectation of one thing and then suddenly declaring that thing to be bad or undesirable. Herodotus begins, after his proem, with a sample of the kind of rationalized mythological aetiology that he intends to reject. As I said earlier, he presents this sample without any indication (at first) that he regards it, and the enterprise it represents, as inane. Even that it is part of a priamel becomes clear only in retrospect.

That Herodotus wanted his audience for the moment to respect the Persian account seems evident. Likewise his motive: the new approach he is about to present will be more effective if the audience has just been seductively reminded of the old. This kind of dramatic, retrospectively polemical introduction is the method and motive of the false-start recusatio generally. It may have had a pedigree almost as long and distinguished as that which Hecataeus claimed for himself; the evidence does not admit proof, but Stesichorus' poem recanting an earlier slanderous (and more traditional) account of Helen (*PMG* 192) will have been an early and relevant instance, provided that the recantation occurred in the same poem as the slander.[39] At any rate, continued fascination with the technique is attested by the use to which Plato put the Stesichorean material in the *Phaedrus*: the complete discomfiting of the "Lysianic" approach is accomplished in the two stages of Socrates' single performance, the first stage comprising Socrates' outdoing of "Lysias" at his own game (as Herodotus mimics Hecataeus in his proem), the second presenting the new and better approach.[40]

III

I now turn to the connection between Gorgias and Herodotus. The similarities of theme and structure so far discussed can all be ascribed either to the coincidence of traditional literary topics and techniques or more narrowly to a debt to Sappho 16, which was certainly a vital presence in those literary traditions. The following matters of detail seem to imply some kind of horizontal connection

---

39. See especially L. Woodbury, "Helen and the Palinode," *Phoenix* 21 (1967) 157–76, 170f.

40. Plato's interest in poetic "self-contradiction" is also shown in the related passage of the *Protagoras* (339aff.).

between the two prose works. These points of contact can best be observed by quoting the relevant excerpts:

Gorgias, *Helen* §5

ὅστις μὲν οὖν καὶ δι' ὅ τι καὶ ὅπως ἀπέπλησε τὸν ἔρωτα τὴν Ἑλένην λαβών, **οὐ λέξω**

τὸν χρόνον δὲ… ὑπερβὰς **ἐπὶ τὴν ἀρχὴν τοῦ μέλλοντος λόγου προβήσομαι**

καὶ προθήσομαι **τὰς αἰτίας, δι' ἃς**

Herodotus, proem–1.5.3

1.5.3: ταῦτα μὲν νυν Πέρσαι τε καὶ Φοίνικες λέγουσι. ἐγὼ δὲ περὶ μὲν τούτων **οὐκ ἔρχομαι ἐρέων**

τὸν δὲ οἶδα… τοῦτον σημήνας **προβήσομαι ἐς τὸ πρόσω τοῦ λόγου**

proem:… ὡς μήτε τὰ γενόμενα … ἐξίτηλα γένηται, μήτε ἔργα μεγάλα… ἀκλεᾶ γένηται, τά τε ἄλλα καὶ **δι' ἣν αἰτίην**

These verbal details by themselves are trivial, comprising as they for the most part do rhetorical clichés.[41] Still, the distribution of the clichés – that is, their use at comparable transitional points for comparable purposes – in combination with the other marked similarities between the passages already noted, gives some ground for suspecting direct influence one way or the other.[42] It is the larger similarities discussed in the previous sections that bind the two works together; the trivial ones suggest direct influence.

The two works also complement one another. In the preface Herodotus dismisses the mythical stories of the heroic age and moves forward to the more recent, and more knowable, past. He appears to reject Helen and the rest out of court as irrelevant and unsuitable to the kind of history he means to write. He does, however, return to the subject and treat it at great length later

41. One of the trivialities can be trivially magnified: according to an Ibycus search of the TLG data base (*Pilot CD Rom · C*), these two passages (and Athanasius, *De decretis Nicaenae synoedi* 40.6.1–2) are the only ones in all the Greek literature recorded in that base in which the form προβήσομαι occurs.

42. It is the second and third items that occur at precisely similar places for similar purposes; the first passage of Herodotus set out occurs at the end of the proem introducing his work; he then proceeds to the foil section, followed by the recusatio, which in turn, by leading into the true beginning of the history, functions as a sort of second proem. The corresponding passage in Gorgias (the first item set out) comes at this last point, viz., at the "second proem." Note that the event of which Gorgias proposes to disclose the reasonable causes (τὰς αἰτίας, δι' ἃς εἰκὸς ἦν γενέσθαι τὸν τῆς Ἑλένης εἰς τὴν Τροίαν στόλον) is that event which Herodotus, in his recusatio, will decline to consider as a cause of the Greco-Persian conflict (δι' ἣν αἰτίην ἐπολέμησαν ἀλλήλοισι).

(2.112–20), and his discussion of the wanderings of Helen constitutes a fairly comprehensive examination of the possibilities, which I shall not summarize. His last word on the subject, however, is worth examining, especially because it reveals in part, at least, the kind of thinking that led him to reject the traditional accounts in the way he did in the preface: in 2.120 he finishes reporting the opinions of others about the Trojan War and delivers his own, which he bases upon a good sophistic argument from probability: Helen could not have gone with Paris to Troy, for if she had, the Trojans would certainly have handed her back to the Greeks, if not immediately, then as soon as it became clear that they would suffer loss on her account. They did not hand her over, but were destroyed; therefore she was not there. QED. Such reasoning leads Herodotus to espouse a version of the Stesichorean solution, as did Euripides in his *Helen*.

Regarded as a defense of Helen, Herodotus' argument constitutes what would have been called in the terminology of Hermagoras the στάσις στοχαστική (= *status coniecturalis*).[43] This type of case rests on a question of fact (disputing what happened), rather than, for example, on definition (στάσις ὁρική = *status definitivus*), which turns on the interpretation of facts conceded by both sides. Now, it is precisely the approach taken by Herodotus, that is, the στάσις στοχαστική (the question of fact), that Gorgias rejects in his section 5: τὸν χρόνον δὲ τῷ λόγῳ τὸν τότε νῦν ὑπερβὰς... προθήσομαι τὰς αἰτίας, δι' ἃς εἰκὸς ἦν γενέσθαι τὸν τῆς Ἑλένης εἰς τὴν Τροίαν στόλον. He explicitly refuses to discuss what happened then – that is, the facts of the case – but, admitting the truth of the traditional account, proposes to rest his defense upon reinterpretation of the events: Helen went to Troy, but I will now prove that it was reasonable for her to do so. The στάσις στοχαστική ("she did not do it") is rejected in favor of another στάσις, that from ποιότης (= *status qualitativus*): "She did it, but it was not her fault."

Again, it is hard to gauge the significance of this coincidence between the two works – and coincidence may well be in this context the right word. First of all, there is dispute about when

---

43. On stasis terminology see R. Volkmann, *Die Rhetorik der Griechen und Römer*[2] (Leipzig 1885) 40ff., G. Kennedy, *The Art of Persuasion in Greece* (Princeton 1963) 307f., and L. Calboli Montefusco, *La dottrina degli "status" nella retorica greca e romana* (Hildesheim 1986).

stasis theory first developed, although there is a general consensus that Hermagoras (first century B.C.) elaborated it into the form in which it appears in later Greek and Roman discussions. As to its existence before Hermagoras, Volkmann correctly inferred from Lysias 13 that, at the end of the fifth century, a skilled speaker, whether or not with the aid of formal theory, will have known the possible approaches to a case, looking both to the construction of his own and to the forestalling of his opponent's.[44] As revealed by Lysias 13, this practical knowledge embraced the possibilities that were eventually to be formally codified by Hermagoras into the theory of στάσεις. If, as I attempted to show earlier, either Gorgias wrote in awareness of Herodotus, or vice versa, then it makes perfect sense that the author who wrote second should have sought a new approach – which will have been, in the juridical fiction adopted by both authors, a different στάσις.[45] The innovation will have been part of the display – perhaps the point of it. This kind of "outdoing" of predecessors, characteristic of

44. Volkmann, (see n. 43 above) p. 48: "Dass indessen die Attischen Redner in ihrer Praxis auf die einzelnen Status Rücksicht genommen und bereits die Unterarten der *constitutio iuridicalis* gekannt haben, wird man nach einer aufmerksamen Betrachtung von Lysias *or.* XIII gegen Agoratos kaum noch bezweifeln können." A. Schweizer, in his study of Lysias' speech, *Die 13. Rede des Lysias* (Leipzig 1936) 57, followed Spengler in denying the existence of an "eigentliche Statuslehre" at this early a period: "denn, wie Quint. 3.6.80 bemerkt, beruht die sogenannte Statuslehre auf sehr natürlichen Grundlagen." Certainly, the imagination can run riot here, if restraint is not exercised, a danger well illustrated by Ledl's attempt to extract evidence for the existence of the theory from the distinction of willing and unwilling murder drawn in the Draconic code (A. Ledl, "Zum drakontischen Blutgesetz," *WS* 33 [1911] 1–36); the possibility had already been raised by O. Navarre, *Essai sur la rhétorique grecque avant Aristote* (Paris 1900) 270, who also believed that he could find clear traces of the theory from Antiphon through to Aristotle and the *Rhetorica ad Alexandrum* (261–71).

45. I suspect that it will be the inclination of most of those who accept my overall claim to hope that the influence worked from the greater author to the lesser. The other alternative should be given its due: see A. Nieschke, *De figurarum, quae vocantur* σχήματα Γοργίεια, *apud Herodotum usu* (Münden 1891), where sufficient evidence is assembled to make plausible a claim that Gorgias did indeed influence Herodotus (even without subscribing to the thoroughly discredited notion that the "Gorgianic figures" are not merely "characteristic of G.", but "originate from = are chronologically later than G."). Compare, for example, with the passage analyzed in n. 11 above, the following passage from Solon's consummately sophistic speech to Croesus in Herodotus 1.32.5–6 (I use bold face for the prefixes ἀ-/ἀν- and εὐ-; underlining for repeated whole words; and italic for repeated elements of compounds): πολλοὶ μὲν γὰρ ζάπλουτοι ἀνθρώπων **ἄνολβοί** εἰσι, πολλοὶ δὲ μετρίως ἔχοντες βίου **εὐ**τυχέες. ὁ μὲν δὴ μέγα πλούσιος, **ἄνολβος** δὲ δυοῖσι προέχει τοῦ **εὐ**τυχέος μοῦνον, οὗτος δὲ τοῦ πλουσίου καὶ **ἀν**όλβου πολλοῖσι· ὁ μὲν ἐπιθυμίην ἐκτελέσαι καὶ ἄτην μεγάλην προσπεσοῦσαν ἐνεῖκαι δυνατώτερος, ὁ δὲ τοιῇσδε προέχει ἐκείνου· ἄτην μὲν καὶ ἐπιθυμίην οὐκ ὁμοίως δυνατὸς ἐκείνῳ ἐνεῖκαι, ταῦτα δὲ ἡ **εὐ**τυχίη οἱ ἀπερύκει, **ἄ**πηρος δέ ἐστι, **ἄ**νουσος, **ἀ**παθὴς κακῶν, **εὔ**παις **εὐ**ειδής.

Greek literature throughout its history, was especially common in the sophistic age, where the need of authors to win audiences was augmented by the desire to acquire pupils.[46] The writers of this period produced speeches for Ajax and Odysseus, Odysseus and Palamedes, and, eventually, defenses and prosecutions of Socrates;[47] these competitive efforts, in which the entire purpose was to discover something brilliantly new to say on the hackneyed theme, reveal precisely the intellectual and cultural context to which the passages of both Gorgias and Herodotus belong.[48] Looked at from this broader perspective, the use by both of the false-start recusatio does not appear a matter of trivial stylistic fashion; the device seems typically to provide a means of connecting innovation to the previous tradition innovated upon; the false-start includes the tradition, the recusatio rejects it, in whole or in part.[49]

ADDITIONAL NOTE: In a book that appeared after I had submitted this article (*The Historical Method of Herodotus* [Toronto 1989]) Donald Lateiner advances an interpretation of Herodotus' preface similar to that recommended here; in a review (*CR* 41 [1991] 24), Stephanie West complains that parody of Hecataeus fails to explain Herodotus' citation of Persian λόγιοι. The question must be examined in light of the opposition, Persian *versus* Greek, already established in Herodotus' first sentence, and, in an obvious sense, well before it; then we should look to the opening of Hecataeus' histories, written, he said, to correct the inconsistent and ridiculous λόγοι of the *Greeks*. It is no good to argue, as some have, that a λόγιος is not a λόγος, as if to see a connection between the two words were the symptom of pitiable naivety; neither is Herodotus a λόγος, and his decision to rebut λόγιοι rather than their λόγοι looks to the personal terms in which he states the climactic contrast: ἐγὼ δέ.

46. On the earlier period, see the article of Mark Griffith cited above (n. 5.)
47. See G. E. L. Owen, "Philosophical Invective," *Oxford Studies in Ancient Philosophy* 1 (1983) 1–25.
48. Cf. Isocrates, *Helen* 12–13.
49. I wish to thank A. T. Cole, F. Dunn, A. Henrichs, A. M. Miller, G. Nagy, and W. H. Race for their criticisms.

Tragic beginnings: narration, voice, and authority in the prologues of Greek drama

CHARLES SEGAL

I. Narration and authority

For Plato and Aristotle drama is a special form of narration, telling its story through enactment or enacted imitation (*mimesis*), sometimes in combination with third-person narration (*diegesis*, *apangelia*).[1] In both epic and lyric the performing bard or chorus addresses the audience directly; in tragedy the poet is absent from the performance.[2] Without such a mediating explanatory voice, whether in the third person (as in epic) or in the first person (as in lyric), the meaning of the story must emerge from the events themselves as those unfold on the stage. The prologue is the place where tragedy comes closest to having a "narrator" on whom it must depend for its basic orientation. Apart from the prologue, the audience receives no direct, explicit guidance about how to interpret these events, although there may be more or less subtle signposts of another sort (e.g. in choral odes or messengers' speeches).[3]

Epic and lyric poets often begin with authority derived from a divine source of truth and power.[4] But at the beginning of a

---

1. See Aristot., *Poet.* 3.1448a 19–29; Plato, *Rep.* 3.392d–94c. In the following notes bibliographical references are intended as exemplary rather than exhaustive.
2. For some of the implications of this absent narrator see Segal (1986) 79ff. (For full references see Works Cited at end of essay.)
3. There is no need to repeat here the obvious and much studied uses of the expository monologic prologue to provide context, suggest a mood, introduce characters, arouse curiosity, awaken suspense, etc. For a good recent summary with relevant bibliography see Erbse (1984) 289, 292f.; Halleran (1985) 8ff.; Meridor (1989) 17f. For older discussions see Decharme (1906) 273–87, especially 279ff.; Murray (1913) 205–9; Stuart (1918) passim. Cf. also Aristot., *Rhet.* 3.14.1415a 11–25.
4. This authority can come from the Muses or the sacred locale of the song or some other divinity related to the occasion: see Pindar, *Ol.* 3, 4, 8; *Pyth.* 8; *Nem.* 8 and 11; Bacchylides 4, 7, 10, 11. On the Muse and the "authority of writing" see Said (1975) 23–25; on the epic invocation and the Muse see Clay (1983) 9–11. Hesiod's Muses may also tell falsehoods (*Theog.* 27f.), but their staff and inspiring breath still give the poet a special power (30–34).

tragedy proximity to the divine is often a source of danger or mystery rather than of comfort.[5] "To begin from Zeus," as the rhapsodes do, calls the highest possible authority into one's song;[6] but no tragedy begins with Zeus, except as a remote and mysterious causality (as in Aeschylus' *Agamemnon* or *Prometheus*).

Tragedy is closer to the philosophical dialogue (which it influenced) than to epic in that it begins with a problem or a conflict, which the ensuing action tries to resolve. To take one of the most celebrated prologues, the *Agamemnon* opens with the beacon signals, an act of signification and communication that dramatizes the problem of meaning in the event itself;[7] but their purpose emerges only with the execution of Clytaemnestra's plot, and their full significance becomes clear only with the answering torchlight procession at the end of the trilogy. Sophocles frequently begins a play with an oracle whose meaning we understand only at the end.[8] Euripides' opening statements of divine order or justice regularly turn out to be painfully different from human notions of order and justice.[9]

Pindar makes it an aesthetic principle to begin radiantly, with a proem like a far-gleaming temple-front (*Ol.* 6.1–4); and his practice is generally consistent with his theory. "Golden Lyre, joint possession of Apollo and the Muses," is literally the "beginning of the radiance," leading the singers to their song and illuminating the poet's way from the very first moment of

---

5. E.g. the uncertainty of the gods' will and divine vengeance in Aeschylus' *Persians* (92–105), the plague in the *Oedipus Tyrannus*, or Apollo's "yoking of Creusa by violence" in the prologue of the *Ion* (10f.). On this last see Whitman (1974) 74.

6. Cf. Pindar, *Nem.* 2.3. To "begin from Zeus" becomes a literary topos later: see Aratus, *Phaen.* 1, Cic., *De Leg.* 2.3.7, Virgil, *Ecl.* 3.60; Ovid, *Met.* 10.148.

7. Goldhill (1986) 4f. remarks on how the beacons, as a scene of "sign-reading," thematize "interpretation and (mis)understanding."

8. E.g. *Trach.* 76ff.; *Phil.* 113ff.; *OC* 46ff., 87ff. Analogously, a prophet's "truth" gains credence only too late, although this motif is generally reserved to a later point in the play (*Antig.* 1091–99; cf. *OT* 298f., 356, and *Ajax* 749ff.). Cf. also the much-discussed oracle in Soph., *El.* 32–37.

9. The *Hecuba*, for instance, opens with images of a clearly organized, hierarchical world order (1–2); but this finds little clear support in the action that follows; and the initial mercy of the chthonic gods only sets off the remoteness and apparent indifference of the Olympians in the rest of the play: see Segal (1989) 15f. and 21. This apparition of Polydorus' ghost echoes the visitation of Patroclus to Achilles in *Iliad* 23.65–107. See Brillante (1988) 433. In both cases the shade of an unburied loved one emerges in a night vision to ask for burial and to inform the survivor of his destiny (cf. πεπρωμένη, *Hec.* 43, and μοῖρα, *Iliad* 23.80). Patroclus' Hades is less obliging than Polydorus' (cf. *Iliad* 23.71–74 and *Hec.* 49f.), but this fact only sharpens the problem of Euripides' Olympian gods.

Tragic beginnings

utterance (*Pyth.* 1.1–4). Such a beginning prefigures the total, present meaning, to be realized in the rest of the poem. In another common epinician image, the poet sees a "myriad path" broadly open before him.[10] The tragic beginning, however, often strikes a mood of constriction and constraint, *aporia* or *ananke*. We may recall the oppressive hushing of speech in the *Agamemnon* or Deianeira's lingering fears from the past in *Trachiniae*, or the muted concern in the exchange between Nurse and Paedagogus in *Medea*, or the reticence of Electra in *Orestes*.[11] The remote geography in the prologue of the *Persians* or the *Bacchae* is a foil to present anxiety or mortal helplessness to come.[12]

In the oral tradition the bard or singer, as the voice of the social memory, preserves details about the past that would otherwise be lost.[13] In the tragic prologue this voice is neither impersonal nor objective. Euripides in particular often begins with what looks like epic objectivity;[14] but this soon dissolves because the speaker is not an impersonal narrator and because the scene must also set up the crisis of the moment. When Andromache narrates the end of the Trojan war, for example, she is telling a tale of personal suffering, full of anxiety about Hermione's plotting against herself and her infant son (Eur., *Androm.* 8–40).[15] The opening account of the epic voyage of the Argo in *Medea* takes the form of a wish by a concerned participant, the Nurse. Amphitryon opens the *Heracles* with an elaborate genealogy and a long account of his son's heroic deeds, but these latter both reveal and contrast with his present need in Heracles' absence (*HF* 37ff.) and with the unheroic threats to his family.[16] Helen's geographical and mythological exposition of Egypt and the background of the Trojan war is soon overshadowed by her anguish over her marriage, her reputation, and her chastity (*Helen* 49–67). The long list of exotic names in the anapaests that open the *Persians* is

---

10. See Pindar, *Isth.* 4.1 and 6.22f.; *Ol.* 6.22–28; Bacchyl. 5.31–34, 9.46–52.
11. On this last see Dunn (1989) 240f.
12. The authenticity of *Ba.* 13–22 has recently been questioned by Dihle (1981), especially 11ff.; but see *contra* Erbse (1984) 91f. and 295f.; see also Verdenius (1980) 3f.
13. See Havelock (1963) chap. 4 and (1982) 122ff.
14. Schmid (1940) 771, for example, commenting on the Euripidean prologue, insists on the "Charakter eines unpersönlichen Sachberichts" and the "Trockenheit eines mythographischen Handbuchs."
15. See Strohm (1977) 125.   16. See Strohm (1977) 129.

like an epic catalogue, but the mood is anxious rather than expansive and is colored by the emotion of the lyric voice.

The Priestess' account of the succession of the Delphic oracle in the *Eumenides* is the earliest extant example of the fact-filled narrative prologue, of the sort that Euripides will use many times. The Pythia's authority is assured by her sacrosanct status and is never questioned. Hers is also an account of events in the distant past that cannot be changed, unlike the Euripidean mixture of retrospect and prediction, where the latter sometimes proves to have been erroneous or partial. Even this earliest manifestation of the expository prologue, however, exploits the situation for extraordinary dramatic possibilities. The Pythia's serene *hieros logos*, with its myths of remote origins, lulls us into a mood of quiet receptiveness and conciliatory harmony that her shocked exit from the temple suddenly shatters (*Eum.* 34ff.).[17]

Even when the prologue-speaker is a god who predicts the future course of events, as often in Euripides, we are far from epic clarity. We are left wondering how the divine plan will be realized in the visible, human form of the theater. How will Aphrodite or Dionysus enter the mortal world of Hippolytus or Pentheus to wreak their vengeance? How will Heracles restore to life one who has already died (*Alcestis* 65–76)?[18] In some cases, as we discover later, the god's account is lacunose, ambiguous, or even misleading – notoriously so in the *Ion* and to a lesser extent in *Trojan Women* and *Bacchae*.[19]

In *Hippolytus*, Aphrodite tells both the beginning and the end of the story. But, contrary to what actually happens, she places Hippolytus' death before Phaedra's and says that she herself and not Phaedra will "show the matter to Theseus" (42). Euripides' purpose is not necessarily to mislead his audience, but rather to reveal the special perspective of anthropomorphic divinity. Aphrodite's concern is Hippolytus' scorn of her power (10–22),[20] which we see enacted in the following scene (73ff.). The "truth of

---

17. Taplin (1977) 358 justly calls this prologue "one of the boldest of its kind in surviving tragedy."   18. See Hamilton (1978) 293ff.

19. On *Ba.* see Hamilton (1974) passim, and on *Ion* Hamilton (1978) 279ff., emphasizing Euripides' manipulation of audience reaction. Erbse (1984), passim, especially 289f., stresses the explanatory function of the prologue and the essential veracity of the gods' account. Both are right, each calling attention to different features of Euripides' complex art. For an older, though still useful, account of "false foreshadowing" see Stuart (1918) passim, especially 297f., 300–3.   20. See Luschnig (1988) 93f.

Tragic beginnings

her words" is not the objective veracity of the events as we will see them onstage (δείξω δὲ μύθων τῶνδ' ἀλήθειαν τάχα, 9), but the more subjective "truth" of the Olympians' obsession with honor and respect from mortals (5–8). Phaedra's death is only a mildly regrettable by-product of this revenge (47–50). As in epic (e.g. the proem of the *Odyssey*), such knowledge demonstrates the gulf between the vast power of the goddess (cf. also 1–4) and the helplessness and ignorance of the mortals. These mortals, however, are not just the generic pitied *deiloi brotoi* of epic but include specific victims against whom the goddess has been plotting her cruel revenge "for a long time" (*palai*, 22), thereby revealing her far from objective engagement.

In the *Bacchae* Dionysus' epiphany-like presence at Thebes seems to assure his authority (1, 5), but the events which he predicts do not occur quite as the god describes them.[21] "Managing things well," he says, "I shall change my path to another land, revealing myself" (48–50). But this god's notion of "managing things well," *themenos eu*, is very different from the Theban view; and the middle voice may prove to be significant: he "manages things well for himself." He tells us at once that he does not appear in his Olympian form; yet within the play this mortal disguise is played off against his polymorphous lability.

In the *Helen* the mortal prologue-speaker, who is also chief protagonist, is unusual in possessing virtually divine knowledge. Helen reports her own genealogy and gives an account of the origins of the Trojan war that one can assume to be common knowledge (23ff.). Yet just how she came by this knowledge in Egypt is left unclear. She knows at first-hand how Zeus replaced her at Troy with a cloud-image (31–36). But when she goes on to describe "Zeus's plans" to relieve earth's overpopulation through the war (*ta Dios bouleumata*, 36f.), the basis of her authority is more problematical. In the *Orestes* this is, as it were, classified information, revealed by Apollo *ex machina* (1639–42).

The heavily Odyssean coloring of the *Helen* may have influenced this closer proximity of a mortal character to the voice of the epic omniscient narrator. Helen belongs to a remote world, close to myth and fairy tale. She has had the company of the prophetess Theonoe, who, in a version of the Homeric formula, "understands

21. See especially *Ba.* 46–52 and in general Hamilton (1974) 148; Erbse (1984) 95.

all things divine, what is, and what will be" (12f.; cf. *Iliad* 1.70, 2.485f.). She has also enjoyed the unusual experience of divine conveyance from Sparta to Egypt "in the folds of aether" (44f.). On this trip, presumably, she learned from Hermes that she will again "dwell in Sparta's glorious plain with (her) husband" (56–59). Euripides does not say explicitly that Hermes gave her this knowledge; but her special proximity to the prophetess and to the god allows her the privilege of giving both a summary of the past and tantalizing hints of the future. By opening with Helen, Euripides can also launch us rapidly into the scene with Teucer, which in turn alerts us to the surprises in store, prefigures the misrecognition scene between Helen and Menelaus (528–96), and gives a foretaste of the half-comic mood.[22]

Euripides withholds some essential background material until the entrance of Theonoe, whom Helen mentions prominently in the prologue. Indeed, Theonoe's entrance is virtually a second prologue (865ff.); and she provides the kind of information that the god often supplies in the prologue.[23] Her account of the present struggle on Olympus (873–91) parallels the more familiar story of the contest among the goddesses on Mt. Ida in Helen's opening speech (23ff.). This event is in fact a direct continuation of that conflict (cf. 880–86). By dividing up the task of supplying privileged information and by postponing the critical portion of it to Theonoe's entrance, Euripides can hold us in suspense and also begin the play with his fascinating mortal character and her involving, if more limited, perspective.

The prologue of *Hecuba* begins by securing sympathy for the victims, in part because the speaker is a child and a ghost, both unusual as speakers of the prologue. But it also introduces a perspective divided between supernatural and normal human

22. The scene with Teucer adds surprise to surprise, for not only is this shipwrecked survivor of Troy astonished to find Helen on this remote shore but, to our even greater surprise, exits without having recognized her. The scene thus dramatizes the contrasts between illusion and truth, image and body, inherent in the motif of the cloud-Helen (cf. 66f., 71–75, 160f.): see Segal (1986) 224–27, 257ff., with the literature there cited. Teucer's report of the rumor of Menelaus' death (*Hel.* 132) also forms part of the important motif of death and renewal and helps build suspense for the attempted recognition and its failure: see *Hel.* 290–92, 319f., 530ff.

23. The scene between Iris and Lyssa in *HF* 823–74 also exemplifies the device of a divine figure who speaks a kind of second prologue at the mid-point of the play. This "second prologue" has the form of the "two-against-one" dialogue discussed below, section V.

knowledge that persists to the end.[24] Polydorus' ghost has a privileged knowledge of his mother's "destiny" (cf. *pepromene*, 43); but with Hecuba herself he can communicate only through nocturnal signs, vivid though they are.[25] She has only vague fears, which are crystallized around the dream-images of the fawn bloodied by the wolf (90–92).[26] The uncertainty intensifies her sorrow, helplessness, and anxiety. True knowledge of her future woes lies on the other side of the divide between living and dead.

Within the prologue Polydorus' shift from his male relations, especially the betrayed tie of *xenia* between Priam and Polymestor, to his concern with his mother anticipates the play's larger movement from the aftermath of the Trojan war to Hecuba's emotions and the sufferings of women. He predicts Polyxena's death and Hecuba's burial of two children, and thus he helps bridge the gap between the two halves of the play.[27] Yet he says nothing about the terrible vengeance that Hecuba will exact for his death, even though the "two corpses of two children" foreshadow it (cf. 45 and 1051). He knows his "dear" and "old" mother (30, 52) as an object of compassion (55–58), not as a vengeful murderess.[28] That is a discovery left for us to make as the play moves from suppliancy and human sacrifice to vengeance. The voice of this prologue is indeed supernatural, but its authority is that of human kinship bonds rather than of divine foreknowledge. Hecuba's determination for revenge can thus emerge gradually, against the background of her maternal nature, rather than as a predetermined event.[29]

If the prologue sometimes withholds information for suspense or surprise, it can also offer a surplus of information. To a modern audience a wealth of mythical, genealogical, or geographical

---

24. Cf. *Hec.* 1259–84; compare also 68ff. with 703–9, and 26–30 with 697–701.

25. Brillante (1988) 445–47 plausibly suggests that the prologue presents two narrative forms of dreams and omens, an "epic" narrative with a linear, coherent description (the speech of Polydorus' shade) that contains its own interpretation, like Oneiros in *Iliad* 2, and a "dramatic" presentation, indicated through a symbolic vision and Hecuba's emotional response.

26. The prologue leaves it somewhat unclear just how much these visions from Polydorus' shade have communicated to Hecuba in his nightly visitations. The question depends, in part, on whether lines 73–77 and 90–97 are accepted as genuine. I tend to agree with Erbse (1984) 49ff. that they should be retained. See also Brillante (1988) 436ff.

27. See Dalmeyda (1919) 128.

28. Strohm (1977) 126f. points out the recurrent addresses to Hecuba as "mother" in the second half of the prologue (30, 34, 36, 50ff.).   29. See Erbse (1984) 58.

detail is boring or confusing. It may have been so for ancient audiences too, some of whom, at least, judged Euripides' prologues "tedious," ὀχληροί.[30] Such details, however, do help establish the authority of the speaker as one who knows the situation and can inform us of its importance, as we have noted in the case of Helen. But, as Helen's example also illustrates, neither the narrator nor his/her knowledge is ever completely external to the plot; and so such an involved telling always raises questions about the narrative's motivation, emphasis, completeness, accuracy, or point of view.

II. Seriousness and cosmicity

To win authority, the prologue must convince us of the seriousness of its contents as well as of the reliability of its speaker. Many plays begin with a gnomic pronouncement, generally somber, about human life (e.g. Soph., *Trach.* and Eur., *Hcld.* and *Or.*). More broadly still, the opening can take a cosmic perspective, extending from earth to heavens: so the watchman in *Agamemnon*, Aphrodite in *Hippolytus*, or Jocasta in *Phoenissae*, who begins and ends with the celestial fires (1–3 and 84). The device was familiar enough by the end of the century to stir Aristophanes to parody it in Praxagora's address to her lamp at the opening of *Ecclesiazusae*.

The *Eumenides*, in keeping with the cosmic themes of its trilogy, begins with founding myths and pre-Olympian deities. The *Hecuba*'s opening, as we have noted, evokes the ancient cosmogonic division of the world between Hades and the upper gods (1–2), whereas the play itself offers little indication of divine order among the living. Achilles' shade in the somewhat similar opening of Sophocles' lost *Polyxena* also calls up the horrid landscape of Hades, but (apparently) without the cosmogonic suggestion of Euripides' prologue.[31] Such beginnings reveal the underlying continuities of tragedy with epic. Both are forms of mythic narration that aim at a comprehensive view of human life seen in relation to nature and the gods, to the world above and the world

---

30. *Vita Eurip.* 3 (p. 4, line 7 Schwartz); see Murray (1913) 206; Decharme (1906) 281–83; Erbse (1984) 4. At the opposite extreme is the silent character of Aeschylus' prologues, criticized by Aristophanes, *Frogs* 911–26.

31. Soph., frag. 523 in *TrGF*, and see Radt's notes ad loc.; also Seneca, *Ag.* 1ff. The priority of *Polyxena* to *Hecuba* is often assumed, but absolute certainty is not possible.

Tragic beginnings

below, to the crisis of the moment and the remote beginnings of all things.

The prologue must tell us where we are, but "place" is not necessarily limited to specific geographical features. *Prometheus Bound* situates us in the midst of cosmogonic conflict at the remote edges of the world. The *Hippolytus* reminds us of the cosmic range of Aphrodite's power. Sophocles' two Oedipus dramas, each rooted in its civic frame, show us divine powers playing about the life of the heroes and the *polis*. The *Bacchae*, though strongly localized in Thebes, makes this city the testing ground of Dionysus' place between mortal and immortal, life-giving liquids and destructive fire (5–12), and East and West (13ff.).[32]

The prologue regularly creates a microcosm of major themes: secrecy and repression of speech in *Agamemnon*, the struggle between life and death in *Alcestis*, family curse and interpersonal conflict in *Antigone*, the meeting of human resources and mysterious divine power in *Oedipus Tyrannus*, and so on. Topographical description may offer images predictive of the human situation that the play will reveal. The "untrodden, uninhabited shore" of Lemnos in the opening lines of *Philoctetes*, the place of the "wandering Oedipus" in the Eumenides' grove at the very edge of Athens, or Egypt's "lovely-maidened streams of the Nile" in the *Helen* all have resonances in the play that extend far beyond topographic detail.[33]

Even small details may hint at themes to be developed later, like vision and pollution in *Hippolytus* (11, 25–31, 35) or what the protagonist is "named" or "called" in the *Helen* and *Oedipus Tyrannus* (*Hel.* 13, 16, 21, 43, 66; *OT* 8, ὁ πᾶσι κλεινὸς Οἰδίπους καλούμενος). Deianeira's background account of her wooing by Achelous in the prologue of *Trachiniae* seems to be drawing us rather confusedly away from the present dramatic situation (9ff.), but it will prove relevant to the violent sexuality and bestiality that circle around her life (cf. 497–530, 555–81). Hermes'

---

32. See Segal (1982) 118–24.
33. In the *Helen* the associations are not only with a distant, exotic world but also with the paradigm of Persephone in the background: cf. 173ff. and 1341ff. On *Phil.* and *OC* see Segal (1981) 295ff. and 364ff. respectively. See also Garner (1990) 147f. and 177 on the atmosphere of the Cyclopean realm of *Od.* 9 in the setting of *Phil.* In comedy, the no-man's-land of the lost and wandering Athenians in the *Birds* has an analogous function, showing the alienation of the protagonists from the *polis* in the real world.

reference to the autochthonous Erechtheids and their golden snakes in the *Ion* makes a picturesque contrast with the young hero's simple life as a Delphic hierodule (cf. 20–27 and 82ff.); but this material is obviously appropriate to a drama based on Athenian foundation myths.[34] Theseus' absence because of blood-guilt in killing kin (*Hipp.* 34f.) not only introduces the important motif of pollution or purity but also prefigures his role in the play as one who kills kin and then suffers some form of punishment.

III. Curiosity and sympathy

To provide information and engage our interest and sympathy, the most direct technique is obviously the appearance of the protagonist who states his or her situation in the first person.[35] The Sophoclean foil character permits a more distanced, objective view of the protagonist (especially in *Ajax* and *Antigone* and less directly in *Trach.*, *Phil.*, and *OC*). Or the prologue can show us a protagonist already fully engaged in the action that will determine his or her tragic suffering, as in Aeschylus' *Septem* or Sophocles' *Antigone* or *Oedipus Tyrannus*.[36]

Euripides sometimes adds a twist of surprise to a prologue's first-person narration by giving us a point of view from which we do not expect the events to be told. In the *Phoenissae*, for example, Jocasta opens the play with a long account of Theban genealogy, including the stories of Laius and Oedipus. But there is a special horror when she comes to the first-person statement, "To my son I bore two sons" (55), especially as this follows upon her third-person account of Oedipus (45–54). The misfortunes of this house do not, then, lie in the remote past but are embodied in the speaker before us who, unlike her Sophoclean counterpart, is still alive.

In like manner, his Iphigenia, in the Taurian play, speaks of herself as "slaughtered" and "sacrificed" (*IT* 8, 20, 24, 27), so

---

34. On these motifs see Whitman (1974) 73 and 97–99.
35. So, e.g., Orestes in *Choephoroe*, Eteocles in *Seven against Thebes*, Deianeira in *Trachiniae*, Andromache, Helen, and Iphigeneia (among the Taurians) in their respective Euripidean plays.
36. This effect will obviously be different for single plays and for the second or third play in a trilogy, like *Choephoroe* or *Septem*, where the characters are to some extent familiar and the action is already underway.

that the audience may be wondering if the speaker is a ghost, as in the *Hecuba*, until she explains Artemis' rescue at line 28. Helen's unique personal perspective on how she became the prize of the Trojan war and her first-person version of the Homeric journey through the aether similarly refresh the old myth in surprising ways (*Hel.* 42–45). The physical presence of the speaker as a living figure before us gives these long and very circumstantial narratives a special dramatic vividness: we see and hear an individual in whose life circumstances we can become directly involved.

First-person narration by a god is, necessarily, more detached; but here too Euripides innovates and experiments, most strikingly in the *Bacchae*.[37] This is the only extant play in which a god, after speaking the prologue, returns to the stage (albeit in disguise) for a major role in the action. The closest parallel comes also at a late point in its genre, namely the figure of Plutus in Aristophanes' comedy, who, though not disguised like Dionysus, is at least reluctant to tell who he is (*Plutus* 58ff.). Dionysus' stage appearance to foretell his disguise is appropriate to his special qualities of fluidity and elusiveness; and it implicitly includes the audience among the victims of the illusionistic power that he brings with him onstage throughout the play. As god of the theater, he can make us see him in many different guises.[38] Even the discrepancies, real or apparent, between Dionysus' plans as announced in the prologue and the events enacted in the play help "reveal" the god: they introduce us to his elusive, multiform divinity (cf. 100–104, 1017–19).[39] His mode of epiphany is mysterious and unexpected, and yet appropriate to his disturbing and ambiguous interventions in human life: shaking Pentheus' palace, leading him on in the form of a bull, and shouting as a disembodied voice from the heavens (585ff., 618ff., 1084ff.; cf. 920f.).

Because Greek tragedy generally (though not always) tells its story within the actual time of its performance, it must get us rapidly into its events. It cannot afford the luxury of a leisurely,

---

37. See the discussions of *Alc.*, *Ion*, *Tro.*, above.

38. On this aspect of Dionysus in the *Bacchae* see Segal (1982) 215ff., 223ff., 260ff.

39. On connections between Dionysus' expressions of "revealing" in the prologue (especially 22, 42, 47, 50) and the modes of epiphany later in the play see Hamilton (1974) 144–49; Segal (1982) 157, 228–32; Erbse (1984) 95–99. For qualifications see Verdenius (1980) 11f., with the bibliography there cited.

indirect beginning, like the ancient novel's ecphrastic account of an art-work (e.g. in Longus or Achilles Tatius) or even the *Odyssey*'s paradigmatic tale of Agamemnon and Orestes (1.28–43). The tragic beginning tends to resemble the proem of the *Iliad* rather than of the *Odyssey*, plunging *in medias res* and into an immediately visible crisis. The *Iliad* asks (1.8), "Who of the gods threw Achilles and Agememnon together to battle in strife?" The prologue of tragedy often seeks to elicit such a question, tacitly, from its audience.

Lacking the external narrator of epic or lyric, the tragic beginning must motivate the audience to ask who or why. But only rarely does it make this interrogative gesture overt, perhaps because it aims at creating a total fiction and at excluding a self-conscious awareness of its aesthetic frame.[40] Comedy, on the other hand, has fewer scruples in this regard and does not hesitate to remind its audience that it is in the theater; and so it often begins with a direct question (e.g. *Wasps, Birds, Thesmophoriazusae, Frogs*). Euripides' Amphitryon opens the *Heracles* by asking, "Who of mortals does not know Argive Amphitryon, sharer of his bed with Zeus?" But the question is rhetorical rather than strongly interrogative, although the epic tone of this genealogy serves as a foil to the very unepic type of hero who emerges at the end of the play.

Competing against other contestants in the big, open, crowded theater of Dionysus, the dramatist is also competing for his audience's attention, and he must get it fast. Success made a lasting impression, as is clear from ancient critics' appreciation of the prologues of Aeschylus' *Eumenides*, Sophocles' *Polyxena*, and Euripides' *Medea*.[41] Failure too made a lasting impression, and the Aristophanic Euripides registers his dismay at the perplexing silences of his rival's grand figures, who by the midpoint of the play have uttered only some dozen massive "ox-words, high-browed and crested" but utterly baffling (*Frogs* 911–26).

Euripides exploits our mixed desire both to know everything and to have the tale told gradually; we want both total revelation

---

40. Late Euripides, however, experiments with breaking this convention: see Zeitlin (1980) passim; Segal (1982) chap. 7, especially 264ff.

41. *Vita Aeschyli* 9; ps.-Longinus, *De Subl.* 15.7; Eur., *Med.* Hypothesis (a), lines 30f. (Diggle).

Tragic beginnings

and the suspense of more to come.[42] His predictive prologues remove suspense in one way but reinstate it in another by withholding crucial details or blurring or eliding events that will occur later. Our curiosity is piqued but not satisfied.

The *Alcestis* is a particularly clear example of this mixture of suspense and prediction. Though a pro-satyric play, it uses the full panoply of tragic techniques.[43] When Apollo tells Thanatos of Heracles' arrival and rescue (65–71), his language is vague enough to leave room for surprises later on, for we do not know just when or how Heracles will "take this woman away" from Death (69), or indeed if she will actually die.[44] Apollo dwells on the imminent death "on this day" (20, 27); and this tension between hope and inexorability becomes even greater as Thanatos brandishes his sword to cut off a lock of his victim's hair and dedicate her to Hades (74–76).[45] Only much later, when Heracles proposes descending to Hades after Alcestis is "recently dead" (τὴν θανοῦσαν ἀρτίως, 840), do we recognize in what sense Apollo's promise is possible.[46]

Even Apollo's opening speech holds a modest surprise: he announces his departure to avoid the pollution of death (23) but then engages the very principle of that pollution, Death himself.[47] Instead of an Olympian god who walks away from the sadness of death as a mortal cannot, Apollo remains and expresses his own "heaviness" of grief in terms that the mortal sufferer will later echo (42; cf. 1048; also 353, 891). Thanatos makes the surprise dramatic by his sharp, indignant questions, suggestive of comedy: "Ah, Ah, why are you in these halls? Why do you roam about here, Phoebus? Are you again doing injustice, appropriating and stopping the honors due to those below?" (28ff.). The buffoonish dialogue that follows, with its allusions to sophistic argument (58), introduces still another unexpected contrast between overhanging doom and the impediment of humorous banter. The light touch

---

42. See Stuart (1918) passim; also Michelini (1987) 104, apropos of *Hecuba*.
43. For an excellent recent discussion of tragic versus satyric elements in *Alc.* see Seidensticker (1982) 129ff., especially 134 on the prologue.
44. See Hamilton (1978) 294f.; Seeck (1985) 151f.
45. See Seeck (1985) 32.
46. See Stuart (1918) 296f.; Hamilton (1978) 297–99.
47. A related contradiction is the fact that Apollo can let Heracles save Alcestis, but cannot do it himself: see Seeck (1985) 148f., with note 9.

then becomes the foil to another surprise in the shift to Thanatos' ominous gesture at his exit, noted above, and in the troubled mourning of the entering chorus (78ff.).

Withholding the protagonist's appearance can be useful for figures who arouse conflicting or ambivalent responses and are not to be judged in black-and-white terms (e.g. Medea, Ajax, Electra). Medea, somewhat reminiscent of the Aeschylean silent character, utters a few offstage cries of woe (*Med.* 96–97), stirring the Nurse's (and our) anxiety for the children (96–121). This technique combines sympathy with distance. Both Hippolytus and Pentheus enter under threat from the prologue-speaking god of their respective plays and can thus appear potentially as both guilty agents and as innocent victims. Hippolytus enters only after Aphrodite's lengthy accusations (*Hipp.* 58–60); Pentheus enters in the middle of the first episode (*Ba.* 215ff.). Hippolytus' brief monologue, followed by his scene with the servant, reveals the weak spot of his character (*Hipp.* 73–120); but he does not return to the stage until the play is nearly half over (601), by which time our sympathies have been much involved in Phaedra. Dionysus' prologue in the *Bacchae* gives little indication of how strongly his quarrel with Thebes will be focused on Pentheus, how vehement the latter's resistance will be (cf. 45f.), or how cruel a punishment the god will exact (cf. 48–54).[48] He is as much concerned with the city of Thebes as with its immature ruler (1, 23, 39, 50). When Pentheus does enter, his tyrannical behavior shows the justice behind Dionysus' threats (215ff.); but our sympathy shifts back again (at least partially) to the mortal sufferer by the end of the play.

Having Polydorus speak the prologue of *Hecuba* is a brilliant stroke. The murdered son can show only Hecuba's helplessness and thus assures our pity for her as the *mater dolorosa*, the "mother" who "will see the two corpses of two children" (45). Only later do we recognize in those "two corpses of children" the other side of her personality, not the victim but the fierce avenger (1051; cf. 897 and 1287). As her son, Polydorus naturally knows and can communicate only this sympathetic side, on which he is still dependent for a mother's last gift, burial of his body. Hence

---

48. See Verdenius (1980) 11–13.

the silence about her other qualities is fully in character, while it also implies the depths of maternal love that forms the tragic link between both of her roles in the play, victim and avenger. Her emotion-filled entrance, in anapaests, expresses her maternal fear and concern (59–97) and thus seems to confirm her son's picture; it certainly gives no hint of her strength and capacity for plotting vengeance.

IV. Suppliant prologues

The scene of supplication is well suited to introduce a tragic situation. It gives a powerful visual and ritual enactment to the helplessness of the weak, and it forces the community to decide how to respond to the demands and possible dangers involved in supplication.[49] The sympathy, however, may be ambiguous and divided, for supplication has an aggressive as well as a dependent component. As John Gould has emphasized, the suppliant is a potentially dangerous outsider, a possible threat to a space or object regarded as inviolate.[50] The suppliant creates a "crisis of indecision," as Gould calls it,[51] that implicates the entire city: Argos in Aeschylus' *Suppliants*, Athens in Euripides' *Heracleidae* and *Suppliants* and Sophocles' *Oedipus at Colonus*. In the most famous suppliant beginning in Greek drama, the prologue of the *Oedipus Tyrannus*, Sophocles reverses the usual terms: the protagonist is the one being supplicated rather than the one making the supplication. The change prepares for the dynamics of the plot, in which the collective crisis of Thebes gradually turns into the personal crisis of its ruler. In a reversal of a different sort, the desperation and helplessness of suppliant status can also set off the courage of one who refuses to surrender to force or injustice, like Amphitryon in the *Heracles* or the stalwart Iolaus in the *Heracleidae* (26–40 and 52ff.).

As these last two plays (and *Hecuba* too) illustrate, the suppliant situation is precarious: there is always the possibility (generally the probability) of a sudden reversal, sometimes in spectacular terms, as in *Oedipus at Colonus*, the most powerful such effect on the Greek stage. Here, as in Euripides' *Heracleidae*, the would-be

---

49. See Strohm (1977) 121, apropos of *Andromache*; also Halleran (1985) 80ff. on Euripides' use of opening tableaux of supplication, especially in *HF*.
50. Gould (1973) 100.   51. Gould (1973) 83f.

suppliant is challenged by a blocking agent who orders him to leave the sanctuary (*OC* 36ff.; cf. *Hcld.* 55ff.). Oedipus' abrupt refusal must have electrified the audience as much as it surprised the citizen of Colonus (44f.). For some forty lines Sophocles keeps us in suspense about Oedipus' reasons for refusing to leave. Only after the exit of the citizen of Colonus, does he reveal Apollo's oracle to Antigone (84ff.). His enfeebled, utterly dependent state as we first see him onstage prepares the ground for the massive *coup de théâtre* in the heroization at the end (cf. 94f. and 1621ff.).

V. The conspiratorial prologue: two against one

A number of tragedies win sympathy for the protagonist by keeping him (or her) absent (or silent) while two other characters talk about him. In this opening dialogue the protagonist is sometimes the object of a plot (as in Sophocles' *Philoctetes*), concern (as in *Alcestis*), or of both together (as in Sophocles' *Electra*). In all cases, he or she is in a position of inferiority, weakness, or subjection to the speakers. This technique has a number of advantages. It involves the audience at once in the dramatic situation through dialogue. It awakens sympathy for the absent protagonist. It visually exhibits the parties in the conflict and the tone that it will have. It also creates suspense as we await the protagonist's arrival onstage, sometimes only after considerable delay (as in *Alcestis* and *Philoctetes*).

The most straightforward and (perhaps) earliest example is the dialogue in *Prometheus Bound* between Kratos and Hephaestus (with Bia standing by in silence) as they chain the silent hero's body to the rock. Though present (in whatever form), Prometheus is effectively absent through his silence.[52] The speakers provide the essential information about his offense and introduce the play's recurrent motifs of fear, pity, and spectacle (e.g. 64–71). Their silence about the additional torment of the eagle leaves room for the development later of Prometheus' strength-in-suffering (cf. 871–73, 1021–29).

The other two early examples of the device, *Ajax* and *Alcestis*, are more complex. Like Hephaestus in the *Prometheus*, Odysseus in

---

52. On the staging and its problems see Taplin (1977) 240ff. The question of Aeschylean authorship does not much affect my argument. I assume a date between ca. 460 and 440.

Tragic beginnings

Ajax carries upon the stage a humane sympathy that contrasts with Athena's vengeful harshness.[53] As in the *Prometheus*, Sophocles brings spectacle and power together.[54] But the god's "devising" (τεχνωμένου, 86), by which Athena renders Odysseus invisible as she calls Ajax onstage, suggests also Sophocles' own craft or *techne* in staging such a complex three-way scene, and Sophocles has called special attention to it (84–88).[55]

The opening dialogue of *Ajax* is reduplicated in a second scene, in which Odysseus is the silent, invisible spectator. The device of two-against-one and the role of Odysseus as the foil-character (like Ismene in *Antigone*) enable us to see Ajax in his still maddened state so that we may both pity and judge him with that mixture of sympathy and horror that often surrounds the Sophoclean protagonist.[56] The closing exchange between Athena and Odysseus repeats the opening situation in an A–B–A structure (118–33). The return, however, has a very different level of feeling and understanding, for we have witnessed the distance between human and divine perspectives and have been led to participate in both.

Euripides uses this distance between human and divine more ironically in the prologues of *Alcestis* and *Trojan Women*. *Alcestis* seems initially to resemble *Prometheus* in its restriction to two speaking actors and its opening dialogue between two divinities about a vulnerable, helpless being in their power. Like *Prometheus* too, it asserts an initial division between an implacable and a gentler attitude, with Thanatos and Apollo corresponding to Kratos and Hephaestus respectively. As in the *Ajax*, the dialogue points up the contrast between mortal and divine worlds.[57] The

---

53. There is a delayed or displaced form of this type of prologue in *HF* 822–74. As in *PV*, there is a dialogue between two divinities (Iris and Lyssa) discussing the future suffering of an "absent" mortal, with a division between a hostile and a more pitying attitude.

54. For these elements as part of the Sophoclean hero's obsession with honor and shame see Knox (1964) 45–47.   55. See Segal (1989/90) 397–98.

56. The comparison of this scene with the opening of the *Prometheus* shows Sophocles' ease and skill in handling three actors. On the problem of the three actors in *PV* see Taplin (1977) 244; also Knox (1964) p. 49, with note 72 on p. 173. The two scenes of opening dialogue are of almost exactly the same length: 87 lines in *PV*, 88 in *Ajax*.

57. *Alcestis*' device of an introductory expository speech followed immediately by dialogue is often repeated by Euripides: e.g. *Medea, Andromache, Troades. Helen, Phoenissae*, and *Orestes* are artful elaborations. The earliest instance (leaving the special effects of the *Eumenides* aside) may be Sophocles' *Trachiniae*.

struggle between Olympian divinity and death-daimon also visualizes onstage the play's basic motif, the struggle between life and death.[58]

In the midst of his promise of the miraculous, however, Apollo implies the restoration of normality: he claims only to be postponing the inevitable (accepting Bursian's ἀμβαλεῖν in 50, with Diggle). His apparently casual way of mentioning survival into "old age" (ἐς γῆρας, 52) is not just a periphrasis but a tacit acknowledgment that even a rescued Alcestis will eventually undergo her mortal lot. The "marvel" (*thauma*, 1123, 1130) of escaping life's most inexorable "Necessity" (962ff., 1076), then, paradoxically reasserts the limits of reality for humans. It cancels out Apollo's obligation to reverse the Fates' decree; and, like Zeus's punishment of Asclepius, it makes future mortals sure of dying when they are supposed to.[59] In this way the prologue not only promises the uniqueness of defeating death but also suggests a kind of tragicomic vision in which normality is restored.

The *Trojan Women*, like *Alcestis*, begins with a god's exposition (though twice as long as Apollo's in *Alcestis*), before he engages another divinity in dialogue. Poseidon and Athena plot together against their human victims, but Euripides again surprises us. The victims turn out to be not the victorious Greeks but the already much afflicted Trojans. Although Poseidon pities the Trojan captives (27–40), Athena's entrance deflects attention to the victors. Poseidon's closing gnomic generalization, on the folly of destroying shrines and cities, encourages us further to expect a tragedy of divine revenge, directed against the Greek sackers of Troy, rather than a play about Trojan war victims.[60] This expectation may have been encouraged by the previous play of

---

58. The motif of life versus death will be replayed between Heracles and Thanatos and, in a remoter way, between Admetus and Pheres: see Burnett (1965) 265. It will return at the end in the contrast between the death-bound Necessity of Alcestis (cf. 962–90) and the "hope" (*elpis*, 1123, 1134, 1160) and resourceful "passage" (*poros*, 1162) implicit in the myth of Orpheus and taken up by Heracles: see in general Segal (1991) 214–18.

59. See Gregory (1979) 268f.

60. Talthybius' command to the Greek captains, near the end, to burn Troy (1260–64), however, may be a warning echo of Poseidon's closing *gnome* of 94–96 and thus return us to the theme of divine vengeance. For this motif in tragedy see Aesch., *Ag.* 338–47 and 524–30; Soph., *Phil.* 1440–44. Eur., *IA* is another case of a collective victim (in this case, the Greek army) of a conspiratorial prologue of "two against one." Here Agamemnon and his old servant meet at night to implement Agamemnon's secret decision to prevent Iphigeneia from coming to Aulis (94ff., 119ff.).

Tragic beginnings

the trilogy, the *Palamedes*, where Oiax, brother of the slain Palamedes, plots to destroy the Greek fleet (cf. frag. 588 Nauck and Aristoph., *Thesmophoriazusae* 770f.).

Within the *Trojan Women*, Poseidon is surprised at Athena's change of mood (56–60, especially καινὸν ἔπος, 55), and this surprise prefigures the greater change in the play's direction, from Athena's concern (vengeance) to Poseidon's (pity: cf. 27–40).[61] The pity of the remote Olympian, however, finds no echo in the human world; and at the end of the play the Athenian audience is drawn to sympathize, with Poseidon, with the Trojans rather than the Greeks.

As Sophocles is more sparing than Aeschylus or Euripides of bringing gods onstage, his two-against-one prologues (with the exception of *Ajax*) are limited to human interlocutors. *Antigone* opens with a conspiratorial dialogue, where (as often in this device) one figure is reluctant. The potential "victim," however, is not a weak or helpless outcast, but the general who commands the loyalty and the army of the entire city (8, 44), while the "conspirator," as Ismene warns, is almost powerless (58–68). Instead of developing into conspiracy, the dialogue leads into the heroine's resolve on *solitary* action and shows her defiant exultation in her doomed and lonely courage (68–96, especially 71–74). The opening mood of conspiracy, then, far from arousing sympathy for an absent victim, only sets off Antigone's isolation and the tragic paradoxes of her strength-in-weakness, her female heroism (72), and her "holy wrongdoing" (74).

The two later plays, *Electra* and *Philoctetes*, are closer to the prologue structure of *Ajax*. In both cases the absent figure is debilitated and trapped in a bleak, corrosive setting while the two speakers are powerful and mobile. Electra's offstage cry (77), just after Orestes has described his stratagem, brings her into the plotters' (and the audience's) purview. The Paedagogus' insistence on putting the deed of vengeance first (80–85) postpones the recognition, in contrast to the Aeschylean and Euripidean versions. But this device also makes Electra the avengers' unintended first victim (cf. 807–23). The "pain" of pretending to

---

61. This prologue, like those of *Hipp.* and *Ion*, is a masterpiece of withheld information: it says nothing about Andromache or Astyanax. Helen, "justly considered a prisoner" (35), will defeat the Trojan demand for justice by escaping that status (1046ff.).

be dead that Orestes had lightly dismissed in the prologue (59f.) proves almost fatal to his sister.[62]

The prologue of the *Philoctetes*, like that of *Prometheus*, unfolds a full-scale plot of two against one. In the *Prometheus*, the protagonist, though physically onstage, is effectively "absent" through his silence. Here the protagonist is literally absent, and there is a division of views between the two conversants, in this case a division between trickery and honesty rather than between hardness and compassion (77ff., 86ff., 100ff.). But compassion also enters, in an unexpected and dramatic way, in Neoptolemus' sudden cry at discovering Philoctetes' rags, wet with the discharges of his wound (38f.). For Odysseus the discovery is merely proof of Philoctetes' potentially dangerous proximity (40f.). We are left to infer Neoptolemus' reactions; but, once introduced, the pity does not disappear. Only much later do we see, in retrospect, how much that first experience of his victim's condition has affected him. His genuine "terrible pity" (*oiktos deinos*, 965), in contrast to the feigned pity of the chorus (507), undoes the plot that has made the whole situation possible. In like manner, Odysseus' explanatory account of Philoctetes' terrible cries at Troy as the reason for the army's having abandoned him (9–11) will contrast with the very different effect of the cries on Neoptolemus within the play (730ff.). Comparing the Sophoclean and Euripidean versions of the "two-against-one" prologue, incidentally, reveals at once how Sophocles tends to situate us immediately in the dramatic situation and engage us emotionally with the protagonists and the conflicts surrounding them.

VI. The detached prologue

Unlike the poet of choral lyric, the tragedian, aiming at the diverse mass-audience of democratic Athens, cannot assume that his hearers will be interested in his story merely because it preserves the traditions of the community or celebrates the origins of aristocratic families. Unlike Homer, he cannot assume an audience well disposed to a panhellenic tradition that embraces the whole field of mythical lore, nor can he presume the

---

62. Soph., *El.* 1108ff., especially 1150f., 1165–70; cf. also 822, λύπη δ' ἐὰν ζῶ. See Segal (1986) 125–27.

audience's acceptance of a code of universally recognized heroic values or behavior. More often than not, such values are called into question, as in Sophocles' *Ajax* and in almost all of Euripides. He can, of course, appeal to another kind of communal solidarity, as is clear from Euripides' Athens-centered plays like *Erechtheus, Heracleidae, Suppliants*, or Sophocles' *Oedipus at Colonus*. The final victory of Aeschylus in the *Frogs* derives from this ethos of civic unity (*Frogs* 1020ff.; cf. 1419–21).[63] Yet such unity may have been far more precarious amid the tensions of the Peloponnesian War (cf. Aristophanes' *Acharnians*), and particularly after the oligarchic revolution of 411. Euripides may have relied increasingly on the detached prologue to meet this problem of a divided and diverse audience and a decreasing identification with the myths as the expression of either panhellenic or communal values.[64]

The detached prologue may result from an inherent tendency within literary genres to evolve toward more complex structures. But, as many scholars have suggested, there are also historical causes: a democratic audience's lessening familiarity with the old myths; an increasingly mixed populace of metics, farmers, and foreigners;[65] cultural factors, like the sophistic enlightenment, literacy, and rationalism. Sophocles, belonging to a slightly older generation, may have been a little less sensitive to these changes, though he too is influenced by them. By formation and temperament, he is inclined to a more totally theatrical and less explicitly intellectualized conception of his art.

Five of Sophocles' seven extant plays either plunge directly into dialogue (*Ajax, Antig., OC*), or move into dialogue after medium-length speeches (*OT, Phil.*). Every extant play has at least some iambic dialogue before the parode, a far higher proportion than in Aeschylus or Euripides. *Electra* has the longest stretch of set speeches in a Sophoclean prologue (twenty-two and forty-four lines, respectively) and the least amount of dialogue. Even here there is a quickening of dialogue and a moment of tense drama at Electra's offstage cry (77–85). Sophocles uses the expository

---

63. For the expression of civic solidarity in the performances of the tragedies at the Dionysia see Goldhill (1987).
64. On the problem of tragedy's relation to the aristocratically oriented myths of the literary tradition see Vernant, "Tensions and Ambiguities in Greek Tragedy," in Vernant and Vidal-Naquet (1981) 6–27, especially 9ff.
65. On this last see Dalmeyda (1919) 121f.

prologue only once in the extant plays, in *Trachiniae*, perhaps because the plot was less familiar to the audience. Yet here too Deianeira's speech – the longest opening speech in Sophocles, with forty-eight lines – immediately becomes part of the action and moves to a three-way exchange of some forty-five lines. As even this scenically stiff play shows, Sophocles tends to make use of all three actors in the prologue.

The *Philoctetes*' deception plot and use of the disguised merchant probably necessitated an explanatory prologue. But Sophocles cleverly makes a virtue of necessity by having Neoptolemus look into the cave that holds both danger for the speaker and surprise for the audience (16). Exposition suddenly becomes exciting stage action as Neoptolemus cries out, *iou, iou*, when he finds the pus-soaked rags (38f.). Sophocles had perhaps learned a lesson from his toughest competitor, Aeschylus, whose *Eumenides*, as we have seen earlier, abruptly transforms an expository prologue into a scene of astonishment and horror.

Euripides' detached expository prologue, while not entirely his own creation (cf. *Agamemnon* and *Eumenides*), is well suited to certain features of his dramatic art: his more sharply articulated structures and his greater conceptualization of issues like divine justice and the nature of the gods. Whereas Sophocles absorbs the literary tradition more or less unobtrusively into the surface of his play, Euripides calls attention to it, self-consciously marking his work's literariness and artifice. Plot here becomes visible as plotting. The god's strategies in divinely spoken prologues, standing above and outside the action, seem devised almost as much by the poet as his speaker. Possibly Euripides is deliberately reacting against the more "organic" Sophoclean form;[66] possibly his melodramatic plots required more preparation of his spectators.[67] But, by the same token, he can also use the prologue to enhance the surprise effects and call attention to the fragmented structure, as *Hecuba, Ion, Trojan Women*, and *Bacchae* illustrate.

66. See Schadewaldt (1926) 105f.; Pohlenz (1954) 1.432; Strohm (1977) 113; also Strohm (1957) 165f. I may mention here the lyric prologues of Aesch., *Pers.* and *Suppl.*, possibly imitated by Euripides as a deliberately archaizing feature in *IA* (if the ms order of the lines is authentic) and *Rhesus* (if by Euripides). On the lyric prologue see Taplin (1977) 61–63.

67. On Euripides' recognition of the fragmented and multiple nature of his plots in relation to the prologue see Michelini (1987) 52–69, especially 65ff. and also 116; also Erbse (1984) 100, on the *Bacchae*.

Tragic beginnings

The detached prologue accompanies the rationalism that created an analytical approach to language and formal techniques of argumentation.[68] There is even evidence for proto-literary criticism of the prologue by the sophist Protagoras.[69] For Aristophanes the prologue is a separate section or "part" of a play and can be analyzed as such.[70] Through the detached prologue, with its outline of the story, the plot itself emerges as an intellectual construct that bears the mark of its creator's craft and artifice. It invites us to view the enacted narrative as a created fiction rather than as part of an inherited, anonymous tradition.

By reminding us of alternative or contradictory versions of his plot, Euripides forces us to recognize how he is transforming or elaborating the inherited tale.[71] He can still claim to celebrate the Muses (*HF* 673–86); but, instead of serving them as an anonymous vehicle of inherited tales, he makes us observe his interventions and selections and to admire his deliberate refashioning of those selected pieces of the tradition.

Amid the growing literacy of the late fifth century, Euripides is probably closer than any ancient writer before Callimachus to being a man of letters, in every sense. He is the first poet who is said to have had a library and whose plays are described as being read (e.g. Aristoph., *Frogs* 52f., 943, 1409). His prologues bear the stamp not only of his literacy but also of his literariness.[72] Agamemnon's writing and then rewriting of his tablet in the prologue of the *Iphigeneia in Aulis* might even be viewed reflexively as the poet's own conscious "re-writing" of the tradition, now marked as distinctively "literary" in this its latest version. Thus Euripides' Agamemnon makes, in letters, exactly the opposite choice from Aeschylus' hero, preferring private, family happiness to war and honor, and putting concern for women in his house ahead of his army.

For the poet aware of writing, the tradition is preserved not by the mysterious, invisible power of memory and its goddesses, but

---

68. Of particular importance here is the sophistic criterion of *sapheneia*, the clarity and articulation of argument: see Schmid (1940) 772.   69. See Segal (1970).

70. *Frogs* 911–26, 1119–248, especially 1120, τὸ πρῶτον τῆς τραγῳδίας μέρος. See also Aristot., *Poet*. 12.1452b 19.

71. Cf. especially the prologues of Eur., *El.*, *IT*, *Hel.*, *Phoen.*, *Or.*, *IA*.

72. On the relation between tragedy and writing in general see Segal (1986) 75–109, especially 92–105.

by direct human intervention at a precise moment of time. Instead of being a gift that comes unbidden and uncontrolled from a divine power, the poem is a "work," an artifact, with a known or knowable moment of production by its human maker. Euripides is indeed such a "maker," or *poietes*, as Aristophanes calls him in the *Frogs*. His later prologues show him not only consciously revising the tradition but also deliberately combining different parts of it, as if the myths have now become a rich resource of delightfully contradictory plots. Far from troubling the poet, as they did Pindar or Herodotus, the differences can be exploited and utilized in a kind of intertextual kaleidoscope.[73]

All the dramatists, of course, range freely over the whole poetic tradition in a rich synchrony of new and old;[74] but in Euripides the critical awareness, sense of distance, and eclecticism are more self-consciously visible. The prologues of his *Electra* and *Iphigeneia in Tauris*, for instance, play against the Aeschylean versions of the myth, as the *Phoenissae*'s prologue plays against the Sophoclean. The prologues also glance consciously toward epic, as the *Helen* does in its Odyssean features or the *Orestes* with its Odyssean motif of the day of Menelaus' return (53–56). The *Phoenissae* shifts surprisingly from Jocasta's narrative of Oedipus to a teichoskopia reminiscent both of *Iliad* 3 and of Aeschylus' *Septem*, with the Paedagogus playing Helen to Antigone's Priam (*Phoen.* 119ff.).

Euripides often matches the literariness of such beginnings with a concretization of the tradition at the end: a closing aetiological narrative or self-conscious memorialization. The ending of *Trojan Women*, for example, provides a tragic version both of the Iliadic monument and of the funeral epigram (cf. 1141ff., 1187ff.).[75] This scene virtually dramatizes the special ability of tragedy to appropriate related motifs in other genres and to stamp them with the special visual and emotional quality of its theatrical art.[76]

By such devices Euripides often makes his play fold back on itself, as it were. The structural arbitrariness of the detached

---

73. On Euripidean intertextuality see Zeitlin (1980) passim (on *Orestes*) and Goldhill (1986) 245ff. on *Electra*. Euripides' uses of Aeschylus continue to be much studied: see Aélion (1983) and Garner (1990) chap. 2.
74. See most recently Garner (1990) passim.
75. On this scene see Pucci (1977) 182–84 and Segal (1989a) 352–54.
76. For this synthetic, appropriative power of tragedy see Herington (1985) passim, especially chaps. 4–6.

Tragic beginnings

beginning is deliberately complemented and amplified by the aetiological monumentalizing of the detached deus-ex-machina speech at the end.[77] The fully articulated predictive summary at the beginning and the aition at the end give the rapid flow of events onstage an almost textual solidity. The poet seems aware here of giving fixity to a fluid tradition and thus achieving a tangible and visible result analogous in its permanence to cult, temple, monument, or institution. Such endings serve as a kind of objective correlative for the play's artifice, innovation, and intervention in the myth. The concretization of the plot in different ways in both the detached prologue and the aetiological epilogue implicitly redefines the poet's voice and function. He is no longer a singer of tales, an impersonal transmitter of inherited lore, but a shaper of plots and maker of myths;[78] and his dramatic work is a self-consciously intertextual form of mythic narration.

Like the prologue, this detached monument at the end asserts the validity of the mythical tradition and its successful, durable transmission from remote antiquity to the present. Like the detached prologue, however, it also shares in the fragility of the play's textuality and the poet's artifice. Like the prologue too, it shares in Euripidean drama's tension between tragedy as continuity with epic (and other forms of mythical narration), and tragedy as interruption of that tradition by its new departures in both form and content. As Euripides is highly sensitive to the shifting moods and currents of his changing times, his way of beginning and ending his plays may reflect a new anxiety about permanence and the traditional forms of monumentalization.

This relation between the detached prologue and the detached closing aition, however, can also be responsive to the still continuing demands of an oral culture for a sense of community and group consciousness in the festive moment of the performance. In both *Ajax* and *Hippolytus*, for example, the isolation of the protagonist as a victim of divine vengeance in the prologue is answered by a communal solidarity of grief and mourning at the end. This ending is also an expression of the community of theater

---

77. On the relation of the Euripidean prologue and epilogue to self-consciousness of intervention in the tradition see Pohlenz (1954) 1.436–39, especially 437f.

78. Both *plattein* and *poiein* mark this new relation of the poet to his myths: e.g. Aristoph., *Thesm.* 193 and Plato, *Rep.* 2.377b.

shaped by the play (cf. *Ajax* 1402–17; *Hipp.* 1462–66).[79] In this way tragedy creates a bond of sympathy among the members of the audience and seeks to unite them in a new community of the theater, constituted by the shared emotions that the performance has aroused. The often conflicting and divided sympathy that the prologue sets in motion for the human actors thus prepares for the fuller, more complex sympathy that holds the members of the audience together, after the resolution of conflict, at the end.

As narrative, the detached prologue often creates a strong temporal continuity. It establishes a more or less clear and well-defined background of past events, and it shows their projection into the future, along with the causal nexus that produces the future. But it also forces its audience to recognize the discontinuity with the past through the modification of familiar myths, the formal disengagement from the rest of the action, the visible crystallization of the play's own plotting, and the reminders of its literary factitiousness.[80]

Works Cited

Aélion, Rachel (1983). *Euripide héritier d'Eschyle* (Paris). 2 vols.
Brillante, Carlo (1988). "Sul prologo dell' *Ecuba* di Euripide," *RFIC* 116: 429–47.
Burnett, Anne P. (1965). "The Virtues of Admetus" (1965), in Erich Segal, ed., *Oxford Readings in Greek Tragedy* (Oxford 1983) 254–71. Originally published in *CP* 60 (1965) 240–55.
Clay, Jenny Strauss (1983). *The Wrath of Athena* (Princeton).
Dalmeyda, Georges (1919). "Observations sur les prologues d'Euripide," *REG* 32: 121–31.
Decharme, Paul (1906). *Euripides and the Spirit of His Dramas*, Eng. trans. James Loeb (New York).
Dihle, Albrecht (1981). *Der Prolog der "Bakchen" und die antike Überlieferungsphase des Euripides-Textes*, SB Heidelberg, part 2.
Dunn, Francis M. (1989). "Comic and Tragic License in Euripides' *Orestes*," *CA* 8: 238–51.
Erbse, Hartmut (1984). *Studien zum Prolog der euripideischen Tragödie* (Berlin).

---

79. See Segal (1988) 62–70, especially 69f.
80. This study was prepared during a Fellowship at the Center for Advanced Study in the Behavioral Sciences, Stanford, California. I am grateful for financial support at the Center, which was provided by the National Endowment for the Humanities (#RA-20037-88) and the Andrew W. Mellon Foundation. I am indebted to the editors of this volume, Thomas Cole and Francis Dunn, for helpful suggestions.

Garner, Richard (1990). *From Homer to Tragedy: The Art of Allusion in Greek Poetry* (London and New York).
Goldhill, Simon (1986). *Reading Greek Tragedy* (Cambridge).
  (1987). "The Great Dionysia and Civic Ideology," *JHS* 107: 58–76.
Gould, John (1973). "*Hiketeia*," *JHS* 93: 74–103.
Gregory, Justina (1979). "Euripides' Alcestis," *Hermes* 107: 259–70.
Halleran, Michael R. (1985). *Stagecraft in Euripides* (London and Sydney).
Hamilton, Richard (1974). "*Bacchae* 47–52: Dionysus' Plan," *TAPA* 104: 139–49.
  (1978). "Prologue Prophecy and Plot in Four Plays of Euripides," *AJP* 99: 277–302.
Havelock, Eric A. (1963). *Preface to Plato* (Cambridge, MA).
  (1982). *The Literate Revolution in Greece and Its Consequences* (Princeton).
Herington, C. J. (1985). *Poetry into Drama*, Sather Classical Lectures, vol. 49 (Berkeley and Los Angeles).
Knox, Bernard M. W. (1964). *The Heroic Temper: Studies in Sophoclean Tragedy*, Sather Classical Lectures, vol. 35 (Berkeley and Los Angeles).
Luschnig, C. A. E. (1988). *Time Holds the Mirror: A Study of Knowledge in Euripides' "Hippolytus,"* Mnemosyne Supplement, vol. 102 (Leiden).
Michelini, Ann Norris (1987). *Euripides and the Tragic Tradition* (Madison, WI).
Meridor, Ra'anana (1989). "Euripides' *Troades* 28–44 and the Andromache Scene," *AJP* 110: 17–35.
Murray, Gilbert (1913). *Euripides and His Age* (Cambridge).
Pohlenz, Max (1954). *Die griechische Tragödie*, 2nd edn (Göttingen). 2 vols.
Pucci, Pietro (1977). "Euripides: The Monument and the Sacrifice," *Arethusa* 10: 165–95.
Said, Edward W. (1975). *Beginnings: Intention and Method* (New York).
Schadewaldt, Wolfgang (1926). *Monolog und Selbstgespräch*, Neue Philologische Untersuchungen, vol. 2 (Berlin).
Schmid, Wilhelm (1940). W. Schmid in W. Schmid and Otto Stählin, *Geschichte der griechischen Literatur* 1.3 (Munich).
Seeck, Gustav Adolf (1985). *Unaristotelische Untersuchungen zu Euripides: ein motivanalytischer Kommentar zur "Alkestis"* (Heidelberg).
Segal, Charles (1970). "Protagoras' *Orthoepeia* in Aristophanes' Battle of the Prologues (*Frogs* 1119–97)," *RhM* 113: 158–62.
  (1981). *Tragedy and Civilization: An Interpretation of Sophocles* (Cambridge, MA).
  (1982). *Dionysiac Poetics and Euripides' Bacchae* (Princeton).
  (1986). *Interpreting Greek Tragedy: Myth, Poetry, Text* (Ithaca, NY)
  (1988). "Theater, Ritual, and Commemoration in Euripides' *Hippolytus*," *Ramus* 17: 52–74.

- (1989). "The Problem of the Gods in Euripides' *Hecuba*," *MD* 22: 9–21.
- (1989a). "Song, Ritual, and Commemoration in Early Greek Poetry and Tragedy," *Oral Tradition* 4: 330–59.
- (1989/90). "Drama, Narrative, and Perspective in Sophocles' *Ajax*," *Sacris Erudiri*: *Jaarboek voor Godsdienstwetenschappen* (Festschrift for Hermann van Looy) 31: 395–404.
- (1991). "Cold Delight: Art, Death, and Transgression of Genre in Euripides' *Alcestis*," in *The Scope of Words: In Honor of Albert Cook* (New York) 211–28.

Seidensticker, Bernd (1982). *Palintonos Harmonia: Studien zu komischen Elemente in der griechischen Tragödie*, Hypomnemata, vol. 72 (Göttingen).

Strohm, Hans (1957). *Euripides. Interpretationen zur dramatischen Form*, Zetemata 15 (Munich).

- (1977). "Zur Gestaltung euripideischer Prologreden," *GB* 6: 113–32.

Stuart, Donald Clive (1918). "Foreshadowing and Suspense in the Euripidean Prolog," *SP* 15: 295–306.

Taplin, Oliver (1977). *The Stagecraft of Aeschylus* (Oxford).

Verdenius, W. J. (1980). "Notes on the Prologue of Euripides' *Bacchae*," *Mnemosyne* 33: 1–16.

Vernant, Jean-Pierre and Pierre Vidal-Naquet (1981). *Tragedy and Myth in Ancient Greece*, Eng. trans. Janet Lloyd (Atlantic Highlands, NJ). (French edn, 1972).

Whitman, Cedric H. (1974). *Euripides and the Full Circle of Myth* (Cambridge, MA).

Zeitlin, Froma I. (1980). "The Closet of Masks: Role-Playing and Myth-Making in the *Orestes* of Euripides," *Ramus* 9: 51–77.

Plato's first words

DISKIN CLAY

Socrates: Ἀλλὰ τόδε γε οἶμαι σε φάναι ἄν, δεῖν πάντα λόγον ὥσπερ ζῷον συνεστάναι σῶμά τι ἔχοντα αὐτὸν αὑτοῦ, ὥστε μήτε ἀκέφαλον εἶναι μήτε ἄπουν, ἀλλὰ μέσα τε ἔχειν καὶ ἄκρα, πρέποντα ἀλλήλοις καὶ τῷ ὅλῳ γεγραμμένα.
Phaedrus: Πῶς γὰρ οὔ;

Plato, Phaedrus 264c

A tail behind, a trunk in front,
Complete the usual elephant.
A. E. Housman, The Elephant, or the Force of Habit

I

In literature beginnings are always an end. They mark the end of a period of indecision and indeterminacy and seal with the stamp of closure the exclusion of all but one possible beginning. The importance of beginnings and of first words for ancient readers and critics is revealed by the significance they attached to the first word of the *Iliad* – μῆνιν. Indeed, the first words of a poem rather than its "title" were enough to identify it.[1] The cult of beginnings in the appreciation of ancient literature was so much a matter of faith that it had to be blasphemed, as it was, by Lucian in his *True History*. Here Lucian as protagonist interrogates the soul of Homer in Hades; his were the burning philological questions of Lucian's age. What city did the poet come from – Chios, Smyrna, or Colophon? Necromancy produces the startling response that he

---

1. Cf. the AbT scholia on *Iliad* 1 1 in Harmut Erbse, *Scholia Graeca in Homeri Iliadem* 1 (Berlin 1969) 3–4 and Horace, *Ars Poetica* 140–43, with Aristotle, *Rhetoric* III 14.1415a13–16 and Quintilian x 1.48. The drinking song Ἐν μύρτου κλάδι (*PMG* 893 Page, with testimonia) is a well-known case of a poem identified by its first words; for others, cf. Lloyd Daly, "The Entitulature of Pre-Ciceronian Writings," in *Classical Studies in Honor of W. A. Oldfather* (Urbana 1943) 20–38.

was not a Greek but came from Babylon, where he was called Tigranes. Well, what then of the athetized verses – did he compose them all? He did. And why did he begin his *Iliad* with "the wrath"? Well, it was the first thing that came to his mind: τί δή ποτε ἀπὸ τῆς μήνιδος τὴν ἀρχὴν ἐποιήσατο, καὶ ὃς εἶπεν οὕτως ἐπελθεῖν αὐτῷ μηδὲν ἐπιτηδεύσαντι.[2] This parable of ancient literary criticism makes it clear that Homer's insouciant answer to the serious question about the meaning of the first words of the *Iliad* was the last response an ancient reader would expect.

We have many confirmations of the critics' faith that the beginning of a work of literature was of great moment to both author and reader. One of the most remarkable is the anecdote Dionysios of Halikarnassos repeats about the beginning of Plato's *Republic*: "For the eighty years of his life, Plato spent his days combing and teasing [at his dialogues] and plaiting them in different arrangements. Everyone with an interest in literature knows the anecdotes told about this untiring author and one in particular – the story about the writing tablet they say was discovered at his death with a number of different versions of the beginning of the *Republic*."[3]

Κατέβην χθὲς εἰς Πειραιᾶ μετὰ Γλαύκωνος τοῦ Ἀρίστωνος... Plato was ultimately responsible for this anecdote and he contributed greatly to the critical attitude that readily accepted it. He might not have died with a writing tablet clenched rigidly in his hand awaiting its *ultima manus* or preserved carefully among his possessions. But he did insist on what Socrates (in the *Phaedrus*) calls the "logographic necessity" of any writing – be this the speech of Lysias Phaedrus reads at the beginning of the *Phaedrus* or the epitaph for King Midas whose four lines can stand in any order or – by implication – the *Phaedrus* itself.[4] If the principle of

---

2. *True History* II 20. For two Platonic descriptions of spontaneous composition, cf. *Phaedo* 60B and *Phaedrus* 264B.

3. Dionysios of Halikarnassos, *De Comp. Verb.* VI 25.32–33 (p. 185) Aujac-Lebel. Cf. Diogenes Laertius III 37 and Quintilian VIII 6.64.

4. *Phaedrus* 264B–D, a passage constantly applied to the interpretation of the *Phaedrus* itself and the Platonic dialogues generally; cf. Hermeias of Alexandria, *In Platonis Phaedrum Scholia*, p. 231.6–9 Couvreur (Paris 1901, Hildesheim 1971); Proclus, *In Platonis Rem Publicam* pp. 6.24–7.1 Kroll, and generally James A. Coulter, *The Literary Microcosm: Theories of Interpretation of the Later Neoplatonists*, Columbia Studies in the Classical Tradition II (Leiden 1976) 78–85. The principle is expanded to the criticism of literature in general by Hermogenes in his *De Ideis* I 12 p. 297.9–21 Rabe.

Plato's first words

logographic necessity decrees that every literary composition should be structured "like a living organism having its own body so that it lacks neither a head nor feet but has a middle and extremities adjusted to one another and to the whole" (*Phaedrus* 264c), then the beginnings – and the ends – of Platonic dialogues are intelligible only once the whole of which they are a part has been understood. And, if this is the scope of Platonic criticism, an essay on Plato's first words could never be written. To write competently about the beginning of Plato's *Phaedo* or *Republic* or of any other Platonic dialogue is to understand the other extremity of the dialogue, its middle, and the unity of the dialogue as a whole. It is also to commit oneself to the belief that the end of Platonic criticism is to discover the unity of a dialogue in the confusion, diversity, and fundamentally elliptical character of its themes.

The interpretative difficulties imposed by the decree of logographic necessity are compounded by two other critical problems that need recognition: the first is that Plato made a fundamental choice of how he would represent the conversations of his dialogues even before he finally settled on the first words that open any given dialogue; the second is that some of his dialogues do not seem to have proper beginnings at all. That is, they begin with the record of a conversation that provides us with the record of the conversation that occupies the rest of the dialogue, but is fundamentally external to it in place, time, and theme. To dwell on this second problem for only a moment before returning to it: the dialogues whose beginnings do not seem to be adjusted to the dialogue they introduce are the frame dialogues which introduce the *Phaedo*, *Symposium*, *Theaetetus*, and *Parmenides*. These frames seem as extraneous to the dialogues they enclose as does the frame (a modern frame) of David's *Death of Socrates* to the canvas it defines and supports.

Even before the first words of a Platonic dialogue break the silence, this silence may suggest a period of deliberation over style and the means of imitating what was said and done in the dialogue that follows. And when Plato's first words are spoken, they are never spoken by Plato,[5] but always, at varying removes,

---

5. Thus "the author is entirely lost in dramatic compositions, and the spectator supposes himself to be really at the actions represented..." as the situation is put forcefully

by one of his characters. Before Plato settled on his final version of the first sentence of the *Republic* he made a decision – he chose one of three possibilities in writing a dialogue. These choices are set out in Socrates' long lesson on literary criticism in Book III of the *Republic* where he moves from a consideration of the theme of discourse (λόγος) to its style (λέξις).[6] Here Plato is introducing a novel conception in the criticism of poetry, and Socrates must stop to make his meaning clear to his interlocutor (Adeimantos). His general term for narrative is διήγησις, and narrative has three varieties: either the poet will speak in the third person throughout, without intruding himself into his narrative, or he will be entirely mimetic – like the tragic and comic poets – and speak nowhere as "himself,"[7] or he will employ a mixed style as does Homer, who speaks both as "himself" (αὐτός) and impersonates his characters. This lesson in literary criticism led inevitably to the ancient classifications of the Platonic dialogues as being "narrative," "dramatic," and "mixed" in their mode of representation.[8] One of the many challenges Socrates articulates for Plato's readers in this discussion of style is to recover the meaning of his aboriginal and unrecorded choice of λέξις.

Open a Platonic dialogue and the character – if not the motive – of Plato's choice becomes apparent: either we stand as the immediate audience to one of Socrates' conversations, or we listen to Socrates as he narrates the words and events of one of his conversations to an unknown audience,[9] or we overhear someone

---

by David Hume in his reflections on the association of ideas in *An Inquiry concerning Human Understanding*, ed. Charles W. Hendel (New York 1955) 37.

6. The Socratic lesson in style is developed in *Republic* III 392C–398B. Inevitably it was applied to the *Republic* itself – by Proclus in his lectures on the *Republic*, p. 14.15–16.25 Kroll. Proclus' own conclusion concerning the style of the *Republic* is that it belongs to Socrates' "mixed" genre of representation and combines, as does the epic, both narrative and *mimesis*. In a fundamental sense, however, all Platonic dialogues are dramatic, if read aloud (as they were in antiquity), since the reader takes the part of even Plato's narrators.

7. Αὐτός, *Republic* III 393B; cf. Aristotle, *Poetics* 3. 1448a19–24 and 24.1460a5–11.

8. The influence of Socrates' discussion of the three possible styles of poetic representation is evident in Diogenes Laertius' taxonomy of the Platonic dialogues, III 50, and is well characterized by Michael W. Haslam in his "Plato, Sophron, and the Dramatic Dialogue," *BLICS* 19 (1972) 20–21. Oddly enough, Socrates' seemingly comprehensive categories do not cover the case of the *Republic* itself, where the narrator is also a character in the dialogue he narrates. The three styles are weighed in Proclus, *In Rem Publicam Commentarii* p. 14.15–15.19 in deciding the style of the *Republic* ("mixed").

9. As is the case of the *Republic*, *Charmides*, *Lysis*, and *Protagoras*. Of the "frame dialogues," two address an unknown audience – the *Symposium* and *Parmenides*, where Apollodorus of Athens and Cephalus of Clazomenae are narrators.

Plato's first words

with an interest in what Socrates does or says (a Phaedo, Apollodorus, Eucleides, or Cephalus) as he recounts one of Socrates' conversations.

The choice of the style of a given dialogue would seem to involve the question of authority, and in the case of at least three of the frame dialogues that authority is questioned. The difficulties of appreciating the first words of one of Plato's dramatic dialogues are not great. We begin with the ultimate authority: the apparent accident of an encounter between Socrates and one of his friends which we overhear – and witness – as its immediate audience. In most cases, Socrates addresses an acquaintance and is thus the first to speak, and at the end of these dramatic conversations it is usually Socrates who has the last word.[10] Of the purely mimetic or dramatic dialogues for which we depend on no narrator we can say – or we feel we can say – that we were there. If an Echecrates were to ask us if we were present at these conversations "ourselves" (cf. *Phaedo* 57A), we would be tempted to say that we were. The effect of Plato's choice of the dramatic mode of discourse is to transport us in time so that we become the audience of a philosophical drama that took place in another age, yet is still immediate.[11]

The effect and the meaning of Plato's choice of the narrative mode of discourse is to distance us from the action and the conversation of the dialogue reported, and for these dialogues, which we know from someone who was present at them or someone who had an account of them from someone who was present, we have two authorities: either Socrates himself, whose word we are not inclined to dispute,[12] or someone else, whose reliability we are sometimes compelled to question. In the first case, the case of a narrative dialogue like the *Republic*, we find

---

10. As in the *Crito*, *Phaedrus*, *Alcibiades* I (and II), *Hipparchus*, *Hippias Minor*, *Ion*, and *Menexenus*.

11. And, by Socrates' conception of *mimesis* in Book III of the *Republic*, we imitate – or impersonate – the speakers of a dialogue like the *Republic* and as a consequence become exposed to the danger – or benefit – of assimilating ourselves to the characters whose parts we play; cf. *Republic* III 395C.

12. Despite his habit of deferring to higher authorities (as in *Apology* 20E and *Symposium* 177A), Socrates stands as the sole authority for the conversation of the *Theaetetus* (*Theaetetus* 142C) and as only one authority for the speeches of the *Symposium* (*Symposium* 173B). In this case, the authority of Socrates would seem to have the stamp of αὐτὸς ἔφα, as is evident in Glaukon's question to Apollodorus: ἀλλὰ τίς σοι διηγεῖτο; ἢ αὐτὸς Σωκράτης; (*Symposium* 173A).

ourselves in Athens and a part of Socrates' audience on the day after he had spent a long afternoon and evening in the house of Cephalus in the Peiraeus. In the case of the *Phaedo*, we find ourselves in Phlius, among the companions of Echecrates, and some considerable time after the trial and execution of Socrates; we also find ourselves in one of the framing dialogues where the authority of the narrator is questioned. Echecrates thus asks Phaedo: "Were you there yourself, Phaedo, on the day Socrates drank the hemlock, or did you hear [of what happened] from someone else?" (*Phaedo* 57A). Here the question of authority, expressed in the first word of the dialogue (Αὐτός) is answered by a single word that seems the ultimate authority (αὐτός), until we realize that Plato is the *author* of the *Phaedo*, not Phaedo himself.

The frame dialogues (*Phaedo, Theaetetus, Symposium*, and *Parmenides*) are properly distinguished from the other Platonic dialogues, either dramatic or narrative, whose central character is Socrates. On first inspection they all seem commemorative and their frames sturdy guarantees of the historicity of the dialogues they memorialize. Such was the assessment of F. C. Bauer more than a century and a half ago: "By their external form they seem to possess a more historical character." But as Kierkegaard, who cites Bauer in his *Concept of Irony* knew, this suggestion of "historicity" is illusory. The frames of these dialogues are Platonic artifacts.[13]

The problem, then, of coming to terms with Plato's first words is not only to understand the beginnings of his dialogues in their relation to the whole of which they are a part – if, indeed, they are a part of a whole;[14] it also entails the difficult task of understanding Plato's choice of the style of a given dialogue and his choice of the purely dramatic dialogue, the dialogue narrated by Socrates, and

---

13. Bauer made this characterization in the *Tübinger Zeitschrift für Theologie* of 1837. It is reprinted in *Drei Abhandlungen zur Geschichte der alten Philosophie*, ed. Eduard Zeller (Leipzig 1876) 228. Kierkegaard discusses the problem of the external drama (*die äussere Handlung*) of such dialogues in *The Concept of Irony*, translated by Lee M. Capel (London 1966) 68–69.

14. This blasphemy has been intelligently argued for in the case of the *Phaedrus* by Malcolm Heath in his *Unity in Greek Poetics* (Oxford 1989) 12–27. Perhaps any unitarian critic who is convinced by the decree of logographic necessity should contemplate the fragment which might well have stood as the conclusion to Heraclitus' "book": "The fairest order in the world is a heap of random sweepings" (CXXV in the ordering and translation of Charles H. Kahn, *The Art and Thought of Heraclitus* [Cambridge 1979]). Or the end of Plato's *Laws*.

the frame dialogue. I shall have little to say in this essay about Plato's motives in choosing one kind of dialogue over another. But, in reflecting on the significance of the setting of the frame dialogue of the *Phaedo* in Phlius and his choice of narrative over drama, something must be said about his choice of this distinctive form of λέξις.

To narrow the scope of this inquiry into the beginnings of Platonic dialogues: in considering the meaning of the frame dialogue of the *Phaedo* and the narrative details Socrates supplies at the beginning of the *Republic*, we are obviously reading these dialogues in terms of Socrates' decree of "logographic necessity." Yet it is possible that we have been misguided by no less an authority than Socrates – that these two dialogues do not constitute organic wholes and that their beginnings have no serious philosophical or literary meaning. This after all is how the beginnings of the *Phaedo* and *Republic* have been read, not by the Neoplatonists, who were careful to attend to Socrates' decree of "logographic necessity," but by competent philosophers and philologists. Even the *Phaedrus* itself has been read not with attention to its dramatic setting and its initial conversation between Socrates and Phaedrus but to the argument that emerges *in medias res*. According to one of his students, Paul Natorp would riffle through the first twenty pages of the *Phaedrus*, put his finger on the first sentence of the proof for the immortality of the soul (at *Phaedrus* 245C), and declare: "Here Plato begins to philosophize."[15] Paul Friedländer, who did take the beginnings of Platonic dialogues seriously, reminds us of Hermann Bonitz and his serene disregard for everything "unphilosophical" at the beginning the *Phaedo*. For Bonitz the properly philosophical dialogue was to be located not in Phlius or what he styled "die Scenerie des Gespräches," but in the sequence of arguments for the immortality of the soul begun at *Phaedo* 62A – seven Stephanus pages into the dialogue.[16] As for the *Republic*, even Paul

---

15. This is the memory of Leo Strauss, who studied with Natorp in Marburg.

16. Friedländer recalls Bonitz in his *Plato: An Introduction*,[2] translated by Hans Meyerhoff (New York 1958) I 232. Friedländer's apology for his own approach to the Platonic dialogues now seems unnecessary, but it can bear repeating to the readers who are impatient with the literary beginnings of the dialogues. His intention was to break down "the barrier between the philosophical content, on the one hand, and what is called dramatic form, on the other. For that is what I intended to do, and it goes without saying

Friedländer could read its entire first book as if it were an early and aporetic dialogue on justice (call it the "Thrasymachus") tenuously attached to the major dialogue we now know as the *Republic*.[17]

II. Phlius

The frame dialogue of the *Phaedo* might in fact serve as a salutary example of how external the beginning of a Platonic dialogue can be to the philosophical issues addressed within and of the conspicuous failure of a Platonic dialogue to respond to the Socratic demand for a motivating logographic necessity that justifies any part as organic to the whole. The *Phaedo* does not begin with the first words spoken by Socrates' jailor on the morning of his execution: "The prison authorities want Socrates unbound and their order is that today he must die" (59E). It begins rather with a much later conversation that is represented dramatically as taking place in another setting. At the beginning of the *Phaedo* we are not in Athens but in Phlius, and not in the early morning of Socrates' last day in prison but some time after Socrates' execution. The first words of the dialogue are spoken by someone identified as Echecrates and addressed to Phaedo and, as we have seen, they pose the question of authority that is typical of the frame dialogues: "Were you there yourself, Phaedo, on the day Socrates drank the hemlock, or did you hear [of what happened] from someone else?" (57A). Phaedo's response, Αὐτός, ὦ 'Εχέκρατες, establishes his authority for what was said and done on Socrates' last day (58c). The only other reports that had reached Phlius from Athens were indirect and brought only the news that he had died (57A). But, paradoxically, the *author* of this frame dialogue and of the *Phaedo* itself was not present on Socrates' last day; he was ill (59B). There are two frame dialogues that recall Socrates after his execution: the *Phaedo* and *Theaetetus*.

---

that it was nothing new, but something quite old. The Neoplatonist Proclus, in his commentary on Plato's *Alcibiades*, makes some very thoughtful remarks about Plato's introductory scenes: they were invented neither for the sake of dramatic suspense nor for the historical subject, but they help determine, from the very beginning, the philosophical objective of the dialogue." Friedländer was thinking of Bonitz' essay on the *Phaedo* in his *Platonische Studien*[3] (Berlin 1886) and particularly, I would guess, of his phrase "In dem Übergang von dieser Erzählung zu dem eigentlichen philosophischen Gespräche...", 313. The phrase *die Scenerie des Gespräches* comes from his treatment of the *Gorgias* on page 1.

17. Cf. his *Plato* (note 16 above) III 63–67 and II 50–66.

Plato's first words

Significantly, they are set outside of Athens and they commemorate a concern for remembering Socrates that is — apparently — not to be found in Athens.

Unlike the beginning of the frame dialogue, the actual beginning of Phaedo's narrative within the *Phaedo* seems inevitable and appropriate — daybreak and the gathering of Socrates' friends outside the prison. As Phaedo tells his audience in Phlius: "I will try to give you a full account from the beginning" (ἐξ ἀρχῆς, 59C). Unlike Bonitz, who would prefer a philosophical dialogue without any scenic preliminaries, Phaedo, who was less philosophical, has chosen the natural moment with which to begin his narrative — the dawn of Socrates' last day on earth; and he concludes in proper "Aristotelian" fashion by observing the unities of both place and time in prison at dusk (cf. ἤδη ἐγγὺς ἡλίου δυσμῶν, 116B).[18] Plato's choice of a beginning for the *Phaedo* is not inevitable and, as we read its first words, we realize that we are "breaking into a conversation already begun."[19] And the conversation of the frame dialogue in Phlius seems irrelevant to the conversation of the inner dialogue which Phaedo narrates. It answers rather to Aristotle's simple test for literary irrelevance: remove it and it will make no perceptible difference to the whole, or so it would seem.[20]

But, as we return to reconsider the frame dialogue in Phlius after listening to Phaedo's narrative of what was said and done in Athens on Socrates' last day, we come to see that the Phliasian dialogue reflects features of the very argument it frames: the strange combination of conflicting emotions that Phaedo describes to Echecrates in Phlius (the laughter and grief at 59A) leads meaningfully to the dialectic of opposites that dominates the argument for the immortality of the soul and that begins in the

---

18. As this fashion was formulated by Lodovico Castelvetro in his *Poetica d'Aristotele vulgarizzata e sposta* (1570): "...tragedy...must have as its subject an action accomplished in a small area of place and a small space of time, that is, in that place and that time where and when the actors remain engaged in acting, and not in any other place or any other time," as translated by Bernard Weinberg (from the edition of 1576) in his *A History of Literary Criticism in the Renaissance* (Chicago 1961) 1 509. Cf. Aristotle, *Poetics* 5.1449b9–16 for the origins of the rule for "unity of time" as applied to tragedy and then other compositions, with Gerald F. Else, *Aristotle's Poetics: The Argument* (Cambridge, MA, 1957) 207–19.
19. As John Burnet observed, *Plato's Phaedo* (Oxford 1911) 57.
20. *Poetics* 8.1451b23–35.

inner dialogue with Socrates' remarks, as he rubbed his legs, on the relation of pleasure and pain (60B); and Phaedo's explanation of the reason for the long delay in Socrates' execution prepares on the level of Athenian cult for Socrates' conception of death as a purification from the contagion of the body and his remarkable devotion to Apollo as a personal divinity within the dialogue. We come to appreciate as well that the logographic requirement for the organic functioning of the parts of a written composition is neither necessary nor sufficient to explain one of the functions of the Phliasian dialogue, which is to provide a point of contact between the age of Socrates and that of his memorialists. In this point of contact Socrates survives. Finally, we can just glimpse in this frame the faint trace of the artist's signature in Phaedo's words "Plato, I think, was ill" (59B).

In Phlius, Echecrates was surprised at the delay of Socrates' execution. Phaedo can explain the delay and his explanation reveals a connection between Socratic religion and Athenian cult. Echecrates' question introduces one of the major themes of what was said – and done – by Socrates on his last day. During the festival of Apollo on Delos to which the Athenians sent an official embassy there was a religious interdiction against any form of pollution in Athens itself, including the pollution involved in the execution of prisoners (58A). The ship carrying the Athenian embassy to Delos had been garlanded and consecrated the day before Socrates' trial, and its return signalled the end of the interdiction and Socrates' execution. "What ship is this?" asked Echecrates. "As the Athenians say, this is the ship which Theseus boarded to transport his 'twice seven' young people to Crete, and he both saved them and was saved himself" (58A). According to the knowledgeable Phaedo, Theseus' vow to Apollo is the origin of the annual Athenian embassy to Delos: "When they begin the period of their sacred embassy, it is their practice to maintain religious purity throughout the city and for the state to put no one to death until the ship sent to Delos has returned to Athens" (58B). The fulfillment of a vow by an Attic hero who had saved the youth of Athens results in the delay of the execution of an Athenian who was convicted of corrupting the youth of Athens.

These seemingly random details in the frame dialogue become

Plato's first words

meaningful only in the context of the inner dialogue in the state prison of Athens. The annual festival of Apollo on Delos is an important festival in the religious calendar of Athens,[21] but the worship of Apollo and the religious purity it entails are also part of an elaborate pattern in the *Phaedo*. When we first encounter Socrates in prison he has just been released from his fetters. And his wife Xanthippe calls out for religious restraint and care in speaking as she catches sight of Socrates' friends: καταλαμβάνομεν τὸν μὲν Σωκράτη ἄρτι λελυμένον...ὡς οὖν εἶδεν ἡμᾶς ἡ Ξανθίππη ἀνηυφήμησε (60A). These gestures are repeated at the end of the dialogue. Now Socrates has taken his last bath and, as had Xanthippe that morning, he enjoins religious decorum on his companions. His death, which had been signalled by the end of the Delia, seems to continue the worship of Apollo; it has become a religious ceremony. If Socrates cannot make a libation from the cup into which the hemlock has been mixed, he can offer a prayer to the gods for a successful passage to another world (117B–C). These gestures at the end of the *Phaedo* remind us forcibly of the gestures of the beginning of the inner dialogue. Release is now followed by purification, and religious decorum of speech is enjoined throughout: ἐκαθίζετο λελουμένος... ἐν εὐφημίᾳ χρὴ τελευτᾶν (116B).

Socrates' religious purity and his last words and actions are proper to a festival of the Delian Apollo. Throughout his life, Socrates had been devoted to Apollo as a personal divinity. Apollo was the god whose oracle declared to Chairephon that none was wiser than Socrates, and Socrates had served this oracle in his paradoxical devotion to testing its truth. It was Apollo who set the gadfly Socrates on the comfortable rump of his sluggish city.[22] In the *Phaedo*, Apollo is the god honored by the unique Socratic hymn composed on the occasion of his festival on Delos (61A–B). And during his last day in prison Socrates is inspired as the priest of this god to offer his swan-song of prophecy concerning the fate of the soul after death (85B).

---

21. Yet the Delia is a festival not usually described in the context of the religious calendar of Athens. Its features can be reconstructed from Thucydides III 104.5, Plutarch, *Theseus* 21 and 23, Xenophon, *Memorabilia* IV 8.2, Aristotle, *Ath. Pol.* 54.6 and 56.3, and Pausanias I 31.2 and I 18.5.

22. *Apology* 21A, 22E, 23C, and 30E.

If we leave the *Apology* and *Phaedo* for the *Cratylus*, Socrates will instruct us, as the god's exegete, that Apollo is the name for the god of purification and release, for this is what his name signifies: ὁ ἀπολούων and ὁ ἀπολύων (405A). This divinity, whose festival on Delos commemorated Theseus' salvation of the "twice seven" young Athenians from their prison in Crete and whose Socratic epithets are "the purifier" and "the releaser," is the god who presides over Plato's *Phaedo*. He is the god who releases the soul from the prison of the body, and this soul, once it has become purified, can attain to the goal of the philosophical life: μηδὲ ἀναπιμπλώμεθα τῆς τούτου φύσεως, ἀλλὰ καθαρεύωμεν ἀπ' αὐτοῦ, ἕως ἂν ὁ θεὸς ἀπολύσῃ ἡμᾶς (67A). In the dialogues of Plato, it seems, nothing is accidental. Καθαρεύωμεν of the inner dialogue reflects Phaedo's word καθαρεύειν in the dialogue in Phlius. And the themes of the *Phaedo* and its seemingly accidental beginning are reflected not only in word but in deed. At the end of his last day, Socrates takes a bath.[23]

In the case of the *Phaedo* it can be argued that the frame dialogue in Phlius connects with the dialogue it serves to introduce and seems to guarantee. But in interpreting the frame dialogue in Phlius it is not enough to stop with admiration of how the extremities of this dialogue connect in elegant and precise junctures with the inner dialogue they introduce. If frame dialogues like that of the *Phaedo* can be shown to respond to the literary demand for logographic necessity, they have another function that has nothing to do with logographic necessity. In the case of the *Phaedo*, *Symposium*, *Theaetetus*, and *Parmenides*, the frame dialogues serve to connect the age of Socrates and his conversations with the age of his memorialists – Phaedo of Elis, Apollodorus of Athens, Eucleides of Megara, Cephalus of Clazomenae, and, we are not allowed to forget, Plato of Athens. Not all of

---

23. The meaning of this gesture is well stated by Douglas J. Stewart in his essay, "Socrates' Last Bath," *Journal of the History of Philosophy* 10 (1972) 253–59; he does not, however, make the connection between the religious purity of the Delia and the major themes of the inner dialogue. Some of the evidence for Apollo as a god of purification is assembled in L. R. Farnell, *The Cults of the Greek States* (reprint New York 1977) IV 295–306. The ritual taboos in force on Delos in connection with the worship of Apollo are described by Philippe Bruneau, *Recherches sur les cultes de Délos à l'époque hellénistique et à l'époque impériale*, Bibliothèque des Ecoles françaises d'Athènes et de Rome 217 (Paris 1970) 48–52.

these memorialists are reliable narrators, but that is another story.²⁴

III. The house of Cephalus

In turning to the *Republic* and entering the house of Cephalus in the Peiraeus, we return to a narrative dialogue and once again to the question of the unity of a Platonic dialogue. In the case of the *Republic*, Socrates himself is narrator; he relates to an audience in Athens the conversation he had had in the Peiraeus the day before. He lays out the details of the setting of his conversation with the guests of Cephalus in what now amounts to less than seven Stephanus pages, but Socrates calls the entire conversation of Book I (including its setting) a "prooemium" (II 357A), and this entire book is sometimes detached from the dialogue as a whole as an early "aporetic" dialogue – the "Thrasymachus." But if Book I as a whole has been viewed by some of Plato's critics as a dialogue first composed without the *Republic* as a whole well in mind, Socrates' introduction could seem an even greater distraction from the theme of the *Republic* as a philosophical argument unified by the principle of logographic necessity. This was not the view of Proclus and his predecessors in the Academy in Athens. Proclus regarded the occasion, the characters, and the setting of the *Republic* as its matter (ὕλη), but do they matter?

The details of Socrates' introductory narrative are not abundant and they are seldom seen as relevant to the *Republic* as a whole: "I descended yesterday to the Peiraeus in the company of Glaukon, Ariston's son, since I wanted to make my prayers to the goddess and also to see how they would stage the festival, as

24. The *Symposium* is the best example of a frame dialogue related by unreliable narrators. Not one but four such narrators are introduced in the frame dialogue of the *Symposium*: the acquaintance of Glaukon, who had heard an account of Agathon's victory celebration from Phoinix, but who was unable to reconstruct it for Glaukon; Phoinix, who obviously had no idea of when this memorable event took place (cf. 173C); our narrator, Apollodorus, who relied for what he can tell us on Socrates' companion Aristodemus and for some points on Socrates himself (173B); and Aristodemus himself who was present at the banquet. Apollodorus cannot recall all that Aristodemus told him (178A), and Aristodemus fell asleep toward the end of the party and could not recall the argument by which Socrates forced Agathon and Aristophanes to agree that one and the same poet could combine the arts of tragedy and comedy (223B). These are our authorities. The author of the *Symposium* was thirteen at the time of the banquet.

this was the first time they were celebrating it" (1 327A). Other seemingly accidental details follow: Socrates and his companion were leaving the Peiraeus for Athens when they were stopped by a slave who asked them to wait until his master, Polemarchus, could catch up with them. When he catches up with them, Polemarchus asks the two companions to stay put: "Either become more powerful than this company or stay here." To which Socrates offers a third choice, persuasion (1 327c). Polemarchus will not be persuaded, and one of his guests, Adeimantos, holds out to Socrates the attraction of a mounted torch race at dusk, to which Polemarchus adds the inducement of a dinner, the spectacle of an all-night festival, and conversation with the young guests at his house (1 328D). Socrates is intrigued by the mounted torch race, but it is Glaukon who finally agrees to stay on in the Peiraeus.

We then enter Cephalus' house and are introduced to the company within and the master of the house. Socrates reports the brief conversation he had with his host, which turns naturally to Cephalus' age and the advantages of both his age and his wealth (1 328c): his age has freed him from the tyranny of passion and his wealth is a comfort to him in old age because it allows him to face the afterlife with good hope: he can pay his debts to both gods and men (1 331B). It is only at this point of their conversation that Socrates asks Cephalus the question on which the entire *Republic* turns: is justice what Cephalus seems to think it is – returning what belongs to another and (we are tempted to forget) telling the truth (1 331c)?

It is in the small and seemingly insignificant details of everyday life – or of life during a festival – that the philosophical issues of the *Republic* begin to take shape. This is the world of commonly held opinions and what Francis Bacon would call the "idols of the cave." The world of *doxa*, delimited by Socrates from the world of reality only in *Republic* VI 508D, is intimated in Polemarchus' conjecture that Socrates and Glaukon must be returning to Athens and Socrates' response to it: δοκεῖτέ μοι πρὸς ἄστυ ὡρῆσθαι ὡς ἀπιόντες. Οὐ γὰρ κακῶς δοξάζεις (1 327c; cf. 328B). The conflict between political power and philosophical persuasion is present, dimly, in Polemarchus' challenge: Ἢ τοίνυν τούτων κρείττους γένεσθε ἢ μένετ' αὐτοῦ (1 327c), and it reveals the attitude that

Plato's first words

would embrace Thrasymachus' conception of justice as "the interest of the stronger."[25] Old Cephalus' conception of the passions as despots leads finally to the paradox of the tyrant as the slave to his passions,[26] and his uneasy fear that the tales the poets tell of the afterlife might prove true (the μῦθοι of I 330D) leads to the very end of the *Republic* and Socrates' myth of Er (x 614B–621B).

The end of the *Republic* returns to its beginning. And as he begins to relate the tale of Er, son of Armenios, to Glaukon, Socrates makes a philosophical apology: 'Ἀλλ' οὐ μέντοι σοι 'Ἀλκίνου ἀπόλογον ἐρῶ (x 614B). That is, he does not intend to tell Glaukon the kind of tale Odysseus told Alcinoos in Phaeacia. His tale will be rather a philosophical version of the Nekuia of Book XI of the *Odyssey*. So it would seem that even as he set down the first word of the *Republic*, Plato had its conclusion in mind. Κατέβην – this verb in preference to any other possible word. Socrates' descent into the Peiraeus is meant to stand as the philosophical analogue to Odysseus' *katabasis* into the underworld. But the shades of Socrates' underworld are the "idols" of his cave in Book VII. Odysseus' word for his descent was κατέβην too (*Odyssey* 23.252), but what Socrates' descent into the Peiraeus signifies is made manifest by his "ikon" (cf. ἀπείκασον at VII 514A) of the cave and its "upward road," which is invisible to the prisoners who are forced to gaze on its back wall. This cave is an image of the reality of our world, and, by his long effort at "conversion" (cf. VII 518c), Socrates finally turns Glaukon back to the "upward path" in the final sentence of the *Republic* (τῆς ἄνω ὁδοῦ ἀεὶ ἑξόμεθα, x 621c). And so the first words of the *Republic* are worth reading with the care Plato invested in writing the entire *Republic*.[27]

25. τὸ τοῦ κρείττονος συμφέρον, I 338c. Polemarchus' challenge also reveals the persuasive powers of majority rule. "We owe then the conversation on justice to a mixture of compulsion and persuasion. To cede to such a mixture, or to a kind of such a mixture, is an act of justice. Justice itself, duty, obligation, is a kind of mixture of compulsion and persuasion, of coercion and reason," as Leo Strauss states the case in "On Plato's Republic," *The City and Man* (reprint Chicago and London 1977) 64.

26. Thus, in the progress of the dialogue, *eros* becomes tyrant over the tyrant, who is capable of ruling all others, but not himself; cf. IX 573B, 575A and D, 577E, 591A, and VIII 553c.

27. An *anabasis* up out of the cave is sighted in VII 515E, 517A–B, and 519D. The architectonic connection between the first word and the last sentence of the *Republic* is firmly established by Hayden Weir Ausland in his dissertation "On the Dialogue–Proem to Plato's Republic" (University of California at Berkeley 1987) 113–14.

There is one last detail and it is remarkable only in Greek: Κατέβην χθὲς εἰς Πειραιᾶ μετὰ Γλαύκωνος τοῦ Ἀρίστωνος προσευξόμενός τε τῇ θεῷ καὶ ἅμα τὴν ἑορτὴν βουλόμενος θεάσασθαι τίνα τρόπον ποιήσουσιν ἅτε νῦν πρῶτον ἄγοντες (I 327A). The verb θεάομαι is repeated twice by Polemarchus in his attempt to persuade Socrates to stay in the Peiraeus (I 328A). We hear no more in the *Republic* of the spectacle surrounding the festival to Bendis in the Peiraeus, of the mounted torch race through the city or the dinner or the all-night festival, and no one observes the shadows the passing torches cast on the walls of Cephalus' house. But spectacle, or θεωρία, will figure as an important philosophical theme in Socrates' discussion of the peculiar passion of the philosopher. And even the prisoners in his cave seem to enjoy the theater of shadows that flickers on the walls of their cave (VII 514B–515A).

Socrates' presence at the new festival to Bendis in the Peiraeus and his interest in observing the spectacle there give us the first intimation of what philosophy will come to mean in the dialogue. We recall that it was Glaukon and not Socrates who was persuaded by the promise of more of the spectacle to stay with Polemarchus in the Peiraeus. And it is to Glaukon that Socrates attempts to explain the passion of the philosopher in Book V of the *Republic*. Glaukon doubts that all those with a passion for spectacle, or observation, οἱ φιλοθεάμονες, can qualify as philosophers, any more than those addicted to the theater of Dionysos and the festivals of this god. But for Socrates the theater-goers resemble the philosopher, because the philosopher has a similar passion for spectacle, but the spectacle he is passionate about is the spectacle of the truth (V 475D).

There seems to be a parable in this. The question "What is a philosopher?" was first asked by Leon of Phlius, who put the question to Pythagoras. We know this anecdote in its fullest form from Cicero, who rehearses it in the *Tusculans* and attributes it to Heracleides of Pontus, the student of Plato (*auditor Platonis*, V 3.8). Leon, who was amazed by the conversation of Pythagoras, asked his visitor what art he practiced. Pythagoras replied that he knew no art, but was a philosopher. To make his meaning clearer, Pythagoras sought an analogy. Human life is like the great games of the Greek states. Some come to it as contestants, some to buy and sell, and some simply to observe: *esset autem quoddam genus eorum, idque vel maxime ingenuum, qui nec plausum nec lucrum, quaererent, sed visendi causa venirent studioseque perspicerent quid ageretur et quo modo.*[28] Socrates was one of these.[29]

28. Fr. 88 in Fritz Wehrli, *Die Schule des Aristoteles VII: Herakleides Pontikos* (Basel 1953). The passage is put in an illuminating context by H. B. Gottschalk in his *Heracleides of Pontos* (Oxford 1980) 13–36.

29. The revision of this essay has been greatly helped by two readers for *Yale Classical Studies*, one of whom very usefully raised the issue of narrative authority. Professor Hayden Weir Ausland has also been generous in allowing me to read and refer to his dissertation and in reading an earlier version of an essay that has benefited greatly from his study of the proem to Plato's *Republic*.

Plautine negotiations: the *Poenulus* prologue unpacked

NIALL W. SLATER

> Once of philosophers they told us stories,
> Whom, as I think, they called—Py—Pythagories;—
> I'm sure 'tis some such *Latin* name they give 'em,
> And we, who know no better, must believe 'em.
> Now to these men (say they) such souls were given,
> That after death ne'er went to hell nor heaven,
> But lived, I know not how, in beasts; and then,
> When many years were passed, in men again.
> Methinks, we players resemble such a soul;
> That does from bodies, we from houses stroll.
> Thus Aristotle's soul, of old that was,
> May now be damned to animate an ass;
> Or in this very house, for aught we know,
> Is doing painful penance in some beau.
>
> Epilogue to *Love for Love*, spoken by Mrs. Bracegirdle

The vision of the soul of the author of the *Poetics* trapped in the body of a Restoration beau and compelled to sit through a performance of Congreve is doubtless one calculated to gladden the heart of any true lover of comedy. But how much greater, we imagine, would have been his sufferings at a performance of Roman comedy. The seventeenth century had at least heard of Aristotle and paid lip service to the French understanding of his dictates upon the drama. Plautus by contrast seems quite unburdened by any anxiety over the philosopher's influence.[1]

---

1. Nor, in the case of prologues, was there any noticeable influence to begin with. Aristotle's only discussion of the term occurs in *Poetics* 12.1452b, where a prologue is defined structurally as everything in a tragedy up to the entrance of the chorus. Presumably he applied the same definition to comedy in the lost portions of the work (if indeed *Poetics* 12 is genuine); on these points, see Richard Janko, *Aristotle on Comedy* (London 1984) 233–34, 239–41.

For in place of the tidy poetic narratives with a beginning, middle, and end which the philosopher recommends (*Poetics* 1450b), the plays of Plautus in particular present us with a bewildering variety of ways to begin (and end) a comedy. The conventionality of Roman comedy in character and plot types and its reliance on Greek models has tended to divert attention from the invention and playfulness which characterizes the beginnings of Plautus' comedies.

What we know of Greek prologues, based on Menander and a few other fragments, suggests a well-recognized, primarily narrative function with a certain sameness of execution.[2] Plautus' practice is much more varied: he can begin with a prologue or not, just as he likes. Where the poets of Greek New Comedy were usually quite careful not merely to announce the happy end in advance but also to explain in detail how one got to it, Plautus can dispense with the plot details altogether. In fact, a rule of inverse proportion may apply: the more we hear of the plot in a Plautine prologue, the less we will see it acted in the course of the play.[3]

The prologues of Menander stand at the end of a long evolution in theatrical practice. His audience came to watch a New Comedy with strongly stamped generic expectations. After all, audiences had been showing up in the Theatre of Dionysos for comic performances at the festival for two centuries. Toward the end of the fourth century BC a certain style and a relatively homogeneous set of plot possibilities had come to dominate the stage. The audience's pleasure lay in watching the ingenious working out of a solution to the lover's dilemma within this established frame of

---

2. The time-honored sport of the hunt for the lost Greek original of a Roman comedy usually includes a careful discussion of its prologue and how Plautus used or misused the narrative material contained in it. Under the term "narrative" I subsume both "exposition" (discussion of events preceding the dramatic time of the play) and "plot" (events within the play). An extensive but not particularly fruitful discussion of these two functions begins with Friedrich Leo, *Plautinische Forschungen*[2] (Berlin 1912) 188–247 and is well reviewed by Niklas Holzberg, *Menander: Untersuchungen zur dramatischen Technik* (Nuremberg 1974) (= *Erlanger Beiträge* 50) 6–100, who is very useful on Menander. Enough material from actual prologues of Greek New Comedy has accumulated so that a general review of the topic is now overdue. R. L. Hunter (to whom I owe the reference to Holzberg) offers a very good short survey of the prologue in his *The New Comedy of Greece and Rome* (Cambridge 1985) 24–35.

3. The prime example is the *Casina* prologue, which describes in detail the happy ending of the romance plot, when in fact neither the hero nor heroine of the romance will appear in the play.

generic expectations.⁴ The prologue in Greek New Comedy gave the audience essential information for the sorting out of the plot and thus allowed the spectators to watch the comedy secure in the expectation of a happy ending. The only puzzle was precisely how one would get there.

The Plautine audience came to a *palliata* performance with very different expectations. They were at best second-generation theatre-goers. Nor was the place of theatre performance within festival celebration anywhere near as secure as in Greece. Theatre might be an *ad hoc* addition to an aristocratic funeral as well as a feature of a regularly scheduled religious festival. More importantly, theatre had no fixed place in the landscape. Unlike the mighty Theatre of Dionysos, massively rebuilt in stone, in which Menander's comedies were framed and anchored, the Roman stage of Plautus' day was a temporary structure, put up for the occasion of the performance only. Cheek by jowl with other competing entertainments (such as the rope-dancers to whom Terence's *Hecyra* once lost its audience), a Roman comedy faced its first challenge simply in securing a hearing.⁵

The prologue to a comedy of Plautus, when he chose to employ one, thus carried a heavy responsibility. It negotiated the conditions of its own reception with its audience. It created the frame through which the audience would view the rest of the performance. It drew the invisible but magic circle surrounding itself and its audience, which (if successful) closed them off from the competing sights and sounds of the festival, and drew the audience into the world of the play. This inductive function might be carried on into scenes of the action as well or might be performed by an opening scene of dialogue (as in the *Mostellaria*),

---

4. It is not too much to suggest a certain resemblance between this form of New Comedy and the more formulaic genres of modern popular literature, such as the romance (a lineal descendant) or the detective novel. Strong formal innovation within the genre (of the order of that displayed in *The Murder of Roger Ackroyd*) is not characteristic of the Greek examples we have; the surprise endings which are *not* resolved by marriage occur only in Roman examples, a fact which deserves more thought than it has heretofore received.

5. For the conditions of theatrical performance in Plautus' day, see G. Duckworth, *The Nature of Roman Comedy* (Princeton 1952) 73–101; W. Beare, *The Roman Stage*³ (New York 1964) 159–95; and A. S. Gratwick, "The Origins of Roman Drama," *The Cambridge History of Classical Literature* vol. II, ed. E. J. Kenney and W. Clausen (Cambridge 1982) 77–84. Especially valuable on the element of competition (alluded to in *Poenulus* 36ff.) is E. J. Jory, "Publilius Syrus and the Element of Competition in the Theatre of the Republic," *BICS Supplement* 51 (1988) 73–81.

but it is in the prologue that we see the operations of induction most clearly.[6]

The prologue to the *Poenulus* offers one of the most interesting examples of Plautus' negotiations with his audience – and a reasonably representative one, given their rich variety.[7] We can divide the text of this prologue into two sections, one which describes and structures the performance situation, and another which narrates the events leading up to the present fictional situation (though to imply any sharp separation between the two in the prologue speaker's performance is false). The narrative material is quite fully represented in the 128-line text of the prologue, which is one of the longer examples in Plautus. The degree of the narrative's elaboration will later raise questions about the structure of the play, since the Carthaginian of the title, whose activities the prologue is at such pains to clarify, does not arrive on the scene until two-thirds of the way through the play.[8] This prologue therefore allows us to study both the process of induction and the power the prologue exerts over the subsequent performance.

There is an inevitable problem in any performance-based reading of a text. Performance proceeds linearly through time. The audience in the theatre does not know when the prologue begins just how it will end. The scholarly reader does – and after the fashion of the Greek audience may well wish from me some statement in advance of how my interpretation of the prologue will turn out. Any detailed declaration of my conclusions here,

---

6. In an earlier discussion of this topic in *Plautus in Performance* (Princeton 1985) 149–54 and *passim*, I implied that there were non-inductive prologues in Plautus. It would be more accurate to say that there are some prologues which complete the process of induction into the world of the play and others which only begin this process. Even the Lar of the *Aulularia* prologue shows some subtle but significant differences from a Menandrean prologue. This thoroughly Roman figure (for there is no Greek equivalent to the Lares) is necessary to set up the theme of community of men and laws versus the untamed state of nature which David Konstan has explored so well in his *Roman Comedy* (Ithaca 1983) 33–46 (first published in *Arethusa* 10 [1977]). Moreover, the Lar's very first line implies an awareness of audience expectation and the need to shape that expectation which we never see in Greek New Comedy: *ne quis miretur qui sim, paucis eloquar* (*Aul.* 1).

7. The standard general study remains K. Abel, *Die Plautusprologe* (Mülheim-Ruhr 1955): on *Poenulus*, 89–96. Two recent studies particularly concerned with questions of narrative are R. Raffaelli, "Narratore e narrazione nei prologhi di Plauto," and *idem*, "Animum advortite: Aspetti della communicazione nei prologhi di Plauto (e di Terenzio)," in C. Questa and R. Raffaelli, *Maschere prologhi naufragi nella commedia plautina* (Bari 1984) pp. 69–83 and 101–20.

8. In fact only in Act V, according to the modern act structure imposed on the text.

however, risks erasing the process of discovery, the twists and turns by which Plautus prepares his audience for viewing the rest of his play. I must therefore beg my reader's patience and indulgence – my argument does have a conclusion, but it is one best reached without having been stated in advance.

Let us begin by examining the performance situation as the prologue invokes it. The relation of text to performance here is particularly problematic: does the text describe or create a performance situation? What begins in parody and easy-going play with the audience (the unnamed and uncharacterized prologue speaker's opening banter) moves to the assumption of authority over the audience (the command to a crier to silence the crowd, before asking the crier in turn to be silent).

The visual forms the first frame of the audience's experience, but how the prologue speaker looked is far from certain. At the conclusion of the prologue, he announces his intention to go costume himself: *ego ibo, ornabor* (123). The natural implication is that he has not been wearing a costume heretofore.[9] Much more puzzling is the question of whether he was wearing a mask. After much debate we seem to have reached a general consensus that masks were already in use in Plautus' day.[10] Given the general practice, it would then be very striking for the prologue speaker to appear without a mask. Lack of a mask would in particular allow the actor to be identified, but it would completely subvert the joke of the opening lines.[11] The play begins:

> Achillem Aristarchi mihi commentari lubet:
> inde mihi principium capiam, ex ea tragoedia.
> "sileteque et tacete atque animum advortite,
> audire jubet vos imperator" – histricus,
> bonoque ut animo sedeant in subselliis,
> et qui esurientes et qui saturi venerint... (1–6)

---

9. So G. Maurach in his admirable and thorough commentary, *Der Poenulus des Plautus*[2] (Heidelberg 1988) 44–45. (I quote the text of the *Poenulus*, however, from the OCT of Lindsay.) Cf. Abel (above, n. 7) 91. Maurach none the less denies (against K. Dowden, *Classical Quarterly* 32 [1982] 428) that the prologue was "uncharacterized." Maurach's view rests on his interpretation of *alius* in line 126 of the prologue (q.v.) but seems to me unpersuasive. We simply do not know how much everyday street costume and theatrical costume were separated in Plautus' day.

10. See Gratwick (above, n. 5) 83–84.

11. It would make possible the joke envisioned by H. Mattingly, *Latomus* 19 (1960) 250 n. 1, who believes that the *dominus gregis* who played in Aristarchus' *Achilles* played the prologue in the *Poenulus* as well. One could, of course, imagine a convention in which

The prologue speaker begins by commenting on beginnings. By referring to another play and playwright, he *seems* to position himself at a moment before performance begins. He is here almost certainly playing off Ennius' adaptation of Aristarchus, and probably a recent performance.[12] The key here is the verb *commentari* in the first line, meaning not Paul Nixon's "imitate" but rather "perform" or "recite."[13] This moment is rather more than simple parody. The prologue is toying with the audience's generic expectations, much as Mercury in the prologue to the *Amphitruo* juggles the notions of tragedy and comedy.[14] The dynamic of movement within just four lines is fascinating. After seemingly casual commentary on performance, he throws himself into the strongly marked performance mode of tragedy, and then slips out of it again. Indeed, until we hear the key word *histricus* at the end of line 4, he seems in danger of hijacking the play and giving a tragic performance.

One must admit to ignorance about the basic production context of this play. We know neither upon what occasion the

prologue speakers were unmasked, though players wore them; after all, to anticipate, the prologue speaker here will leave to put on his costume at the end of the prologue. Yet this will not do as a general rule. Mercury in the *Amphitruo* prologue (see further n. 14, below) must be identifiable as the god for his opening joke (his contract with the audience) to work, and that identification must have included mask as well as costume. One could then argue that uncharacterized prologue speakers were unmasked, others masked, but nothing else supports this conclusion. One could also imagine a special mask, just for the prologue (cf. the costume for a prologue speaker suggested for a later period, see n. 26, below), but it is doubtful that masking conventions were as developed or rigid in the Roman performance tradition of this period as in the Greek. The play with genre in both *Amphitruo* and *Poenulus* prologues also suggests that comic and tragic masks were not sharply differentiated from each other in Rome (as those in Greece would be by the presence or absence of the *onkos*).

12. Maurach (above, n. 9) 44–45; cf. Abel (above, n. 7) 95. It will soon become clear that my approach to the *Poenulus* prologue is the antithesis of that of H. D. Jocelyn, "*Imperator histricus*," *YCS* 21 (1969) 97–123. Jocelyn attempts to divide its lines among at least three different poets. He awards lines 1–2 and 50–54 to a poet with "more scholarly knowledge than dramatic sense" (123). I believe that the *Poenulus* prologue *is* playable as it stands; my argument against the analyst view is the interpretation of the prologue's dynamics which follows and consequently I will not attempt to answer Jocelyn point by point.

13. See Maurach (above, n. 9) *ad* 1. Nixon's translation appears in the Loeb edition of Plautus.

14. Mercury first announces a tragedy, then pretends to change the nature of the play to a comedy (later labelled a tragicomedy) in the face of a negative reaction from the crowd (lines 51–63). For a detailed discussion of this passage and the play with genre in the *Amphitruo*, see my "*Amphitruo, Bacchae*, and Metatheatre" (*Lexis*, forthcoming, and also appearing in a collection called *City and Stage*). This is the first of many parallels between the prologues of the two plays.

Poenulus was performed nor how such productions were advertised and announced. There is no evidence that there were designated days for tragic performances as opposed to comic ones. The prologue speaker then apparently teases the audience with the notion that they might be about to hear a performance of Aristarchus' *Achilles* and does not dispel the notion until he states that we are under the command of the *imperator histricus*.[15] The actor is presumably masked and ready to perform in either tragedy or comedy.

The dynamic of these opening lines, an alternation of casual conversation with assumed authority, will soon be repeated. The prologue speaker seizes power by making himself an *imperator* but seems to yield it again. After all, he is only a stage *imperator* – but he has not in fact discarded the role. Having established the good will of the audience (5–6), the prologue speaker begins to act like a commander. He orders the *praeco* into action:

> exsurge, praeco, fac populo audientiam.
> jam dudum exspecto, si tuom officium scias:
> exerce vocem, quam per vivisque †et colis.†
> nam nisi clamabis, tacitum te obrepet fames.
> age nunc reside, duplicem ut mercedem feras. (11–15)

This passage has the ring of plausibility to it – as well as pomposity, once again immediately undercut.[16] A Roman holiday crowd was doubtless boisterous, and securing a hearing for a play was no easy task, as Terence learned to his cost. Where Terence makes a straightforward appeal for a hearing, Plautus stages a playlet. The *imperator* exercises his authority, urges the crier on with a crude joke about starvation, and then cuts him off in a way that will once more draw the audience's sympathies.[17] Authority

---

15. The prologue to the *Captivi* says (61–62) that it is unfair to the audience to give them tragedy when they expect comedy. This joke would be impossible at Athens; time and place of comic and tragic performances were fixed, and the notion that a comedy could appear in the place of a tragedy at the City Dionysia or the Lenaia would be unimaginable. That the joke can be made at all in Rome, though, implies that performance there was not so regulated and systematized as to preclude the possibility that an audience would come expecting one genre and find the other instead. See also n. 11, above.

16. See Jocelyn (above, n. 12) 114 on *exerce vocem*, 13.

17. What, if anything, happens between lines 14 and 15? The joke works best if the *praeco* cries for silence only a few times before being cut off. The notion that the crier also announced didascalic details here (see Maurach, above, n. 9, *ad* 15) seems dubious in the extreme.

is exerted and almost immediately subverted; the prologue gets the silence he needs but directs any hostility the audience may feel at this imposition on their holiday mood against the figure of the *praeco*.

The prologue speaker then proclaims his "edict," using the formula a praetor entering upon office might,[18] but produces a thoroughgoing parody instead. His edict prescribes the proper behavior in the theatre: no walking around during the performance, no slaves pushing their way in in front of free men, no crying children, and no women talking. Within the tensions of authority and submission so pervasive in this prologue, it is well worth noting that essentially all of these objects of the histrionic edict are society's powerless: slaves, children, and women. While the prologue speaker does object early on to the lictor and his rods making noise (18), he soon switches to safer objects for his severity. The message of order is made palatable by being directed ostensibly at everyone except the majority of the audience.

The edict seems to culminate with an appeal for the audience to deal fairly with the performers, a direct comment on the performance conditions:

> quodque ad ludorum curatores attinet,
> ne palma detur quoiquam artifici injuria
> neve ambitionis causa extrudantur foras,
> quo deteriores anteponantur bonis. (36–39)

Such moral seriousness is not the province of comedy, however. This appeal and its potential commentary on the *deteriores* and *boni* in the society at large is immediately undercut by the Plautine spirit of subversion:

> et hoc quoque etiam, quod paene oblitus fui:
> dum ludi fiunt, in popinam, pedisequi,
> inruptionem facite; nunc dum occasio est,
> nunc dum scriblitae aestuant, occurrite. (40–43)

The final two lines of this first part close the ring with an allusion to the *imperator histricus* of line 4; these, says the prologue speaker in summary, are the orders which apply *pro imperio histrico* (44), and each participant (both performers and spectators) must

---

18. See Maurach (above, n. 9) *ad* 16, who cites *TLL* 2, 2094, 17ff., and Suetonius, *Div. Julius* 80.2.

Plautine negotiations

internalize them. The magic circle around the performance is now completed, and the play can begin.[19]

Next, within the performance space the boundaries of the play must be laid out, and the prologue speaker is the properly appointed surveyor (48–49). He jokes that he will tell the spectators the name of the play, whether they wish it or not (50–51), because he has been authorized by the festival management. We may feel that the play proper – that is, preliminary matter specific to this and no other comedy – is about to begin, when once again the balance of power shifts:

> nunc rationes ceteras
> accipite; nam argumentum hoc hic censebitur:
> locus argumentost suom sibi proscaenium,
> vos juratores estis.   (55–58)

The praetor is now a simple citizen, giving account of his property to the *juratores*, the censors' assistants charged with making property assessments.[20] The audience, whom he earlier presumed to order about, now sits as an IRS auditor in authority over him. This simple reversal is a prolepsis for the whole performance of the play: the players exercise their hour's authority upon the stage but must submit themselves to the audience's judgement at the end.

Theatrical and political spheres here mirror and reinforce each other. The completeness of the power reversal on stage (the praetor reduced to an average citizen, the audience he ordered about elevated to *juratores*) undergirds the notion of popular control over the magistrates of the Republic – even as practice historically moved ever further from that ideal.[21]

The prologue finally turns to the *argumentum* proper at line 59. This narrative is extensive, so detailed that it needs to be enlivened with a few jokes,[22] and – what the audience cannot

19. This ring composition might also suggest the boundaries of a Plautine expansion, but in fact clearly Plautine material continues in the next section.
20. See Maurach (above, n. 9) *ad* 55–58.
21. The degree to which (or indeed whether) Plautus' plays take cognizance of contemporary politics has been hotly debated. The best discussion now (with full bibliography) is Erich Gruen's chapter on "Plautus and the Public Stage" in *Studies in Greek Culture and Roman Policy*, Cincinnati Classical Studies n.s. VII (Leiden 1990) 124–57; see especially his discussion (pp. 134–37) of trials over accounting for campaign booty, which might provide a partial parallel to the census inquiry here.
22. E.g., jokes about knowing the undertaker who buried the dead father (61–63) and metatheatrical banter with the audience, offering to carry out commissions for them in

know at this point – almost wholly irrelevant to the play that follows. Irrelevant, that is, in the sense that it tells us a great deal we will not see enacted and would not strictly need to know: this complicated tale of three abducted children, their family relationships, and the property inheritances which will eventually come to them is prologue to a thoroughly conventional play of lovers, clever slave, boastful soldier, and a scheme to deprive the pimp of both money and girl. Only in the last third of the play does the Carthaginian of the title appear to recognize his daughters and his cousin's son and therefore to provide money and status to make the resulting marriage possible.

The structure of the play which follows this prologue does present certain problems at first glance, and not just to the analyst critic.[23] The two halves of the *Poenulus* are virtually complete in and of themselves. In the first part Agorastocles' slave Milphio concocts a scheme whereby the pimp Lycus is tricked into denying possession of Agorastocles' slave or money, when in fact he unknowingly has both at his house. Lycus thereby makes himself liable to a court action, the profit from which would finance Agorastocles' purchase of the girl he loves. In the second part of the play Hanno, the Carthaginian of the title, arrives, meets Milphio and Agorastocles, recognizes the latter as his cousin's long-lost son, and further, when enlisted to *play* a father in another (and unnecessary) scheme to cheat Lycus, recognizes and claims the girls as his own lost daughters. The second part of the action, then, is merely a series of revelations with little or no development

Carthage (79–82). These jokes are one of several similarities between the *Poenulus* and *Menaechmi* prologues. On these and the *Poenulus* prologue in general, see E. Stärk, *Die Menaechmi des Plautus und kein griechisches Original* (Tübingen 1989) 60–64.

23. Certainly enough to have aroused suspicions of contamination, though recent scholarship has tended to favor a single Greek original. Even such a defender of the play's unity as W. H. Friedrich, *Euripides und Diphilos*, *Zetemata* 5 (Munich 1953) 233–54 (= *Die Römische Komödie: Plautus und Terenz*, ed. E. Lefèvre [Darmstadt 1973] 146–72; I cite the pages from this latter version as the more accessible), admits that it is "mithin gefährlich, von 'zwei gegen den Kuppler gerichteten Intrigen' zu sprechen, denn damit wird eine Konkurrenz der beiden Teile behauptet..." (155). Any consideration of this question detailed enough to be useful would lead us too far afield. Particularly helpful on the subject, though, is the up-to-date discussion in J. C. B. Lowe, "Plautus *Poenulus* I 2," *BICS* 35 (1988) 101–10 (with thorough bibliography). Gratwick (above, n. 5) 96–103, makes a most interesting case for Plautus' use of a scene from Menander's *Sikyonios* in his adaptation of the original *Karchedonios*. Our concern is with the play as performed for the Roman audience, not any possible antecedents. I argue that the prologue anticipates and does much to forestall any feeling on the part of the audience that the play does fall into separate halves.

Plautine negotiations

or complication. Once the second part of the play has begun, the audience doubtless accepts it and follows it with interest, but what prevents the sense of an ending after the first part? The text as we have it further presents two alternative endings to the play. Both yield the same result: Hanno's recognition of his daughters and betrothal of Agorastocles to the elder, Adelphasium. The two endings do, however, portray the final discomfiture of the pimp by his opponents (including the *miles* Antamonides, in love with the other of the two girls) with differing degrees of emphasis.

We cannot expect the prologue to sort out all these problems of structure for us, but we can ask how well it prepares us for the play as it unfolds. It is perhaps only in retrospect that the critical viewer will see Plautus' strategy behind the apparently useless plot information provided in the prologue. The *argumentum* has a difficult job. It must hold the two disparate halves of the action together. It must catch the interest of that portion of the audience more interested in the conventional complications of Roman comedy while holding onto (or generating) the interest of those who prefer the sentimental recognition plot which only the second half will deliver. It does so by focusing on the pivotal figure from each plot: Lycus and Hanno respectively. The first narrative builds to the introduction of the pimp as villain and the revelation of his name, Lycus (92). The second relates the curious method Hanno uses to search for his daughters: he hires *meretrices* in each new town he visits to inquire after them.[24] The narrative also touches on his remarkable language abilities, which he nonetheless knows how to conceal to his own advantage (*dissimulat sciens se scire*, 112–13). The prologue speaker is not content merely to hint that the old man will find daughters and nephew (115),[25] but spells it out quite explicitly (121–22; 124–25).[26]

24. We see none of this action in the play itself. On what this reflects of the Greek original, see Maurach (above, n. 9) 60–61.
25. Given Roman objections to first cousin marriages (cf. Gratwick [above, n. 5] 113), it seems almost certain that Plautus altered the story to make Hanno and Agorastocles' father cousins (*fratres patrueles*, 59; cf. 70) rather than brothers, but here at the end he slips.
26. Lindsay in his OCT edition assigns 121–23 to a retractator, though I can see no reason for deleting 123. Both Jocelyn (above, n. 12) and Maurach (above, n. 9) *ad loc.* take one couplet to be the doublet of the other, and this may well be the case. Plautus can, however, be surprisingly repetitive: even this could have been playable in the prologue as it stands. Abel (above, n. 7) 91 would assign all of 124ff. to a production in a later period, when the Prologus wore a special costume, and thus must *change* costumes, not merely put on his costume.

We must return to the first half of the prologue to examine two themes which, though at first apparently unrelated, also succeed in tying the two parts of the play together. The first is Plautus' metatheatrical fascination with the process of play-making, the second the nature and interrelations of law, power, and justice. As we examine the workings of these two themes in the body of the play, the skill with which Plautus has constructed his prologue should become more apparent.

From the opening tragic parody to the parting reference to getting into costume (123), the prologue calls attention to its own status as dramatic performance. Its careful negotiations with the audience, laying out the boundaries of the stage and introducing the players, do *not*, as a Greek prologue would, close an illusionistic frame around the subsequent action. This is a play whose fundamental plot mechanism is role-playing, and whose characters, just like the prologue speaker, are well aware of their status as players, not only within their own schemes but within Plautus' play as well. A few examples should suffice. The bailiff Collybiscus, slave of Agorastocles, is costumed as a foreigner in order to induce Lycus to take him in. When quizzed by Milphio, Collybiscus insists he knows his part in thoroughly theatrical terms: *quin edepol condoctior sum quam tragoedi aut comoedi* (581). Only a few lines later the counsellors assure the audience directly that the "gold" they are using is only stage money:[27]

> aurum est profecto hic, spectatores, comicum:
> macerato hoc pingues fiunt auro in barbaria boves;
> verum ad hanc rem agundam Philippum est: ita nos
> adsimulabimus.   (597–99)

Such theatrical self-consciousness is quite frequent in Plautus, but we should not be too eager to dismiss it as stock comedy. The use of role-playing in the play's two different schemes helps to tie the two halves together. The conventional Roman comedy plot against Lycus turns on Collybiscus' deception: Lycus believes him to be a genuine foreigner (a mercenary on the dodge, in fact) and takes him in, hoping for a considerable profit, but instead is duped into perjuring himself and becomes therefore liable at law to

---

27. Leo would like to add another metatheatrical reference. When Hanno expresses surprise at 1167 that his daughters have grown so tall, Leo emends Agorastocles' reply to say *tragicae sunt; in calones sustolli solent* (1168).

Agorastocles. In the recognition plot in the second part of the play, Milphio proposes to enlist Hanno in another role-playing scheme to cheat Lycus by having Hanno *play* the father of the two girls and claim them as his long-lost daughters.

Role-playing by its very nature, however, is endlessly multiplicable. Two plots are required for this play because the first yields only the answer that satisfies, not the answer that is true. The first will provide money and/or power over the pimp to force him to yield up the *meretrix* Agorastocles loves. A conventional Roman comedy could end right here. It requires the second plot, however, to produce the real recognition which supersedes role-playing. I suggest then that the prologue foregrounds metatheatrical issues, not simply because the audience is unused to theatre and requires explicit negotiations of the conditions of watching a play,[28] but in order to make more satisfying the later occurrences of the sort of reversal we repeatedly experience in the prologue. As the prologue speaker assumes and discards roles, the audience is drawn deeper into the realm of playing: the succession of roles somehow succeeds in suggesting a "reality" behind multiplicity. Paralleling this in the body of the play, our heightened self-consciousness of theatrical form will there ultimately be suppressed by a conventional romance ending, the recognition of the lost children and the inauguration of a new, legitimate marriage. The discovery that Hanno, the master of many roles, is in reality what he proposes to play, yields a powerful sense of an ending. Theatre turns out to have been miming a deeper reality.

Is that suppression of metatheatrical consciousness quite complete, however? And how does it relate to the second of the prologue's themes, the nature and workings of law and justice? It may seem a modern, anachronistically sentimental worry, but what are we to make of a play which not only regards the pimp Lycus as subhuman (*si leno est homo*, 89) but also finds the law (the *leges populi*, as Agorastocles pointedly terms them at 725) a splendid instrument for cheating him? After all, the first plot is simply an elaborate fraud, requiring the knowing and malevolent

---

28. On the capabilities and the degree of sophistication of Plautus' audience see E. W. Handley, "Plautus and his Public: Some Thoughts on New Comedy in Latin," *Dioniso* 46 (1975) 117–32.

participation of Collybiscus, Milphio, Agorastocles, and the counsellors to induce Lycus to perjure himself – and then make capital out of this technical perjury. The second plot starts out to be a fraud every bit as cold-blooded: find an old foreigner to play the girls' father and perjure them away from Lycus. Lycus may be an enemy to gods and men,[29] but it is a bit unnerving for the law to appear to be nothing more than a comic plot device. Perhaps it is not too far-fetched to suggest that the two alternative endings to the play (1355–71 and 1372–422) suggest an unease in the Roman audience as well – or at least two different responses to the problem.

Lines 1355–71 present the simpler and shorter of the two endings.[30] It focuses on the pimp's complete overthrow and humiliation and even prefaces an apology for the play's long-windedness to its appeal for applause:

> multa verba fecimus;
> malum postremo omne ad lenonem reccidit.
> nunc, quod postremum est condimentum fabulae,
> si placuit, plausum postulat comoedia. (1368–71)

By placing line 1369 where it does, this ending grounds that appeal completely on the story of Lycus' fall. Lycus will not only suffer financially but must be confined in stocks (*lignea in custodia*, 1365) at Agorastocles' house. The moral universe of this ending is simple: the pimp is a villain who gets his just deserts. In such a play, as Lycus says himself, "what need for the judge?" (*quid praetore opust?*, 1361).

That question carries us back to the prologue and the mock praetorian edict. There we saw the mirroring of theatrical and political orders as mutually reinforcing, the justice of the praetor a pledge for the good qualities of the play. After a play in which law has been so thoroughly subverted, the question *quid praetore opust?* begins to sound dangerously ironic.[31]

---

29. The sacrifice at the temple of Venus shows this clearly. Lycus tells us that, unable to get favorable omens at the sacrifice, he went off in a rage without giving Venus her share (449–69). He hubristically mocks the *haruspex* for foretelling disaster for him (463–67; 746–50) but later acknowledges that the latter foretold sooth (791–93). On this theme, see my forthcoming "The Market in Sooth: Divine Discourse in Plautus," in *City and Stage*.

30. A full review of the problems of the two endings is beyond our scope here. See Maurach (above, n. 9) for discussion.

31. There is certainly much more here than the general theme of the uselessness of legislative activity discussed by Gruen (above, n. 21) pp. 141ff., a corollary of the

Plautine negotiations

It is perhaps not surprising that the other ending to the *Poenulus* is more to modern taste (and that of a perhaps significant segment of the Roman audience as well). In it Hanno, having regained his daughters, forgives Lycus, as do Antamonides and, apparently, Agorastocles. He considers the possibility of pursuing vengeance in the courts but knows he is at a disadvantage as a foreigner:

> si volo hunc ulcisci, litis sequar in alieno oppido,
> quantum audivi ingenium et mores ejus quo pacto sient.
> (1403–4)

There is a sense that this ending is fragile and ought not to be tested too far. Though Lycus may not be invited to the feast (as is the pimp Labrax in Plautus' *Rudens*), neither is he thrown into the stocks. The play ends in a spirit of reconciliation, appropriate to the recognition and marriage theme of the play's second part.

This movement was anticipated. The *Poenulus* prologue begins boisterously, with mock authoritarianism and comic incitement to riot (urging the *pedisequi* to storm the bakeshops, 41–43), but gradually calms the holiday audience and focuses their attentions and energies on the narrative of recognition and romance. The emotional tenor of the play itself follows the same development, from the inverted, Saturnalian world of the first plot against Lycus to the recognition and the restoration of just, "normal" order. The prologue speaker's exaggerated enactment of putting on and discarding various roles (tragedian, praetor, humble tax-payer) is no random series of comic bits or *lazzi*; it is a negotiation, devoted to determining the proper roles for both actors and audience, and an induction, drawing both into the world of the play and setting its action in motion. On a deeper level, the double structure of the prologue anticipates the double structure in the body of the play: a conventional role-playing plot (corresponding to the role-playing games of the prologue's first part) is followed by a recognition (prepared for by the prologue's narrative) and the revelation of "reality."

All of Plautus' prologues, from the two-line warning prefixed to the *Pseudolus* up to the lengthy plot expositions of plays such as the *Rudens* or the *Amphitruo*, bid for the audience's sympathy for, and

opposition between the worlds of forum and festival so brilliantly explicated by Erich Segal, *Roman Laughter*, 2nd edn (Oxford 1988). The boundaries of the community which law governs are here at issue (cf. on *Aulularia*, above, n. 6).

participation in, the project of creating the play. While the means may vary (compare Mercury's "contract" with the audience in the *Amphitruo* with the praetorian edict here), the basic process of induction is the same. The audience must be separated from its workaday concerns and drawn into the temporary holiday world (*dum ludi fiunt*, 41). The *Poenulus* prologue faces the additional challenge of knitting together almost independent plots, aimed perhaps at two quite different audiences or tastes. The prologue does not, and cannot, carry that burden by itself, but it creates a frame and introduces themes which make the task much easier. As for the details of that process:

> quod restat, restant alii qui faciant palam.
> valete atque adjuvate ut vos servet Salus.   (127–28)[32]

[32] I am deeply grateful to the editors of this volume and my colleagues Carolyn Dewald and Amy Richlin for their most helpful comments on this essay. The errors and infelicities that remain fall to my own account.

Proems in the middle

GIAN BIAGIO CONTE

I

How to begin a poem forms an established part of rhetorical theory. But in practice poets know that the solemn celebration of a beginning is something that far transcends rhetoric: the exordium is an inauguration, almost a liturgy which mediates the text's passage and thereby permits it to escape from silence and to enter into the literary universe. At the border between fully poetic speech and speech still outside of poetry, the proem – the preliminary announcement of a poem which follows – is already song and is not yet song. When the poet invokes the Muse to inspire him (or in hymns invokes the divinity to whom the hymn is addressed), he imposes a precise delimitation upon the "contents" of his poem. By indicating its essential themes (this or that story – or part of a story) he outlines the limits of a discourse which was undefined as long as it was merely virtual. In his discussion of the proem, Aristotle defines it in this way: δεῖγμά ἐστιν τοῦ λόγου, ἵνα προειδῶσι περὶ οὗ ὁ λόγος, καὶ μὴ κρέμηται ἡ διάνοια ("the proem provides a sample of the subject, in order that the hearers may know beforehand what it is about, and that the mind may not be kept in suspense," *Rhet.* III 1415, a12f.).

If the inauguration of poetic discourse is an act regulated by a literary ceremony, the empirical function which this act at the same time fulfills is to inform the public of the song's object – its *quid* – by serving as a periphrastic substitute for the title itself, or a plot-summary of the contents. Among its various possible functions, and aside from many others which could be added, this is the most characteristic function of the proem, the only necessary and constant one. Indeed – if I may be permitted to oversimplify for a moment – this is in substance the structural defining feature of almost all the proems found in Greek literature until the fourth century B.C. – the indisputable sign of an immediate and as yet unproblematized relation between poet and public. The community recognizes in the speech of its poets its own literature, and not only do the poets recognize in this community a unanimous and homogeneous public, but, what is more, it does not even occur to them to doubt the nature and modes of their own poetic production. From time to time, in different ways, these poets will have a more or less clear sense of the dignity which belongs to their function; but all of them, in substantially the same way, know how poetry is produced.

But the political and social upheavals of the Hellenistic age created a markedly different cultural system in the course of a very short time: the ecumenical community of this new world shared a cultural horizon which was likewise ecumenical (an indication of this, and to a certain extent a condition for it, is the diffusion of the book as that medium which most directly answers to the changed requirements of cultural communication). Within this horizon, the position of literature takes on a new configuration; the relation between poet and public changes, for the very destination of poetry changes. And if the poet no longer addresses himself to that community within which he was directly integrated (his existential space now takes on the shape of the court, of the libraries, and of the schools), the audience becomes – as though responding to the new cultural "professionalism" of the poet – a specialized public of connoisseurs.

The literary code, even more than serving to communicate, now functions as a means of selecting and qualifying its users. The audience is ecumenical, but it is selected and restricted; speaker and listener are the peaks of a mountain range which is immensely extended, but whose valleys are excluded from communication. The awareness that not only a political epoch has ended, but also a cultural one, leads to reconsideration of the whole complex of "tradition" as a legacy to be recovered – by evaluating and selecting, by taking this, refusing that. The philological meditation which derives from this busies itself with erudite classifications and with laborious textual systematizations, but it also generates both a sophisticated rhetorical theorizing and a consciousness attentive to the procedures of poetic creation. Literature is no longer something obvious: whoever practices it must say what he is doing, because everyone does it differently. The result is not merely marginal asseverations, but literary professions of faith, ambitious and all-embracing. *Programmgedichte* like Theocritus' *Thalysia*, Herodas' *Mimiamb* 8 (the Dream), Callimachus' *Epigram* 28, and especially the prologue to his *Aetia*, are manifestos of the new poetry, of the new way of conceiving and formulating the problematic relation between literature and reality. And the poet invents a new liturgy in the act of inaugurating his poetry, so that the public will know not only the object – the *quid* – of the incipient poem, but also and above all its individual artistic character – its *quale*. In this second aspect we can see the announcement of a new literary vocation (which polemically desires to renew itself even in its artistic materials) and the proposal of a new form of expression and of contents (comprising a liberty which refuses canonical measures and distinctions and which contaminates diverse modes of poetic discourse). At the same time, the restricted public of competent readers is practically required to adopt a role of jealous connivance. All this is the ambitious affirmation of the poet's ego, which far from hiding itself behind any sort of cover, now comes forward in the first person to proclaim everything which might serve to characterize him and to distinguish him from others.

The ancient structure of the proem is ready to welcome this new function, to turn itself on occasion into a declaration of poetics as well. Side by side with the thematic proem exists the programmatic proem. To be more precise, we often find a programmatic proem interwoven with and superimposed on the thematic proem. Thus, alongside the *quid*, the *quale*.

Up to this point I have generalized, and a lot. But perhaps my doing so has made one thing clear: that these two forms of proem are functionally opposed in such a way that, even if both perform the ceremony of opening, one is concerned with what will be said, the other with how poetry will be made. This synchronic oppositional pair is, as often happens, the result of a diachronic evolution. On the one hand, that is, we find the persistence of an ancient feature, one virtually congenital with poetry (the expository proem), and, on the other hand, the insertion of a new proemial nature, in which a different culture comes to light (the programmatic proem).

II

This distinction will remain valid for the artistic consciousness of poets to come – both a constraint and the sign of an artistic responsibility necessary for making poetry. At Rome such a consciousness is fully revealed in the literary practice of Virgil. The architecture of the *Georgics* is exemplary: four books, each one with a single subject that is announced each time by a brief, precise proem, a specific *deigma*, which takes up "in variando" the plot-summary of contents prefixed to the work as a whole in the first proem:

> Quid faciat laetas segetes, quo sidere terram
> vertere, Maecenas, ulmisque adiungere vitis
> conveniat, quae cura boum, qui cultus habendo
> sit pecori, apibus quanta experientia parcis
> hinc canere incipiam. (1.1–5)

Each of these four verses proposes one of the four themes. Then follows the hymnal invocation to the divinities of the countryside and to Caesar.

The proem of the second book has an analogous structure and identical function. It is a naked *propositio* of the argument, cultivation of the vines (followed by a dedication to Bacchus). Likewise the proem to the fourth book is reduced to the exposition of the *summa rerum*, the raising of bees.

On the other hand, the third book does not open with this type of structure, a thematic proem; it has a programmatic proem which is a genuine declaration of poetics:

> Cetera, quae vacuas tenuissent carmine mentes,
> omnia iam volgata: quis aut Eurysthea durum
> aut inlaudati nescit Busiridis aras?
> cui non dictus Hylas puer et Latonia Delos
> Hippodameque umeroque Pelops insignis eburno,
> acer equis? Temptanda via est, qua me quoque possim
> tollere humo victorque virum volitare per ora.
> Primus ego in patriam mecum, modo vita supersit,
> Aonio rediens deducam vertice Musas;
> primus Idumaeas referam tibi, Mantua, palmas
> et viridi in campo templum de marmore ponam
> propter aquam, tardis ingens ubi flexibus errat
> Mincius et tenera praetexit harundine ripas.

Proems in the middle

> In medio mihi Caesar erit templumque tenebit.
> Illi victor ego et Tyrio conspectus in ostro
> centum quadriiugos agitabo ad flumina currus.
> Cuncta mihi Alpheum linquens lucosque Molorchi
> cursibus et crudo decernet Graecia caestu.
> Ipse caput tonsae foliis ornatus olivae
> dona feram.   (3.3–22)

By now practically everything a poet can say has been said (*omnia iam vulgata*, 4). For the man who would rise to new regions of poetry, and to flattery on the mouths of men as a winner (*victorque virum volitare per ora*, 9), only a road which has never yet been tried can guarantee ascent to the mountain of the Muses; and it is Virgil, *primus*, who will know how to bring them to Italy.

This ambitious new poetry includes all the programmatic topics – in the proper order: the motifs of the *recusatio*, of *primus ego*, and of the Muses, once Greek, now finally Latin. And the path that leads to the temple dedicated to Caesar, the path of a great new epic poem, follows in the footsteps of the greatest of all Roman literary traditions, that of Ennius.[1] Precisely because he has chosen his own direction, the poet can reject a large part of what has already been said. The new song will arise, built following the lines of that symbol in which Pindar had several times embodied the grandeur of poetry: an architectural monument, with the limpid proportions of a temple.

Here in Virgil the Pindaric metaphor takes on the form of a grandiose programmatic allegory: Caesar, the divinity of that temple, and Caesar's glorious deeds will be the object of the future poem; but the marble building will rise on the green banks of the Mincio River.[2] In this declaration, the poet Virgil is entirely present: he promises something completely new, but neither his memories nor his *Eclogues* have abandoned him. This emergence

---

1. Besides the obvious presence of Ennius' epitaph (*volito | vivo' per ora virum*), the magnificent poetry of the *Annals* is also indirectly evoked by 10–11, *Primus ego in patriam mecum, modo vita supersit, | Aonio rediens deducam vertice Musas*, where there is an echo of Lucretius' praise of Ennius at 1.117f., *qui primus amoeno | detulit ex Helicone perenni fronte coronam*.

2. The water of the Mincio performs here the same symbolic function – it contributes to the poet's investiture – as the river Permessus performed in the landscape of Helicon, the Muses' mythical seat, just as Mantua will be the new Helicon of the Virgilian Muses. Cf. W. Wimmel, *Kallimachos in Rom*, Hermes Einzelschriften 16 (Wiesbaden 1960) 222–38; less useful is A. Kambylis, *Die Dichterweihe und ihre Symbolik* (Heidelberg 1965) *passim*, esp. 98ff., 110ff.

of the poet's own identity from his programmatic awareness is directly related to the Alexandrian and Neoteric experience, the cultural soil upon which the new edifice of Augustan literature was being constructed.

But there is another proem of Virgil's, or rather a proem in the middle, which shows much more immediate ties with that Alexandrian experience. I am referring to the beginning of the sixth *Eclogue*, almost as Alexandrian as the prologue to Callimachus' *Aetia* itself, to which it adheres quite closely.[3] The programmatic topics to which the poet has recourse in order to establish his declaration are, in this case also, the *primus ego*, the *recusatio* of what is extraneous to the new song (*cum canerem reges et proelia*), and the choice of what is appropriate for his new intentions. But the connections with that Alexandrian culture remain so close that – in contrast to his promise in the *Georgics* – this Virgil still rejects the grand themes so as to confine himself to small ones.

But I am not so much interested here in showing how contents that are related in substance become actualized in forms that are opposed. What I would like to point out instead is the persistence within different poetic genres – and distinct moments in the poet's career – of an identical function performed by the proem placed in the middle of the work: that of offering a specific declaration of poetics. In other words, the position inside the compositional architecture – just at the beginning of the second half of the *Georgics* and of the bucolic collection – corresponds to a specific function, distinct from the one belonging to the proem placed normally at the beginning of the work. I shall explain its meaning in greater detail soon; now we must still consider, within the Virgilian corpus, the proem placed at the beginning of the seventh book of the *Aeneid*, at the transition from the Odyssean part to the Iliadic one. Here the poet takes another and a deeper breath, he invokes the Muse anew – in short, this is a new beginning, one which would seem to find its only rationale in the objective caesura which divides the material of the poem.

---

3. Always fundamental is E. Reitzenstein, "Zur Stiltheorie des Kallimachos," *Festschrift R. Reitzenstein* (Leipzig 1931) 23–69; see also R. Pfeiffer, "Ein neues Altersgedicht des Kallimachos," *Hermes* 63 (1928) 302ff.; cf. Wimmel (above, note 2) 132ff., and finally E. A. Schmidt, *Poetische Reflexion: Vergils Bukolik* (Munich 1972) 19ff., 239ff.

Certainly, the empirical necessity of signalling in some way the passage from the adventures of Aeneas by sea to the harsh battles of Rome's destiny was easily solved by inserting a new proem.[4] But it would be a serious misunderstanding of the poetic architecture of Virgil to reduce it all to such mechanical requirements of composition; the poet says now what he will sing, and the proem declares the *quid* of the new narrative. So at least it seemed to Heyne who, commenting on the anaphoric lines *dicam horrida bella, | dicam acies actosque animis in funera reges*, explained *reges* with the annotation "Latinum, Turnum, Mezentium." I suspect that the commentator, anxious to give an objective denotation to every Virgilian word, misunderstood the meaning and the specifically literary function of the formula *bella et reges*, its implicit programmatic and declaratory connotation. It is the very formula which Horace employs in *Ars Poetica* 73 to designate the highest kind of heroic poetry: *res gestae regumque ducumque et tristia bella*. Heyne, in other words, misunderstood the *quale*, the qualities and characteristics of the Iliadic part which is about to begin, characteristics which Virgil, after a couple of lines, emphatically and explicitly announces with the words *maior mihi nascitur ordo, | maius opus moveo* (44–45). Here Virgil finally agrees to sing of *reges et bella*, he no longer refuses *tristia condere bella* (the formulas of *recusatio* prefixed to the sixth *Eclogue*), and he also satisfies the promise made in the proem in the middle of the *Georgics*. Thus the proem to the seventh book of the *Aeneid*, joined horizontally in a synoptic relation to the thematic topics of the other two proems in the middle, not only refers to the contents of what the poet is about to sing, but is also enriched with a meaning which touches on the *qualitas* and the modes of poetry.

III

The regular recurrence in Virgil of the proem in the middle as the privileged locus of literary consciousness allows us to recognize in it a function of a systematic character, not different from those performed by other formal literary conventions. Now that the phenomenon has been identified, the philologist would be

---

4. And of course we should not neglect the specific connection with the verses which open the proem to the third book of Apollonius Rhodius.

concerned at this point to discover its "source"; and perhaps not wrongly, if it is true that – as one of the few Italian philosophers maintained – the nature of things often "is in their birth." One thinks immediately of Ennius, as is only natural, the true or presumptive *pater* of so great a part of Latin literature. Because of the fragmentary form in which his *Annals* have come down to us, no certainty can be attained; nevertheless, I believe that the hypothesis I shall formulate has a certain degree of plausibility.

Several books of the *Annals* opened with single thematic proems. But among these there is one which seems to have contained many of the very same programmatic topics with which we have been concerned up to now: it is the celebrated proem to the seventh book. What remains is little but, perhaps, sufficient:

> scripsere alii rem
> Versibus quos olim Fauni vatesque canebant,
> Cum neque Musarum scopulos...
> ...nec dicti studiosus quisquam erat ante hunc.
> Nos ausi reserare...
> Nec quisquam *sophiam* sapientia quae perhibetur
> In somnis vidit prius quam sam discere coepit. (213–19 V²)

Here is the poet's rejection of his predecessors and his separation of himself from them; here his difficult ascent to the mountain of the Muses, a boast which inevitably precedes the motif of *primus ego* (connected with the symbolic theme of the fountain), and which proudly declares the new poetics of the *dicti studiosus* – the literary profession of the poet-philologist of the Alexandrian school.[5]

After the first six books (it matters little whether the publication proceeded by triads or hexads), Ennius was obliged to declare the differences which separated him from his predecessor Naevius (since his own treatment of the Punic Wars began with the seventh book), and he was also obliged to respond to the attacks

---

5. That the verb *reserare* was completed by an object like *fontes* (the appropriate *Wassersymbol* of poetic initiation) has been proposed by G. Pascoli, *Epos* I, 2nd edn (Livorno 1911) 34, on the basis of comparison with Virg. *Georg.* 2.175, *ingredior, sanctos ausus recludere fontes*, and has been supported by F. Klingner, *Virgil* (Zurich 1967) 241, who cites Stat., *Silv.* II 2.38f., *reseretque arcana pudicos | Phemonoe fontes...* The resulting image seems to me well suited to this context, *pace* O. Skutsch, *Studia Enniana* (London 1968) 124f. For a good discussion of these verses, with full bibliography, see W. Suerbaum, *Untersuchungen zur Selbstdarstellung älterer römischer Dichter: Livius Andronicus, Naevius, Ennius*, Spudasmata 19 (Hildesheim 1968) 249–95.

which inevitably came from the belated resistance of traditionalist schools. The circumstances required, in short, an open profession of literary faith, which found its most natural locus in a new proem, at the beginning of the new part which was now being published. And Ennius, now becoming polemical, in declaring his literary ideals again evoked his splendid allegory of the dream, the investiture (in the first proem) from which he had derived his own poetic *sophia*. Thus in Ennius also we find a proem which is inserted into the body of the poem with the specific function of declaring the author's program – and which would have remained a genuine proem in the middle if the "old Olympian racehorse" had in fact completely exhausted his forces, and had not instead unexpectedly taken on new energy and a poetic second wind. Consider the close of the twelfth book:

> Sicut fortis equus, spatio qui saepe supremo
> vicit Olympia, nunc senio confectus quiescit. (374–75 V²)

Upon finishing his work, at the farewell, the poet speaks about himself (the concluding *sphragides* of Callimachus' *Aetia* or of Virgil's *Georgics*, for example, are no different). Ennius compares himself to a strong but old horse, once victor at Olympia, but now obliged by age to take a well-earned rest. Even if it turned out that the old Olympian racehorse would after all find the energy for six more books, it is probable that at first he believed that the twelfth book would mark the end of his *Annals*.[6] This is, in short, the

---

6. The edition of the *Annals* edited by O. Skutsch (Oxford 1985) places the two lines that Vahlen put at the end of Book 12 among the *sedis incertae fragmenta* (lines 522–23). Vahlen's reconstruction was based mainly on a reading (*duodecimum annalem* in Gellius XVII 21.43) which Skutsch has shown to be wrong (pp. 674–75). This now makes possible various collocations of these two lines: the end of Book 15 (this seems to me to be the most attractive), the end of Book 18, or even the beginning of Book 16. I do not, however, believe that my line of argument is greatly affected by this. Two different problems must be distinguished. The first is the diachrony of composition, the ups and downs that accompanied the composition of the *Annals*, and the resulting collocation of those two lines at one or another stage in the process of composition; the second is the definitive form in which the *Annals* appear (or, rather, appeared to its ancient readers) at the end of that process. It is possible to make out within this definitive form the great initial proem, one or more endings to sections of the text, and further proems in the course of the work. Of these, the proem to Book 7 (which at least with respect to the whole plan of fifteen books had a collocation which can be called "medial") must certainly have possessed – in length and in scope – a function comparable to that of the general proem, so that it appeared complementary to it. Thus the problem is not one of rigid geometry or numerical schemes (even if Ennius can hardly have been displeased that a formulation of his poetic ambitions found its place near the middle of his work); rather, the proem to the seventh book sprang

architectonic structure which the future reader of Ennius would have found in the *Annals*; and I suspect that, to make it even more perspicuous, there was probably a sort of *retractatio* at the beginning of the thirteenth book, designed to justify Ennius' renewed commitment to sing even the most recent history of Rome. This is just what Ovid does when he adds the third book of his *Ars Amatoria*, missing in the original plan; and in the same way Manilius justifies his fifth book.[7]

It is the lucid desire for proportion – typical of the new Roman classicism – which attaches an aesthetic value to this empirical and contingent opposition between two proemial functions and their respective collocations in the economy of the work, attributing to it a specific formal meaning. In other words, the empirical opposition will achieve pertinence: the circumstantial collocation will become a convention – a rhetorical institution – and win a place among the possible models of the literary system.

Roman classicism, and Virgil in particular, have a clear awareness of the difference in functionality between the two types of proem: the ancient proem of contents and the programmatic proem, Alexandrian and modern. These poets know the Alexandrian experience and have learned its lesson, but they seek a direct relation with that ancient essentiality which at the beginning of the song simply said "what" would be sung. Yet they also, in the fashion of the Alexandrians, feel the need to say "how." Hence the need for a distinction – splitting into two the proemial utterance – for which the architecture of Ennius' gradually evolving poem opened up an opportunity for a difference in location. To speak in the middle is also to assign an

from Ennius' practical need to compare himself with Naevius, his predecessor and rival, in treating a common subject. We are thus dealing with a fortuitous process and a contingent collocation which eventually served as a model in composition – which acquired, in other words, a paradigmatic function.

7. Ovid justifies the addition to his original plan (cf. *Ars Am.* 1.36–40) on the clever grounds of fair play: "Now that I have instructed the men, it is fair that the women too should know the weapons of amorous seduction, so that they can wage a fair battle" (cf. *Ars Am.* 3.1–6). Manilius justifies his fifth book thus: *Hic alius finisset iter...me properare...mundus iubet, Astron.* 5.1ff.; he seems to have added to the plan of a work probably conceived in four books, following the model of the didactic poem represented by the *Georgics*; cf. E. Romano, "Struttura degli *Astronomica* di Manilio," *Acc. Scienze Lett. Arti, Palermo Classe Sc. Mor. Filolog.*, Mem. 2 (1979), esp. 64ff. See further the way in which, according to Pliny (*Nat. Hist.* 7.101), Ennius himself motivated his decision to add Book 16: *Q. Ennius T. Caecilium Teucrum fratremque eius praecipue miratus propter eos sextum decimum adiecit annalem* (cf. Vahlen[2] *Ann.* XVI fr. 1, p. 74).

appropriate place (a secondary position) to a function which must remain secondary with respect to the effort to perform an unmediated utterance, not a self-reflective discourse. It was necessary to create a poetry which would again seem to be a "naive" and, as it were, natural utterance. This is the *tour de force* of the poets of Roman classicism after the literary sophistication of the Neoterics.

But they could no longer ignore their self-reflective consciousness. What they had to do was confine it to a position of lesser conspicuousness – of concealed conspicuousness. This seems to me the same toned down emphasis that we find in the figure of litotes, where an idea is shrewd enough to express itself indirectly, where it is so sure of reemerging later in the ultimate meaning of the sentence that it agrees to eclipse itself in an attenuating circumlocution.

The proem in the middle, in short, permits the poet to declare himself, but with less conspicuousness. Horace too seems to have profited from this possibility, when he located in the center of the fourth book of his *Odes* the eighth poem (the solemn motif of *dignum laude virum Musa vetat mori*, 28), joining it immediately to the ninth, the ode of the *vate sacro*; or when in the group of the six Roman Odes he reserved the fourth place (the beginning of the second half of the cycle) for the invocation of Calliope and for a Pindarizing profession of a poetics of the sublime. (But often Horace's professions of his poetic vocation are placed deliberately at the close of the books: a delayed and conclusive presentation of himself and of his own poetry rather than a problematic declaration of poetic rationales, the author's seal in the Alexandrian fashion but also a confident farewell to his readers.)

IV

The dossier of "proems in the middle" could be enriched by other examples, which all point, as has already been noted, towards the Alexandrian character of this technique. Thus, examining the relations between the new Lille papyrus of Callimachus and Roman poetry, Thomas has shown how the central proem of the *Georgics* was influenced by the beginning of Book 3 of the *Aetia* of Callimachus; and he has pointed out the notable "Callimachean" continuity of the proems of *Eclogue* 6, *Georgics* 3, and *Aeneid* 7.[8] It should also be noted that the imitations of the "medial Proem" of the *Aetia* are all located, according to Thomas, in initial or functionally programmatic positions (besides *Georgics* 3, also Propertius 3.1 and Statius, *Silv.* 3.1). It is important to note that in all these Latin examples (Virgil, Propertius, Statius), the imitation of Callimachus, in a conspicuous position, takes on a precise character of metaliterary enunciation; Callimachus offered nothing more than a compositional framework, which the Latin poets transformed to create a new proemial institution.

Instead, I should like to conclude with a final hypothesis. It involves the famous proem to the fourth book of Lucretius – famous, unfortunately, not only for the grandiose beauty which makes it one of the most enthusiastic declarations of poetics in all of Latin literature, but also for the jungle of philological opinions and counter opinions which has luxuriated around these verses. The problem, certainly, exists, and is neither of easy nor of sure solution.[9] The problem, in a nutshell, is this. Verses 1–25, which constitute the proem to the fourth book, also figure, with two or three tiny changes, in 1.926–50, where they are preceded by verses 921–25, which are tightly connected to them. Was it the poet who wrote them in both places? Or were they written in only one place and then transferred to the other by an editor or interpolator, surviving also in their original location? In that case, which was their original location? Some scholars have found it in Book 1; others have maintained that these verses, written as a proem to Book 4, were later transferred to 1.926–50; and among these there are some who think it was Lucretius himself who transferred

---

8. R. F. Thomas, "Callimachus and Roman Poetry," *CQ* 33 (1983) 92ff.

9. But it is equally certain that the creation of a now suffocating *lukrezische Frage* has been fueled by the scruples of some philologists (primarily German) who hesitate to rid themselves at the outset of baseless or arbitrary hypotheses, if only to make show of a laborious "scientific" apparatus. I agree in substance with the arguments of K. Gaiser, "Das vierte Proömium des Lukrez und die lukrezische Frage," in *Eranion: Festschrift H. Hommel* (Tübingen 1961) 19ff., who after an analysis of the context in which the disputed verses are found, and noting the evidence provided by study of the manuscript tradition, traces the difficulties presented by the text back to the very beginning of its transmission. Lucretius seems to have left his work by and large completed, but apparently without having been able to submit it to an organic revision; hence his manuscript was probably loaded with additions and corrections, second thoughts and improvements. The first editor of *De rerum natura* (perhaps Cicero), intervening in this text with an excessive conservatism, in a mechanical and not always critical manner, seems to have paved the way for many of the incongruities and errors of the tradition.

them, some who think it was an editor, and some a late interpolator.¹⁰

What has been outlined up to now, the specifically programmatic function which belongs to the proem in the middle, can perhaps contribute a new piece of evidence towards solving this question. In the fourth book, a declaration of poetics like this one is in exactly the right place. It is densely interwoven with programmatic *topoi*: among others, the new roads of Callimachus, the still untouched fountains of poetry and the coronation of the poet, and the motif of *primus ego*. It is Lucretius' solemn enunciation of his literary credo; it occupies the proemial position at the beginning of a book; and at the beginning of the fourth book it is conspicuously placed in the middle of the poem. This location, therefore, is typical; but one cannot say as much if the original location of these verses is sought in the first book. Will so much evidence of compositional care betray the intention of the poet (in that case Lucretius would have made those verses expressly for the fourth book, or at least it would have been he who transferred them there)? Or if that care does not betray the intention of Lucretius, does it not betray the critical intervention of the reviser?¹¹

10. For the essential points of this problem, see the Oxford commentary of Bailey *ad* 1.925ff. The complex procedure of proposals and discussion can easily be reconstructed with the help of the text and notes of Gaiser (above, note 9).
11. The present article is a slightly revised version of an essay earlier published in *Il genere e i suoi confini* (Turin 1980) 122–36, 2nd edn (Milan 1984) 121–33. I should like to thank Professor Antonio La Penna for the gratifying fall-out initiated by his keen interest in this essay; curious readers may consult A. La Penna in *Maia* n.s. 33 (1981) 217–33 and 35 (1983) 115–21, and G. B. Conte in *Materiali e Discussioni* 8 (1982) 123–39 and 9 (1983) 153–54.

Openings in Horace's *Satires* and *Odes*: poet, patron, and audience

BARBARA K. GOLD

Maecenas is a preeminent figure in Horace's poetry. Theirs is the most famous, most documented, and most studied of all relationships between an ancient writer and his patron, and it hardly needs to be said that Maecenas' name always appears in Horace's poetry in the right and obvious places: *Epodes* 1.4, *Satires* 1.1.1, *Odes* 1.1.1, and *Epistles* 1.1.3.[1] Formally, Horace makes it very clear that Maecenas is to be a focal point of his audience's attention. Yet, the poet's relation to his patron is in general complex (witness the *recusatio*),[2] and this is true even in the ostensibly straightforward dedication at the beginning of each work.

Although at first glance the patron appears to be both the major catalyst for the poems and the sole person in whose praise these poems have been written, a more careful reading of the dedicatory poems reveals a multiplicity of audiences and voices, including but not limited to patron and poet, all of which are important for an understanding of Horace's works. My interest here will be in two specific opening poems, *Satires* 1.1 and *Odes* 1.1 (the opening poem of *Odes* Books 1–3, published as a collection in 23 B.C.). I will argue that one of the main functions of these poems is to establish the authorial voice of the poet by delineating the

---

1. These are only the introductory poems in which Maecenas' name occurs; Horace also addresses key poems to him throughout all of his works except the *Carmen Saeculare*. See B. Gold, *Literary Patronage in Greece and Rome* (Chapel Hill 1987) 113ff., 220 n. 14; M. Santirocco, *Unity and Design in Horace's Odes* (Chapel Hill 1986) 54–55, 154–68; E. Fraenkel, *Horace* (Oxford 1957) 69 n. 1, who points out that Horace often delays the mention of Maecenas by name for several lines or longer but alludes to him earlier in the poem (cf. e.g. *Epodes* 1 and *Epistles* 1.1).

2. For the *recusatio*, see W. Wimmel, *Kallimachos in Rom: Die Nachfolge seines apologetischen Dichtens in der Augusteerzeit*. *Hermes Einzelschrift* 16 (Wiesbaden 1960); Gold, *Literary Patronage*, 65, 220 n. 2; J. E. G. Zetzel, "The Poetics of Patronage in the Late First Century B.C.," in *Literary and Artistic Patronage in Ancient Rome*, ed. Barbara K. Gold (Austin 1982) 96ff. *Odes* 2.12 is a good example of an Horatian *recusatio*; on this poem, see P. Smith, "Poetic Tensions in the Horatian *Recusatio*," *AJP* 89 (1968) 61.

various levels of audience to be addressed, and further, that the programmatic nature of these poems lies in their shifting addresses and polyvocality, a technique that identifies the poems as peculiarly Horatian. The primary audience in *Sat.* 1.1 and *Odes* 1.1 is Horace's patron, Maecenas, but there are at least three other equally important levels of audience, which are usually addressed directly or indirectly without being named. I will begin by looking at the function of *Sat.* 1.1 as an opening to Book 1 of the *Satires*, at Maecenas' role in it, and at the importance of Horace's audiences. I will then discuss *Odes* 1.1 as an opening to *Odes* Books 1–3 and examine the rather different role that Maecenas and Horace's other audiences play there.

I

In his discussion of *Satires* 1.1–3, Niall Rudd makes the following statement: "these satires are all straightforward diatribes in the sense that *the poet speaks directly to his audience* and takes responsibility for what he says. But while his manner is direct and unequivocal, his material is so general that we learn practically nothing about himself" (italics mine).[3] With this as my starting point, I would like to inquire about the nature of the alleged "audience" and about the possibility of speaking directly to one's audience. Which audience does Rudd mean? What kind of audience is Maecenas? Are there audiences besides Maecenas?

We can delineate in any piece of literature different groups for whom the author is writing and from whom he might expect to elicit very different responses. Part of our task as readers is to perceive different dimensions of a work by examining the kinds of readers or audiences to whom the author speaks. In Horace the relative importance of these audiences varies from genre to genre. In *Satires* Book 1, there are at least four potential audiences:

the primary audience, the dedicatee, who appears only in-
frequently and is mentioned briefly, though prominently;[4]

---

3. N. Rudd, *The "Satires" of Horace* (Cambridge 1966) 35.
4. In fact, few of the *Satires* are addressed to anyone at all; the exception is 1.6, also to Maecenas. Several of the satires in Book 2 appear to be addressed to a second party (2.1, 2.4, 2.5, 2.8), but these "addressees" turn out to be characters in a dialogue with Horace or someone else. I am indebted to Peter Rabinowitz' discussion of audience response for

the internal audience, whom Horace has contrived to play the straight man, to pose as the interlocutor for his rhetorical questions, and to misunderstand the ironies of the satire;[5]

the authorial audience, the first-century B.C. Roman upper-class writers and politicians to whose experience and values Horace appeals and who could be counted on to understand the full effect of Horace's mixed signals and ironic tone;[6]

the actual audience, the person who is reading or hearing a text at any given moment.

In *Sat.* 1.1, then, the first audience on whom our attention is focused is Maecenas, the primary addressee who is named only three words into the poem:

> Qui fit, Maecenas, ut nemo, quam sibi sortem
> seu ratio dederit seu fors obiecerit, illa
> contentus vivat, laudet diversa sequentis?   (1-3)

Since ancient works were often known by their first line or partial first line, the name of Maecenas would have been a prominent part of the title of *Sat.* 1.1 and probably of the book as a whole once it was put together.[7] Thus he is immediately invested with a formal importance for the work itself as well as for Horace's life and career. It is unclear at the outset whether Maecenas is more important as one of the prominent themes which traditionally receive mention in any programmatic first line of poetry (e.g. *arma virumque cano*) or as an external referent who lends dignity and authority to the poem by his name and presence. We should ask whether the satire enhances Maecenas' importance or Maecenas lends to the satire a different dimension and tone.

---

some of my terms and ideas (although his treatment discusses contemporary fiction and drama, not classical poetry). See P. Rabinowitz, "Truth in Fiction: A Reexamination of Audiences," *Critical Inquiry* 4 (1977) 121-41; "Shifting Stands, Shifting Standards: Reading, Interpretation, and Literary Judgment," *Arethusa* 19 (1986) 115-31. See also the introduction to this issue of *Arethusa* by N. S. Rabinowitz and V. Pedrick.

5. See A. J. Pomeroy, who discusses *Odes* 1.1 and proposes as a critical strategy "a 'naive' reading which will cooperate with the poet by accepting his vision of his methods" ("A Man at a Spring: Horace, *Odes* 1.1," *Ramus* 9 [1980] 37). This is the reading that my internal reader would have.

6. For Horace's creation of an incoherent persona, see J. E. G. Zetzel, "Horace's *Liber Sermonum*: The Structure of Ambiguity," *Arethusa* 13 (1980) 70-73 and passim.

7. For the importance of the first lines of books of poetry and their use as titles, see Gold, *Literary Patronage*, 230 n. 77; E. J. Kenney, "The Incomparable Poem the '*Ille ego*'?," *CR* 20 (1970) 290.

We know that Maecenas was a wealthy, important statesman, close to Augustus and one of the inner circle, friend and patron to the leading literary lights of Rome, a man of dignified lineage and standing. Thus his name connotes wealth, power, and influence, and it gives added meaning to the ensuing discussion of greed, contentment, and choice of vocation.[8] In contrast to such qualities and attributes, however, the tone of the opening lines is almost studiedly casual, as if Horace were trying to reproduce a conversation in progress.[9] Maecenas is presented here not as a patron, but as a friend who is interested in philosophical disquisitions on contentment and greed and is the suitable recipient of a diatribe on these subjects. The tone of the satire, underscored by the choppy phrasing of the first three lines, which imitates everyday speech, establishes the unpoetic or even antipoetic character of satiric style and counters the dignifying potential of Maecenas' persona. These words seem to be the *disiecti membra poetae* that Horace accused himself of producing instead of writing weighty, Ennian-style verse (*Sat.* 1.4.62). Words and phrases like *qui fit* and *nemo*, which are colloquial and conversational in nature, also add to the informal tone of the satire.[10]

Thus the tone of Horace's address to Maecenas is unclear from the beginning. Even more puzzling, Maecenas drops out of the poem entirely after the first line. His name is not mentioned again nor is any direct allusion made to him or his relationship with Horace. What replaces Maecenas is the vague second-person addressee, recipient of Horace's constant questions and exhortations.[11] This is Horace's internal audience, the group of listeners

---

8. We might compare, for example, the impact of a contemporary work on business ethics addressed to "Dear Joe Smith" and one addressed to "Dear Mr. Rockefeller."

9. See Rudd, who comments on the satire's "informal aspect" (13).

10. For the colloquial words used here, see P. Lejay, *Oeuvres d'Horace: Satires* (Paris 1911) ad loc.; B. Axelson, *Unpoetische Wörter* (Lund 1945) 76; A. Kiessling and R. Heinze, *Q. Horatius Flaccus, Satiren*, 8th edn (1957) ad *Sat.* 1.1.20–21.

11. Horace complicates matters even further, however, by often using the pronoun *tu* to refer not to his internal audience but to the framed character inside the vignettes in the satire. For example, in lines 16–17, a *deus* appears with an offer of exchange for the soldier and the lawyer whom he addresses by *tu*, then *vos* (Horace, the author, refers to these characters in the third person [*nolint*, 19]). We might call this the *framed audience*. Elsewhere, *tu* refers to the internal audience (e.g. lines 38–42). See Pomeroy's remarks (p. 37) on the change of addressee in *Odes* 1.1 from Maecenas to "the general second person" (in line 13) to "the ideal second person singular of the future" (in line 35). Zetzel is wrong to say that Horace changes addressees frequently in order to show a failure of tact and logic ("Horace's *Liber Sermonum*," 70). Such a change of address is quite common in most of the

on whom Horace can count to fall into his traps, follow his leads, and believe that he is genuine each time he changes tone. It is also the group that displays the very set of qualities that Horace has set out to admonish and correct (in this case, greed and discontent). They embody the traits shown within the vignettes (e.g. lines 4–8, 15–19, 43, 51, 64–67, 80–83, 95–100) which we, the actual audience, and Horace's authorial audience can scorn and mock. This of course is part of the fun of satire: while it appears to attack vice in a general way, it does so by singling out specific (although often unnamed or falsely named) people in whom this vice is embodied.[12] Horace's internal audience offers this kind of sympathetic target.

The third layer of audience (moving out from the center of the satire) is the authorial audience, the specific external audience at whom Horace is aiming his comments and upon whom Horace can depend to understand the overall effect of the satire. This audience is nowhere referred to specifically but is implied throughout. The artistic integrity of the work depends on the existence of this group of readers.[13] They are the ones for whom the somewhat confusing and disingenuous asides are written: "I don't want to keep you – this is the point I want to make" (14–15); "What's wrong with being honest and enjoying myself? – I'm like the teachers who used to bribe their pupils with treats to learn their letters – but let's stop fooling around now and get serious" (24–27). This audience is sophisticated enough to understand the overall drift of the satire since it is not mired in its details and expected to respond to its attacks as is the internal

Roman poets; see W. Abel, *Die Anredeformen bei den römischen Elegikern* (Berlin 1930). Furthermore Horace purposely makes such frequent changes of address in *Sat.* 1.1 and elsewhere not to exhibit a lack of logic but to express many different levels of meaning to different types of audience.

12. Niall Rudd, in his discussion of the features of Roman satire, says that it deals with the behavior of "the individual in society" but in "a suitably general way." The particularized characters in Horace's *Satires*, like Tigellius in 1.2 and 1.3, are "cartoons," characters who are "etched with a few quick strokes" and then "vanish in the wake of the argument" (15). While this may be true of the characters in the vignettes, the internal reader enables Horace to give a more substantial portrait of a specific individual who represents the general type of vice. See also Rudd's remarks about the effects of detailed, personal illustrations (27–28).

13. This is the same group of readers that understands the tensions, inconsistencies, ironies, and contradictions that Zetzel claims for *Satires* Book 1 ("Horace's *Liber Sermonum*," 69–73) and also corresponds to Pomeroy's "general reader," who is not, I think, to be confused with Maecenas (Pomeroy, 37–38).

audience. The authorial audience would also appreciate Horace's jokes and such clever lines as *frontibus adversis componere: non ego avarum* (103). Here the "miserly" rhythm and elision at the end force us to put together two words that are not grammatically connected, and they thus underline Horace's personal rejection of *avaritia*. Finally, this audience would know when Horace was serious in his discussion of maintaining the proper limits and keeping a reasonable and sane perspective (106–07). It might even have enough aesthetic distance and appreciation to connect Horace's brief and perfect analogy between the contented person and the well-filled guest with his later portrayals of himself and his friends dining simply but well, content with the meal and with what life has brought (*Sat.* 1.6, 2.2, 2.6).

The fourth audience, which is farthest removed from the text, is the actual audience. By this I mean any person embedded in a particular time and cultural context who sits down to read Horace, bringing his or her personal, historical, and social conditions to a reading of the text. Each one of us who has read, is reading, or will read Horace *Sat.* 1.1 interprets the details, the motivations, and the message in a different way. Horace's frequent references to posterity are evidence that he was highly aware of this particular audience (see e.g. *Sat.* 1.10, *Odes* 1.1, 3.30, 4.6, 4.7, *Ep.* 1.20).[14] This, of course, is also the most difficult audience for the author to anticipate, since he could not have imagined his future readers and their many different perspectives and sets of assumptions.

I would like now to return to Rudd's statement that Horace in *Sat.* 1.1 is speaking directly to his audience and takes responsibility for what he says. If we posit several audiences (as we must for all of Horace's works), how can Horace be speaking *directly* to all of them at once? Or can he speak directly to any of them? What Rudd seems to mean is that, in a diatribal style of satire, the author wishes to give the impression that he is actually speaking in person to the addressee of the satire, who corresponds to the listener of a verbal diatribe. Horace's commentator Porphyrio noted this characteristic of satire when he said *in sermonum nomine vult intellegi quasi apud praesentem se loqui*, but, by the use of the word

---

14. See Zetzel's statement that "Roman poets had their sights set not on contemporary social approbation but on eternity" ("Poetics of Patronage," 101).

quasi, he makes a clear distinction between addressing someone in writing and actually delivering a verbal diatribe.[15] Rudd thus draws attention to the speaker's diatribe against his internal audience, and Porphyrio acknowledges the fictional status of this audience, but neither seems to recognize that the full effect of the satire depends upon the involvement of other audiences.

The most important audience in *Sat.* 1.1 is, of course, Maecenas, but his relationship to the speaker remains ambiguous.[16] In line 1 of *Sat.* 1.1 Maecenas' name is immediately identified with the idea of contentment or discontent with one's lot; Horace assumes him to be a suitable recipient for a question about such matters because of his qualities and background. The material in the satire was a commonplace in philosophical diatribes, but it is given a new face in this Roman and more personal context.[17] For underneath the generalizing, moralizing tone of the diatribe and the deliberately impersonal references is a focus on the subject that would occupy Horace throughout his poetic life: the basis for contentment and happiness. For Horace, this subject was inextricably tied to the name of Maecenas, who would provide Horace with the physical, emotional, and literary means to achieve the state that his exemplars in *Sat.* 1.1 could never achieve.

Horace starts this opening satire with what seems to be a sweeping categorical statement:

> Qui fit, Maecenas, ut nemo, quam sibi sortem
> seu ratio dederit seu fors obiecerit, illa
> contentus vivat, laudet diversa sequentis? (1–3)

He states that *nemo*, no one, ever remains content with the life dealt out to him; presumably *nemo* must also refer to Horace and Maecenas. But Horace carefully excludes himself and Maecenas from this group. For, although they are included in those referred to by this inclusive negative pronoun, they also have an existence

---

15. R. J. Baker contrasts the *Satires* with the *Epistles*, which, as written letters, never claim to be face-to-face conversations, but take the rhetorical stance of addressing a listener who is at some distance ("Maecenas and Horace's *Satires* II.8," *CJ* 83 [1988] 214).

16. The picture of Maecenas in *Sat.* 1.1 is clarified and brought into perspective by later satires in the book, particularly 1.9 (the companion piece to 1.1 according to Zetzel, who discusses the arrangement of Book 1 in "Horace's *Liber Sermonum*," esp. 67–73). According to Zetzel, the purpose of the satires is to create "a portrait of the speaker."

17. See Rudd, 20, 30.

outside of the group, as the observer-addressee and the observer-speaker. If they can objectivize "nemo" in their conversation, they cannot themselves be identified with the group of people to which the word refers.[18] So Horace has at the opening formed a privileged group of two, who are not quite included with the rest of mankind. By the end of the satire, Horace softens the categorical *nemo* even further when he says "*rarely* is anyone found who leaves the world a contented guest":[19]

> inde fit ut raro qui se vixisse beatum
> dicat, et exacto contentus tempore vita
> cedat uti conviva satur, reperire queamus.   (117–19)

As the satire progresses, there is a gradual but clear shift in focus from the primary audience to the internal audience. After several examples in the opening lines (4–12), which introduce characters other than Maecenas and Horace and put more actors onto the stage, Horace says *ne te morer, audi/quo rem deducam* (14–15). We might easily understand the *te* here to refer to Maecenas, but the intervening lines have dimmed the focus on him, and the referent for *te* is somewhat ambiguous. The succeeding lines (15–19) contain a framed vignette in which the second-person pronouns refer not to Maecenas or to the internal audience, but to the framed audience in the story, the interlocutor of the *deus* (15).[20] This audience is distanced by the third-person verb *nolint* (19), which objectifies the people addressed here and makes them into a part of the story rather than direct addressees.

The effect of this self-sustaining vignette is to remove us farther from the primary addressee, Maecenas, and to prepare us for a shift to the internal audience. Horace uses the introduction of the angry Jupiter (20–21) to change the tone. He assimilates himself to the image of the god presented here, dropping the neutral stance and easy-going banter that characterize the early part of the satire and declaring that he will adopt a sterner demeanor

---

18. See Pomeroy for a discussion of a similar technique used in *Odes* 1.1 (46–47). He says that in *Odes* 1.1 Horace tries to remove himself from the system which he is investigating, but that he cannot escape his own rhetoric in his description of himself.

19. Note that the phrases *contentus vivat* and *contentus...vita* (these do not go together grammatically but are placed suggestively close to each other), key thematic words for Horace, are repeated in *Sat.* 1.1.3 and 118 and provide a positive focus in a satire more generally connected with the theme of μεμψιμοιρία and *avaritia*.

20. See the discussion in note 11 above.

(27). After several more *exempla*, including the sympathetic portrait of the industrious little ant (32–35), Horace's tone shifts again, to outright abuse, and here, for the first time, he addresses the internal audience directly:

>   cum te neque fervidus aestus
>   demoveat lucro, neque hiems, ignis, mare, ferrum,
>   nil obstet tibi dum ne sit te ditior alter.
>   quid iuvat immensum te argenti pondus et auri
>   furtim defossa timidum deponere terra?   (38–42)

The addressee is characterized in this passage as *timidum* (42) and accused of being miserly, greedy, and foolish.

It is difficult to imagine that Horace would adopt so abusive a tone toward Maecenas or call him *timidum*. We can therefore assume that Horace is no longer addressing Maecenas here, and the progress of the satire substantiates this by distancing us from Maecenas after line 1 and certainly after line 15. Horace continues from this point to lambast his internal addressee, who argues in a stupidly obtuse manner giving Horace a chance to set forth the correct position. The abuse continues (68–91) until finally Horace calls a halt to it (*denique sit finis quaerendi*, 92), slows down the pace with one final story, and comes back full circle to the beginning (*illuc unde abii redeo*, 108). He means to imply that he is returning to his original subject, but his statement also brings us back to the initial and primary addressee, Maecenas.

Thus although Maecenas' name has not been mentioned for 119 lines when Horace interrupts with *iam satis est* in line 120, we are prepared for the concluding frame in lines 120–21 which returns us to the opening address and gives the impression that Horace is now ending the conversation he had started in line 1 with *qui fit, Maecenas*:

>   iam satis est. ne me Crispini scrinia lippi
>   compilasse putes, verbum non amplius addam.   (120–21)

So the final paradigm of the satisfied dinner guest appears to be directed to the same pair of ears as was the initial question and to be given by way of an answer to Maecenas. *Avari* (103, 108) are never satisfied with life, but Horace, as we have seen, has separated himself and his primary addressee from this group and pronounces himself, for the first of many times to come, as satisfied, content with what he has said, and wanting no more (*non amplius addam*, 121).[21] The stark contrast between the internal and authorial audiences helps to emphasize the bond between Horace and Maecenas and their shared values. And, although Maecenas loses his primacy of place after the opening lines of the satire, he clearly fulfills a very important function in *Sat.* 1.1. He helps to define the reader's role by offering a model of the privileged position enjoyed by the authorial audience. As Maecenas recedes from view, we take over his role, becoming Horace's private accomplices in mocking the follies of others, who are embodied in the internal audience. Horace must remove Maecenas from the satire in order to change his tone and to make way for the internal audience he needs as a foil, but he maintains Maecenas' presence and importance in a number of ways.

At the end of *Sat.* 1.1 Horace leaves himself an opening into the remaining nine satires of Book 1. The final second-person address in *putes* (121) could refer to any one or all of the audiences set up between lines 1 and 121. The referent is likely to be, but is not necessarily, Maecenas. Thus Horace leaves himself both a structural opening and a rhetorical opening into the next satire so that the attention again shifts away from Maecenas and onto the subject matter and the reaction of the other audiences. By this technique, Horace displaces Maecenas from his privileged position, and he begins to widen his circle of acquaintances, setting the stage for depicting a complex set of relationships between himself and many others, including but not limited to Maecenas.

The treatment of Maecenas in *Sat.* 1.1 foreshadows his role in the rest of Book 1. He appears every so often in the later satires, but as just one of many addressees and not in a dominant position. In the third satire, on the right treatment of friends, Maecenas makes a brief but memorable appearance. In the midst of complaining that we often turn good qualities on their heads and unfairly mislabel our friends' virtues as vices, Horace portrays himself as a person with failings who could nonetheless be

---

21. Cf. with *Sat.* 1.1.121, *Sat.* 2.6.4: *nil amplius oro*. For a discussion of the much disputed line 108 of *Sat.* 1.1, printed in Wickham and Garrod's Oxford text as *illuc unde abii redeo, qui nemo, ut avarus*, see Fraenkel, 97–101. I agree with Fraenkel's decision to return to the reading of all the other manuscripts except V: *illuc unde abii redeo, nemon ut avarus*.

charitably painted in a better light by a true and tactful friend (63–66). Maecenas is used as an example of the kind of friend who would be gracious enough to call Horace *simplex* rather than *molestus*. Maecenas is simply part of the exemplum here, but he is not wholly objectivized because he is paired with *me*, the author himself. As in *Sat.* 1.1, Horace cleverly makes himself and Maecenas a part of the satire as well as external observers, identified with the themes and yet commentators on them, both of them cast in several roles at the same time. First, Horace is the *simplex* and *molestus* who is taken to task for being so gauche as to disturb an important man's concentration; Maecenas is the *grand seigneur* who should not have been disturbed. But Horace is also an example of someone who should be forgiven for his *faux pas*; isn't that after all the lesson of the satire? The third role that Horace plays, and Maecenas along with him, is that of the authorial audience ("we") which passes judgment on the *simplex*: "*communi sensu plane caret*," *inquimus* (66). And fourth, Horace, Maecenas, and his authorial audience are themselves taken to task for finding fault with another person when they themselves are far from perfect (66–69). Thus Maecenas is worked cleverly into the satire, given the roles of objectified exemplum, coopted authorial audience, and respected patron.

Maecenas appears at brief but regular intervals in the remainder of Book 1, identified with Horace's major themes, other important friends, and typical situations. In *Sat.* 1.5 Maecenas is a fellow traveler on the famous trip to Brundisium; he is never directly addressed but is glancingly referred to as one of the retinue on this famous journey (27, 31). As in *Sat.* 1.1, Maecenas' importance is at once downplayed by the trivialized context in which he appears (Horace contracts an eye inflammation) and yet magnified by the subject matter (political and personal friendship), the great importance of this political mission (*magnis de rebus*, 28), the grand presentation of his name and person (*huc venturus erat Maecenas optimus atque/Cocceius...*, 27–28), and the company he keeps (Cocceius, Fonteius Capito, Virgil, Plotius Tucca, and Varius).[22]

Sat. 1.6, a difficult and intricate piece and the first since *Sat.* 1.1

---

22. See C. J. Classen, "Eine unsatirische Satire des Horaz?," *Gymn.* 80 (1973) 235–50; Gold, *Literary Patronage*, 134–35.

to have a direct address, is dedicated to Maecenas. This address is clearly meant to recall the opening line of *Sat.* 1.1,[23] and it seems to be a ringing acknowledgment of Maecenas' glorious ancestry, cast in highly rhetorical language hardly befitting satire:

> Non quia, Maecenas, Lydorum quidquid Etruscos
> incoluit finis nemo generosior est te,
> nec quod avus tibi maternus fuit atque paternus
> olim qui magnis legionibus imperitarent... (*Sat.* 1.6.1–4)

Yet the formal endorsement of Maecenas, who again takes the honored position of primary audience, is undercut at once by the negative frame in which he is cast and the ambivalence expressed about his grand titles and lineage.[24] In fact, Maecenas will be praised here *not* because of his good breeding but for quite the opposite reason: because he realizes that matters of rank and birth are of little consequence in the face of true moral integrity. This sets the stage for the appearance of the poem's real subject: Horace, an *ignotus*, *libertino patre natus* (6), but not scorned on that account by the discerning Maecenas. As in *Sat.* 1.3, Maecenas' principal outstanding characteristic seems to be his uncanny ability to judge his friend correctly and to appreciate him. The remainder of the satire focuses on Horace's father, his upbringing, his emergence as one of Maecenas' friends, and his ethical values,[25] and Maecenas becomes a substitute father for Horace.

Maecenas is not addressed directly again but appears in two more satires, both times in close conjunction with Horace. *Sat.* 1.9 gives a portrait of another *molestus*, this time not Horace but a character invented to make Horace appear to be a part of the in-group.[26] This unpleasant and bumptious fellow gives the outsider's view of Maecenas and his friends so that Horace, now an insider, can set the record straight. As in the earlier satires, Maecenas' presence here is made all the stronger by his near absence. The longer Horace waits to mention Maecenas by name in such a

---

23. For *Sat.* 1.6 as a mid-book rededication, see Fraenkel, 101.
24. Horace's ambivalence about Maecenas' lineage seems to have some basis in fact; see L. A. MacKay, who talks about the "elegant neurotic" hiding the "shabby paternal shadow of Perperna's scribe" in the luster shed by the "legendary glories of Etruscan royalty" ("Notes on Horace," *CP* 37 [1942] 80).
25. See Gold, *Literary Patronage*, 132–33 for a discussion of the social and moral ambiguities of the language in *Sat.* 1.6.
26. See Zetzel, "Horace's *Liber Sermonum*," 67, 71 on the correspondences between *Sat.* 1.1 and 1.9. Both describe approaches to Maecenas but from different points of view.

Openings in Horace's "Satires" and "Odes"

setting as *Sat.* 1.5 or 1.9, where we would expect to find him, the clearer it becomes that he is a focal point of the satire. A famous remark of Sherlock Holmes illustrates the focusing power of an expected but missing name or incident:

"Is there any point to which you would wish to draw my attention?"
"To the curious incident of the dog in the night-time."
"The dog did nothing in the night-time."
"That was the curious incident," remarked Sherlock Holmes.[27]

We could almost say that Horace invents yet another readership in such circumstances, the absent audience (which is Maecenas here).

Maecenas makes his last appearance in the tenth and final satire of Book 1. Other members of the group appear here (Virgil and Varius), but it is not until the end that Maecenas is mentioned in a list of political and literary luminaries and friends, the *docti amici* for whose approbation Horace has written the book (82–83, 88–90). Mention of Maecenas' name is once again delayed and given only the briefest notice, but that name is nonetheless highlighted, placed in a sonorous roll call of famous men and sandwiched between Varius and Virgil, whom Horace has already praised in the highest terms as those best of men who introduced him to Maecenas (*Sat.* 1.6.54–55). In *Sat.* 1.10 Horace is no longer in direct conversation with Maecenas as he pretends to be in *Sat.* 1.1, nor does he create an intimate vignette in which he and Maecenas can interact freely as in *Sat.* 1.3. Instead Horace gives the emphasis to himself, and his major dialogue is with a dead but influential character, Lucilius, and with the internal audience which, Horace implies, has reacted to his earlier pronouncements. Maecenas would never ask such foolish questions or need such explanations; he has been moved to an external group of *pauci lectores* (74), the authorial audience, who can be counted on along with us to take Horace's satires in the appropriate spirit (*arridere*, 89).

Thus, as we track Maecenas through *Satires* 2–10 of Book 1, his significance and appearances there seem to parallel the roles assigned to him in *Sat.* 1.1. And, although he recedes from

---

27. See A. Conan Doyle, *Memoirs of Sherlock Holmes* (London 1893) vol. III, 22 (cited by R. J. Baker with remarks about a similar phenomenon in *Sat.* 2.8 in "Maecenas and Horace *Satires* II.8," 226).

prominence in the remainder of the book just as he does in 1.1, Horace makes clear his continued importance. After losing his primacy as dedicatee and primary addressee in *Sat.* 1.1, having offered us access to a superior position, Maecenas is identified in the succeeding satires with all of Horace's various audiences, becoming at alternate moments primary, internal, authorial, actual, and absent audience.

How then is *Sat.* 1.1 programmatic and important as an opening poem? As Fraenkel points out, this satire seems to lack the character of a prelude to the book that it introduces (as opposed, for example, to *Sat.* 2.1 or *Odes* 4.1).[28] Fraenkel finds a few explicit references to later satires (1.1.24f. and 1.10.14f.; 1.1.74 and 1.6.111ff.; 1.1.104 and 1.2.12; 1.1.101ff. and 1.2.24) and several characters who reappear (Fabius in 1.1.14 and 1.2.134; Nomentanus in 1.1.102 and 1.8.11; Crispinus in 1.1.120 and 1.3.139, 1.4.14). I would add to this list clear and important cross-references between *Sat.* 1.1 and the final satire, 1.10: *contentus* in 1.1.118 and 1.10.74, describing Horace's state of mind to Maecenas, and *arridere* in 1.10.89, which characterizes the effect that Horace wants his satires to have on his *docti amici* ("I hope they laugh at them") and reminds us of Horace's important description of his method in 1.1.24–25: *quamquam ridentem dicere verum quid vetat?* Another intertextual reference is the important repetition of Maecenas' name in *Sat.* 1.1.1, 1.3.64, 1.5 passim, 1.6.1, 47, 1.9.43, and 1.10.81. Fraenkel also tries to uncover formal qualities that make *Sat.* 1.1 "eminently suitable to represent the new – or renewed – literary genre": its polish, variety, length, and comico-serious tone. Finally, Fraenkel sees the theme, a plea to avoid *avaritia* and πλεονεξία and to espouse moderation, as a key to the rest of the satires.[29] But apart from the important theme of *Sat.* 1.1, these specific references and more general formal properties could be found in most of the remaining satires of the book (apart perhaps from 1.7 and 1.8). Fraenkel's obvious lack of ease with trying to explain why this poem heads

---

[28]. Fraenkel, 96. See also Zetzel's article, "Horace's *Liber Sermonum*," for a discussion of the correspondences between *Sat.* 1.1 and the other satires in Book 1.

[29]. On the importance of the moral issues addressed here and elsewhere in *Satires* Book 1, see I. M. Le M. DuQuesnay, "Horace and Maecenas: The Propaganda Value of *Sermones* 1," in *Poetry and Politics in the Age of Augustus*, ed. T. Woodman and D. West (Cambridge 1984) 19–58, esp. 33–36.

the book is not put to rest by any of the vague programmatic qualities he finds.

I think that we will discover the basis for the opening position of *Sat.* 1.1 not in the minor details of correspondence, which operate on a superficially structural level, nor in the formal artistic properties of the satire, which are too general to be convincing, but rather in Horace's development of his various audiences in this satire and in his use of Maecenas in this context. The first satire displays Horace's great virtuosity in addressing an astounding variety of audiences and in thereby identifying different levels of meanings to be discerned. It is a paradigm of the satiric technique that Horace will continue to use throughout the rest of Book 1 to explain his positions, values, and interests. Horace uses Maecenas as a familiar name and a model for this technique. Maecenas can be all types of audience and can interact with Horace on many different levels. Horace maintains his own identity and primacy as author by constantly shifting Maecenas from one position to another, while cleverly magnifying Maecenas' importance along the way, and he uses these interactions between himself and his audiences (Maecenas prime among them) to create both a personal and an artistic identity.

II

In *Odes* 1.1 the roles played by Horace's audiences are simpler, yet more problematic. As in *Sat.* 1.1, the poem is framed by a prominent address to Maecenas in the opening lines and an implied return to this primary audience at the close. But instead of leading us into the poem as accomplices to the speaker, these framing lines seem extraneous to it, while the body of the ode is addressed to no one in particular.

The ode opens impressively and resoundingly with Maecenas' name, a description of his noble lineage, and an effusively complimentary address which seems strained in its formality:

> Maecenas atavis edite regibus,
> o et praesidium et dulce decus meum... (1–2)

There is no clear structural relationship between the opening pair of lines addressed to Maecenas and the priamel that follows, nor is there necessarily any semantic connection between lines 1–2 and the subject matter of the priamel. The poem veers sharply away from Maecenas in line 3 and does not return to him, even implicitly, until the *inseres* of line 35:

> quodsi me lyricis vatibus inseres,
> sublimi feriam sidera vertice. (35–36)

Maecenas is not integrated into the subject matter as he is in *Sat.* 1.1; rather, the ode encourages us to forget about Maecenas between lines 2 and 35.

The final pair of lines (35–36) are as uneasily connected to the body of the poem as the first pair. As critics have complained, these four lines are not a necessary part of the poem, but seem oddly detachable and awkward. Hermann was the first to suggest that the first and last pairs of lines, which he called *inepta et ridicula*, should be excised, thus leaving the priamel in lines 3–34 to stand as a more coherent unit.[30] Landor would move the first two lines (which "would be better anywhere else") and delete the last two lines, thus ending the poem with *barbiton*.[31] Collinge, in discussing the structure of *Odes* 1.1, points out that the "first and last couplets certainly look to be outside the general scheme; they might be read continuously were it not for the *quodsi*."[32] This is not, however, evidence of artistic weakness but rather a device that Horace uses to frame the ode with lines that have meaning by themselves as much as in the context of the poem. Taken apart, the lines are a rather standard, formal dedication to Maecenas, expressing the respect and devotion of the poet to the patron and the poet's desire to excel with his patron's help. When read together with the rest of the poem, Maecenas' name gives added resonance to the list of vocations in the priamel, particularly those of idler and poet, but the priamel can easily stand on its own.

The apparent awkwardness and detachability of the framing lines reflect a more problematic relationship between Horace and Maecenas than was present in the satires and a greater sense of the poet's independence here. Even the address at the end in *inseres* (35), which seem to point back to Maecenas and to complete the

---

30. G. Hermann, *De Horati primo carmine dissertatio* (Berlin 1842) = *Opuscula* (Leipzig 1877) vol. 8, 395–401. His suggestion was picked up by Nauck, who is often mistakenly credited with the idea.

31. See A. LaVonne Ruoff, "Walter Savage Landor's Criticism of Horace: The *Odes* and *Epodes*," *Arion* 9 (1970) 200.

32. N. E. Collinge, *The Structure of Horace's Odes* (London 1961) 108.

frame, could be addressed to patrons of an entirely different order: the Muses and the gods referred to in the previous lines and posterity, of whom Horace is always aware and never so much as in *Odes* 1.1 and its counterpart 3.30.

After the address to Maecenas in lines 1–2, the only other explicit second-person address in the poem occurs in line 13, *dimoveas*, which is aimed at Horace's internal audience. The verb is imbedded in an exemplum, and it has a completely different rhetorical function than the many second-person addresses found in *Sat.* 1.1. There, Horace actually seemed to be addressing an interlocutor who was introduced to play the straight man. Here, the address in *dimoveas* has the function of varying the discourse rather than giving the impression of a genuine conversation, and the internal audience is reduced to an idiomatic expression:

> gaudentem patrios findere sarculo
> agros Attalicis condicionibus
> *numquam dimoveas* ut trabe Cypria
> Myrtoum pavidus nauta secet mare.   (11–14)

("*You could never*, even with a million dollars, *induce* a man who loves to hoe his father's fields to become a fearful sailor ploughing through the Myrtoan sea with his Cyprian boat.")

There is no attempt to convince us here that there is any interchange between Horace and his interlocutor, and Horace's detachment from his internal audience is clear. This detachment is reinforced by Horace's assertion that his poetic identity separates him from the crowd:

> me gelidum nemus
> nympharumque leves cum Satyris chori
> secernunt populo...   (30–32)

The other types of audience detailed in the discussion of *Sat.* 1.1 above are also found in this ode. The authorial audience is a less obvious outside observer than it was in the satire, but its presence is felt in various satiric nuances and humorous touches throughout the ode. Many of the ironies that appear at various points in the priamel are clearly calculated to attract the authorial eye. For example, the noble career of the soldier (23–25) is devalued by its placement next to the less admirable career of the idler (19–22), war is problematized by its description as *matribus detestata*

(24–25), and the hunter, seeking life-sustaining wild game, shivers in the cold with no thought for his warm, tender wife (25–28).[33] The authorial audience would also have appreciated such touches as the connection Horace draws between the idler in lines 19–22 and himself as he is described at the end of the poem, and the humorous note in the last line, which deflates the pomposity and gives a nod to Virgil's ninth *Eclogue* (line 29).[34]

Finally, Horace recognizes his actual audience in the closing lines of the ode, particularly in the verb *inseres* (35). The subject here could be Maecenas, but could as easily be the Muses or the readers of posterity who are not limited, as each of Horace's specific addressees are, by specific historical, political, and social conditions and who as a group can bring to Horace the many modes of discourse that would cause his poetry to live on and to flower.

Despite the fact that these four types of audience are all present, however, Horace in the *Odes* stands somewhat uneasily removed from them, maintaining the fiction of address while announcing his independence. The differences in stance and tone between *Odes* 1.1 and *Satires* 1.1 are quite striking. Horace opens *Sat.* 1.1 by starting a conversation; midway through the first line he inserts the name of his interlocutor, Maecenas. The language and style here are colloquial and casual, the address to Maecenas downplayed. Although Maecenas begins as the main focus, Horace then goes on to address many other audiences, and the conversation begins to take on a life of its own, addressed to everyone and to no one in particular. There are a multiplicity of voices heard, and Horace seems to be engaged in a genuine conversation with Maecenas and with his other audiences. By the end of the satire, the *putes* in line 121 could refer to the authorial audience as well as to Maecenas, and thus we are left unsure which of his audiences (if any one in particular) Horace has in mind here. The frame of the satire is left incomplete, with *putes* pointing not back to the opening address in line 1 but outside of *Sat.* 1.1 to the authorial audience and to the other satires in Book 1. Thus in *Sat.* 1.1 Maecenas is important as the first person

---

33. See H. James Shey, "The Poet's Progress: Horace, *Ode* 1.1," *Arethusa* 4 (1971) 186–87 for further examples of satiric elements in *Odes* 1.1.

34. See Santirocco, *Unity and Design*, 25.

mentioned and the well-known figure whose attributes and relationship with Horace give added meaning to the subject matter; he is clearly well integrated into the body of the satire. He offers a model of the privileged position taken by the authorial audience and stands in contrast to the internal audience as one who shares Horace's values and friendship and is in sympathy with what Horace desires to achieve. However, he is only one of many participants in the dialogue, and his particularity and importance diminish by the end.

Odes 1.1 proceeds in a very different fashion. Horace remains throughout detached from all of his various audiences except for Maecenas. The grandiose address at the beginning emphasizes Maecenas' importance for Horace and provides a contrast with Horace's detachment from his other audiences. Yet, in the final lines, Horace does not quite return to his patron; rather his personal relationships with his Muse, his patron, his readers, and posterity become melded into one.

Many of these differences in stance and tone between *Odes* 1.1 and *Satires* 1.1 can be attributed to the generic considerations of satire versus lyric poetry. Others are due to the peculiar history of lyric poetry. Horace must have felt certain tensions with the kinds of lyric which he had inherited: monodic (I–You), meditative, and narrative.[35] Unlike the dialogue situation that Horace was striving to recreate in *Sat.* 1.1, *Odes* 1.1 is more univocal, with its roots in the lyric of Sappho, Alcaeus, and Pindar. This was in general a more private kind of poetry but poetry that had been performed for an audience, and Horace had to juggle the essentially paradoxical nature of this verse and find a way to introduce it to a Roman readership unused to such performance poetry. He had to blend together the static and crystallized images and sounds of Roman lyric with the original live, aural conditions under which Greek lyric was performed. Horace found many ways to accomplish this illusion of dynamism: unfinished images and situations that continue to unfold in succeeding poems, varying styles, multiple and ever-changing personas, and dialectical modulations.[36] He also used the constant shifts from

---

35. See W. R. Johnson, *The Idea of Lyric* (Berkeley 1982) 1ff., 123–45.
36. See A. Y. Campbell, *Horace* (London 1924) 5–7, 76–81, 224–28; S. Commager, *The Odes of Horace* (New Haven 1962) 50–58; Pomeroy, 46–47; Johnson, 127–28. See also

one addressee to another, which are more implicit than explicit in *Odes* 1.1, as a means of creating the illusion of dynamic, living poetry. Unlike *Sat.* 1.1, where, in imitation of a discursive conversation, both the voice of the poet himself and the voices of the various audiences are diffused and never quite brought together, *Odes* 1.1 speaks in a single voice with the identity of the poet unified, as lyric demands, and set apart from his patron and other audiences. Maecenas too maintains a unified identity as patron and dedicatee, but he is separated from Horace in a way that he is not in *Sat.* 1.1.

It is puzzling that both of these introductory poems, standing in significant places in their respective collections and obviously considered important by their author, have suffered harsh words of condemnation from the critics. Although *Odes* 1.1 is more clearly programmatic than *Sat.* 1.1,[37] its artistic merit and its structure have been questioned and its praises of Maecenas have been viewed as intrusive and contrived. Fraenkel's statement that "in the greater part of the ode Horace does not say anything especially original" (232) sounds like a compliment compared to Walter Savage Landor's remark: "The worst in the book, excepting the second."[38] Even David West, who praises the poem, says that all the odds are against it since it treats a hackneyed theme and takes on the difficult task of praising other people's enthusiasms.[39]

The weakness of the poem that is most often criticized apart from its lack of coherence is its traditional and hackneyed subject matter. Commentators have wondered why Horace chose to open his carefully elaborated set of poems with one that has for its subject a well-worn theme. We might have expected Horace to open Books 1–3 of the *Odes* with a more original poem, but, as in the case of *Sat.* 1.1, he returns to a theme and form used by many

---

Nietzsche's famous description of Horace's lapidary style: "this mosaic of words in which every word, by sound, by placing, and by meaning, spreads its influence to the right, to the left, and over the whole" (cited by Commager, 50).

37. See Fraenkel, 230 for a list of the verbal correspondences between *Odes* 1.1 and the other odes in Books 1–3. Fraenkel says that the ode is obviously a "real 'overture' to the three books" [of odes].

38. W. S. Landor, "Tibullus and Messala," in *Imaginary Conversations* (1824), reprinted in *The Complete Works of Walter Savage Landor*, ed. T. Earle Welby (New York 1969) vol. 2, 165. For further discussion of Landor's opinions about Horace, see Ruoff, 189–204.

39. D. West, *Reading Horace* (Edinburgh 1967) 78.

of his Greek predecessors. *Odes* 1.1 develops the classic priamel, in which a series of pursuits is listed, each one inferior to that which the writer favors. Such priamels, some with close parallels to Horace, can be found in Sappho, Solon, Pindar, Bacchylides, and Euripides, and Horace himself uses similar catalogues in *Epodes* 2, *Odes* 1.7.1–14 and *Ep.* 1.1.77–82 (the first and last are parodies of a priamel).[40]

There are several reasons why Horace might have chosen to open these *Odes* dedicated to his patron with such a widely used form (and this form in particular). First and more important, he, perhaps more than most poets, is highly conscious of his place in a long poetic tradition, and in fact it is his identity as a poet that becomes his major theme in *Odes* 1.1 and throughout his work. He desires both to pay tribute to and to align himself with the Greek masters of lyric poetry (Pindar, Sappho, and Alcaeus in particular) and to mark himself off as different and Roman.[41] A perfect formulation of these two conflicting desires brought into harmony is the phrase *lyricis vatibus* in 1.1.35. *Lyricus*, a Greek word, reminds the reader of Horace's Greek predecessors, while *vates* is a very Roman word for poet which, unlike the Greek *poeta*, had the additional connotations of priest and prophet, a man with magical powers.[42] This clear statement of an alliance to two different but related traditions is subtly echoed by the subject matter of the priamel, which shows Horace to be one of the list of people whose careers are mentioned in metonymic relationships but also outside of the list, separated from the rest of mankind and protected in his private grove, a special and unique figure.[43]

---

40. For priamels in the Greek authors, see Sappho fr. 16 (L–P); Solon fr. 1.43ff.; Pindar fr. 221 (Snell); Bacc. 10, 14.1ff. (Snell); Eurip. fr. 659 N. See also H. Musurillo, "The Poet's Apotheosis: Horace, *Odes* 1.1," *TAPA* 93 (1962) 235–37 for a discussion of an Egyptian papyrus containing such a vocation catalogue which compares many professions unfavorably to that of scribe.

41. See Santirocco's comments on this aspect of Horace (20–23). He cites contemporary critics such as Harold Bloom and W. Jackson Bate who talk about "the anxiety of influence" and "the burden of the past" (20).

42. See Pomeroy, 42; R. G. M. Nisbet and M. Hubbard, who give references to other similar collocations in Horace's *Odes* (*A Commentary on Horace: Odes Book I* [Oxford 1970] 3); Shey, who says that in this ode Horace "will be unswervingly traditional and at the same time highly individualistic" ("The Poet's Progress," 193).

43. Pomeroy says that the lives portrayed in the priamel in *Odes* 1.1 should be seen as metonymical rather than synecdochal as they usually are (45–46). According to him, Horace does not dismiss the other lives and elevate his as the only type of any value, as most critics think; rather he views his profession as one that has similarities with the others.

Horace's double status both inside and outside of the catalogue is further emphasized by an irregularity in this priamel. A straightforward priamel would have given a list of things that other people desire and privilege; these various alternatives would then be rejected one by one and replaced at the end or climax of the priamel by what the poet determines to be the best or most desirable thing.[44] Horace's priamel is not so straightforward. There are certain similarities between Horace and many of the other types described here (e.g. Horace and the athlete both seek glory, Horace and the small farmer both take delight in their farms), but there is a particular and striking resemblance between Horace and the person described in lines 19–22, who has been called an "idler," a "gentleman of leisure," a "wine drinker," and an "epicurean," *inter alia*:[45]

> est qui nec veteris pocula Massici
> nec partem solido demere de die
> spernit, nunc viridi membra sub arbuto
> stratus, nunc ad aquae lene caput sacrae.   (19–22)

The importance of this vignette is marked by its position in the exact center of the poem and by the echo of *sunt quos* from line 3 in *est qui* (19). Although any identification between this character and the poet upsets the formal arrangement of the priamel, we cannot ignore the similarity between the man who whiles away the day in pursuit of *otium* under a tree and Horace.[46] Reckford remarks that the very language here reminds us of the Horace we see in other odes and suggests that, whereas lines 19–22 reveal the private side of Horace, lines 29–34 show us Horace's public persona.[47] Dunn explores an even closer connection, saying that the "idler" in lines 19–22 is Horace and that the language is

---

44. For a discussion of the priamel form, see Wm. H. Race, *The Classical Priamel from Homer to Boethius*, Mnemosyne Supp. 74 (Leiden 1982) esp. 122–23 on Horace *Odes* 1.1. For other interpretations of Horace's use of the priamel in *Odes* 1.1, see K. Vretska, "Horatius, Carm. 1.1," *Hermes* 99 (1971) 323–35; A. Setaioli, "Il proemio dei Carmina oraziani," *Atti e Memorie dell'Accademia Toscana di Scienze e Lettere* 38 (1973) 50–59.

45. "Idler," see F. M. Dunn, "Horace's Sacred Spring (*Ode* 1.1)," *Latomus* 48 (1989) 98, 104, and passim; "gentleman of leisure," see Commager, 331; "wine drinker," see J. V. Cody, *Horace and Callimachean Aesthetics* (Brussels 1976) 53; "l'epicureo," see A. Ghiselli, "Lettura dell' *Ode* 1.1 di Orazio," *Lingua e Stile* 7 (1972) 117.

46. See Race, 122 n. 13, who tries to explain away the potential violation of the priamel form by saying that the indolence of the man described in lines 19–22 contrasts with the nobler aspirations of an intellectual and artistic man such as Horace.

47. K. J. Reckford, *Horace* (New York 1969) 15–16.

meant to suggest poetic inspiration (*ad aquae lene caput sacrae*, 22) and Epicurean, contemplative values.[48] If we accept this identification or even a partial identification, we again have Horace painting a double portrait of himself as an idler and poet, inside and outside the catalogue, part of the priamel (object) and creator of it (subject).

The priamel is important, then, both for its form, which links Horace to his Greek predecessors and yet has unique Roman elements, and also for its content, which portrays Horace as one of mankind and yet as set off from other men. Its paradoxical gestures of inclusion and exclusion parallel the ode's relationship to its audiences as the poet participates with the various audiences but also maintains a position detached from them at the same time.

A second reason for using the priamel is that it provides an unmistakable reference back to *Sat.* 1.1 and to the person addressed there, Maecenas.[49] *Odes* 1.1 and *Sat.* 1.1 are closely linked by their opening and closing addresses to Maecenas and by their subject, an occupational catalogue. The types of occupations listed vary somewhat (e.g. *Odes* 1.1 adds a hunter and politician to the list given in the satire), and the rhetorical strategy is different (greed and discontent do not figure large in the ode), but the similarities are striking.[50] In the most general terms, Horace indicates in the *Odes* a continuing interest in the philosophy that dominates many of the satires, particularly *Sat.* 1.1–3. In the *Satires* Horace shows a concern with philosophy and poetics but keeps them separated to a larger degree than in the *Odes*, where they achieve a closer synthesis.[51] In *Odes* 1.1 Horace, the *vates*,

48. Dunn, 97–109, esp. 108–9.
49. Both poems start with an explicit reference to Maecenas and end with an address to a second-person addressee, whom I take to be Maecenas, although he has now been transformed into a general reader or "the ideal second person singular of the future" (Pomeroy, 37–38, 47–48 n. 8). See also Johnson, 127, who calls the formal addressee of Horace's poems "a metaphor for the readers"; Santirocco, 21; my discussion above of *Sat.* 1.1.
50. For similarities between *Odes* 1.1 and *Sat.* 1.1, see Shey, 190–93; Santirocco, 16–17; Musurillo, 230–33; for the discontinuity in tone between the *Satires* and the *Odes*, see Johnson, who discusses Horace "the suave satirist" being replaced in the *Odes* by "an arrogant, affected stranger" (129).
51. See Zetzel, "Poetics of Patronage," who claims that Book 1 of the *Satires* "shows a clearly delineated progress from...philosophy to literary criticism" (94). Although this may be partly true, I would not put Horace's two abiding concerns in quite such discrete compartments.

takes a clearly defined moral and ethical position in enumerating satirically the limitations of the various pursuits and in so doing provides formal, verbal, rhetorical, and generic continuity with the *Satires* and especially with *Sat.* 1.1.[52]

A third and related reason for Horace's use of the priamel is that, by the time of the composition of the *Odes*, Maecenas' name was beginning to be identified with such a catalogue of occupations. This identification becomes for Horace almost a signature or *sphragis*.[53] The priamel, an implicit *recusatio* which rejects other occupations in favor of the composition of poetry, blends well with the dedication to Horace's patron, who has made his life as a poet possible and whose continued benefactions Horace seeks.

A fourth reason for the use of this classic form is Horace's usual desire, so consonant with the persona he presents throughout his poetry, to mock gently his own pretensions and ambitions. By including himself in a group of others with somewhat questionable occupations (while he is separating himself from them), making it clear that he needs the assistance of Maecenas, the gods, and the Muses to accomplish his task, and ending with the comic vision of himself bumping his head on the stars when he arrives at that exalted position, he preempts and blunts any possible criticism of his arrogance and allows Maecenas a major role in his development.[54] His demeanor here, in a poem which was surely written after Books 1–3 of the *Odes* were completed but which maintains the fiction of prior composition, had to be different from that displayed in his final, climactic poem, *Odes* 3.30. The rhetorical stance to be taken in 1.1 was a difficult one and had to be treated with the utmost delicacy, and the role to be given to Maecenas was particularly problematic.[55]

Thus the use of the priamel in *Odes* 1.1 serves both to highlight Maecenas' significance and to parallel Horace's important and difficult relationships with his audiences in the ode. Although the

---

52. For Horace's ethical viewpoint and his synthesis of poetry and philosophy, see Cody, 48–53, and the bibliography cited in n. 18 (p. 53); for the moral continuity of the *Satires* and *Odes*, see Santirocco, 17–18, 155; Shey, 190–93.

53. See Zetzel, "Poetics of Patronage," 94. *Sat.* 1.1, *Odes* 1.1, and *Ep.* 1.1 are all dedicated to Maecenas and all contain priamels. See Shey, 193.

54. See West, 79.

55. For a good discussion of the status of *Odes* 1.1 as prefatory and yet epilogic chronologically, see Pomeroy, 36–37.

priamel serves the function of marking *Odes* 1.1 as programmatic and dedicatory, neither the ode nor *Sat.* 1.1 is programmatic in any conventional sense. Rather, the two poems act as guides and introductions to Horace's characteristic method of shifting audiences frequently within and between poems. In *Sat.* 1.1 and *Odes* 1.1 Horace creates several different audiences: the primary audience (Maecenas), the internal audience, the authorial audience, and the actual audience. Although the audiences are used in very different ways, they perform the same general functions in these two poems. From each of his audiences Horace expects to elicit different responses, and it is through attention to these audiences that Horace's reader perceives all the various dimensions of his work. Horace uses his opening poems to begin to characterize these audiences, including his patron, in order to create a persona and an artistic identity for himself through the relationships that evolve between poet and listener/reader.[56] Horace casts Maecenas in several roles, first as addressee and dedicatee and later (particularly in the satire but also in the ode) as various other types of audience. Horace's interactions with and separations from Maecenas allow the poet to be perceived as both creator and created element and to have, as Maecenas does, both a unified and a multidimensional, constantly unfolding identity. The opening poems of *Satires* Book 1 and *Odes* Books 1–3 are programmatic and uniquely Horatian, not because of their content or detail, but because Horace reveals in them a special model of the technique he will use in his shifting changes of address and thereby introduces us to the various audiences through whose eyes he will develop and be defined as a poet and an artist.[57]

56. See Pomeroy, 36–37 and 46–47 on the necessity of reading Horace as an open-ended text which is continually revised as the reader receives new information from later poems.
57. I would like to thank the referees for *Yale Classical Studies* for their helpful comments and criticisms.

An aristocracy of virtue: Seneca on the beginnings of wisdom

THOMAS N. HABINEK

In the matter of birth, as in other matters, Roman society of the early Principate exhibits a tension between ideology and practice. Implicit in the Roman notion of an *ordo senatorius*, into which members are inscribed at birth, or in the distinctions between slave and free, *Romanus* and *municeps*, is a premium on beginnings, of self, family, and nation. At the same time, the relative frequency of movement across what might appear to be rigid boundaries (slave/free, decurion/equestrian/senatorial) weakened the authority of beginnings to the advantage of achievement, connections, and luck. This tension, which might have been expected to dissolve with the transition from one social system to another, was in fact perpetuated by the political stagnation and retrogressive modes of acculturation characteristic of the era. Politics of the period can be described as an equilibrium of balanced antagonisms between princeps, aristocrats, and arrivistes, while education promised social mobility to those most skilled at manipulating the symbols of an ossified cultural tradition.

It is in this context of a competition or tension between the age-old authority of birth and the birth of new forms of authorization that the Senecan invitation to begin to live (*incipere vivere*) must be understood.[1] The readers of Seneca's dialogues and letters – like virtually all readers in the Roman world – would have been members of the economic elites, and thus benefited from certain aspects of the fixity and stratification of the Roman social system.[2] Yet as ambitious adolescents,[3] or self-made adults,[4] his audience

---

1. *Brev.* 3.5; *Ep.* 13.16–17; 23.9–10. Related to the idea of beginning to live is the claim that we are not born wise or innocent, but make ourselves so: e.g. *Clem.* 1.6.4; *Ira* 2.10.
2. W. V. Harris, *Ancient Literacy* (Cambridge, MA, 1989), 175–284.
3. Quint. *IO* 10.1.126. Tac. *Ann.* 12.8 offers general confirmation of Seneca's popularity.
4. M. Griffin, *Seneca: A Philosopher in Politics* (Oxford 1976) describes Lucilius, Seneca's most frequent addressee, as a "self-made eques" (p. 91) and (more tentatively) Aebutius

could be expected to appreciate and capitalize on opportunities to break free of the limits of birth and surpass the achievements of their predecessors. By posing the challenge of beginning to live, Seneca confirms and appropriates the very power that authorizes the reader's privileged existence while at the same time holding forth the promise of a life that transcends the limitations of each reader's beginning.

Roman society's paradoxical approach to beginnings – as locus of privilege and problem to be overcome – is reflected in Senecan beginnings variously conceived. Whether we regard the "beginning" of a Senecan treatise as its origin in the literary and cultural tradition, its intervention in the lives of its readers, or simply the words with which it opens, the Senecan beginning manifests its ambivalence with regard to its own powers of authorization. Ultimately, as we shall see, Seneca seeks to escape the problem of beginnings in his own era by positing an ur-beginning, a beginning of beginnings, that authorizes and sustains precisely the contradictory project on which he is engaged. But for the present it will be useful to examine in as much detail as space permits the Senecan beginning in its literary, cultural, and textual instantiations.

The literary point of departure for the Senecan philosophical project is the upper-class Roman tradition of exhortation.[5] By writing in Latin, by directly addressing friends and relations, by posing practical moral dilemmas, and exhorting to new forms of behavior, Seneca situates his treatises in the hortatory tradition

---

Liberalis, addressee of *De Beneficiis*, as "a provincial who rose through the ranks quickly" (p. 456). Other addressees include Annaeus Serenus who served as praefectus vigilum; Seneca's brother Novatus, of senatorial rank; Seneca's father-in-law, Pompeius Paulinus, who reached the rank of praefectus annonae; his mother Helvia; Marcia the daughter of the senatorial historian Cremutius Cordus; Polybius the freedman of Claudius; and the young emperor Nero. The addressees were no doubt of loftier status than the average reader, but the latter would certainly have been a member of the educated, propertied, urban elites.

5. I know of no single comprehensive work on the Roman tradition of exhortation. Helpful on aspects of the topic are the following: J. André, *La philosophie à Rome* (Paris 1977) 40ff.; H. Cancik, *Untersuchungen zu Senecas epistulae morales*, Spudasmata 18 (Hildesheim 1967); S. Dill, *Roman Society from Nero to Marcus Aurelius* (London 1904) 289–333; A. Guillemin, *Pline et la vie littéraire de son temps*, Collection des études latines 4 (Paris 1929) chapter 1; I. Hadot, *Seneca und die griechisch-römische Tradition der Seelenleitung*, Quellen und Studien zur Geschichte der Philosophie 13 (Berlin 1969). See also T. N. Habinek, "Greeks and Romans in Book 12 of Quintilian," *Ramus* 16 (1987) 192–202 and "Science and Tradition in Aeneid 6," *HSCP* 92 (1989) 223–55.

and thereby claims for his own texts the authority of that rich and variegated mode of discourse. His treatises lay claim to the authority of parental advice, mentor's guidance, national and familial exempla, and self-interrogation in the presence of intimates – all conventional aristocratic modes of control over thought, word, and action, in Rome as in other traditional societies.[6] The social function of such exhortation is both to transmit the dominant ideology in readily comprehensible form and to correlate specific instances of ethical choice with the general principles it prescribes. Its criterion of validation is neither truth nor beauty, but effect; hence in Seneca's case it is the origin of his project in the tradition of exhortation that legitimizes the relentless flow of aphorisms, the shifts of stylistic register, and the logical contradictions characteristic of his works.

Even the arrogance of self-advertisement, damaging to Seneca's later reputation, in ancient as in modern times, has its beginning in his assumption of the hortatory mantle. If effect is the measure of advice, where better to seek it than in the person of the adviser? The Epicureans understood this well, with their promulgation and circulation of letters of the master. Seneca acknowledges it in his identification of the source of authority in Demetrius the Cynic ("not a teacher but a witness of the truth is he")[7] and in his reference to the enhancement of consolatory authority to be derived from consoling oneself.[8] Thus the use of self as exemplum in Seneca's philosophical works, especially his letters, is authorized by the literary tradition in which he writes. At the same time, the literary imperative toward self-exemplification is supplemented by the social and cultural imperative to match, even outstrip, one's predecessors.[9] Hence Seneca's claim to equal Epicurus in talent and influence,[10] the need to embrace and thereby restrict

6. See, for example, the parainetic oratory of the Aztecs, discussed by D. Abbott, "The Ancient Word: Rhetoric in Aztec Culture," *Rhetorica* 5 (1987) 251–64.
7. *Ep.* 20.9; cf. 62.3.
8. *deinde plus habiturum me auctoritatis non dubitabam ad excitandam te, si prior ipse consurrexissem* (*Helv.* 1.1).
9. An old feature of aristocratic culture (see Habinek, "Science and Tradition" [above n. 5], 237). This drive to outstrip one's predecessors is transferred by the Romans to competition in the cultural arena: see the brief discussion in Habinek, "Greeks and Romans" (above n. 5), 236–38.
10. *Ep.* 21. Throughout the early letters Seneca calls attention to Epicurus as a way of assimilating the philosopher's influence to his own as well as a means of signalling generic

Demetrius,[11] the competitive urge, in the final texts, to advertise familiarity with the least compelling aspects of the Ciceronian exemplum.[12] The beginning of Seneca's project in the Roman tradition of exhortation is a circumstance whose presence is felt everywhere: no feature of the treatises ever quite escapes it.

Yet escape is precisely what the text seeks. By writing in Latin instead of Greek and by opting for exhortation, Seneca misses out on the opportunity to participate in the technical debate of specialists. The hortatory mode itself, which Seneca clearly differentiates from the exposition of dogma, does not readily lend itself to the clear exposition of technical topics. Yet, in numerous passages, from the meditation on time in *De Brevitate Vitae* to the analysis of the corporeality of the good in letter 106, Seneca struggles to develop a dogmatic approach within a hortatory framework.[13] The tensions and fault lines in Seneca's prose, sometimes ascribed to the drama of the soul's encounter with evil,[14] have a more mundane explanation as the predictable outcome of the writer's struggle against the authority of his own text's beginnings, a struggle that (not accidentally) parallels that

competition with antiquity's most famous writer of philosophical letters. On Seneca's assimilation of Epicurus' teachings and authority, the bibliography is extensive. Particularly helpful is W. Schmid, "Eine falsche Epikurdeutung Senecas und seine Praxis der erbauenden Lesung," *Acme* 8 (1955) 119–29. Seneca's attempted assimilation of Epicurus is probably not simply of antiquarian or aesthetic interest, but a part of Roman Stoicism's attempt to insist on the totality of its own explanatory (and hence political) power. For the extent of Epicureanism in the Principate, see P. Innocenti, "Per una storia dell'epicureismo nei primi secoli dell'era volgare: temi e problemi," *Rivista critica di storia della filosofia* 27 (1972) 123–47. On the connection between explanatory and political power see B. D. Shaw, "The Divine Economy: Stoicism as Ideology," *Latomus* 44 (1985) 16–54.

11. Seneca's references to Demetrius are extensive, but consist chiefly of brief citations or allusions. He treats him as something of a freak whose distance from normal Roman social behavior is emphasized in order to keep the logical consequences of carrying out Seneca's teaching from becoming apparent.

12. At *Ep.* 21.4ff. Seneca contrasts by implication the true glory he offers Lucilius with the political glory sought by Cicero. At *Ep.* 23.1 and *Ep.* 67.1 he criticizes epistolary commonplaces of the sort found in Cicero's letters. At *Ep.* 97 he quotes an extensive passage of *Ad Atticum* 1.16.5 as evidence of the corruption of the times and at *Ep.* 118.2 he specifically objects to Cicero's tendency to write whatever pops into his head (*quod in buccam venerit*). The allusions to Cicero would have been especially functional as part of a campaign of self-glorification if the letters to Atticus had just become widely available. For publication in the Neronian period see D. R. Shackleton Bailey, *Cicero's Letters to Atticus* (Cambridge 1965) 1.59–73; opposed by A. Setaioli, "On the Date of Publication of Cicero's Letters to Atticus," *SO* 51 (1976) 105–20.

13. Note for example the use of the terms *in partes*, *argumenta diducere*, and *probem*, introducing the expository section of the *De Brevitate Vitae* (10.1).

14. A. Traina, *Lo stile "drammatico" del filosofo Seneca* (Bologna 1978); M. Bellincioni, *Educazione alla sapientia in Seneca* (Brescia 1977).

Seneca on the beginnings of wisdom

of Seneca's insecure yet upwardly mobile readers. Seneca's treatises seek to maintain the privileges of their inception while denying the limitations that follow therefrom.

Given the inherent contradictions of Roman society and the ambivalence Seneca reveals towards the literary form he adopts, we should not be surprised to learn that the new beginning he proposes for his readers is equally ambiguous with regard to the social and cultural environment in which it is created. As Edward Said has observed, virtually all beginnings contain elements of that which they intend to disrupt or replace.

It is, however, very difficult to begin with a wholly new start. Too many old habits, loyalties, and pressures inhibit the substitution of a novel enterprise for an established one. When the Old Testament God chooses to begin the world again he does it with Noah; things have been going very badly, and since it is his prerogative, God wishes a new beginning. Yet it is interesting that God himself does not begin completely from nothing. Noah and the ark comprise a piece of the old world initiating the new world.[15]

What God chooses, Seneca cannot avoid: the creation of a new life out of the materials of the old. A life that purports to be egalitarian, carefree, and at ease is in fact fashioned out of the political, aesthetic, and economic anxieties afflicting the very audience Seneca seeks to liberate. Although these anxieties are apparent throughout Seneca's treatises, our focus here will be on their urgent and intrusive expression at the (literal) commencement of Senecan texts.

The standard rhetorical strategy of the opening of a Senecan treatise – the claim to privileged knowledge – contradicts the repeated assertion that wisdom or virtue is available to all.[16] In *De Providentia*, the cause of the gods (which Seneca will plead) is juxtaposed with the brief developed by doubting mortals.[17] At the outset of *De Brevitate Vitae*, the greater part of mortals (*maior pars mortalium*) reveals its ethical ineptitude, in implicit contrast to the knowledgeable author.[18] In *De Vita Beata*, Gallio is informed that while all men desire the good life, they are blind to the means of

---

15. E. Said, *Beginnings: Intention and Method* (New York 1985) 34.
16. Virtue available to all: *Ep.* 44.3, 66.3; *VB* 24.3; *Ben.* 3.18.1, 3.28.1–3 etc.
17. *manente lite...causam deorum* (*Prov.* 1.1).
18. *Brev.* 1.1–4, where the greater part of mortals is said to include even noble men (*clarorum virorum*) and the philosopher Aristotle.

achieving it[19] – the implication being that Seneca and Gallio are exempt from the company of the ethically sightless. Life, the passage continues, is not a simple country byway which anyone can traverse with ease, but a well-traveled highway whose very popularity is its danger. Along it moves the crowd, leaderless as sheep, following rumor this way and that until their journey turns into a stampede in which each is led to destruction by others, and in turn destroys those around him. In their behavior the masses of humanity simply repeat the political folly of the electoral assemblies who are surprised to hear the names of the candidates they have elected. Reliance on majority opinion, the reader is reminded, is the logic of the lowest in society.[20] Seneca and Gallio seek what is best (*optimum*)[21] and look forward to the fulfillment of the aristocratic dream of secure possession of eternal well-being (*possessione felicitatis aeternae*).[22] The distinction between the stampeding crowd and the followers of Seneca, soon to be secure in their permanent estate, is both a slur against the critics who prompt Seneca to defend his moral authority in the second half of the *De Vita Beata* and an assimilation of the philosophical life to the political prejudices of the rich and high-born. Virtue may create its own nobility; but it is a nobility that mimics the old nobility's strategies of exclusion and contempt.

In a similar vein, the obsession with orderliness and decorum revealed at the outset of *De Ira* runs contrary to the numerous injunctions elsewhere against concern with appearance and style.[23] Anger, we learn at the commencement of the treatise devoted to its exclusion, is to be condemned because it violates the aristocratic norms of decorum and taste.[24] It cannot control itself (*inpotens sui est*),[25] forgets decorum (*decoris oblita*), ignores relations (*necessitudinum immemor*), persists beyond reason in its undertakings (*in quod coepit pertinax et intenta, rationi consiliisque praeclusa*), is set in motion by trivialities (*vanis agitata causis*), and is unfit for the investigation of the just and true (*ad dispectum aequi verique*

---

19. *Vivere, Gallio frater, omnes beate volunt, sed ad pervidendum quid sit quod beatam vitam efficiat caligant (VB* 1.1).   20. *argumentum pessimi turba est (VB* 2.1).

21. *VB* 2.2.   22. *VB* 2.2.

23. E.g. *Ep.* 40, *Ep.* 52.14, *Ep.* 114. Note the paradoxical expression at *Ep.* 100.4: *oratio sollicita philosophum non decet*. How can one achieve decorum without being *sollicitus*?

24. On decorum as a process of exclusion see E. Oliensis, "Canidia, Canicula, and the Decorum of Horace's *Epodes*," *Arethusa* 24 (1991) 107–38.

25. This and the quotations that follow are from *De Ira* 1.1.2–4.

inhabilis). The angry man is recognizable by his hideous appearance, which Seneca catalogues and anatomizes for the reader's edification. Gleaming eyes, red face, quivering lips, clenched teeth, bristling hair, forced breathing, crackling joints, groans and bellows, spluttering speech, pounding fists, and stamping feet render the *iratus* deformed as well as detestable.[26]

Only secondarily is the issue of anger's destructiveness raised, and then with a recurrent emphasis on its danger to the upper echelons of society. Anger causes murder and poisoning – and the auctioning of goods of leading citizens (*principum sub civili hasta capita venalia*).[27] Anger destroys the notable foundations of noble cities, creates wastelands, and turns mighty generals into examples of bad fortune (*memoriae proditos duces mali exempla fati*).[28] When directed against large groups it has led to the slaughter of assemblies, the butchery of the plebs, and the promiscuous condemnation of whole populations (*in perniciem promiscuam totos populos capitis damna⟨tos⟩*).[29] It is anger's potential to destroy order, dissolve boundaries, and trample on hierarchies that makes it peculiarly dangerous and singularly inappropriate for members of the aristocracy. Thus, in the very act of condemning the reckless violence of Rome's dominant classes, Seneca reasserts their claim to privileged treatment.

In the area of economics, Seneca's evasion of the tension between birth and achievement is betrayed in a particularly spectacular manner. Philosophical *otium*, although proffered to the reader as a way of avoiding the risks and losses inherent in social and economic competition, merely opens space for re-enacting the property owner's anxiety over loss of capital and for redeploying the contradiction between personal acquisition and aristocratic inheritance. From the opening of the collection of moral letters, Lucilius is commanded to lay claim to his birthright (*vindica te tibi*)[30] and to seize control of the one possession that is truly his, namely time (*omnia aliena sunt, tempus tantum nostrum est*).[31] Yet to do so he must involve himself in the business of wisdom (*sapientiae negotium*),[32] in the calculation of profits and losses (*ratio mihi constat impensae*).[33] No matter how diligently the *proficiens*

---

26. nescias utrum magis detestabile vitium sit an deforme (*Ira* 1.1.4).   27. *Ira* 1.2.1.
28. *Ira* 1.2.2.   29. *Ira* 1.3.1.   30. *Ep.* 1.1.   31. *Ep.* 1.3.
32. *Ep.* 85.37; cf. 35.1, 68.9, 75.7.   33. *Ep.* 1.4.

works, he cannot make headway against the dissipation of time's capital. He is reduced to poverty in spite of himself.[34] The most he can hope for is an augmentation of philosophical or ethical capital through the creation of memorable sayings.[35] Even then, the capital will not be his to enjoy, for like a good paterfamilias he must leave behind more than he has received so that others will be able to enjoy the privileges of inheritance.[36]

Even the process of giving and taking advice is implicated in the revised economic order of the early Principate. What Cicero regards as an essential characteristic of aristocratic friendship (the unfettered exchange of honest advice)[37] is commodified in Seneca's relationship with Lucilius. "Here's a little something for the plus side."[38] "I owe you another installment."[39] "Here's my payment for this letter."[40] Financial obligation replaces social. In the course of exercising his own prerogative as retired statesman, cultural leader, and *amicus maior* to Lucilius, Seneca contradicts the aristocratic standards by which that prerogative was initially assigned.

Sexuality offers a final perspective from which to explore the Senecan text's failure to liberate itself from its cultural origins and the strategies Seneca employs to mask the dependence of his new life on the material and psychological make-up of the old. For the Romans birth established a dividing line between the sexually privileged and the sexually compelled, with freeborn men on one side and women and slaves on the other.[41] The special treatment of two marginal or transitional groups – freeborn youth and freedmen – reinforced the central divide: young *ingenui*, who as *pueri* might be mistaken for legitimate targets of sexual aggression, were protected by the identifying *bulla*, while freedmen, slaves by birth but free in status, could jokingly be described as performing sexual duties for their former masters.[42] Yet just as in the realms

---

34. *causas paupertatis meae reddam* (*Ep.* 1.4).   35. *Ep.* 64.8–10; cf. *Ep.* 52.7–8.
36. *mihi ista adquisita, mihi laborata sunt. Sed agamus bonum patrem familiae, faciamus ampliora quae accepimus; maior ista hereditas a me ad posteros transeat* (*Ep.* 64.7).
37. The role of exhortation in friendship is implied from the very setting of the *Laelius*. More particularly, see sections 17 and 88.
38. *lucellum* (*Ep.* 5.7).   39. *diurnam tibi mercedulam debeo* (*Ep.* 6.7).
40. *pro hac epistula dependendum* (*Ep.* 8.7).
41. E. Cantarella, *Secondo natura: La bisessualità nel mondo antico*, Nuova biblioteca di cultura 289 (Rome 1988) 129ff.
42. Sen. *Contr.* 4pr. 10; cf. the discussion by A. Richlin, *The Garden of Priapus* (New Haven 1983) 220–26, esp. n. 11.

of economics, politics, and aesthetics, the transitional status of Roman society can be seen as authorizing new forms of behavior, and creating alternative modes of evaluation to those established by a hereditary aristocracy, so in the area of sex roles and sexual behavior, the possibility of a non-aristocrat's rise to power through sexual services[43], the expanded opportunities for female participation in the economy and in court politics,[44] and the adoption on the part of the tyrants Caligula and Nero of sexually subversive practices such as cross-dressing, incest, and homosexual marriage[45] created, at least at the upper levels of society, a new type of conflict between birth and achievement.

Neither Seneca's text nor his reader escapes enmeshment in the sexual tensions and cross-currents of the era. In a series of passages, the sexual prerogatives of freeborn males and the *verecundia*, or reserve, designed to veil those privileges from the less fortunate, are taken for granted as essential components of the Stoic dispensation. Thus, the opening sentence of the *De Constantia Sapientis* informs us that there is as much difference between Stoics and other philosophers as there is between males and females (*tantum inter Stoicos, Serene, et ceteros sapientiam professos interesse quantum inter feminas et mares*).[46] Each group is useful, but one was born to command, the other to obey (*altera pars ad obsequendum, altera imperio nata sit*). Some wise men seek to flatter and cajole (*molliter et blande*), like slave doctors (*domestici et familiares medici*); the Stoics, in contrast, take the manly approach (*virilem ingressi viam*), avoiding the pleasures of digression. The differentiation here, expressed in the sexual code words *molliter*, *blande*, and *virilis*,

---

43. E.g. Tigellinus, as described at Tac. *Hist.* 1.72. This motive is imputed to Messalina's "husband" Silius at Tac. *Ann.* 11.28. Caligula is said to have seduced Ennia Naevia in order to have influence over her husband (Suet. *Cal.* 12). Mnester seems to have gained influence over Caligula this way (Suet. *Cal.* 36 and 55). Strategic seduction figured in the careers of Sejanus (Dio 57.19.5 and Tac. *Ann.* 4.1.2, 4.3.2f.) and perhaps Seneca (cf. the charges of adultery with Agrippina). Even if such charges are mere malicious gossip, the possibility of their being taken seriously points to the uncertainty concerning the enforceability of the aristocratic code of sexual ethics.

44. E. Cantarella, *Pandora's Daughters*, tr. M. Fant (Baltimore and London 1987) 135ff. While Roman women played an important role in the politics of the late Republic, the elevation of a single household to supreme power expanded the opportunities for influence on the part of aristocratic women.

45. The charges are scattered throughout the accounts of the period by Dio, Suetonius, and Tacitus. For an analysis of the political implications of the emperors' untraditional sexual behavior, see M. Cazenave and R. Auguet, *Les empereurs fous* (Paris 1979).

46. This and the quotations that follow are taken from *Cons. Sap.* 1.1.

plays upon the contrasting sexual behaviors expected of the *cinaedi*, or sex-slaves of the Roman household, and the businesslike Roman *pater*.[47] So too, in *De Providentia*, Seneca reminds the reader that slaves are admired for their sexual forwardness (*licentia, audacia*), sons for their modesty and self-restraint (*modestia, disciplina*).[48] The women who are lucky enough to be beneficiaries of Seneca's advice owe their good fortune either to the inescapable bonds of motherhood (i.e., Helvia), or, in Marcia's case, to distance from the weakness of womanly spirit and a long-proven hardness (*exploratum iam robur animi*).[49]

The discussion of Seneca's transferral of contemporary economic concerns into the new life of the Stoic *proficiens* alluded to the commodification of the relationship between author and reader. In the sexual realm, this conflict between the ideology expressed by the text and the behavior demanded of the reader encountering it becomes acute, and involves not just the internal reader (i.e., the addressee of the treatise or letter), but the external reader as well (i.e., the audience, ancient and modern). To put it simply, while proclaiming the values of conventional upper-class male sexuality Seneca in fact sets in operation a mode of reading that requires the reader to be an accomplice in his own violation – a humiliating state of affairs according to Roman sexual ethics.[50]

Here is Seneca's account of his own encounter with a text of Lucilius:

Librum tuum quem mihi promiseras accepi et tamquam lecturus ex commodo adaperui ac tantum degustare volui; deinde blanditus est ipse ut procederem longius. Qui quam disertus fuerit ex hoc intellegas licet: levis mihi visus est, cum esset nec mei nec tui corporis, sed qui primo aspectu aut Titi Livii aut Epicuri posset videri. Tanta autem dulcedine me tenuit et traxit ut illum sine ulla dilatione perlegerim. Sol me invitabat, fames admonebat, nubes minabantur; tamen exhausi totum. Non tantum delectatus sed gavisus sum. Quid ingenii iste habuit, quid animi! Dicerem "quid impetus!" si interquievisset, si ⟨ex⟩ intervallo surrexisset; nunc non fuit impetus sed tenor. Compositio virilis et sancta; nihilominus interveniebat dulce illud et loco lene. Grandis, erectus es:

---

47. On the behavior expected of *cinaedi*, see J. Colin, "Juvenal, les baladins et les rétiaires d'après le manuscrit d'Oxford," *Atti della Accademia delle Scienze di Torino*, Classe di scienze morali, storiche e filologiche 87 (1952–53) 315–85.

48. *Prov.* 1.6. 49. *Marc.* 1.1.

50. On the shame associated with being penetrated and, worse, with enjoying it, see the evidence collected by W. A. Krenkel, "Fellatio and irrumatio," *Wissenschaftliche Zeitschrift der Wilhelm-Pieck-Universität Rostock* 29 (1980) 77–88.

hoc te volo tenere, sic ire. Fecit aliquid et materia; ideo eligenda est fertilis, quae capiat ingenium, quae incitet.

(*Ep.* 46.1–2)

I received your book as you had promised me, and I opened it at leisure with the intention of reading it. I wanted just to take a little taste, but it so charmed me that I decided to go further. Very skillful it was, as you can tell from this: its delicacy – not like your body or mine – made me think at first glance that it belonged to Livy or Epicurus. But then with such sweetness it took control of me and drew me on that I read it all the way through without taking a break. The sun called, hunger admonished, clouds threatened; and still I swallowed it whole. I wasn't just pleased – I was overjoyed. What talent it had, what spirit! I would say "what thrust", if it had ever quieted down, ever risen up after taking a break. But this wasn't thrust, it was endurance. Your way of fitting things together was manly and determined; yet still somehow charming and at times even gentle. You're big, you're taut:[51] stay that way, keep at it. And the subject matter had something to do with it too. Make sure you pick a fertile topic, one that will captivate and stimulate that talent of yours.

A remarkable passage. The writer begins as the controller, the subject of active verbs, the one who explores a new text at his convenience, and determines to sample only a portion. The text itself is smooth (*levis*), like a beardless boy, not like the mature and rugged Seneca and Lucilius. Then somehow the tables are turned, the controller becomes the controlled (note the switch to accusative *me* and the passive *delectatus*); the only action left for him is to swallow it whole, drink it all down. Yet far from being humiliated by his passivity, Seneca rejoices in what he has encountered – the force, the endurance that take him by surprise. Lucilius is congratulated on a job well done, and offered tips on preparing for the next encounter. Seneca the reader is not only penetrated by Lucilius the writer, but becomes a willing accomplice in the continuation and repetition of that act of intrusion.[52]

In the passage just quoted, the sexually subversive nature of the Senecan enterprise is muted by ascription of passivity to the author himself in the uncharacteristic role of reader. But can we

51. For the connotation of *grande*, cf. *Ep.* 92.35, where Maecenas is said to have had a genius that was *grande et virile* – if only prosperity hadn't undressed him: *habuit enim ingenium et grande et virile, nisi illud secunda discinxissent*.

52. On reading and penetration, see J. Svenbro, *Phrasikleia: anthropologie de la lecture en Grèce ancienne* (Paris 1988).

doubt that the same process is initiated when an unsuspecting reader begins a Senecan text? *Arma virumque, Cynthia prima, Aeneadum genetrix* the poets sing, fashioning an external reality, access to which authorizes the poet to continue. Cicero, too, imagines a world beyond the intercourse of writer and reader, one peopled with the likes of Q. Mucius augur,[53] resonant with the voices of Atticus, Quintus, and Marcus himself,[54] in which the intrusion of the author's voice is cause for apology.[55] Senecan openings, in contrast, are invasive and unmediated: they situate the reader in a conversation already ongoing and refer to a world outside that defined by speaker and interlocutor only to deny its claim to validity.

Consider the beginning of the *De Providentia*:

Quaesisti a me, Lucili, quid ita, si providentia mundus ageretur, multa bonis viris mala acciderent. Hoc commodius in contextu operis redderetur, cum praeesse universis providentiam probaremus et interesse nobis deum; sed quoniam a toto particulam revelli placet et unam contradictionem manente lite integra solvere, faciam rem non difficilem, causam deorum agam.

You have inquired of me, Lucilius, why it is, if the universe is directed by providence, that many evils befall good men. This would more appropriately be considered in the context of a work in which we could prove that providence presides over everything and that god is involved in our affairs. But since it is pleasing to pluck one small portion from the whole, and to resolve a single issue while leaving the rest of the brief intact, I will accomplish no difficult task, I will plead the cause of the gods.

Proclamation of the interlocutor's confidence in the author; clear articulation of a problem; implied dismissal of alternative solutions: such rhetorical strategies we might expect of any moral exhorter, ancient or modern, and can find paralleled throughout the Senecan corpus. More striking here is the absolute irrelevance of the external reader to description of the project at hand. It is Lucilius' question and Seneca's answer that together provide the opportunity for and set the limits to the discourse that is to follow. As if to advertise this insouciance with respect to the reader, Seneca employs the impersonal verb *placet* (it is pleasing) without explicitly mentioning whose pleasure is served by the restriction of

---

53. *Laelius* 1.1.   54. *Leg.* 1.1.   55. *Fin.* 1.1.

the treatise to one portion (*particula*) of a whole (*totum*).⁵⁶ Whereas conventional apostrophe, as found in hymns, or the dramatization of a figure from the past, as in Ciceronian dialogue, serves to draw a distant figure closer, to make familiar and apprehensible the sources of religious or ethical authority, Seneca's enstrophic play of *tu* and *ego* creates an inaccessible dialogue, inward directed and self-sustaining.⁵⁷

Yet for all its independence of the reader, the discourse between Seneca and his addressee intrudes itself upon us unapologetically and insists upon our cooperation in this very intrusion. To do otherwise, we quickly discover, is to side against the gods, to miss the moment of access, the window of opportunity, the *particula* that promises us insight into all the mysteries of the ethical universe.

The opening of the *De Beneficiis* engages the reader in a similar interplay of part and whole, exposure and concealment, violation and seduction.

Inter multos ac varios errores temere inconsulteque viventium nihil propemodum ⟨indignius⟩, vir optime Liberalis, dixerim, ⟨quam⟩ quod beneficia nec dare scimus nec accipere.⁵⁸

Among the many and various errors made by those who live rashly and without plan, my good man Liberalis, almost none would I call more unfitting than the fact that we do not know how to give or receive benefits.

Humans make many mistakes, we learn, but only two types of error are to be of concern in this treatise. Why? What qualifies the writer to make this decision? By what criterion was the selection made? These issues are of no interest to the self-possessed voice of authority.⁵⁹ An opposition is established, or at least implied, between those who live rashly and those who do not (cf. the

---

56. Cf. the comments of Shaw (above n. 10), 54, concerning Stoicism generally: "The doctrine faced the listener and reader, even the occasional one, with the fearsome and challenging possibility of the whole world being explicable by an idea that systematically excluded, even threatened, other interpretations of it. On the other hand, the enticement was that you actually knew what you were doing and knew that it was right."

57. On lyric apostrophe see J. Culler, "Apostrophe" in *The Pursuit of Signs* (Ithaca, NY 1981); on hymnic apostrophe see A. L. T. Bergren, "Sacred Apostrophe: Re-presentation and Imitation in the Homeric Hymns," *Arethusa* 15 (1982) 83–108.

58. I follow the text of F. Haase in the Teubner edition (Leipzig 1852).

59. The textual corruption makes it impossible to say that Seneca does not specify the basis for selection; but the lacuna/e cannot be lengthy because of the reference to the addressee (always early in Seneca) and the close connection between *quod* and *nihil*.

beginnings of *De Brevitate Vitae, De Vita Beata*, and *De Providentia* discussed above), only to be dissolved in the first person plural *nec...scimus* ("we do not know..."). Are we, then, among the rash in need of correction? Or are we asked to take a stand with the one whose powers of discernment allow him not only to make corrections but also to decide what needs correcting? Before we can answer, even before the question is fully posed, we learn that the two categories are one, the arrogant intruder is nothing but a fellow-sufferer, soliciting our empathy and companionship. Within a single sentence we have been insulted, disarmed, and seduced – a more concise version of the process of reading to which Seneca himself is subjected in letter 46. Thus the act of reading as Seneca describes it and initiates it requires of the reader a receptivity and engagement at odds with the conventional male sexual ideals of aggression and detachment promulgated elsewhere in the treatises.

Of the relationship between ideology and mythology Pierre Bourdieu has written that "unlike myth, a collective product collectively appropriated and consumed, ideologies serve particular interests which they tend to present as universal interests, common to the whole group."[60] Of Stoicism more particularly, Brent Shaw has argued that its proponents seek to generalize "the traditional idea of values and good behaviour, once restricted to a narrow elite of the city...as a good for everyone."[61] "Stoicism was thus cosmic social metaphor positing a Divine Economy, in which everything and every person had its proper place and function."[62] Shaw is unwilling to go as far as Bourdieu and the Marxist analysts on whom Bourdieu relies and suggests instead that Stoicism, *qua* ideology, rather than serving as a weapon "in the unique possession of certain individuals or groups," provides "external signposts or referents shared and used by various, even divergent, social groups."[63] Shaw's stricture may be applicable to Stoicism conceived as a timeless system, but it is surely not far-fetched to regard the particular version of Stoicism inscribed by

60. P. Bourdieu, "Symbolic Power," translation by R. Nice of a lecture given at Harvard in 1973; printed as part of Centre for Contemporary Cultural Studies, *Stencilled Occasional Paper*, no. 46 (University of Birmingham 1977): quotation taken from p. 2.
61. Shaw (above n. 10) 36.   62. Shaw (above n. 10) 37.
63. Shaw (above n. 10) 48.

Seneca as functioning as a weapon, both offensive and defensive, in the hands of the class for whom it is designed.

In this capacity, however, Seneca's philosophy makes exactly the universalizing gesture predicted by Bourdieu, for it presents the contemporary tension between birth and achievement as characteristic of human civilization from its outset. By implication, then, the Senecan text assimilates the elite Roman's vested interest in preserving the power of both birth and achievement to the interest of the whole of human society, past and present. This linkage between a chronological and sociological fraction, on the one hand, and the whole of human society on the other is most clear in letter 90, concerning the end of the Golden Age and the commencement of philosophy, and in the immediately succeeding letters, which elaborate on the association between Senecan philosophy and the originary force of desire. Thus we may conclude our survey of Senecan beginnings – literary, cultural, and textual – with a brief consideration of yet another type of beginning, one which we may call either cosmic (following Shaw) or mythological (following Bourdieu).

The apparent aim of letter 90 is the rejection of the Posidonian claim that philosophers invented the arts or technologies of human society during the Golden Age.[64] Posidonius' position is to be rejected because the arts he ascribes to philosophers are trivial and/or subject to ethical misuse, and because there could not have been philosophers in the Golden Age, since there was (by definition) no desire in that era, hence no room for the exercise of virtue, which it is the function of philosophy to instill. In other words, Seneca criticizes Posidonius' claim concerning philosophers' invention of arts in the Golden Age through an analysis, expressed or implied, of philosophy, of the other arts of human society, and of the meaning of the Golden Age.

In the context of his criticism of Posidonius Seneca develops a positive account of philosophy and its origins. Philosophy, we learn, is active and involves achievement: this is why it cannot have been part of the effortless lifestyle of the Golden Age (*quamvis egregia illis vita fuerit et carens fraude, non fuere sapientes, quando hoc iam*

---

64. On Seneca's encounter with Posidonius in this letter, and the letters surrounding it, see A. D. Leeman, *Mnemosyne* 4 (1951) 175–81; 5 (1952) 57–78; 6 (1953) 307–13; 7 (1954) 233–40.

in opere maximo nomen est, Ep. 90.44). The best thing about philosophy is precisely that one does not stumble upon it by chance (*sapientia quod in se optimum habet perdidisset, inter fortuita non esse,* 90.2). These passages display an explicit privileging of achievement, a strategy that serves the immediate purpose of the argument against Posidonius, but also makes a more general claim about the nature and significance of philosophy.

Yet despite the attempt to link philosophy to the self-fashioning tendencies of the ethically upwardly mobile, its real claim to authority, in this letter and those that follow it, seems to be its connection with the originary force of desire. Philosophy would not exist if there were no desire. And, concomitantly it would seem, philosophy is available to human beings, from the outset, as a potential therapy of desire. The Golden Age came to a conclusion when vice insinuated itself (*subrepentibus vitiis,* 90.6) and avarice thrust itself onto the scene (*inrupit... avaritia,* 90.38).[65] In an era without vice, there was also no wisdom or philosophy. "Through ignorance of affairs were those men innocent. But there is a great difference between choosing not to sin and not knowing how to sin" (*ignorantia rerum innocentes erant; multum autem interest utrum peccare aliquis nolit an nesciat,* 90.46). The end of the Golden Age, not the Golden Age itself, marks the commencement of human civilization through the agency of desire. And so philosophy cannot have come into existence until the time at which desire had prompted the transition from the Golden Age to human history. By assigning philosophy to the Golden Age, Posidonius has not only ascribed a laborious project to an age of inertia; he has also ascribed a remedy for desire to an era in which desire does not yet exist.

Philosophy's intrinsic connection with desire is reinforced in succeeding letters in which it is described as mimicking in the individual soul the techniques that desire once deployed against the Golden Age and continues to deploy in each succeeding generation. In mimesis of desire's irruptive force, philosophy lays hold of the emotions (*adfectus ipsos tangunt,* 94.28), takes the listener

---

65. The word *subrepens* describes the action of snakes. For the erotic implication, see W. Krenkel, "Tonguing," *Wissenschaftliche Zeitschrift der Wilhelm-Pieck-Universität Rostock* 30 (1981) 37–54 (esp. 41–42). For the erotic significance of *inrumpo,* see Krenkel, "Fellatio and irrumatio" (above n. 50).

by force (*vim praeceptorum, occursus... sapientium*, 94.40), and penetrates more deeply (*altius penetrat*, 94.44). If desire instead creeps in and seduces, then philosophy, too, can press itself upon the chest (*paulatim descendit in pectora*, 94.40), and insinuate virtue (*insinuanda virtus*, 95.35). Such language, particularly in the context of advice to separate oneself from the mob (94.69–74), gain control of one's own affairs (*liberet, potestate*, 91.21), and become a new incarnation of the traditional *vir bonus* (95.72ff.), reinforces both the paradoxical sexual implications of the Senecan project and the cosmic connection between philosophy and desire.

Posidonius' position concerning the place of wise men in the Golden Age had been a strongly elitist one; the arts of human life, vulgar as well as noble, had been invented by sages during the Golden Age. Seneca resists that elitism by emphasizing the effort involved in philosophy and its availability to all. Yet in so doing, he relies on a distinction between philosophy and the vulgar arts and re-enacts Posidonius' aristocratic gesture by privileging philosophy on the basis of its origin. What appears to be an acknowledgment of the claims of achievement is undercut by a rhetorical focus on beginnings. Seneca transforms and mythologizes the anxieties of his immediate audience into the originary tensions between the Golden Age and history, and nature and desire. "If the gods had made wisdom a common good and we were born prudent, wisdom would have lost what it possesses best in itself" (*nam si hanc quoque bonum vulgare fecissent et prudentes nasceremur, sapientia quod in se optimum habet perdidisset...*, 90.2). "Inclined toward the highest, but not in possession of it, are we born, and even among the best, until you civilize them, there is the material of virtue, not virtue" (*ad hoc quidem, sed sine hoc nascimur, et in optimis quoque, antequam erudias, virtutis materia, non virtus est*, 90.46). The distinction between the good and the vulgar or the best and all the rest frames a letter that purports to describe philosophy as a matter of effort or achievement. Seneca's aristocracy of virtue supplements, even as it seeks to supplant, the age-old aristocracy of birth.

Beginnings in Plutarch's *Lives*

THOMAS G. ROSENMEYER

I

"Men can do nothing without the make-belief of a beginning."[1] "Make-belief," because in the world of action it is objectively impossible to isolate a putative first step within the chain of contiguous causes and consequences. Current thinking frowns upon the axioms of origin, of authorship, of the unitary validating enactment. In the swirl of contextualization and dialogicity, a genuine starting point will go down as a dubious fiction. "The genesis...is never more than a transition from one structure to another, but also a formative transition that leads from a weaker to a stronger structure."[2] Edward Said borrows Hayden White's deprecatory coinage "inaugural gestures" to convey the artificiality and delusoriness of a sense of beginning.[3] He lists the various ways in which "beginning" can be understood: as physical exigency, as a departure from an antecedent, as a moment in time, a place, a principle, an action, a verbal stratagem of easing into sequence. His expansive temper and his commitment to renewal condition him to see in a genuine beginning a revolutionary element, challenging the conventions but also harnessed by the structures of the context. Nowhere in his massive book does Said provide a discussion of how a writer's first paragraph relates to the larger enterprise; his concern is with the total enterprise *as* a beginning.

---

1. George Eliot, quoted by H. Abzug in Veninga (1983) 21. The present essay had been sent to the editor when, through the kindness of Philip A. Stadter, I received a copy of his detailed, learned and generous "The Proems of Plutarch's *Lives*." Thanks to it my discussion has profited from a few last minute changes and additions. Unavoidably our papers evince some duplication, but the perspectives and the results seem to me sufficiently distinct to warrant proceeding with the submission of my piece.

2. Piaget (1968) 121, cited by Said (1975) 192. Said's book remains the most detailed analysis of the complexities of the notion of a beginning. (For full references see Works Cited at end of the essay.) 3. Cf. White (1978) 5.

My interest is in first paragraphs, or even first lines. By what initiatory tactic does the writer open a window on the desk top of literature to frame the construct upon which he is engaged? Do his "inaugural gestures" suggest that he is aware of the linkage of his project to a larger context or tradition, and that his construct is, more or less violently, torn from that tissue of indebtedness, or, on the contrary, fuelled by that tradition? Again, what yardstick, if any, do we apply in deciding where a beginning, a head, comes to its end and the body of the work supervenes? These are difficult questions, to be answered, if at all, variously, depending upon the organizational perspicuity of the work studied, or, often, upon the properties of the genre with which we might be willing to associate a particular work or writer.

In the case of Plutarch's *Lives*, one might suppose, a scrutiny of beginnings promises some rewards. Plutarch is not one of those who, in Harold Bloom's phrase, write against writing. There is nothing in the *Lives* to suggest, even at a submerged level of composition, a demonic wrestling with authority. Plato's authority, as Plutarch understands it, he accepts unreservedly; others he rifles or opposes in his disciplined, academic, appreciative or dismissive manner. His "awe in the presence of a classic"[4] is restrictive only in the sense that he chooses not to recapitulate everything his sources have reported in authoritative detail.[5] His own uncomplicated sense that in writing biography he is doing something that has not been done in quite the same manner before has been vindicated by those specialists who have condemned attempts to fold Plutarch's achievement into an earlier evolution of the genre.[6]

A brief reminder of the material involved. We have twenty-two sets of *Parallel Lives*, each containing two biographies, of a Greek and a Roman, followed, with some exceptions, by a concluding comparative-contrastive analysis (σύγκρισις); one set of four

---

4. Wardman (1974) 154. Wardman has in mind Plutarch's respect for Thucydides, Xenophon, and Philistus.

5. *Artaxerxes* 8.1. Plutarch criticizes Timaeus in *Nicias* 1.2–4 for replicating the material drawn from his sources in a spirit of competition. As for himself, he proposes to summarize the findings of his authorities, and bring in only those details that may have escaped their scrutiny. Cf. Pelling (1980); de Romilly (1988).

6. Cf. especially Dihle (1956) and (1987); Erbse (1956); Krischer (1982); Momigliano (1971); Russell (1966a); Wardman (1974); Ziegler (1951).

Beginnings in Plutarch's "Lives"

biographies (*Agis*, *Cleomenes*, and the *Gracchi*); and a set of two (*Galba* and *Otho*) rescued from another collection, the *Lives of the Emperors*.[7] The *Lives* were almost certainly written in the later period of Plutarch's career, between c. 96 and c. 120 CE. An impressive attempt has been made to date the *Lives* in relation to one another,[8] but no definitive consensus about these relations exists, and in this paper chronological considerations will be disregarded. Nine of the twenty-four Greek figures, from Theseus to Demosthenes, are drawn from the history of Athens. Only one of the contrasting heroes is not a Roman but a Persian: Artaxerxes; and in one case (*Galba* and *Otho*) the two figures juxtaposed (not paralleled) are both Romans. The conspicuousness of the Romans in the *Lives* is noteworthy in the light of Plutarch's admission, in *Demosthenes* 2.2–4, that he came late to the study of the Latin language, and that he lacked the leisure to master the niceties of the tongue.[9] He hastens to add that his understanding of the meaning of the words was facilitated by his practical experience. And it is evident that his knowledge of Roman materials is indebted to authorities who wrote in Greek.

Why did Plutarch compose his *Lives*? There is no doubt about the didactic intention.[10] By putting on the stage the imitable (and, occasionally, the cautionary) examples of outstanding public figures, Plutarch installs mirrors, not just for magistrates, but for all men who prize the products of excellence (ἀρετή) and character (ἦθος). In the wake of Plato and Aristotle and the Hellenistic ethical philosophers, Plutarch accepts a vital connection between these moral staples, experience, habituation, and behavior under pressure. In the *Lives* he focuses on actions and decisions

---

7. *Demosth.* 3.3–5 presents the best formulation of why Plutarch wrote parallel lives: he is interested in ὁμοιότητες φύσεως, similarities of natural endowment, but also in πολλὰ τῶν τυχηρῶν, the frequency of the coincidence of circumstance. Cf. also *Pelop.* 2.9–12 and *Aemil.* 1.6. In my discussion I will deal with *Galba* and *Otho* as if they were part of the collection of *Parallel Lives*.

8. Jones (1966). Some of the *Lives*, including, probably, the first written, have not been preserved. The order in which the extant *Lives* have come to us in the manuscripts, or in the so-called catalogue of Lamprias, is demonstrably not the order in which they were penned. In one case, *Aemilius Paulus* 1, Plutarch's statement of why he continued with the series suggests that there had been a break, and that the *Life* constitutes a new beginning.

9. Pelling (1979) 74–76 argues that for the Roman *Lives* Plutarch lacked the ready fund of recollections he was able to invest in the Greek *Lives*.

10. See especially Ziegler (1951) coll. 903–05. Also Erbse (1956) 419, who cites confirmatory evidence from the *Moralia*.

and elicits from them the evidence he seeks concerning the qualities needed to lead a good life. This immediately raises a historiographic problem that may turn out to be reflected in Plutarchan beginnings. Is it not true that the closer a student gets to the intricacies and the opacities of biographical reality, the more refracted the moral entities become? An understanding of ethics sharpens the suspicion that the practicalities and the necessary compromises of a successful public life are the least likely arena in which to uncover exemplary manifestations of virtue. Perhaps the *Lives of the Philosophers*, a prominent Hellenistic literary genre, and certainly the Christian *Lives of the Saints* would prove more bountiful in rendering up prototypes of the exercise of excellence. Plutarch does not see it that way. His own uncomplicated sense of what is right and the experience gained as a leading citizen persuade him that successes achieved against great odds and in the taking of risks are equally effective and perhaps superior indices of moral assets. Nor is he inclined to ferret out the negatives in the careers of the ancients; note his objection to the practice of Herodotus (*de malign. Herod.* 874B): he compares his malice, his βλασφημία and κακολογία, to the activity of a rose beetle ravaging the smooth and delicate tissues.

It is here that the biographer's art of selection comes into its own. Nepos, in the preface to his *Life of Epaminondas*, worries that readers, not in tune with the customs of the Greeks in Epaminondas' time, might be turned off by the prominence of music and dancing which was part of his hero's education. We may compare Plutarch's disdainful comments about poets and musicians at the beginning of his *Pericles* and elsewhere. Nepos insists that he cannot omit these details: "when...we wish to produce an impression of the habits and the life of Epaminondas, we must not appear to omit anything that might be relevant to its fulfillment." This target of inclusiveness or totalization is not one that Plutarch acknowledges. His declaration that he will not reiterate what his sources have already delivered, but will look for additional materials they might not have caught,[11] permits him to shape the details of his *Lives* so as to elicit the significant moral patterns with a minimum of interference. His occasional hesitation

---

11. Herodotus 6.55 shows that this is an authentic historiographical move.

about which version or judgment to adopt has to do with the lack of a decisive motive, or the lack of documentary evidence.[12] And where the lives inspected prove to furnish negative rather than positive paradigms, as in the cases of *Demetrius* and *Antony*, Plutarch, a Corneille *avant la lettre*, reserves to himself the right of admiration, in the belief that even here there is enough promising material for a discerning emulator to take heart. The cautionary or deterrent ingredient in his didacticism is, for the most part, distinctly understated.

Plutarch's decision to organize his biographical sketches in tandems, many of them culminating in comparative-contrastive analyses or summaries, is a further mark of the confidence with which he handles his task. For if his purpose is didactic, to establish embodiments of achievement for imitation, the coupling of two embodiments would seem to make the task more difficult. Elsewhere, in his *On the Virtues of Women* (243B–D), addressed to a distinguished woman friend, Plutarch talks about the principles involved in comparing the accomplishments of women with those of men. We must juxtapose lives, and actions, like great works of art, and compare them for successes, intelligence, nobility, and other goods. Their divergent natures produce different hues; so do the contemporary mores, personal temperaments, upbringing, lifestyles. Achilles was brave in one way, Ajax in another. But this does not mean that the two heroes exhibited two distinct kinds of bravery, only dissimilarities in their instantiation of the same bravery. One may wonder whether in this varied lumping together of men and women, of people and art objects, of properties split and unsplit, Plutarch has given the problem of comparing all the thought it deserves. The argumentative discourse indicates that he is aware of the difficulties. But the problem recedes in the face of his assurance.

Later we will have occasion to ask whether the manifest assurance of the method is gainsaid by what happens in the introductions to the *Lives*. Meanwhile let us ask another question. How does Plutarch's procedure measure up against what we understand by biography? The partiality for the stars of one's culture is still discernible in the vulgate variety represented by the

12. Barbu (1934) 143ff.

National Inquirer and *People Magazine,* and again in the interbellum pattern biography chronicling the corruption of the hero by the power he seeks.[13] It is not difficult to think of the *Lives* as the ancient counterpart to the seductive tales of glamorous success and rightful fall our mass culture has spawned. But Plutarch's practice is superior to these bastard varieties in that it conforms more closely to the four principles which according to Leon Edel sustain serious biography: the biographer must understand his subject's dreams; he must preserve a critical distance from the spell of his hero; he must analyze his materials for the keys to the deeper truths about his subject; and he must discover the unique literary form that will express the special quality of the life considered.[14] Plutarch's fascination with virtue and character, and his special mix of admiration for what the hero has achieved, tempered by limited but firm reservations in the face of the subject's shortcomings, bring him close to a realization of Edel's requirements. So does his control of the literary means whereby the data of the life are turned into a compelling *Life*. Only Edel's further comment that a biographical account "need no longer be strictly chronological... Lives are rarely lived that way" would not earn Plutarch's consent. Chronological sequence is Plutarch's major organizing device for what happens after the introduction; without the equivalent of an *ab ovo* the body of the work would not set itself off from the introduction.

Albrecht Dihle has put us in his debt by venturing to circumscribe the characteristics of the biographical tradition to which, he argues in the face of doubts, Plutarch subscribes. Biography, he says, trains its sights on the totality of a man's life, in its before and after, not *necessarily* in all its details; it is shaped to capture the attainment of moral values *commensurate* to the *experience* of the reader.[15] I have italicized what seem to me the principal points on which further questions might be raised. In what sense is biography more compellingly entitled to the claim of commensurateness than any other form of verbal or indeed

---

13. The most popular writer of this type of biography was Emil Ludwig. For an entertaining critique, see Lowenthal (1980), who considers this species, with its hypostasis of an iron-willed history creating its own figures, a travesty of sociology.

14. Edel (1984) 28–30.

15. Dihle (1987) 8–9; cf. also Dihle (1956) 88, who puts a greater emphasis on the inclusion of the insignificant (*unscheinbar*) events of daily life.

non-verbal communication registering upon a consciousness readied by the experience of living? In fact, commensurability has recently become the object of philosophical inquiry, with one critic asserting that it can be said to exist only for insignificant options.[16] It could further be argued that, far from "not necessarily" maximizing coverage, Plutarch has no interest whatever in producing a critical mass of details. On the contrary, the didacticism and the foregrounding of the tension between moral values and the risks of fortune (τύχη) require a strenuous selectiveness. Some *Lives* are considerably shorter than others; it is unlikely that the availability of source material had anything to do with this variance. Details of intimate and domestic conduct may be just as important for the clarification of character as actions of state (*Cato min.* 37.10). But precisely because they are designed to clarify the moral dimensions of the man, they must not be allowed to take on a life of their own. The didacticism of the genre, and its pliable selectiveness, continue to be with us, though rarefied and adjusted to our more skeptical temper.[17]

More crucially, we often prefer writers and texts that incorporate struggle, tension, recalcitrance, the lure of the unfinished and the disoriented. Plutarch, on the contrary, gives us heroes who, it is understood if not overtly stated, know what they want, and experience brief though repeated disappointments only because history and luck do not always wait upon them. Plutarch does not capitulate to the temptation of vitalism, the surrender before the irresistible fulness of life, which tends to detach the hero of serious modern biography from the moorings of social accountability and descriptive transparency.[18] Because of these restraints, Plutarchan biography has about it the air of the predictable. Both the nature of the challenges to which the hero is exposed and the choices he makes in response to the challenges are severely limited. Though each hero has his own special qualities, his function as a role model within the limitations of a homogeneous scene of politics and military ventures renders his life virtually collapsible into that of his peer in the parallel match-up; and together the two lives are once again collapsible into the

16. Raz (1986) ch. 13.   17. Scheuer (1979) 6.
18. Cf. Lowenthal (1980) 243–44. The liveliness of Plutarch's writing is not easily identified with the relative simplicity of the conceptual design; cf. Russell (1966a) 143.

larger pool of lives of Plutarch's heroes. It is against the foil of the relative sameness of the lives, or better: of the *Lives*, that the beginnings, the first paragraphs, will have to be studied.

Yet ancient biography is not the same as encomium. Isocrates' *Evagoras* is "rhetorische Heldendichtung" (the term is Krischer's[19]), with all negative features omitted from the idealized portrait. To avoid a possible trespass upon the utopian arena of the encomium, biography must always try to avoid the impression that the life portrayed is both satisfactorily unified and independently meaningful.[20] Plutarch's choice of the dual structure, the governing feature of his *Parallel Lives*, makes it easier for him to abide by this warning.

Plutarch is aware of the need to distinguish between biography and history, though his admiration of Thucydides makes it difficult for him to stipulate a clear boundary between the two genres. His statement early in *Galba* is symptomatic of a reluctance to leave historiography entirely behind: "The precise reporting of what happened in each case is a function of the history of events (πραγματικὴ ἱστορία); but I too must not pass over the noteworthy moments in what was done or experienced by the Caesars." Perhaps we might say that biography, for Plutarch, is a convenient and appealing mechanism for cutting history, the potentially overwhelming and infinite stream, up into cameo units furnishing the comforting semblance of beginning, middle, and end, with the agents, rather than the actions, providing the nuclei of orientation. "We do not write histories but lives. The most visible actions do not carry within them a foolproof index of virtue or its opposite; that is furnished often by a limited act or utterance or pleasantry. They give a greater insight into character than battles with mountains of dead or gigantic confrontations or investments of cities" (*Alexander* 1).[21] Plutarch adds an Aristotelian comparison with painters who go out of their way in their attention to facial

---

19. Krischer (1982). The encomiast, unlike the biographer, is constantly aware of the risks of exaggeration and attendant φθόνος, the resentment triggered among the audience.

20. Kracauer (1963) 75-80.

21. Wardman (1974) 4 suggests that Plutarch's remarks are motivated as much by the special case of Alexander (and Caesar) as by more general considerations. Dihle (1987) refers to Polybius 10.21.1-8 and Cicero *ad fam.* 5.12 for revealing discussions of the difficulty of distinguishing biography from historiography. Cf. also Nepos' proem to *Pelopidas*.

expression rather than taking account of the full outline of the body. The comparison is intriguing, but one wonders whether history, as practiced by Plutarch's admired predecessors, is greatly different in this respect from his own practice, or, conversely, whether in his own practice he can ever get away from the historical materials he proposes to remodel. It is almost touching to see him apologize, *after* detailing the pincer movement at Cannae, the dismounting of the Roman cavalry, Hannibal's reaction, and the heroism of Paulus Aemilius, for the disproportionate fulness of a battle account that cannot be said to help us to a better understanding of the peculiar greatness of Fabius Maximus (*Fab.* 16).

II

We are now in a better position to look at the choices Plutarch makes to launch his biographies.[22] The issues to which we need to be alert include the extrication of the great individual from the enveloping events of his time; the recognition, or the lack of it, of data that might conflict with the paradigmatic intention of the *Lives*; the inclusion, or the lack of it, of references to the childhood of the hero, to demonstrate the presence, already plottable, of the man in the child; and generally an anticipation of the several rubrics which Friedrich Leo, the founder of the modern study of Greek biography, proposed to find in the tradition from the start: lineage, family, looks, character, lifestyle, education, evidence of intelligence.[23] A question of a different sort, alluded to above, concerns the indispensability of "beginnings." Can Plutarch ever be said to start *in medias res*, without the flourish of an introduction? If so, will this allow us to gauge the limits of the prefatory statement in cases where he does not?

22. I am deliberately leaving aside the question of the comparability of beginnings in other writers, including post-classical historians and essayists. The challenge to Plutarch's beginnings is greater and distinct because of the relative invariability, even predictability, of the pattern of the *Lives*. So even if it is true that Ephorus or Lucian or Dio or Philostratus practiced a comparable versatility in their introductions, a preliminary and isolated scrutiny of Plutarch's procedure has its value.

23. Leo (1901). Leo admitted that not all of the subheadings are found in any one life or in the same order. The exceptions acknowledged by Leo are generally thought to subvert the case for a generic scheme; cf. Barbu (1934) 5–6.

Let us call the prefatory statement, coming before the systematic description of the hero's ancestry or birth or early life, "proem,"[24] understanding that Plutarch himself is unlikely to have regarded his initial remarks as analogous to the clearly articulated proems of forensic oratory.[25] Typically, we shall find, the *Lives* that are headed by prefatory matter (and by no means all of them are) begin with a proem of about two or three chapters' length (counting the modern organization of the text), a not unreasonable delay of the beginning of the *Life* proper. Finally, the concept of the *Parallel Lives* provokes a question peculiar to it: does the proem do justice to the specificities of both of the lives celebrated, or, if one of them is more clearly intended by the prefatory remarks, is it that of the Greek or the Roman?[26] Does the second *Life* of the pair get its own proem, of equal weight with the proem of the first? A special problem is of course set by the quadruple treatment of Agis, Cleomenes, and the Gracchi. It is just as well to begin with this document. It is hoped that the reader will not be put off by a series of summaries, highlighting the diversity of content, structure, and control, whereby Plutarch initialled his *Lives*.

III

In the first two chapters of *Agis and Cleomenes* Plutarch establishes the ethical and political maze within which the lives of the Spartan kings and of the Gracchi promise interesting test cases for the reflection and potential emulation of the readers.[27] Plutarch starts with the image[28] of Ixion, who desired Hera but embraced

---

24. Plutarch's own term, in a case where the articulation approaches the rhetorical division (*Pelopidas* 2.5), is προαναφώνησις. But cf. Lucian's προοίμιον and φροιμιάζεσθαι: *de conscr. hist.* 53. Stadter (1988), folding Plutarch's practice back into the rhetorical tradition, also adopts the term "proem" for the introductory section, whose precise limits he chooses not to discuss. For the conceptual and textual properties of the proems, and a possible distinction between "formal" and "informal" proems, see Stadter 276; he counts thirteen "formal" proems. My limitation of the confines of the proem to the material that comes before the canonic sketch of the hero's pedigree, birth, or youth is responsible for my omission of much that Stadter considers proemial.

25. For the earlier proemial tradition, see the valuable summary of Stadter (1988) 277–82. For ancient theory, see the materials cited by Stadter n. 12, and by Lausberg (1960) 150–63, all of which, of course, go back to Aristotle, *Rhetoric* 3.14.

26. Stadter (1988) 284 finds that "The thirteen formal proems...each respond to the particular needs of a pair of lives..." But contrast his remarks on p. 291.

27. Cf. Marasco (1981) 42 and 175ff. 28. For imagery, see below, n. 35.

a cloud, to characterize those who yearn for high position and authority but in working for it take their guidance from the untutored masses whose admiration they wish to attract. The emphasis is on influenceability and corruptibility. "For these men, attaching themselves to prestige which is a sort of mirror of virtue, accomplish nothing genuine or authoritative, but much that is spurious and half-bred; they are uncertain in their directions, slaves to resentments and passion." To drive home his point, Plutarch cites a passage of Sophocles[29] and brings in an analogy from shipping, where the lookout, though more informed about what lies ahead than the captain, takes his orders from him. In Chapter 2 the influenceable and therefore corrupt man is contrasted with the man of inherent virtue. Plutarch immediately qualifies this by conceding that in their younger years good men need the applause of others to develop their native virtue; but then returns to his strong condemnation of men whose political lives are lived in obedience to popular approval. This section is garnished with references to a work by Theophrastus, to a conversation between Phocion and Antipater, and to a fable about a snake whose tail rose up against its head. We cannot fault Plutarch for larding his discussion with literary, philosophical, visual, and anecdotal materials.[30] But a closer look at the sequence of ideas, and the application of the moral in the balance of Chapter 2, leave us with serious questions.

To take up the latter point first: my remarks about the dangers of looking for popularity, Plutarch concludes, are prompted by considering the effect of what happened in the case of the Gracchi: their character, education, and political philosophy were above reproach, but they were undone, less by a craving for acclaim than by a fear of not living up to it. So it turns out that the proem is primarily designed to prepare the *Lives* of the two Romans (but even they, Plutarch admits, were not really the slaves to popular approval to whom the reflections of the proem

29. For Plutarch's use of quotations, see Helmbold and O'Neill (1959). The evidence does not suggest that quotations are more likely to be found in proems than elsewhere.
30. Stadter (1988) 290 says that Plutarch's proems employ many rhetorical devices including "χρεῖαι, γνῶμαι, comparisons, digressions, metaphors, and indirection." My understanding of what constitutes a proem in the *Lives* suggests that "digressions" goes awkwardly with the rest of the devices. The proem is digressive or, perhaps better, ingressive by definition.

would apply). To find his way back to the Greeks, Plutarch, at the end of Chapter 2, has to say that, like the Gracchi, Agis and Cleomenes also in increasing the power of the people and trying to restore a commonwealth that had turned sick, drew upon themselves the hatred of the powerful. The parallel is less than adequate; corruptibility is not one of the vices with which either Agis or Cleomenes (or the Gracchi) could be charged. By this unsatisfying transition Plutarch manages to close his proem and to open Chapter 3, which details the forebears of Agis. Such genealogies or pedigrees are to be found in the great majority of the *Lives*; they form a convenient starting point for detailing the career of the hero, via a minimal reference to his childhood and upbringing. They are found at the start of the *Life* proper, after the prefatory remarks. Neither ancestry nor childhood is anticipated in the proem. In the present case the genealogical details that follow the proem are unusually extended and intricate, as if Plutarch owed Agis a debt for his earlier focus upon the Gracchi.

This is not the only proem in which the organization is determined by the questions to be asked about the Roman rather than the Greek.[31] On more than one occasion, it seems, it was the Roman life that was selected first, and the Greek life suggested by it was consequently placed ahead of it for reasons of chronology.[32] Could it be that Plutarch's information about the Romans was less hymnodic or more detailed, so the paradigmatic objective was more easily enriched by means of interesting caveats? Does the Roman life lend itself to "an initial crude presentation... which is then [sc. within the parameters of the Greek life] developed and refined?"[33] Better yet, does Plutarch start to think about the Greek, but quickly turn to the Roman to gain the distance and the perspective that a good beginning requires? This last explanation, though accounting for only a minority of the cases, would do

---

31. See also *Theseus, Nicias, Cimon, Alcibiades, Timoleon, Eumenes*. Pace Geiger (1981), when Plutarch proceeds from the figure cited first to the figure to be matched with it, he does not say that he is looking for a parallel life, and thus initiate us into the process of selection, but merely states that such and such a person is comparable. The points of similarity will be detailed, but we gain no insight into Plutarch's working method.

32. Cf. Marasco (1981) 178, who also remarks that the association of the Gracchi with Greek counterparts is already found in Cicero and earlier.

33. The quotation is from Pelling (1986) 96.

justice to the view that a true beginning calls for a deflection, a move away from the context in which the topic to be dealt with is imbedded. Whatever the reason, the surprise displacement of the Greeks by the Romans in the proem leaves the reader wondering.

Equally important, to return to the *Life of Agis*, the combination of moves in support of the condemnation of the love of acclaim, φιλοδοξία, offers its own surprises. The analogy from navigation, which clearly derives from Plato's *Republic*, is turned upside down by finding fault with the proposition that the deckhand is to be answerable to the captain. And as Plutarch turns to Theophrastus for the notion that in the child's development of character praise is a necessary nutriment, he evades the possible objection that such praise might not be dangerous to a grown man by adding that excess (τὸ ἄγαν) is always a trap, and it is a killer for men who want political acclaim. I suspect the difficulty Plutarch has with the logic of his proem has something to do with the snags of the Greek tradition of fame, κλέος. From Homer onwards a man's, and particularly a leading man's, standing in the community is measured by how people talk about him. By itself, the desire for popular acclaim is easily squared with the requirements of an excellent character, of virtue. By suggesting that the desire for acclaim can be an instrument for descending to the moral level of average people, Plutarch maneuvers himself into a precarious seesaw between moral approbation and moral warnings, precisely the kind of mixture that will make a biography interesting, but that will also obscure the ethical tenor of a proem. His mercurial willingness to accommodate negatives within his models and to proceed as if the models were eminently imitable is, as always, worrisome. But in this case the proem comes down heavily on negatives which the *Lives* themselves fail to sustain. It appears, then, that Plutarch has built more than enough surprises into the structure and the argument of this particular proem to fashion it into an appropriate vehicle for introducing his readers to some of the issues in his practice of biography. Or should we rather say that the surprises constitute an overkill, leaving a needless disparity between the asymmetries of the proem and the more shapely text that follows? May we speak of overdetermination, or even of counterproductiveness?

On the same topic of currying popular favor, the proem to *Phocion* extends over three chapters and constitutes a complex argument: Plutarch begins with a comparison of Demades, a quisling under the Macedonians and a most unattractive character (at least so Plutarch thinks), with the respected Phocion for the constraints under which they lived, and which darkened their reputation. He proceeds, with the help of an assortment of images and similes, to recommend a compromise between steering a wilful course and taking one's guidance from the populace; and finds the same tough mixture of moral goodness and public concern in both Phocion and Cato. "Cato's lineage, as will be shown, derives, by general agreement, from distinguished ancestors; Phocion's, I find, is by no means humble or without honor." Thus Plutarch slides, by means of a characteristic chiasmus, into the customary genealogy, after a proem more vivid than most, and once again conforming to the usual prescription of quotations from the authors, pregnant comparisons, references to persons or institutions only remotely connected with the lives at issue, and moral judgments in excess of covering the fates about to be featured.

I next turn to the proem of the *Life of Cimon*, an equally complex structure, though, for once, a straight narrative. The story is full of adventure and erotic strife, a peculiar overture to the life of a man whose conservatism might be thought to invite a less colorful introduction. It is a tale of gang violence in Plutarch's Chaeronea; of the city being taken to court for killings consequent upon the sexual intrigue between a Roman officer and a rugged and handsome adolescent; of the Roman general, Lucullus, finding for the city; of the adolescent, now matured, invited back but promptly assassinated; of ghosts haunting the city and soot-faced revellers recalling the ancient mayhem; and of the Chaeroneans setting up a marble statue of Lucullus in recognition of his clearing them of a charge brought against them by their rival Orchomenus. This story, even more erratic than my summary would let on, covers the first chapter and the start of the second. In the balance of the chapter Plutarch narrows his focus upon the statue: his aim, prompted by continuing gratitude to Lucullus, is to do better than a sculptor, who concentrates on externals, and to compose an image that gives shape to (ἐμφανίζει = "suggests" and "emphasizes": the term is from rhetoric) the hidden qualities, character, and temperament. Painters, he continues, in the interest of truthfulness would not pass over small imperfections though of course they would not blow them up. We must do the same, in the case of mistakes or even horrors (κῆρες) arising out of misfortune or public constraint. They will figure in our treatment as imperfections of virtue rather than as the active enhancements of vice. This particular formulation of the tension between imitability and realism takes Plutarch to the beginning of Chapter 3, in which he finally turns to Cimon and explains why he is the most suitable pendant to Lucullus. And in Chapter 4 the genealogy of Cimon inaugurates the *Life* proper.

Once again, then, Plutarch introduces the Roman of the dyad before he turns to the Greek. But the line of reasoning is remarkably tortuous. The soot-faced emulators of the ancient murder gang occupy a disconcertingly large space side by side with the honorary state of Lucullus; the local pride and embarrassment celebrating the native rowdyism clash with the deference shown the Roman general. The aetiological expansiveness coloring the antecedents of what in his own time, by his own account, was a staid and quiet country town is in stark contrast with the standard move of the comparison between biography and the visual arts. If the proem to *Agis and Cleomenes* seemed problematic in its inconsequentiality and its displacement of the Greeks, what are we to make of the preamble to *Cimon*, mixed as it is of equal measures of thuggery, sexual violence, ritual charade, and methodological considerations that appear to fly in the face of the very purpose of the *Lives*, which is not to monitor defects and trace disasters that are thrust upon people, but to sketch the accomplishments of the much better than average. To be sure, the *Lives*, as we learn on many occasions, allow for the inclusion of πάθη, of what is done to the heroes, as well as of what is done by them. But the bedlam of this particular horror story far exceeds the usual limits of πάθη, of the sufferings experienced by the individuals who attract the biographer's attention. One can only gather that Plutarch was not interested in fashioning a prologue suited to the quality of the heroes of the hour, and that he saw nothing wrong with bringing in material that could as easily have been used in some of the more sensationalist portions of his

Moralia. Perhaps it was the consciousness of the peculiarity of taking his cue from the Roman of the dyad that prompted him to resort to the circuitry evident in the proem to *Cimon*.[34]

The three proems we have analyzed are unusually complex. I hasten to repeat that their complexity is not demanded by the complexity of the *Lives* they introduce. Other *Lives*, of equal or greater resistance to normative expectations, such as *Alcibiades* and *Alexander*, receive less ambitious proems or none at all. Why Plutarch chose to endow one *Life* with a substantial proem and leave another to sail along without such an introduction or with a lesser brand we cannot tell. Plutarch disposes of no standard technique to introduce his *Lives*; each occasion calls for a reconsideration of the form and the quantity to be invested in the initiatory statement. Another issue raised earlier should, however, be settled at this point: as a rule, the second *Lives* – and that means, usually, the *Lives* of the Romans – carry no proems of their own. Of the second *Lives* we have, only those of Romulus and Marius are granted brief introductory remarks. Clearly Plutarch felt that one proem covering the dual composition was sufficient, especially since that proem usually claims to cover the needs of both heroes of the tandem structure.

The affection for Chaeronea, Plutarch's sleepy home town, demonstrated in *Cimon* also plays a role in the *Life of Demosthenes*. The proem starts out by asserting that the stature of the native city is unimportant for the rise of the public hero; his excellence could originate and flourish in any environment. But the arts, and that includes the work of historians and essayists, are dependent for their success on the logistical support and the resonance they are more likely to find in large cities, with their cultivated readerships and their well-endowed libraries. For myself, Plutarch continues, I am content to stay in Chaeronea, if only because my departure would make the town even smaller than it is. But I did have some experience with living in Rome – and at that point

---

34. One is tempted to invoke the ancient category of the shocking, the παράδοξον σχῆμα or *admirable* (or *turpe*) *genus*, used by orators to enhance the moral defensibility of the case (Lausberg [1960] 58). Could the strangeness of the proem be an instance of *insinuatio*? Cf. Lausberg 160: "Die *insinuatio* besteht darin, dass durch listige Verwendung psychologischer Mittel...das Unterbewusstsein des Publikums in einem für uns günstigen Sinne beeinflusst wird..." Hardly; there is no live audience; readers do not need to be inveigled into reading.

Plutarch proceeds to his account of the lateness of his exposure to the Latin tongue, to which I have already referred. In Chapter 3 we are introduced to Demosthenes and Cicero. In what Plutarch says about them – and for once they enter the discussion together, on a level of parity – there is no link whatever with the matters taken up in the first two chapters. He says that he will look at their public lives and not at their speeches; he compares them for their appetite for honors, their love of freedom, their reluctance to take risks, and their involvement in strokes of bad luck. Only glancingly does he revert to the topic of small-town birth, by saying that they became powerful from obscure beginnings. To drive the reference harder would have been impossible in the case of Demosthenes, whose birth in Paeania was tantamount to birth in Athens. The arguments of the first two chapters, then, are largely unrelated to what follows; and my summary of those arguments has skimmed lightly over a number of smallish dislocations and erudite notes which distance the proem even more radically from the concerns of the subsequent *Lives*.

The proem to the *Life of Pericles*, one of the longest and most contrived, is too well known for me to need to rehearse its contents at length. Unlike the proems we have inspected, it has a certain standing as an introduction to what Plutarch considers important and what he considers counterproductive in the writing of biography. It is notorious for its Platonizing critique of the arts, especially of music and sculpture, but also of poetry: we may appreciate good verse but we cannot admire its creators. Nobody wants to be another Phidias or Anacreon, but each of us desires to be another Pericles or Fabius Maximus. We all love to learn and see, but we disapprove of those who love to learn and see unworthy objects. The whole proem, full of anecdote and simile and rife with class prejudice against working with one's hands, shows Plutarch at his most skittish and disconcerting, as if the *Life* itself, with its allowance for the relation between Pericles and Phidias and its inclusion of the hero's family experiences, gave him cause to worry ahead of time that the greatness of the hero's virtue might not in the end emerge with sufficient brilliance. What is more, the long shadow thrown by the majesty of Pericles blocks any serious consideration of Fabius in the proem.

Demetrius starts out with a peculiar analogy drawn between the sensations and the arts: both of them are capable of distinguishing contraries. Vision registers the light and the dark; by the same token the art of medicine studies sickness and health. Plutarch's own art is capable of focusing on both positive and negative paradigms. The students of human behavior must know both; the Spartans made helots drunk in order to parade them before their young as warning examples. Plutarch concedes that one might quarrel with the ethics of this practice. But, he continues, as long as history offers us paragons of imperfection, it may be useful to bring a few to the notice of his audience. Hence the *Lives* of Demetrius and Antony, men who confirm Plato's view that great natures (αἱ μεγάλαι φύσεις) are capable of exhibiting great vices along with their virtues. Before they reached their unhappy end, both these men distinguished themselves by their love life, their drinking, their warring, their generosity, their extravagance, and their violence. Next Plutarch leads into the pedigree of Demetrius with an extended passage on both men, a procedure which is normally found in the contrastive analyses at the end of the pair of *Lives*. His willingness to make room in the *Lives* for high rollers as well as paragons, though a natural consequence of the Aristotelian insight that perfectly good characters make for indifferent drama, comes through in this instance with particular clarity. By the same token, Plutarch cannot be said to make any clearer how the career of the gambler works within the didactic scheme of the *Lives*.

Up to now I have touched on proems introducing the *Lives* of the Greeks. Of the twenty proems giving Plutarch a chance to pose as an essayist before the *Life* settles down to an account of the lineage or the youth (and looks) or both of the hero, fifteen are attached to the *Lives* of the Greeks, although, as we have seen, they may take their cue from the Romans; only five have the function of introducing the *Life* of the Roman. This is of course largely due to the fact that the *Life* of the Greek as a rule precedes that of the Roman (*Demosthenes* 3.5 baldly states: we must begin with the one who came first), no matter which of the two heroes looms larger in the author's imagination. The three exceptions to this rule are *Sertorius*, which unaccountably precedes *Eumenes* (the proem awkwardly advertises the coincidence of events, and of personal identities; both Eumenes and Sertorius were one-eyed!);

Beginnings in Plutarch's "Lives"

Aemilius, whose equally curious precedence over *Timoleon* was inverted by the Aldine; and *Galba*, which is matched, or better followed, by *Otho*. (*Romulus* and *Marius* are, as we have seen, second *Lives*.) The proem of *Galba* anticipates several of the themes taken up again in the body of the work, with a major emphasis on the importance of discipline and obedience in the military. It was, we learn, because of the disorganization and the viciousness of the military machine and the empire that Galba, a virtuous man, was undone. For once, the proem, introducing a set of lives deriving from another cycle, does not indulge in imagery or digressions or wit.[35] And in as much as it consists of statements that with equal or better justice could have come by way of commentary on Galba's death, its pertinence to the demonstration of Galba's personal qualities is dubious, and its anticipation of the terminal expression of sorrow may be regarded as out of place and wasteful.

A few additional examples, briefly summarized, will attest further to the inventiveness and the eccentricity of the proems. At the beginning of *Lysander* Plutarch "corrects a popular fallacy current at Delphi: the statue at the door of the Treasury of the Acanthians represents, he tells us, not Brasidas but Lysander."[36] *Romulus* gets underway with seven different accounts given for the naming of Rome; the last account, designating Romulus as the most qualified source, carries over easily if speciously into the standard discussion of Romulus' ancestry. The proem of *Theseus* openly declares, once again, that the Greek hero is being selected to form a pair with Romulus, the primary paradigm, and offers a colorful and unhurried discourse on the murkiness of the distant past, more distant than the periods in which Plutarch had found

---

35. I differ profoundly with Georgiadou (1988) 351: "Plutarch's moralizing introduction in the *Life of Galba* 1.1–2.1 closely resembles the introductory chapters of many of the *Parallel Lives*, which open with one or more moral concepts and then describe the heroes in accordance with the concept, as far as possible." For imagery in Plutarch, see Fuhrmann (1964). Fuhrmann has nothing to say about imagery in the *Lives* as distinct from the rest of the corpus, or about the positioning of the imagery in the *Lives*. A cursory check suggests that the frequency and the kind of imagery in the proems are no different from those in the bulk of the *Lives*. But the topic deserves further study.

36. Russell (1966a) 151. Russell continues: "Let us call this προοίμιον ἀπὸ οἰκείου, following a hint in Lucian (*de conscr. hist.* 53) about historians' prefaces: they should aim, he says, at securing προσοχή and εὐμάθεια, though they need make no special effort for εὔνοια; and προσοχή is secured if the topic broached is 'great', 'essential', 'familiar', or 'useful'. Plutarch chooses the familiar."

his earlier subjects. He hopes, he says, to be able to convert these opacities into believable history; but if the material does not submit to this kind of naturalization, he begs his listeners to be tolerant. The proem to *Pelopidas* is a more narrowly focused if also more prolix construct. Anticipating a possible reservation concerning Pelopidas and Marcellus, namely that in demonstrating their personal bravery they substituted recklessness for courage, Plutarch agrees and lists a number of authorities, including Simonides and Homer, who warned that a good fighter must protect himself and not rashly throw away his life. The proems of the *Lives* of Nicias, with its uncharacteristically savage invective against Timaeus and his spurious etymologies, and of Aratus, with its sententious appeal to a descendant of the Sicyonian who, Plutarch argues, knows the material already but who might want the essay for his children, are further evidence of a desire to diversify and to hang the biographies upon pegs that are icons of the distance Plutarch needs to travel before homing in on his subject.

Having canvassed at some length the varied stratagems Plutarch employs in his proems, we now come to one that may give us a deeper insight into the reasons for his inaugural surprises. This is the proem of *Aemilius Paulus*, a *Life* which has attracted to itself an introduction that might equally well have been attached to *Timoleon*, the second of the pair. Plutarch muses that he started the *Lives* for the pleasure of others, but that he has come to enjoy and draw profit from staying with the project, "trying, somehow or other, to use my research as a looking glass by which to embellish and improve my life in the light of the achievements registered in the *Lives*." He makes each of the heroes his guest, admires him as Priam admired Achilles, and gets moral advantage out of the encounter. Since, he says on this occasion, he selects the best figures and what is best about them, he avoids the risk of being corrupted that may attach to a different kind of biography. With respect to the particular work at hand, the two heroes about to be featured are outstanding both in quality and in their luck. In fact, readers will find it difficult to decide whether excellence or circumstance was responsible for their successes.

This bare summary of the contents of Chapter 1 shows Plutarch in the curious role of posing as his own appreciative reader. As a collector of models to be emulated and as a miner of earlier records Plutarch is always a reader, a reader of other authors' texts. Here, for once, he spells out the advantages and the risks of perusing his own materials. He has been improved, not merely by the example set by Aemilius and Timoleon, but by reflecting upon his own presentation and interpretation of their lives. Conversely, because he must be included among the readers appealed to at the end of the proem, the author cannot tell whether the achievements chronicled are triggered primarily, or exclusively, by the characters' native excellence or by the good luck without which, Aristotle teaches, no lasting accomplishment is possible. Plutarch, then, as both composer and reader, interpreter and consumer, must leave certain basic questions unanswered. His control over the material is limited (cf. also the uncertainties in the proem of *Theseus*, cited above); the information transmitted by his sources counts for more than any analysis or perspective furnished by him. More important, the proem equips the space in which he becomes the critic of his own composition. Unlike the post-modern, Barthesian critic, he refuses to transcend and eclipse the writing.[37] But he is made uneasy by what he reads, and by the project as such. His authorial "I" is transformed into the reactive middle voice. This is our clearest case in any of the *Lives* of an authorial disclaimer, of the sense that the *Lives* write themselves, and that it is their automaticity that guarantees their authority, but also baffles the interpretive control of the biographer. Whether this might also explain why the proem is displaced and attached to *Aemilius* rather than to *Timoleon*, which lacks the honor of a proem, is a question we cannot answer.

IV

The assortment of *Lives* we have considered should suffice to demonstrate the variety of ways in which Plutarch eases himself into the orderly accounts of the public careers in which he is interested. The proems, by their diversity and inventiveness as

---

37. Wright (1984) 123: "Barthes is the reader of his own writing, self-consciously displaying the various effects of transference." The reference is to Roland Barthes, *A Lover's Discourse* (New York 1979).

much as by their risk-taking, serve to hide from view, at least initially, the routine pattern, the repetitive quality of the *Lives* which, as records of model careers, must fall into line within a narrow range of imitability. Plutarch, the Platonist, is mildly conscious of the absurdity of a model life that, because of the compromises of history and because of the needs of a minimal degree of realism, must be flawed.[38] Hence a touch of discomfort, which translates into the gyrations exercised in the proems. Unlike Nepos, who in a proem like that of his *Epaminondas* sets out the order in which he is going to proceed within the work,[39] Plutarch luxuriates in an enlargement, or distortion, of the focus before the mandatory narrowing called for in detailing the genealogy or the first emergence of the hero. I use the term "luxuriate" deliberately, for when Plutarch, at the end of the proem, enters into the heart of his enterprise, he renounces the leisureliness of the preliminary amble and resigns himself to selection and focusing and restriction.[40]

But let us note once again that in thirty of the *Lives* Plutarch proceeds as Nepos and Suetonius customarily do: instead of creating a cushion of diversification before launching into his tale, he immediately sets to work upon the family background or the upbringing and the looks of the young hero, or other vital statistics such as offices held (*Camillus*), with lucubrations about the uncertainty of evidence furnishing a routine softening of the fabric. Many of these unprefaced *Lives* are, as I have said, found among the seconds, the Romans, of the pairs, whose need of an introduction may be thought to be satisfied by what is said at the start of the dyad. But note *Romulus* and *Marius*, discussed above, second pieces endowed with proems of their own.[41] And some of the most celebrated of the Greek *Lives* are without proems, notably *Solon, Themistocles, Aristides*, and *Alcibiades*. The lack of a

---

38. See Ferrari (1989) 122: "For the young Guardian, the models of virtue are scarcely distinct from the actual human paragons whom he begins by emulating and whose ranks he can hope...to join." Human paragons in history are not unflawed paragons.

39. It should be mentioned that only two of Nepos' twenty-nine *Lives*, *Pelopidas* and *Epaminondas*, are prefaced. Not even *Atticus*, by far the longest and most substantial of Nepos' compositions, has a proem. Of the initial chapters of Suetonius' twelve extant *Lives* of the Caesars, from Julius Caesar to Domitian, only that of Galba strays from the standard focus upon family and birth by exhibiting Livia in her encounter with an eagle chasing a white hen.   40. Schneeweiss (1985).

41. Note also *Pompey*, which combines lineage and character *e contrario*.

proem to the last is particularly noteworthy; one might have expected Plutarch to use his prefatory art of poetic citation, simile, anecdote, and tribal wisdom to lead into a story well calculated to show off the pitfalls of the facile combination of talent and good looks. Some of this is done in the comparative-contrastive analysis which brings the dyad to a close. Not all dyads conclude with a σύγκρισις; and there appears to be no correlation whatever between the lack or presence of a proem and the presence or lack of a final stocktaking.[42]

There is, I fear, no way of explaining why some *Lives* are preceded by an expansive prefatory section, and others are not. And where we might wonder about the absence of a proem, as in *Caesar*, we might further wonder why Caesar is not even found worthy of the stock privilege accorded to all (except Otho), a pedigree of his own, but is thrust into midlife as a mature man.[43] In the end it is as if Plutarch wanted to frustrate modern critics intent on reconstructing a biographical *schema*, a formal canon available to him and readily, if with some modifications, put to use. Whether purposely or because no need is felt, Plutarch defeats our expectation of formal consistency, except that where proems are supplied, their length is roughly the same.[44] He refuses to introduce a *Life* in the manner of a modern journalist, by anticipating and giving dramatic exposure to a specific act within the hero's career that might serve as a beacon for the *Life* as a whole, and then retracing his steps to the beginnings. The sayings

42. Erbse (1956) demonstrated that σύγκρισις is a crucial element in the body of the work, guiding the selection of *topoi* and themes. In fact, the final σύγκρισις is often less interesting than its anticipations. This last point is emphasized by Pelling (1986), who draws attention to the "extemporizing" in the final sections. Erbse's pronouncement, p. 416, that "Jede Aussage der Rahmenkapitel [sc. proem and σύγκρισις] manifestiert sich...wenigstens einmal, meist öfter, in den erzählenden Teilen der Syzygie," strikes me as unduly optimistic, considering the eccentric scope of some of the proems. Further, "Rahmenkapitel" assumes a regular affinity between proem and σύγκρισις that does not seem to me to exist.

43. Ordinarily "Plutarch deals with his subject's γένος even when there is little to say": Pelling (1988) 117, on *Antony*, where Pelling finds the coverage remarkably unhurried. See also Pelling (1979) 91–96 for valuable suggestions concerning Plutarch's method in composing the *Lives*. For the view that the beginning of *Caesar* is lost, see the literature cited by Scardigli (1979) 198, note 704.

44. I am puzzled, therefore, by Russell's remark (1966a) 143 that an "elaborate preface" is distinctive of the *Lives*. But one of the best appreciations of the virtual structure of the *Lives* is Russell's composition (1966a) 149 of a *Life of Churchill* along Plutarchan lines. See also Russell (1966b) 47, commenting on *Alcibiades* 1–16: he characterizes the composition as "a loose structure, alarming in its incoherence."

or actions of *others* cited in many of the proems (prime specimen: *Pericles*) serve the same purpose of providing a moral jumping-off point, but the frequent lack of manifest relevance makes them into temporary enigmas waiting to be solved, with a definitive solution only rarely in evidence. The classical historians begin by identifying themselves, or their methods, or they provide a résumé of the events and the conditions of the era preceding the period in which they are interested. Philosophical writers after Plato head their treatises and their essays with generalizations designed to trigger the problems to be taken up. Plutarch himself, as an essayist, is capable of a "brisk opening" furnishing the necessary information, and then going on to justify the writing of the essay.[45] The biographer has no proemial method. The substance of the life to which he hopes to give literary shape takes its organization from the personality and the career of a public figure celebrated or considered remarkable by earlier writers, not the kind of material that lends itself either to inventive restructuring or to systematic exploitation, and hence inhospitable to an orderly preface. I would go further and say that Plutarch has to be ill at ease in the face of the disproportion between the didactic intention of the *Lives*, announced on several occasions, and the subjects' resistance to moral reduction. The great versatility of his opening gambits is a documentation of the wealth of his learning and of his creative flexibility in making connections. But it may also be the index of an embarrassment felt in the face of a task that offered no precedent for cushioning or naturalizing the routine beginning of pedigree and youth. Perhaps it is not unfair to conclude that the drifting and the freakishness of many of Plutarch's proems vindicate, to a degree, the sense of Said and Hayden White that "inaugural gestures" are deeply problematic. Plutarch, I said earlier, *appears* to exhibit remarkable assurance in fashioning his *Lives*. This assurance, I daresay, does not extend to the proems, whose unsteadiness may well reflect a larger uncertainty. The proems are full of the most fascinating material, but *as* proems many of them must be declared failures. Perhaps Plutarch should be commended for this also, for clearly demonstrating to us that in so ambitious a project as the setting

---

45. Hillyard (1981) 37, on *aud. poet.* I am not sure about Hillyard's "brisk," but he is right about the pragmatic relevance of the opening.

up of models for imitation, a patently unrevolutionary act, beginnings are bound to stumble.

Works Cited

Barbu, N. I. (1934) *Les procédés de la peinture des caractères et la vérité historique dans les biographies de Plutarque* (Paris).
Dihle, A. (1956) *Studien zur griechischen Biographie* (Göttingen).
— (1987) *Die Entstehung der griechischen Biographie* (Heidelberg).
Edel, L. (1984) *Writing Lives: Principia Biographica* (New York).
Erbse, H. (1956) "Die Bedeutung der Synkrisis in den Parallelbiographien Plutarchs", *Hermes* 84: 398–424.
Ferrari, G. R. F. (1989) "Plato and Poetry," in G. A. Kennedy, ed., *Cambridge History of Literary Criticism*, vol. 1 (Cambridge) pp. 92–148.
Fuhrmann, F. (1964) *Les images de Plutarque* (Paris).
Geiger, J. (1961) "Plutarch's *Parallel Lives*: The Choice of the Heroes," *Hermes* 109: 85–104.
Georgiadou, A. (1988) "The *Lives of the Caesars* and Plutarch's Other *Lives*," *Illinois Classical Studies* 13.2: 349–56.
Helmbold, W. C. & O'Neil, E. N. (1959) *Plutarch's Quotations*, APA Philological Monographs 19 (Baltimore).
Hillyard, B. P. (1981), ed. comm. *Plutarch: De audiendo*, Monographs in Classical Studies (New York).
Jones, C. P. (1966) "Towards a Chronology of Plutarch's Works," *Journal of Roman Studies* 56: 61–74.
Kracauer, S. (1963) "Die Biographie als neubürgerliche Kunstform," in *Das Ornament der Masse* (Frankfurt) pp. 75–80.
Krischer, T. (1982) "Die Stellung der Biographie in der griechischen Literatur," *Hermes* 110: 51–64.
Lausberg, H. (1960) *Handbuch der literarischen Rhetorik*, vol. 1 (Munich).
Leo, F. (1901) *Die griechisch-römische Biographie* (Leipzig).
Lowenthal, L. (1980) "Die biographische Methode" = "Sociologica I," in *Schriften 1* (Frankfurt) pp. 231–57.
Marasco, G. (1981), ed. comm. intr. *Commento alle biografie plutarchee di Agide e di Cleomene* (Rome).
Momigliano, A. (1971) *The Development of Greek Biography* (Cambridge, MA).
Pelling, C. B. R. (1979) "Plutarch's Method of Work in the Roman Lives," *Journal of Hellenic Studies* 99: 74–96.
— (1980) "Plutarch's Adaptation of his Source Material," *Journal of Hellenic Studies* 100: 127–40.
— (1986) "Synkrisis in Plutarch's *Lives*," in F. E. Brenk & I. Gallo, eds. *Atti del I. Convegno di studi su Plutarco* (Ferrara) pp. 83–96.
— (1988) ed. comm. intr. *Plutarch: Life of Antony* (Cambridge).

Piaget, J. (1968) *Le structuralisme* (Paris).
Raz, J. (1986) *The Morality of Freedom* (Oxford).
Romilly, J. de (1988) "Plutarch and Thucydides or the Free Use of Quotations," *Phoenix* 42: 22–34.
Russell, D. A. (1966a) "On Reading Plutarch's *Lives*," *Greece and Rome* 13: 139–54.
  (1966b) "Plutarch, *Alcibiades* 1–16," *Proceedings of the Cambridge Philological Society* 192: 37–47.
Said, E. W. (1975) *Beginnings: Intention and Method* (New York).
Scardigli, B. (1979) *Die Römerbiographien Plutarchs* (Munich).
Scheuer, H. (1979) *Biographie: Studien zur Funktion und zum Wandel einer literarischen Gattung vom 18. Jahrhundert bis zur Gegenwart* (Stuttgart).
Schneeweiss, G. (1985) "Gegenstand und Absicht in den Biographien Plutarchs," in M. Suerbaum & F. Maier, eds. *Festschrift...Fr. Egermann* (Münster) pp. 147–62.
Stadter, Ph. A. (1988) "The Proems of Plutarch's *Lives*," in *Illinois Classical Studies* 13.2: 275–95.
Veninga, J. F. (1983) ed. *The Biographer's Gift: Life Histories and Humanism* (College Station, Texas).
Wardman, A. (1974) *Plutarch's Lives* (London).
White, H. (1978) *Tropics of Discourse: Essays in Cultural Criticism* (Baltimore).
Wright, E. (1984) *Psychoanalytic Criticism: Theory in Practice* (London).
Ziegler, K. (1951) "Plutarchos von Chaironeia," in *Realencyklopädie der klassischen Altertumswissenschaft* 21.1: coll. 636–962.

Initium mihi operis Servius Galba iterum T. Vinius consules...

THOMAS COLE

So begins Tacitus' famous account (*Hist.* 1.1ff.) of the year of the four emperors and, with it, the major phase in the author's career as a historian. Both beginnings, like so much else in Tacitus, are at least partially grounded in Sallustian precedent. The sentence itself, so we are informed, is an echo of the *res populi Romani M. Lepido Q. Catulo consulibus ac deinde...gestas composui* with which Sallust began his own *Histories*.[1] Both works sought to give a general account of events over a significant period of years during the author's boyhood or youth; and each had been preceded by two preliminary studies devoted to, respectively, prominent individual Romans active toward the end of the period destined for treatment in the *Histories* (Agricola, Catiline) and prominent foreign enemies of Rome (the Germans, Jugurtha, and the Numidians).

The parallels are striking and perhaps sufficient in themselves to explain what might otherwise be inexplicable in Tacitus' choice of when and how to begin.[2] Why start – unless out of deference to Sallustian, annalistic precedent – by recounting events from the beginning of a particular consulship?[3] The two weeks (January 1–16, 69) during which Galba and Vinius held that office fell roughly in the middle of the period of rebellion and unrest which began in early 68, once it became apparent that Nero could no

---

1. Fr. 1. Cf. Klingner (1928) 167ff. and, most recently, Petrone (1976). (For full references see Works Cited at end of chapter.)

2. Well stated by Hainsworth (1964), the problems raised by Tacitus' decision have not, I think, been satisfactorily solved in any subsequent effort to deal with them. Cf., for earlier treatments, the survey in Fuhrmann (1960) 251–52, n. 2. Syme (1958) 145 seems virtually alone in finding the choice of January 69 so "vital and inevitable" as to merit little or no discussion.

3. One cannot, of course, know how rigidly Sallust and other annalists adhered to the year-by-year articulation of events announced in his opening sentence. One can only make inferences from the two representatives of the tradition that survive in extenso (Livy 1.60.4ff., Tacitus, *Ann.* 1.55ff.), where the arrangement is maintained almost without exception.

longer command the loyalty of his military and civilian subordinates, and ended only in 70, with the consolidation of the power of a new dynasty. Compare any other account of the period and you will find a continuous narrative articulated around one or the other of these points[4] or, more often, the death of Nero in June 68.[5] Either procedure would have simplified the task of Tacitus' readers, who are now condemned to move back and forth constantly between the narrative of 69 (1.1; 1.12ff.) and the allusive, intermittently obscure survey (1.4–11) of the background information on Rome and the provinces that is required if *non modo casus eventusque rerum... sed ratio etiam causaeque* are to be known (1.4). Why, moreover, abandon the plans announced earlier (*Agr.* 3.3) for a work on Domitian's tyranny and its happy sequel (*memoriam prioris servitutis ac testimonium praesentium bonorum*) in favor of one that begins with the fall of one of Domitian's predecessors and ended – presumably – with Domitian's death?

Tacitus' own answer, in so far as he gives an answer, merely indicates January 69 as one among a number of suitable starting points:

> The eight hundred and twenty years that preceded [Galba and Vinius], beginning with the founding of the city, were treated by many writers with both frankness and eloquence – so long as the subject was the history of the Republic; after the battle of Actium, when for the sake of peace all power had to be consolidated into the hands of one man, that era of great talents came to an end. At the same time standards of accuracy were compromised in various ways: at first because of ignorance of public affairs as if they were someone else's business; later from a desire to curry favor or else out of hatred for those in power. Between the embittered and the beholden there was no one with any concern for posterity's right to know...[6]

Central to Tacitus' argument here is the distinction between historiography before and after Actium: many and good treatments before, few and unsatisfactory ones after. This contrast marks out the entire imperial period, at least down to the death of Domitian, as a subject desperately in need of the attention of historians – provided they are historians who, like Tacitus, are in

---

4. As in Greenhalgh (1975) and Bengtson (1979).
5. So Dio Cassius 63; Merivale (1851–) ch. lvi; Henderson (1908); Wellesley (1975).
6. Translations of this and subsequent portions of *Hist.* 1.1 are my own.

"Initium mihi operis..."

a position to resist the double temptation of malice and favoritism:[7]

> I for my part experienced neither benefit nor injury at the hands of Galba, Otho, and Vitellius. My beginnings, I admit, were owed to Vespasian, my rise to Titus, my further career to Domitian. But a promise of strict adherence to truth forbids partiality toward anyone, and rancor too must be avoided.

Hence, presumably, the decision to begin much earlier in the imperial period than originally planned and to postpone, perhaps indefinitely, the promised history of Nerva and Trajan:

> I have reserved for my old age, in the event I should live so long, the principates of the late Nerva and of Trajan: a richer and easier theme, given the rare good fortune of an age in which both thought and expression are free.

That Tacitus still refrained, at this stage in his career, from extending the range of his work to include the earliest part of the imperial period as well was natural enough, given the strong emphasis, in the tradition of writing to which he belongs, on history as a record of the events of one's own lifetime.[8]

This interpretation of Tacitus' opening paragraph becomes somewhat easier if one assumes that the *DCC et XX* printed by all editors before Rycke and Jakob Gronovius[9] restores what Tacitus wrote, as against the Mediceus' *octingentos et viginti*:

> post conditam urbem DCC et XX [: octingentos et viginti *M*] prioris aevi annos multi auctores rettulerunt, dum res populi Romani memorabantur, pari eloquentia ac libertate.

One is thereby relieved of the necessity of giving to *dum res populi Romani memorabantur* a corrective or restrictive as well as a temporal force: "The eight hundred and twenty years prior to the consulship of Galba and Vinius were well covered by many historians – those years, that is [or 'those of them, at any rate']

---

7. Why – in two sentences not translated here (*sed ambitionem scriptoris facile averseris... malignitati falsa species libertatis inest*) – Tacitus insists that *adulatio* arouses more hostility among readers than *malignitas* has not, I think, been satisfactorily explained. The sentences form a kind of parenthesis, however, the interpretation of which does not affect one's analysis of the entire argument.

8. Only such a tradition – to which Sallust, Sisenna, Asinius Pollio, Aufidius Bassus, Cluvius Rufus, Fabius Rusticus, and the elder Pliny among others belong – is subject in the crucial way Tacitus has in mind to the twin vices of *adulatio* and *odium*.

9. See the commentaries of Gronovius and Ernesti *ad loc*. The ultimate source of the "restoration" is unknown: it may derive from inadvertence, or conjecture, or some manuscript tradition independent of the Mediceus.

which fell within the period of the republic. The situation changed after Actium." As emended, Tacitus' approximate total will not refer to the 753 + 68 years preceding the consulship of Galba and Vinius, but to the 753–31 preceding Actium, a century earlier: "the seven hundred and twenty years of the antecedent period that were immediately subsequent to the founding of the city – years during which republican history was what one wrote about" (or, eliminating the comma after *memorabantur*, "during which the writing of Roman [not republican] history was distinguished for both eloquence and outspokenness").[10] The sequence of thought thereby becomes exactly parallel to that developed later in the preface to the *Annals*:[11]

post conditam urbem septingentos et viginti PRIORIS AEVI annos MULTI AUCTORES rettulerunt dum res POPULI ROMANI memorabantur pari eloquentia ac libertate.	VETERIS POPULI ROMANI prospera vel adversa CLARIS SCRIPTORIBUS memorata sunt.
POSTQUAM BELLATUM APUD ACTIUM. magna illa ingenia cessere...primum inscitia...MOX LIBIDINE ADSENTANDI	TEMPORIBUS AUGUSTI dicendis non defuere decora ingenia DONEC gliscente ADULATIONE deterrerentur. Ann. 1.1.4

Even without the emendation, however, the paragraph is most plausibly understood in the manner suggested; and whether emended or not, it gives, as indicated earlier, only an approximate explanation for Tacitus' choice of where to begin.[12] Granting that

---

10. Cf., for example, I. Baudoin's translation (Paris 1619), made from a pre-Gronovian edition of the text, "l'on n'a pas manqué d'auteurs lesquels, pendant qu'on pouvait raconter les faits du peuple romain avec une éloquence et une liberté pareille, ont écrit les choses durant les sept cent vingt années depuis que Rome a été batie. Or, après la bataille actiaque..."   11. On the parallels see, in general, Kierdorf (1978).

12. Precision is only possible if one assumes (see, most recently, Leeman [1973] 176–77) that Tacitus is contrasting (a) the few writers who treated events after January 69 with (b) the *multi scriptores* who wrote of events before – very well during the period of the republic (b1: *dum res populi...memorabantur pari eloquentia ac libertate*) and rather badly thereafter (b2: *postquam bellatum apud Actium magna illa ingenia cessere*). He is thus is beginning at exactly the point where earlier accounts began to be few in number (a) as well as poor in quality (b2). With this interpretation, however, precision (and a strictly temporal sense for *dum res populi...*) is achieved at the price of two implausible assumptions: 1) that there was a relative dearth of accounts of the year of the four emperors (a dearth hard to accept in the light of the stirring episodes involved, and of which there is no hint either in the reference at 2.101 to the *scriptores temporum qui potiente rerum Flavia domo monimenta belli huiusce* [i.e., that

"*Initium mihi operis...*"

there were good reasons for starting as early as his commitment (above, p. 233) to writing the history of his own times would allow, and that this would mean, given the natural articulation of events during the early principate, some point which would exclude all the Julio-Claudians but include all the Flavians, why the consulship of Galba and Vinius? And so we are thrown back on the Sallustian explanations indicated at the start – or on others yet to be considered.

Two such explanations have figured in Tacitean scholarship thus far – one literary, one "ideological."[13] The "Sallustian" beginning point, it has been maintained, positions Tacitus more advantageously than any other for an immediate plunge into the chronicle of horrors which he promises in 1.3: *opus...opimum caedibus, atrox proeliis, discors seditionibus, ipsa pace saevum...quattuor principes ferro interempti, trina bella civilia* etc. The reader is thereby invited to experience events as a contemporary observer might, for their immediate dramatic impact; he is not expected to take a historian's perspective and locate them in the larger process by which the issues raised by the *Bellum Neronis* of 68 and its immediate sequel were finally worked out to a kind of settlement through the violent upheavals of 69.[14]

To this "psychological" literary explanation for Tacitus' choice of opening one might add a formal one as well: the elaborate fugal structure thereby imparted to his text, as four versions of the same imperial theme pursue each other in a homicidal romp throughout the initial sections of his work. The successive versions are introduced at intervals of a half-book (Otho at the start of Book 1, Vitellius in its center, Vespasian at the beginning of Book 2), gather momentum over regularly lengthening intervals (respectively, one, two, and three half-books) to the point of decisive encounter with each one's immediate predecessor (the battles fought midway through Books 1, 2, and 3 at Rome, Bedriacum,

---

leading to the fall of Vitellius] *composuerunt*, or in Pliny when he speaks [*Ep.* 2.1 and 9.19] of historical accounts dealing with the career of Verginius Rufus); and 2) that this dearth was the primary consideration determining Tacitus' choice of where to begin (in which case the entire qualitative contrast between historiography before and after Actium becomes irrelevant to the main subject of the paragraph).

13. A third, which would have Tacitus begin where some earlier historian (Cluvius Rufus, Fabius Rusticus) left off, is now generally rejected. Cf. the suggestions of Mommsen and Hirschfeld discussed by Syme (1958) 145.

14. Shotter (1967) 162–63; Martin (1981) 68.

and Cremona), then make their exit in concluding sections which show a similar pattern of increasing lengths (half a book for Galba, two half-books for Otho, three for Vitellius). Of Galba we are able to hear only the concluding section, and of Vespasian only the beginning: but the half of each that we do hear conforms to the pattern – which means that Galba's exit has to be brief enough to be accommodated within a single half-book and so conterminous with a relatively short period of his reign.

Both these considerations may have had a share in determining the ultimate shape of Tacitus' work, hence his choice of where to begin; but both are, I believe, of less consequence in the long run than a specific political program with strong claims on the historian's allegiance. Two particular instances of the influence of this program, though not the program itself, have been commented upon in earlier scholarship. They involve Galba and one other important protagonist of the events of 68–69, Verginius Rufus. A connected treatment of the earlier of these two years would almost certainly have committed Tacitus to a more forthright judgment about the character and career of both men than he now gives – or, I would argue, wanted to give. His presentation of isolated episodes instead – retrospectively as need arises and often as what was later thought or alleged to have occurred in that year – is best seen as a calculated stratagem, politically motivated, for ignoring or glossing over certain crucial pieces of evidence.

By defeating Galba's earliest ally, the Gaulish rebel Vindex, in the spring of 68 Verginius removed the principal military challenge to Nero's authority. The decision he made at this point – neither to support the regime nor to accept his own soldiers' bid to make him emperor in Nero's place, but rather to back whichever alternative imperial candidate the senate might choose to name – was probably the single most important factor in determining the course which events took during the succeeding year and a half. By withdrawing the support of the German legions, it insured Nero's downfall; by removing the prospect of active candidacy on the part of Verginius himself, it gave a powerful impetus to Galba's claims; at the same time, by withholding open support from Galba at a crucial point, it created the impression in certain quarters that the support when it eventually came was unwilling or half-hearted. The result was mutual distrust and, later, Galba's recall of Verginius from his German command – an act which contributed, in turn, to the discontent and plottings on the part of Verginius' former subordinates that were to culminate in the revolt of the Rhine legions in January 69.[15]

Tacitus, however, has almost nothing to say of the crucial consequences of the decision or its possible motives. An obvious and plausible explanation[16] is his reluctance to include any material which might call into question the official reason given, at the time and later, by Verginius and his friends (of whom Tacitus' own close friend Pliny was one). It was maintained that Verginius had acted at this crucial juncture out of pure patriotism: in order that *imperium* should belong, in the words of his epitaph, *non sibi sed patriae* (cf. Pliny, *Ep.* 9.19). Whether or not a more detailed Tacitean account would have given color to the extreme suggestion[17] that makes Verginius a covert ally of Galba and Vindex, induced by perfidy or prudence to a temporary desertion of their cause, there would have been, almost inevitably, intimations of timidity, indecision, and bad judgment. Relegated to the background status which Tacitus assigns to all the events of 68, the episode can either be ignored (as it usually is) or dismissed (as it is at 1.8) with a brief *an [Verginius] imperare noluisset dubium: delatum ei a milite imperium conveniebat*. And even here we are probably right to detect "a sign of embarrassment, an effort both to honor factual truth and to avoid a lapse in taste or tact."[18]

There is no single incident of comparable importance that Tacitus passes over in Galba's career prior to January 69. Yet it is possible to put together from brief references in the *Histories* and from more detailed ones in the biographies by Suetonius and Plutarch, a disturbing collection of cruelties, crimes, and follies that go well beyond the *severitas, parsimonia*, and *segnitia* that figure in the account of his principate in 1.15–34 and in the famous

---

15. Murison (1979) 187–94 has argued convincingly, on chronological grounds, against Tacitus' presentation (1.55ff.) of the revolt as almost exclusively the work of the two Galban appointees, Valens and Caecina.

16. So Hainsworth (1964).

17. Cf. John of Antioch's story (fr. 91 Mueller [= Dio Cassius, vol. 3, p. 87 Boissevain]) of a secret pact giving Gaul to Verginius, Spain to Vindex, and the rest of the empire to Galba, or – more elaborately – the reconstruction offered in Daly (1975).

18. Rudich, 833.

epitaph at 1.49. Political necessity may have justified the assassination of Clodius Macer (*in Africa haud dubie turbantem*, 1.7); but the same cannot be said of the murder of Fonteius Capito in Germany, or the executions without trial of the Neronian commander Petronius Turpilianus and the associates of Nymphidius Sabinus, or the slaughter of large numbers of unarmed soldiers in the outskirts of Rome just before Galba's entry into the city. And there was also, in the other direction, the decision not to take any action against Tigellinus and Halotus, two of the worst and most hated holdovers from the previous regime. None of these episodes occurred in 69, and so Tacitus can – as he does in every case except that of Macer – either ignore them altogether or treat them as simple allegations. True or false, their existence helps explain the emperor's subsequent unpopularity, and this is the only thing relevant to the matter at hand.

There can be, I think, little doubt that "the division of the historical narrative...into a general introductory survey of the period leading up to the 1st of January...followed by a detailed account of events from that date serves Tacitus' purpose of improving Galba's image"[19] – just as it improves that of Verginius. It is easy to see, moreover, how a shared enthusiasm for republican *virtus* in the one instance and personal friendships in the other could have blinded Tacitus to some of his subjects' faults. But these explanations fail to take into account the degree to which the cases of Galba and Verginius are simply parallel manifestations of a single larger phenomenon. The nature of this phenomenon, concealed by Tacitus' reticence, is quite clear in the context of the general picture that emerges as soon as one looks at the events of 68 in the logical and chronological sequence which the decision to begin with Galba and Vinius never allows to appear.

The picture thereby revealed is of a protracted, complex struggle between a number of would-be emperors or emperor-makers, all aspiring to fill the vacuum left by the collapse of the

---

19. Shochat (1981a), 202. To Shochat's valuable inventory of these and additional crimes ignored or obscured in Tacitus' account one may add the sending of assassins against Vespasian (the official reason [Suet., *Gal.* 23] for the latter's subsequent refusal to sanction the senatorial deification decree) and – less spectacular though perhaps more plausible – the removal of tribunes suspected of pro-Flavian sympathies inferred by Birley (1977) in his discussion of *Hist.* 1.20.

"*Initium mihi operis...*"

Neronian regime. The four who eventually came to the throne owed their success as much to chance, or the ability of advisers, or the crimes and follies of enemies, as they did to their own popularity or merits; and of none was this more true than Galba. Without such help, even the accident of lineage, which gave him an advantage over other contenders at the start, would probably have been insufficient to guarantee the outcome. Matters had actually gone so far at one point, according to Suetonius (*Gal.* 14), that he was only saved from suicide by his freedman Icelus, arriving posthaste from Rome with the news of Nero's death. And the event which brought him to the verge of suicide, Verginius' defeat of his ally Vindex, was, paradoxically, just enough (in conjunction with the successful lobbying of senators and praetorians by the pro-Galban prefect Nymphidius Sabinus) to destroy Nero, while at the same time not enough (given Verginius' unwillingness to further his own candidacy) to destroy Galba himself. Similarly, Nymphidius' subsequent desertion of Galba may have been just late enough to doom the chances of Clodius Macer[20] while, at the same time, not quite early enough to allow Nymphidius any hope of success in his own bid for power.

Galba's reference (1.15) to this successful combination of ruthlessness, ineptness, and luck as a *deorum hominumque consensus* summoning him to *imperium* would have been nothing short of grotesque had the events of 68 been presented in connected detail as a preface to those of January 69. Tacitus does not, of course, intend that self-congratulatory evaluation – or its later echo by Piso (1.30: *Galbam consensus generis humani...Caesarem dixit*) – to be accepted without reservations. It is inconsistent with, among other things, the historian's own epigrammatic reference to the events of 68 ten chapters earlier (1.4): *evulgato arcano imperii posse principem alibi quam Romae fieri*. Yet the only explicit refutation he supplies is made to come from the most suspect of sources: Otho's speech of thanks to the praetorians upon receiving their oath of allegiance (1.37).[21] It is essential to Tacitus' purposes that Galba

20. For the possibility, often suggested, of close links between Nymphidius and the attempt of Clodius, as legate of Africa, to gain acceptance of his own claims by cutting off the Roman grain supply, see now Bossone (1979).

21. Tacitus' regular preference for the *deterior interpretatio* whenever Otho is involved (Shochat [1981b] 365ff.) is as striking as his reluctance to adopt this attitude in dealing with Galba.

appear in the opening chapters as the embodiment of legitimate imperial authority, duly grounded in senatorial choice and popular ratification. His elevation to the throne by a process that involved neither usurpation nor hereditary succession is, as has often been pointed out,[22] a clear anticipation – the only such anticipation in imperial history up to that point – of the process by which Nerva came to the throne in 96. And the arguments for succession by adoption which Galba presents in the speech to the emperor-elect Piso at 1.15–16 can be paralleled in those brought forward thirty years later by Pliny when, in the *Panegyricus*, he praises Nerva's choice of Trajan to be his heir.[23] That Galba, unlike Nerva, made poor use of the imperial power conferred upon him by the senate, and applied a correct principle of succession disastrously when his choice fell on Piso, does not alter the paradigmatic role which he plays *vis-à-vis* a regime and a policy which received – whether out of conviction or hope or prudence – at least open endorsement from Tacitus.[24]

There was every reason not to allow the position of this exemplary model to be undercut by too close or too prolonged a look at Galba's crimes, or at the haphazard, unedifying sequence of events that brought him to power. Sallustian precedent and the annalistic tradition, by suggesting the opening of a consular year as a natural, almost inevitable *terminus post quem* for material to be included in a major piece of continuous historical narrative, supplied the ideal solution for Tacitus' problem. Those earlier events, with the questions raised about both Galba and Verginius, were a thing of the past by January 69, and Galba himself on the verge of performing the act of adoption which would turn him into a kind of martyr in the cause of "constitutional" *imperium*. The literary gains realized by beginning at this point are none the less real if the choice itself was the result, ultimately, of considerations that had nothing to do with literature.

That the choice had equally little to do with the problem of where, for whatever reason, one *should* begin – as distinct from the problem of where one should *not* begin – is also possible in view of

---

22. See, for example, the discussion in Syme (1958) 150.
23. See Bruère (1954) 170.
24. For the difficulties in assuming that the views assigned to Galba in 1.15–16 are Tacitean pure and simple, see Chilver (1979) *ad loc.*

"*Initium mihi operis...*"

everything that has been said thus far. But negative considerations have their positive counterpart, still to be discussed. It is not only Galba, Otho, and Vitellius, on the one hand, and, on the other, Tacitus' career as a major historian that make their entrance with the consuls of 69. In a sense, the history of Nerva and Trajan begins there as well – the promised *testimonium praesentium bonorum* which has been made to form a kind of counterpoint to the *memoria prioris servitutis* by the decision to begin the latter at exactly the point where the false dawn (as it turned out) of 68–69 most closely anticipated the true dawn (as it was hoped) of 96–98.[25] The indirect method of treatment permitted Tacitus to compliment the recent inauguration of a new regime without fear of what might come to seem, in retrospect, excessive or self-seeking optimism. Men and events which promised well in 98 might ultimately turn out badly, like their precursors in 69.

Tacitus' model for this two-tiered structure of reference was not Sallust but Cicero, as imitated and updated in the work, the *Dialogus*, whose composition is generally thought to have preceded most closely his embarking on the *Histories*.[26] Though its dramatic

---

25. The counterpoint could obviously not be maintained except at isolated points beyond the opening of Book 1. Note, however, the frequent references (1.14, 31, 39, 45, 71, 77, 87, 90; 2.23–25, 33, 39–40, 44, 60) to the career of Marius Celsus, consul designate under Galba and consul under Otho and Vitellius. These are perhaps intended as a compliment to the Marius Celsus, presumably his son, who was consul in 106, when the first installment of the *Histories* may have been published (see Shotter [1978]). If so, the stress placed throughout on the elder Celsus' exemplary loyalty to a succession of regimes will have been both a compliment and a means of foreshadowing what the Nervan and Trajanic union of *libertas* and *principatus* was to make possible on a much larger scale. The younger Celsus' father, like Tacitus' own father-in-law Agricola, is a man before his time.

26. The argument of this paragraph is not seriously affected if one accepts the recently proposed (Murgia [1980] and [1985]) redating of the *Dialogus* from 102 or thereabouts to 97. In general, however, I find Murgia's arguments against 102 as a date of publication, and for 100 (the delivery date of Pliny's *Panegyricus*) as a *terminus ante quem*, much stronger than those by which he seeks to make the *Dialogus* Tacitus' earliest work – post-Domitianic but antedating both *Agricola* and *Germania*. The close resemblances noted by Murgia and others between passages in those two works and the *Dialogus* are unlikely to be fortuitous, but are as easily explained by echoings by the *Dialogus* as vice-versa. And, *pace* Murgia (1980, 101–103), it is unlikely that anyone who had already published the *Dialogus* would refer to himself, as Tacitus does in the *Agricola*, as a writer from whom one can still expect compositions in a "crude and unpracticed style" (*rudi et incondita voce*). I find it equally hard to believe, either that Pliny's *motu...excitatur* (in a letter [1.6.2] addressed to Tacitus in 97) and the *motibus excitatur* of *Dialogus* 36.1 are sufficiently peculiar pieces of Latinity to justify the assumption that one of the two writers has imitated the other (Murgia [1985] 174–76, following Bruère [1954] 167), or that the straightforward, unselfconscious reference in the same letter to *silvae et solitudo* as *magna cogitationis incitamenta* could have been made (as Murgia argues [1985] 176–80) by anyone who had read with care the passages in the *Dialogus* that refer to the *solitudo* and *secretum* (9.6, 12.1) of *nemora* and *lucos* as suitable

date (75 A.D. or thereabouts)[27] is not too far from the consulship of Galba and Vinius, the *Dialogus* is, as has been recently pointed out,[28] a work concerned quite as much with the Nervan or Trajanic present as with the Flavian past. Just as Cicero had projected his personal prescription for the sort of literary or political leadership required in his own day into conversations among Roman *nobiles* in 91 (*De oratore*) or 129 B.C. (*De republica*), so Tacitus closes his work with an obituary for oratory that he ostensibly heard from Curiatius Maternus in 75, but that can only be fully understood against a contemporary background. In dismissing oratory as the product of disorderly, licentious times whose disappearance should be a cause for rejoicing, Maternus must be thinking, anachronistically, of Trajan's suppression, whether accomplished or anticipated, of the most conspicuous beneficiaries of oratorical license, the public informers or *delatores*,[29] and so welcoming in a new age, in which imperial prudence and benevolence will chastise the bad and protect the good far more effectively and reliably than the eloquence of isolated private citizens was able to do in the past.[30] The obituary – like Galba's proclamation of the principles of constitutional *imperium* – is premature in its Flavian or pre-Flavian context; and Maternus' own end – also like Galba's – may have been hastened by his failure to recognize this fact.[31] Once again, as in the

backgrounds for poetic composition. Contrast the *poemata...quae tu inter nemora et lucos commodissime perfici putas* of *Ep.* 9.10.2, addressed to Tacitus at a time when Pliny evidently *had* read the *Dialogus* or (see Lefèvre [1978] 43–46) became aware of Tacitus' endorsement of this fairly commonplace notion (cf. Horace, *Ep.* 2.2.77–78; Quintilian 10.3.22) in some other way.   27. See, most recently, Letta (1985).

28. Williams (1978) 32–45.

29. Pliny, *Paneg.* 34–35; cf. Williams (1978) 35–37.

30. Against this interpretation, Murgia (1980, 119–21) argues that, since one type of oratory at least, that in cases *de repetundis*, seems to have shown no signs of imminent decline in the early years of Trajan, the pessimistic estimate of oratory's prospects should be taken as applying exclusively to the Flavian period. If this is so, however, it becomes very difficult to reconcile Maternus' contempt for contemporary oratory with his apparent praise for an imperial system which continues to require and reward its services (on Vespasian's encouragement of the *delatores*, see Winterbottom [1964] 93). One can only assume, rather improbably, that his speech is a heavy-handed piece of irony: an argument, drawn out at un-Tacitean length, to show (ostensibly) that things are so good no oratory is needed but (in fact) that things are so bad no oratory would do any good.

31. See Cameron (1967) or, most recently, Barnes (1981 and 1986, 240–43), where it is suggested that Maternus was not, as had been argued by Cameron and others, one of the victims of Vespasian's quarrel with the senate in the mid-70s but, rather, the Maternus executed or driven to death by Domitian in 91 or 92 (Dio Cassius 67.12.5).

"Initium mihi operis..."

Histories, indirect references to the present seem to be a means for expressing loyalty to the current dispensation without endangering, through risky prognosis, one's credibility as a historian. Maternus' fate, like Galba's, serves as a stern, if unspoken, reminder against facile optimism.[32]

Intimately linked to his own hopes, fears, and reservations about the new regime, Tacitus' reasons for starting with Galba and Vinius could hardly be spelled out in detail. Hence the vagueness of the preface, whose explanations do no more than put the historian in the general vicinity of where he must begin, leaving the exact spot unaccounted for. The rest was left to his readers, and to their dawning shock of recognition as "scenes, persons, and events leapt into life, startling and terrifying."[33] It would be apparent soon enough that the point at which the historian began was also the point at which they themselves had begun – awakening in the manner described at the outset of the *Agricola* from the long Domitianic night, and hoping that their generation, unlike Galba's, would not lose its way once again, almost before being properly embarked upon it. History for Tacitus is perpetual repetition; every beginning a beginning again: *eadem...deum ira, eadem hominum rabies, eaedem scelerum causae* (2.38). And so it is much more than the desire to complete a formal piece of ring composition that makes him lead into his actual account of the consulship, after the retrospective digression of 1.4–11, with a magnificently somber variation on the language of 1.1. We are thereby brought back to a point where we as readers have, like Galba, already been (*initium...Galba iterum* [*1.1*] ... *iterum Galba... incohavere* [*1.11*]), beginning where we as Romans began once before, but also where we or our descendants may find ourselves beginning once again; and, immediate appearances to the contrary, it may prove even harder, this time

---

32. The double reference – Flavian and Nervan – of the *Dialogus* is not altered if one follows Barnes (1986) in taking the concluding obituary of oratory as directed primarily against Quintilian's call for a Ciceronian revival which will restore to eloquence both the style and the moral and political pretensions it enjoyed in the late republic. Such an attack presupposes, as Barnes notes, the position enjoyed by "Quintilianism" in the mid-90s. Its anachronistic transfer to the early 70s, when Quintilian's career as professor and arbiter of taste was just beginning, would be yet another instance of Tacitus' tendency, whether out of politeness or prudence, to address contemporary issues indirectly.

33. Syme (1958) 150.

around or the next, for the *res publica* as a whole to avoid the wrong path which turns beginnings into endings:

hic fuit rerum Romanarum status, cum *Servius Galba iterum T. Vinius consules incohavere* annum sibi ultimum, rei publicae prope supremum.[34]

Works Cited

Barnes, T. D. (1981) "Curiatius Maternus." *Hermes* 109: 382–84.
  (1986) "The significance of Tacitus' *Dialogus de oratoribus*," *HSCP* 90: 225–44.
Bengtson, H. (1979) *Die Flavier* (Munich).
Birley, E. (1977) "The Aftermath of an Incident of A.D. 69," *Chiron* 7: 275–81.
Bossone, L. (1979) "Clodio Macro e la fine di Nerone," *Rivista storica dell' antichità* 9: 39–59.
Bruère, R. T. (1954) "Tacitus and Pliny's 'Panegyricus'," *CPh* 49: 161–79.
Cameron, A. (1967) "Tacitus and the Date of Curiatius Maternus' Death," *CR* 17: 258–61.
Chilver, G. E. F. (1979). *A Historical Commentary on Tacitus' "Histories" I and II* (Oxford).
Daly, L. J. (1975) "Verginius at Vesontio: The Incongruity of the *Bellum Neronianum*," *Historia* 24: 75–100.
Fuhrmann, M. (1960) "Das Vierkaiserjahr bei Tacitus," *Philologus* 104: 250–78.
Greenhalgh, P. A. L. (1975) *The Year of the Four Emperors* (London).
Hainsworth, J. B. (1964) "The Starting Point of Tacitus' Histories – Fear or Favour by Omission," *Greece and Rome*: 128ff.
Henderson, B. W. (1908) *Civil War and Rebellion in the Roman Empire* (London).
Kierdorf, W. (1978) "Die Proömien zu Tacitus' Hauptwerken: Spiegel einer Entwicklung?", *Gymnasium* 85: 20–36.
Klingner, (1928) Fr. "Über die Einleitung der Historien Sallusts," *Hermes* 63: 165–92.
Leeman, A. D. (1973) "Structure and Meaning in the Prologues of Tacitus," *YCS* 23: 169–208.
Lefèvre, E. (1978) "Plinius-Studien II: Diana und Minerva. Die beiden Jagdbillette an Tacitus (1, 6; 9, 10)," *Gymnasium* 85: 37–47.
Letta, C. (1985) "La data fittizia del *Dialogo de oratoribus*," in F. Broilo (ed.) *Xenia, Scritti in onore di Piero Trèves* (Rome) 103–109.
Martin, R. H. (1981) *Tacitus* (London).
Merivale, Ch. (1851–) *History of the Romans under the Empire* (London).

---

34. My argument and its presentation have both benefited from the valuable criticism and suggested improvements offered by my co-editor and by Joseph Solodow and Vassily Rudich.

Murgia, C. E. (1980) "The Date of Tacitus' *Dialogus*," *HSCP* 84: 99–125.
—— (1985) "Pliny's Letters and the *Dialogus*," *HSCP* 89: 171–206.
Murison, C. L. (1979) "Some Vitellian Dates: An Exercise in Methodology," *TAPA* 109: 187–97.
Petrone, G. (1976) "Per una ricostruzione del proemio delle *Historiae* di Sallustio," *Pan* 4: 59–67.
Rudich, V. "The Subvertible Virtue: Political Dissidence under Nero" (unpublished typescript).
Shochat, Y. (1981a) "Tacitus' Attitude to Galba," *Athenaeum* 59: 199–204.
—— (1981b) "Tacitus' Attitude to Otho," *Latomus* 40: 365–77.
Shotter, D. C. A. (1967) "Starting Dates of Tacitus' Histories," *CQ* 17: 158–63.
—— (1978) "Tacitus and Marius Celsus," *LCM* 3: 197–200.
Syme, R. (1958) *Tacitus* (Oxford).
Wellesley, K. (1975) *The Long Year* (London).
Williams, G. (1978) *Change and Decline* (Berkeley and Los Angeles).
Winterbottom, M. (1964) "Quintilian and the *Vir Bonus*," *JRS* 52: 90–97.